P9-DOB-414

Archaeology

04/05

Seventh Edition

EDITOR

Linda L. Hasten

Linda Hasten received both her B.A. and M.A. from the University of California, Los Angeles. Her background is in archaeology, and she has done fieldwork in several areas, including California, the southwest United States, Peru, Europe, Mexico, and British Columbia. She formerly taught anthropology and archaeology as a full-time professor at Pasadena City College from 1971 to 1992. She has also taught experimental anthropology classes to children at UCLA. Currently, she is continuing her career as the author of both fictional and nonfictional works. Ms. Hasten is a member of the American Anthropology Association and the Author's Guild of America.

McGraw-Hill/Dushkin

2460 Kerper Blvd., Dubuque, IA 52001

Visit us on the Internet
http://www.dushkin.com

Credits

1. **About Archaeologists and Archaeology**
   Unit photo—© 2004 PhotoDisc, Inc.
2. **Problem-Oriented Archaeology**
   Unit photo—© United Nations/Rothstein
3. **Techniques in Archaeology**
   Unit photo—© Eigeland, Egyptian Antiquities Organization/Saudi Aramco World/PADIA
4. **Historical Archaeology**
   Unit photo—© Courtesy of Israeli Tourist Office
5. **Contemporary Archaeology**
   Unit photo—© United Nations Photo Library

Copyright

Cataloging in Publication Data
Main entry under title: Annual Editions: Archaeology. 2004/2005.
1. Archaeology—Periodicals. I. Hasten, Linda L., *comp.* II. Title: Archaeology.
ISBN 0–07–294960-0   658'.05   ISSN 1092–2760

Seventh Edition

Cover image © 2004 Nick Koudis/Getty Images
Printed in the United States of America   1234567890QPDQPD987654   Printed on Recycled Paper

Editors/Advisory Board

Members of the Advisory Board are instrumental in the final selection of articles for each edition of ANNUAL EDITIONS. Their review of articles for content, level, currentness, and appropriateness provides critical direction to the editor and staff. We think that you will find their careful consideration well reflected in this volume.

EDITOR

Linda L. Hasten

Staff

To the Reader

In publishing ANNUAL EDITIONS we recognize the enormous role played by the magazines, newspapers, and journals of the public press in providing current, first-rate educational information in a broad spectrum of interest areas. Many of these articles are appropriate for students, researchers, and professionals seeking accurate, current material to help bridge the gap between principles and theories and the real world. These articles, however, become more useful for study when those of lasting value are carefully collected, organized, indexed, and reproduced in a low-cost format, which provides easy and permanent access when the material is needed. That is the role played by ANNUAL EDITIONS.

This seventh edition of *Annual Editions: Archaeology* consists of a number of readings that were specifically selected to present a vivid overview of the field of archaeology as it is practiced today. Every article was chosen to make the old bones, shards of pottery, and stone tools pop into the present. The purpose of this book is to present an approach in which archaeologists speak for themselves of their own special experiences. The student is shown that archaeology is a historical, living, and public science. The idea is to show the student the necessary basics to enable the student to transform passive learning into active learning. This way, information is both perceptualized and conceptualized. Hopefully, the light bulb will go on when students read these articles.

This book is organized into five units, each of which contains several articles on various themes on "doing" archaeology. At the beginning of the book a *table of contents* provides a short synopsis of each article. This is followed by a *topic guide* that cross-references general areas of interest as they appear in the different articles. At the end of the book is a comprehensive *index*. In addition, there are *World Wide Web* sites that can be used to further explore the above articles.

Each unit is introduced by an *overview* that provides both commentary on the unit topic and *key points* to provoke thought and discussion. It is highly recommended that the student read these *unit overviews*. They are presented for the student with humor and contain challenges and even puzzles to solve.

The organization of this book is both suggestive and subjective. The articles may be assigned or read in any fashion that is deemed desirable. Each article stands on its own and may be assigned in conjunction with or in contrast to any other reading. For introductory archaeology courses, *Annual Editions: Archaeology 04/05* may serve as a supplement to a standard textbook, or replace it altogether. This book may also be used in general, undergraduate, or graduate courses in anthropology. This book would also be useful to the lay reader in anthropology.

The people involved in the production of this book wish to make each edition a valuable and provocative teaching tool. We welcome your criticisms, advice, and suggestions in order to carefully hone each edition into a finer artifact of education.

We suggest you use the *postage-paid* form at the end of this book for your comments and article ratings. We would be most grateful for the time you take to give your feedback. Each year these comments and ratings are carefully read by me and the advisory board in creating the next edition. Your responses would truly be appreciated and seriously considered.

It is humbling to realize that today is tomorrow's yesterday and that evidence abounds of truths whose questions we have not yet asked.

Linda L. Hasten
Editor

Contents

UNIT 1
About Archaeologists and Archaeology

Eight articles present overviews of the history and definition of archaeology and how archaeologists view themselves and each other in their attempt to practice science. Brief human aspects of archaeologists are presented.

The concepts in bold italics are developed in the article. For further expansion, please refer to the Topic Guide and the Index.

UNIT 2
Problem Oriented Archaeology

Twelve articles deal with the contemporary goal of archaeology, which is to solve problems rather than to make discoveries. Problems range from general issues such as peopling of the New World, to explaining the social complexities that underlay hunting and gathering and/or agricultural subsistence economies, to learning if human cannibalism was once a cultural practice.

Unit Overview   42

The concepts in bold italics are developed in the article. For further expansion, please refer to the Topic Guide and the Index.

The concepts in bold italics are developed in the article. For further expansion, please refer to the Topic Guide and the Index.

UNIT 3
Techniques in Archaeology

Eight selections demonstrate how modern archaeologists set up experiments that reenact past events. By such things as diverse as collecting modern garbage, living with Bushmen, or recreating Eastern Island moai, a whole new body of fundamental information about archaeological processes is generated.

The concepts in bold italics are developed in the article. For further expansion, please refer to the Topic Guide and the Index.

UNIT 4
Historical Archaeology

Seven articles consider the use of the studies of contemporary societies, including but not limited to primitive societies, in an attempt to extrapolate back to the past in order to recreate a kind of livng social archaeology.

Unit Overview 138

The concepts in bold italics are developed in the article. For further expansion, please refer to the Topic Guide and the Index.

UNIT 5
Contemporary Archaeology

Nine selections examine who has what rights and responsibilities with respect to archaeological sites. Nationalistic and local politics, developers, economic needs, and greed come into play in attempting to solve these various and often conflicting demands. Archaeologists must learn to take on new roles as they move into the areas of salvage, private business, cultural resource management, preservation of sites, conservations, and public archaeology.

The concepts in bold italics are developed in the article. For further expansion, please refer to the Topic Guide and the Index.

The concepts in bold italics are developed in the article. For further expansion, please refer to the Topic Guide and the Index.

Topic Guide

This topic guide suggests how the selections in this book relate to the subjects covered in your course. You may want to use the topics listed on these pages to search the Web more easily.

On the following pages a number of Web sites have been gathered specifically for this book. They are arranged to reflect the units of this *Annual Edition.* You can link to these sites by going to the DUSHKIN ONLINE support site at *http://www.dushkin.com/online/.*

ALL THE ARTICLES THAT RELATE TO EACH TOPIC ARE LISTED BELOW THE BOLD-FACED TERM.

About archaeologists and archaeology

1. Metaphors We Dig By
2. The Awful Truth About Archaeology
3. The Quest for the Past
4. Distinguished Lecture in Archeology: Communication and the Future of American Archaeology
5. First Lady of Amazonia
6. Archaeology's Perilous Pleasures
7. The Travails and Tedium of Conflict-Zone Fieldwork
8. All the King's Sons

American Indians

9. Prehistory of Warfare
13. Who's On First?
14. The Slow Birth of Agriculture
15. Archaeologists Rediscover Cannibals
30. Reading the Bones of La Florida
33. Life in the Provinces of the Aztec Empire
36. Burying American Archaeology
37. Ownership and Control of Ethnographic Materials
38. Last Word on Kennewick Man?
39. Tales From a Peruvian Crypt
40. Guardians of the Dead

Art and religion

8. All the King's Sons
11. In the Beginning Was the Word
15. Archaeologists Rediscover Cannibals
32. Case of the Colorado Cannibal
33. Life in the Provinces of the Aztec Empire
34. Legacy of the Crusades
35. Israel's Mysterious Stone
39. Tales From a Peruvian Crypt
40. Guardians of the Dead
42. Land Can Be Divided. Histories Cannot

Burials, reburials and human remains

3. The Quest for the Past
6. Archaeology's Perilous Pleasures
13. Who's On First?
15. Archaeologists Rediscover Cannibals
16. New Women of the Ice Age
22. High-Tech "Digging"
25. Profile of an Anthropologist: No Bone Unturned
26. 'Let the Bones Talk' Is the Watchword for Scientist-Sleuths
28. The Archaeologists Who Wouldn't Dig
30. Reading the Bones of La Florida
31. Living Through the Donner Party
34. Legacy of the Crusades
36. Burying American Archaeology
38. Last Word on Kennewick Man?
39. Tales From a Peruvian Crypt
40. Guardians of the Dead
43. The Past as Propaganda
44. Proving Ground of the Nuclear Age

Ceramic analysis

3. The Quest for the Past
21. Camera Bodies
28. The Archaeologists Who Wouldn't Dig
33. Life in the Provinces of the Aztec Empire

Classical and biblical archaeology

3. The Quest for the Past
8. All the King's Sons
11. In the Beginning Was the Word
14. The Slow Birth of Agriculture
22. High-Tech "Digging"
28. The Archaeologists Who Wouldn't Dig
29. Alcohol in the Western World
34. Legacy of the Crusades
35. Israel's Mysterious Stone

Cognitive and ideological archaeology

3. The Quest for the Past
4. Distinguished Lecture in Archeology: Communication and the Future of American Archaeology
5. First Lady of Amazonia
33. Life in the Provinces of the Aztec Empire

Cultural Resource Management (CRM)

6. Archaeology's Perilous Pleasures
22. High-Tech "Digging"
23. Space Age Archaeology
36. Burying American Archaeology
37. Ownership and Control of Ethnographic Materials
38. Last Word on Kennewick Man?
39. Tales From a Peruvian Crypt
40. Guardians of the Dead
41. In a Box
42. Land Can Be Divided. Histories Cannot

Epistemology (method and theory)

2. The Awful Truth About Archaeology
3. The Quest for the Past
4. Distinguished Lecture in Archeology: Communication and the Future of American Archaeology
5. First Lady of Amazonia
6. Archaeology's Perilous Pleasures
7. The Travails and Tedium of Conflict-Zone Fieldwork
8. All the King's Sons
12. Who Were the First Americans?
13. Who's On First?
14. The Slow Birth of Agriculture
16. New Women of the Ice Age
17. Woman The Toolmaker

Ethics and laws

3. The Quest for the Past
8. All the King's Sons
13. Who's On First?

Public archaeology

Salvage and conservation

Techniques in archaeology and forensics

Tombs and pyramids (also see burials)

Public archaeology

Salvage and conservation

Techniques in archaeology and forensics

Tombs and pyramids (also see burials)

World Wide Web Sites

The following World Wide Web sites have been carefully researched and selected to support the articles found in this reader. The easiest way to access these selected sites is to go to our DUSHKIN ONLINE support site at *http://www.dushkin.com/online/*.

AE: Archaeology 04/05

The following sites were available at the time of publication. Visit our Web site—we update DUSHKIN ONLINE regularly to reflect any changes.

General Sources

Anthropology Resources on the Internet

http://www.socsciresearch.com/r7.html

This site provides extensive Internet links that are primarily of anthropological relevance. *The Education Index* rated it "one of the best education-related sites on the Web."

Archaeological Institute of America

http://www.archaeological.org

This home page of the AIA describes the purpose of the nonprofit organization. Review this site for information about AIA and AIA/IAA–Canada and other archaeological-research institutions and organizations around the world.

How Humans Evolved

http://www.wwnorton.com/college/anthro/bioanth/

This site presents a good overview of human evolution, with links to *Science* and *Nature* magazines, access to e-mail chat groups, and other topics of archaeological interest.

Library of Congress

http://www.loc.gov

Examine this extensive Web site to learn about resource tools, library services/resources, exhibitions, and databases in many different subfields of archaeology.

The New York Times

http://www.nytimes.com/

Browsing through the extensive archives of the *New York Times* will provide you with a wide array of articles and information related to archaeology.

USD Anthropology

http://www.usd.edu/anth/

Many topics can be accessed from this site, such as South Dakota archaeology. Repatriation and reburial are just a few examples of the variety of information available.

UNIT 1: About Archaeologists and Archaeology

Ancestral Passions

http://www.canoe.ca/JamBooksReviewsA/ancestral_morell.html

This is review of Virginia Morell's book *Ancestral Passion*, a biography of the fabulously dysfunctional Leakey family, that will encourage you to learn more about the history of paleontology and the thrill and trials of archaeological fieldwork. It is the evolutionary detective story that is the book's true drama. Jump over to *http://url.co.nz/african_trip/tanzania.html* to read an individual's account of a recent trip to "Leakey territory" in "In the Cradle of Humankind."

Anthropology, Archaeology, and American Indian Sites on the Internet

http://dizzy.library.arizona.edu/library/teams/sst/anthro/

This Web page points out a number of Internet sites of interest to archaeologists. Visit this page for links to electronic journals and more.

Cult Archaeology Topics

http://www.usd.edu/anth/cultarch/culttopics.html

This fun site provides information on interesting pseudoarchaeological theories that often have attracted scholarly attention. These endeavors are sometimes called cult or fantastic archaeology. The Moundbuilder Myth is one theory that is debunked here.

GMU Anthropology Department

http://www.gmu.edu/departments/anthro/

Look over this site for current listings of scientific papers dealing with anthropological and archaeological studies. The site provides a number of interesting links, such as a listing of archaeological fieldwork opportunities.

Smithsonian Institution Web Site

http://www.si.edu/

This site, which will provide access to many of the enormous resources of the Smithsonian, will give you a sense of the scope of anthropological and archaeological inquiry today.

UNIT 2: Problem Oriented Archaeology

Archaeology Links (NC)

http://www.arch.dcr.state.nc.us/links.htm#stuff

North Carolina Archaeology provides this site, which has many links to sites of interest to archaeologists, such as the paleolithic painted cave at Vallon-Pont-d'Arc (Ardeche).

www.dushkin.com/online/

Archaeology Magazine
http://www.archaeology.org

This home page of *Archaeology* magazine, the official publication of the AIA, provides information about current archaeological events, staff picks of Web sites, and access to selected articles from current and past editions of the magazine.

UNIT 3: Techniques in Archaeology

American Anthropologist
http://www.aaanet.org

Check out this site—the home page of the American Anthropology Association—for general information about archaeology and anthropology as well as access to a wide variety of articles.

Ancient Economies II
http://www.angelfire.com/ms/ancecon/

This site addresses ancient economies and in so doing reveals the importance of archaeology in discovering the cultures and practices of people who lived long ago.

NOVA Online/Pyramids—The Inside Story
http://www.pbs.org/wgbh/nova/pyramid/

Take a virtual tour of the pyramids at Giza through this interesting site. It provides information on the pharaohs for whom the tombs were built and follows a team of archaeologists as they excavate a bakery that fed the pyramid builders.

UNIT 4: Historical Archaeology

GIS and Remote Sensing for Archaeology: Burgundy, France
http://www.informatics.org/france/france.html

This project has been an ongoing collaboration between Dr. Scott Madry from the Center for Remote Sensing and Spatial Analysis at Rutgers University and many other researchers. A period of over 2,000 years in the Arroux River Valley region of Burgundy is being analyzed to understand long-term interaction between the different cultures and the physical environment.

Petra Great Temple/Technology
http://www.brown.edu/Departments/Anthropology/Petra/excavations/technology.html

The introduction of a field reporting system using computers in fieldwork holds promise for resolving the dilemma between recording much information or recording accurate data. At this site, surveying, is done using a computer-controlled theodolite and ground-penetrating radar.

Radiocarbon Dating for Archaeology
http://www.rlaha.ox.ac.uk/orau/index.html

This Web site describes the advantages inherent in using radiocarbon dating to promote mass spectrometry over the older decay counting method.

Zeno's Forensic Page
http://forensic.to/forensic.html

A complete list of resources on forensics is here. It includes DNA/serology sources and databases, forensic-medicine anthropology sites, and related areas.

UNIT 5: Contemporary Archaeology

Ancient World Web
http://www.julen.net/ancient/

Extensive categories at this site include Alternative Theories, Art, Daily Life, History, Mythology and Religion, and Science.

Archaeology and Anthropology: The Australian National University
http://online.anu.edu.au/AandA/

Browse through this home page of the Anthropology and Archaeology Departments of the Australian National University for information about topics in Australian and regional archaeology and to access links to other resource centers.

WWW: Classical Archaeology
http://www.archaeology.org/wwwarky/classical.html

This site provides information and links regarding ancient Greek and Roman archaeology.

General Sources

Al Mashriq-Archaeology in Beirut
http://almashriq.hiof.no/base/archaeology.html

At this site the links to the fascinating excavations taking place in Beirut can be explored. Reports from the site, background material, discussion of the importance of the site, and information on other Lebanese sites are included.

American Indian Ritual Object Repatriation Foundation
http://www.repatriationfoundation.org/

Visit this home page of the American Indian Ritual Object Repatriation Foundation, which aims to assist in the return of sacred ceremonial material to the appropriate American Indian nation, clan, or family, and to educate the public.

ArchNet—WWW Virtual Library
http://archnet.asu.edu/archnet/

ArchNet serves as the World Wide Web Virtual Library for Archaeology. This site can provide you with access to a broad variety of archaeological resources available on the Internet, categorized by geographic region and subject.

Current Archaeology
http://www.archaeology.co.uk

This is the home page of *Current Archaeology,* Great Britain's leading archaeological magazine. Its various sections provide links about archaeology in Britain.

www.dushkin.com/online/

National Archeological DataBase
http://www.cast.uark.edu/other/nps/nagpra/nagpra.html
  Examine this site from the Archeology and Ethnography
  Program of the NAD to read documents related to the Native
  American Graves Protection and Repatriation Act.

Society for Archaeological Sciences
http://www.socarchsci.org/
  The Society for Archaeological Sciences provides this site to
  further communication among scholars applying methods from
  the physical sciences to archaeology.

We highly recommend that you review our Web site for expanded information and our
other product lines. We are continually updating and adding links to our Web site in order
to offer you the most usable and useful information that will support and expand the value
of your Annual Editions. You can reach us at: *http://www.dushkin.com/annualeditions/.*

UNIT 1

About Archaeologists and Archaeology

Unit Selections

Key Points to Consider

- When was archaeology recognized as a science? Does anyone really understand postmodernism?

- What is an antiquarian: grave robber, and looter? Give examples of each.

- What is a modern archaeologist? Give some examples of what is meant by archaeological methods, fieldwork, theory and ethics.

- How is culture viewed by anthropology?

- What is the general relationship between anthropology and archaeology? Please give specific examples.

- What is public archaeology? How could archaeologist better communicate with the public? What role should archaeology play in public education? Give some examples.

- What is the difference between academic and non-academic archaeologists? What is the potential for non-academic archaeologists?

- What kinds of problems do archaeologists have with questions of legal entitlement? What kinds of conflicts occur between contemporary native groups and archaeologists over the rights to excavate? Give some examples.

- What kind of conflicts do archaeologists have while doing their work in a combat-area zone? How do they archieve a normalization of violence?

- What is the biggest find in Egypt since Kind Tut-ankh-Amun's tomb? Why is digging in Egypt considered to be a cliché among archaeologists? Is this an example of academic archaeology? Give some examples.

 **Links: www.dushkin.com/online/**
These sites are annotated in the World Wide Web pages.

Ancestral Passions
http://www.canoe.ca/JamBooksReviewsA/ancestral_morell.html

Anthropology, Archaeology, and American Indian Sites on the Internet
http://dizzy.library.arizona.edu/library/teams/sst/anthro/

Cult Archaeology Topics
http://www.usd.edu/anth/cultarch/culttopics.html

GMU Anthropology Department
http://www.gmu.edu/departments/anthro/

Smithsonian Institution Web Site
http://www.si.edu/

Ozymandias [1817]
I met a traveller from an antique land,
Who said: Two vast and trunkless legs of stone
Stand in the desert. Near them, on the sand,
Half sunk, a shattered visage lies, whose frown,
And wrinkled lip, and sneer of cold command,
Tell that its sculptor well those passions read
Which yet survive, stamped on these lifeless things,
The hand that mocked them, and the heart that fed;
And on the pedestal these words appear: "My name
    is Ozymandias, King of Kings:
Look on my works, ye Mighty, and despair!"
Nothing beside remains. Round the decay
Of that colossal wreck, boundless and bare,
The lone and level sands stretch far away.
                          —Percy Bysshe Shelley

About Archaeology. What is the difference between archaeology and anthropology? Would the archaeologists or anthropologists who have not been asked this question please stand up and be counted!

If human behavior were a baseball game, the anthropologist would be in the broadcaster's booth. But long before the game was over, in a seeming paradox, the anthropologist would run into the stands to be a spectator, chow down on a good fresh steamy mustard-covered hot dog, and then rush onto the field to be a player and catch a high fly to left field. This is the eccentric nature of anthropology. This is why anthropology is so interesting.

If one compares anthropology, psychology, sociology, and history as four disciplines that study human nature, anthropology

is the one that takes the giant step back and uses a 360-degree panoramic camera. The psychologist stands nose to nose with the individual person, the sociologist moves back for the group shot, and the historian goes back in time as well as space. However, the anthropologist does all these things, standing well behind the others, watching and measuring, using the data of all these disciplines but recombining them into the uniqueness of the anthropological perspective: much the way meiosis generates novel genetic combinations.

Anthropology is the science of human behavior that studies all humankind, starting with our biological and evolutionary origins as cultural beings and continuing with the diversification of our cultural selves. Humankind is the single species that has evolved culture as our unique way of adapting to the world.

Academically, anthropology is divided into the two major fields of physical and cultural anthropology. Cultural anthropologists hold in common a generally shared concept of culture. The basic tenet that cultural anthropologists share is to generate a behavioral science that can explain the differences and similarities between cultures. In order to achieve this, cultural anthropologists view people within a cross-cultural perspective. This encompasses comparing the parts and parcels of all cultures, present and past, with each other. This is the holistic approach of anthropology: considering all things in all their manifestations. A grand task, indeed. One that requires, above all, learning to ask the "right" questions.

What is culture? Culture is the unique way in which our species adapts to its total environment. Total environment includes everything that affects human beings—the physical environment, plants, animals, the weather, beliefs, values, a passing insult, or an opportunistic virus. Everything possible that human beings are capable of is by culture.

Culture is the human adaptive system. It is an ecology in which all people live in groups defined by time, space, and place. They pass on shared values and beliefs through common language(s), and manipulate things in their environment through tool use and tool making. Cultures change and evolve through time. And perhaps most enigmatically cultures, all cultures, be they high civilizations or small tribes, do eventually cease to exist.

Archaeology is the subfield of cultural anthropology that studies these extinct cultures. Archaeologists dig up the physical remains, the tools, the houses, the garbage and the utensils of once-living cultures. And from this spare database, archaeologists attempt to reconstruct these past cultures in their material, social, and ideological aspects. Is this important to anthropology? Yes, this is anthropology. Because these once-living cultures represent approximately ninety-eight percent of all cultures that have ever existed. They tell us where we have been, when we are there again, and where we might go in the future.

How do archaeologists do this? Today the mass media is the major source of the epistemology in the modern world and thus underscores cultural values as well as creating the necessary cultural myths by which all humans must live. The media is as much a response to our demands as we are to its manipulations. Its themes play a medley in our minds over and over again, until they fade into our unconscious only to be recycled again, pulled up, and laid before us like the ice cream man's musical chimes of our childhood. But the media mind is characterized by fuzzy thinking and credulity. The essence of archaeology is scientific thinking and skepticism. If minds are trained to be articulate, thought and action will follow suit. Scientific thinking involves a very strict set of rules and regulations that test the veracity of conclusions. A kind of operationalized language emerges, codified similarly to mathematics, that allows apples to be compared to apples.

Postmodernists may argue that knowledge is only knowable in a relative sense. But we know what we know in a very real and pragmatic sense because we are, after all, humans—the cultural animal. It is our way of knowing and surviving. Let us proceed now to see how archaeologists ply their magical trade.

Metaphors We Dig By

by Warren R DeBoer
Queens College Cuny

In addressing the theme "As Others See Us," I surveyed undergraduate students enrolled in my introductory archaeology classes at Queens College

during the 1998–99 academic year. The survey is based on pen or pencil-on-paper drawings collected from 76 students, 43 males and 33 females from 19 different countries of birth, a diversity reflecting the large immigrant population of the Borough of Queens. During the first class session, each student was asked to

"draw an archaeologist." In presenting the results, I follow the journalistic formal of who?, what? and where?

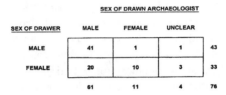

	SEX OF DRAWN ARCHAEOLOGIST			
SEX OF DRAWER	**MALE**	**FEMALE**	**UNCLEAR**	
MALE	41	1	1	43
FEMALE	20	10	3	33
	61	11	4	76

WHO ARE ARCHAEOLOGISTS?

As drawn, most archaeologists are males (61:11). Although females are more likely to draw female archaeologists, they also choose to draw males by a 2:1 margin. Whether this result—which does not accurately reflect the actual composition of the archaeological profession—indicates a significant male-domination of perceptions of archaeology, or merely a more pervasive and general sexism, could only be explored through additional tests (eg, drawings of doctors, lawyers, but probably not "Indian chiefs").

More telling is how the male-dominated sample is rendered. As shown in the drawings, archaeologists tend to be hirsute. Beards and moustaches are common. Coupled with hairiness is the wearing of glasses, usually of the rimless sort.

There are also sartorial motifs. Hats, especially wide-brimmed ones, are virtually obligatory; boots underscore that archaeologists are outdoor types who, above all, *dig;* "jungle suits" complete the profile.

A word about somatotype. As pointed out many years ago by Alfred Kidder, archaeologists come in two varieties: the hairy-chested and the hairy-chinned. The first is an emblem of carnal virility, while the second is a skinny wreak of a somatotype with scholarly, mad or otherwise weird tendencies. The same polarity can be found in novels and films. Although a few of the drawings are clearly inspired by Indiana Jones or other popular icons, it would be a mistake to believe that these media-based stereotypes determine popular perceptions. More likely, both the popular media and public participate in a enduring structure that was already there.

WHAT DO ARCHAEOLOGISTS DO?

Archaeologists dig holes (7 cases), or work in caves (3+; recall that both *cavern* and *excavate* are rooted in Latin *cavus*, "hollow" or "hole"), and to do so they need tools. In fact, the archaeologist is the quintessential "Man the Tool-User." Tools are dominated by shovels (16), picks (15) and trowels (4). Brushes (5), a notebook and a magnifying glass intimate a softer, more studious touch, but the overall impression is one of vigorous digging facilitated by an "extended phenotype" of sharp, earth-penetrating devices. With some exceptions, archaeologists themselves rarely publicize the tool-centered nature of their activity. Such technical matters of craft are relegated to oral tradition. Finally, the inclusion of beer mugs (2) suggests that some archaeologists like to drink.

What are archaeologists looking for anyway? Although unsolicited, paraphernalia in the drawings allow us to address this question. Apparently archaeologists are looking for bones. Bones (16) far exceed pots (4), "rocks" (4), or other artifacts. The quest for bones suggests that archaeologists (like a few of their brethren in physical anthropology) are basically fossil-hunters—a wincing thought in this NAGPRA era. Although archaeologists constitute only about 25% of American anthropology departments and physical anthropologists another 15% (estimates based on the AAA *Guide*), the deep-seated image of dry, dusty bones pervades public images of anthropology at-large. However, resented by cultural anthropologists, archaeologists have been, and continue to be, central metaphor-givers of the profession.

WHERE DO ARCHAEOLOGISTS DIG?

Real archaeologists do not work in Illinois, Alabama, New Jersey or New York. According to Queens College students, they dig in exotic lands where there are mountains (3), "natives" (3), cave paintings (3), and hieroglyphs and pyramids (2). To supplement their drawings, I asked the same students to indicate the most likely place to find an authentic archaeological "dig." The responses are informative.

Martin Bernal, author of *Black Athena,* would be pleased that Egypt (with 33 votes) wins hands-down, followed by the Near East (12), African "early man" sites (9), and European "caveman" (6). In contrast, Stonehenge, Chaco Canyon and other "cliff-dwellings", the Maya, Machu Picchu and Easter Island are but dimly registered in mental maps of the archaeological landscape.

A crucial aspect of archaeological authenticity, therefore, entails a spatial metaphor involving a journey to exotic and distant lands. As book titles suggest (*Corridors in Time, New Roads to Yesterday* and *In Pursuit of the Past* are examples that could easily be multiplied), this journey in space is likened to a journey back in time. The drawings call attention to another trope. Following a cartoon format, several students attached speech scrolls to their archaeologists. Their gist is either one of exhilarating

discovery ("I've found it!") or, alternatively, one of frustrating disappointment ("I still haven't found anything!"). The unifying theme is clearly one of *loss,* as in *lost civilizations.* The space-time metaphor is activated to suggest a wrenching loss that took place in either the phylogenetic or ontogenetic past.

ARCHAEOLOGISTS DEFINED

The above portrait of the archaeological enterprise can be summarized as follows. Archaeologists tend to be spectacled, hirsute males who brandish sharp implements for digging holes. They do this in exotic, forbidden locales to seek—or re-find—a lost bone! The astute, whether disposed toward Freudian analysis or not, will sense the oedipal and castration anxieties at the core of this picture. For instance, the bone as "lost phallus" is more transparently rendered here than in any Lacanian text that I've not been able to understand. Furthermore, the archaeologist, much like the Native American figure of the Trickster, seems confused about body orifices and gender. He appears to have trouble distinguishing his ass from a hole-in-the-ground.

By emphasizing the matter of sexual identity, I do not offer archaeology as a test case in Queer Theory. Nor am I es-

WHERE DO ANTHROPOLOGISTS DIG?	
Egypt	33
Near EastBiblical	12
"Early Man"	9
"Cave Man"	6
US Southwest	2
Maya	2
"Amazon"	2
Easter Island	2
Machu Picchu	2
Mexico	1
Stonehenge	1
Indus Valley	1
China	1
"Local Indians"	2

Archaeologists tend to be spectacled, hisute males who brandish sharp implements for digging holes. They do this in exotic, forbidden locales to seek—or re-find—a lost bone!

pousing a psychoanalytic archaeology—although Freud likened his own work to that of an archaeologist—and a Freudian perspective continues to be a powerful source of metaphor for shedding light on the human condition. The more general critique is stated aptly by Gísil Pálsson:

"the Baconian imagery of sexual assault, of entering and penetrating holes and corners, is a recurrent one. The literature on modern science is replete with passages that describe human-environmental interactions by means of an aggressive, sexual idiom; nature appears as a seductive but troublesome female. Anthropology is not exempt from modernist, sexual jargon and predator-prey metaphors" (*Nature and Society* 1996, page 63)

Nor is such exemption illustrated by the case reported here.

Warren R DeBoer, *professor of anthropology at Queens C, CUNY, Flushing, has interests in the prehistory of the Americas. He is recipient of the 1999 Society for American Archaeology's Excellence in Ceramics Award.*

The Awful Truth about Archaeology

Dr. Lynne Sebastian

"Ohhhh! You're an Archaeologist! That sounds soooo exciting!" Whenever I tell someone on a plane or at a dinner party what I do for a living, this is almost always the response that I get. Either that, or they want to talk to me about dinosaurs, and I have to explain gently that it is paleontologists who do dinosaurs; archaeologist study people who lived long ago.

The reason people think archaeology must be exciting is that they have spent WAY too much time watching The *Curse of the Mummy*, *Indiana Jones* and the *Temple of Doom*, and *Lara Croft, Tomb Raider* (do you suppose that she actually has that printed on her business cards?). Perhaps it is a flaw in my character or a lapse in my professional education, but I have never once recovered a golden idol or been chased through the jungle by thugs, and I appear to have been absent from graduate school on the day that they covered bullwhips, firearms, and the martial arts. I have not even, so far as I can tell, suffered from a curse, although I have had few nasty encounters with serpents, scorpions, and lightening.

I'm sure that members of every profession are exasperated by the way that they are portrayed in movies and on television, and archaeologists are no exception. Every time we see Sydney Fox (*Relict Hunter*, another great job title) fly off to an exotic country, follow the clues on the ancient map, and rip-off some fabulous object to bring home to the museum, we want to root for the bad guys who are trying to bring her career to an abrupt and permanent halt.

What would really happen if a mysterious man wearing an eye patch showed up at Sydney's university office and gave her the map, just before expiring as a result of slow-acting poison? Well, of course, first there would be a lot of unpleasantness with the campus police ... but leaving that aside, she would spend months writing grant proposals to get funding for a research expedition and more months getting the needed permits and authorizations from the government of the exotic country. Then she would have to persuade the Dean and her department Chair to give her release time from teaching. And when she and her research team finally arrived in the exotic country, they would spend months meticulously mapping the site, painstakingly re-

moving thin layers of soil from perfectly square holes, and recording every stone, every bit of stained earth, every piece of debris that they encountered, using photos, maps, sketches, and detailed written notes. Finally, at the end of the field season, the team would return to the university with 70 boxes of broken pottery, bits of stone, and all manner of scientific samples to be washed and cataloged and analyzed. And in the end, all that material would be returned to a musuem in the exotic country.

Now, of course, nobody would want to watch a TV show where even the beauteous Sydney did all that, but this kind of tedious, detailed work is one important aspect of "real" archaeology. Just about every archaeologist that I know has a copy of an old Calvin and Hobbs cartoon somewhere in his or her office. In it, Calvin, who has spent an exhausting day doing a make-believe archaeological excavation in his backyard, turns to Hobbs in disgust and says, "Archaeology has to be the most mind-numbing job in the world!!" And some days it is. Worse yet, it is detailed work that involves a lot of paperwork and delicate instruments but has to be done outdoors in every sort of adverse weather. When it is 20 degrees and you are hunched down in a square hole in the ground trying to write a description of layers of dirt with a pen that keeps freezing solid or when the wind is blowing sheets of sand straight sideways into your face while you are lying on your stomach using a dental pick to expose a broken shell bracelet so you can photograph it before you remove it - these are experiences that can cause a person to question her career choice.

But you know what? Archaeology really IS exciting, and not for any of the reasons that Indy or Lara would suggest. Archaeology is exciting because it connects with the past in a way that nothing else can, and sometimes that connection can be stunningly immediate and personal. I worked one year on the Hopi Reservation in Arizona, excavating a site that was going to be destroyed by road construction. We found that one of the three "pithouses" or semi-subterranean structures on the site appeared to have been cleaned out and closed up, presumably in the expectation that someone would return to live in it again. A flat slab had been placed over the ventilator opening, perhaps to keep out dirt and debris and critters, and the slab was sealed in place with wet mud. But no one came back, and eventually the small pithouse burned.

When we excavated the pithouse, we found the imprint of human hands, perfectly preserved in the mud, which had been hardened by the fire. That little house was built in AD 805, but I could reach out and place my hands in those handprints left there by someone a thousand years before. And more important, the Hopi school children who visited the site could place their small hands in those prints made by one of their ancestors, 50 generations removed. We lifted each one of the children into the pithouse, and let them do just that—like children everywhere, they were astonished that they were being encouraged to touch rather than being forbidden to do so.

Afterward we sat together on the site and talked about what life was like for that Hisatsinom (the Hopi term for the people we call Anasazi) person. We talked about food and looked at the burned corn kernels and the squash seeds that we had found. We talked about shelter and tools and looked at the three houses and the broken bits of stone and bone and pottery that we were recovering from the trash areas at the site. One of the houses had burned while it was occupied, and we looked at the fragments of the rolled up sleeping mats and baskets of corn and other possessions that the people had lost. We talked about the family that had lived there, how much the parents loved their children and how they must have worried about providing for them after such a terrible loss. And we talked about the migration stories that are a central part of Hopi oral history, and about what the Hopi elders had told us about the place of this particular site in those stories. I like to think that those children, who reached back across the centuries and touched the hand of their fifty-times-great grandmother, came away with a stronger sense of who they were and where they came from and a richer understanding of the oral traditions of their people.

But what if I had been not me, Dr. Science, purveyor of meticulous and mind-numbing archaeological techniques, but rather Lara Croft, Tomb Raider? If Lara had been rooting about in this site, searching for "treasures," she would have quickly dismissed that small pithouse, although she might

have smashed that burned mud with the handprints in order to rip away the slab and check for hidden goodies behind it.

No, she would have focused on the other house, the one that burned while it was being used. She would have pulled out all those burned roof beams whose pattern of rings enabled us to learn that the houses were built in AD 805, probably using them for her campfire. She would have crushed the remnants of the burned sleeping mats and baskets of corn. She would never have noticed the stone griddle still in place on the hearth or the grease stains left by the last two corn cakes cooking on it when the fire started. She would have kicked aside the broken pieces of the pottery vessels that were crushed when the burning roof fell, the same pots that we put back together in the lab in order to estimate the size of the family and to recover traces of the items stored and cooked in them.

No, Lara would have missed all that we learned about that site and the people who made their homes there. Instead, she would have seized the single piece of pottery that didn't break in the fire and clutching it to her computer enhanced bosom, she would have stolen away into the night, narrowly escaping death and destruction at the hands of the rival gang of looters.

Is archaeology the most mind-numbing pursuit in the world, as Calvin claims? Or is it "sooo exciting" as my airline seatmates always exclaim? Both. And much more. What Lara and Indy and the others don't know is that archaeology is not about things, it is about people. It is about understanding life in the past, about understanding who we are and where we came from—not just where we came from as a particular cultural group, but what we share with all people in this time and in all the time that came before.

Lynne Sebastian is Director of Historic Preservation with the SRI Foundation, a private nonprofit dedicated to historic preservation, and an adjunct assistant professor of Anthropology at UNM. She is a former New Mexico State Archaeologist and State Historic Preservation Office, and she is currently the President of the Society for American Archaeology.

The Quest for the Past

Brian M. Fagan

Archaeologists are commonly thought to be eccentric people who wear rumpled khaki shorts and sun helmets and spend their lives unearthing crumbling ruins in the shadow of mighty pyramids. They live in a world of lost civilizations and buried treasure, deep mysteries and unexplained phenomena. The archaeologist of novel and television seems to be continually off on a "dig," searching for missing links and unwrapping innumerable Ancient Egyptian mummies. Sometimes, too, the angry mummies chase the unfortunate archaelogists, intoning dreadful curses that lead to their premature deaths. Many of us, at one time or another, have dreamed of pursuing such a romantic—if, in fact, mythical—career.

This is ... about actual archaeological discoveries, about remarkable archaeologists whose explorations have dramatically expanded our understanding of human history. It is ... about the excitement of archaeological discovery about a scientific world that many consider to be one of the most engrossing frontiers of science. Its heroes are archaeologists of extraordinary ability who have made fascinating discoveries, often after years of patient effort. Each was a pioneer who pursued a dream, a conviction that spectacular archaeological finds awaited his or her spade.

The face of archaeology has changed considerably in recent years. Archaeologists of the 1840s, and even as late as the 1930s, could hope to uncover hitherto unknown civilizations: the Assyrians and Sumerians of Mesopotamia surfaced in the mid-nineteenth century, the Maya of Mexico in the 1840s, the Mycenaeans of Greece in the 1870s, the Shang civili-

zation of China in the late 1920s. All of these discoveries captured the public imagination, for they were made under conditions of great difficulty, conditions that often required near-heroic efforts. The early archaeologists had few resources and no advanced excavation techniques. By constant improvisation, by drawing on their own wealth, and by acute political maneuvering, they frequently achieved miracles. They learned digging the hard way, made brilliant finds, and, regrettably, sometimes irreparably damaged vital clues to the past.

Some of our archaeologists belong to this heroic era, others to our own generation, where there are simply no lost civilizations left to find. But today's archaeologists still make remarkable discoveries, often as a result of applying such advanced tools as the computer to archaeological data. Modern archaeology is big business; thousands of people all over the world are currently involved in digging up the past. Practically every nation now employs a few archaeologists—as museum curators, university professors, or conservators of national culture. All of these archaeologists use excavation techniques that have evolved over generations of archaeological discovery. The newer techniques enable them to tackle problems that would have boggled the mind even a few years ago.

One of Mexico's earliest cities, Teotihuacán, is a case in point. Early archaeologists could only gasp at the size of Teotihuacán, sample a portion of a pyramid or a few houses, then turn away in despair. They simply did not have the technology needed to carry their explorations further. It has taken a team of

modern archaeologists over a decade to map the entire twelve-and-a-half square miles of Mexico's largest prehistoric city. Their task would have been impossible without a mosaic of air photographs and highly sophisticated computer programs that enabled them to store inventories of archaeological finds and millions of other items of information on computer tape. When the time came to put the data together, the archaeologists could recall and classify thousands of data items in a few seconds. The result: a whole new picture of Teotihuacán.

How do archaeologists dig up the past? What makes archaeological excavation different from ditch digging or the treasure-hunting activities of our mythical, sun-helmeted archaeologist? To get some idea of just how far the field of archaeology has progressed, let's look back over its colorful history.

Archaeology has a long and disreputable line of descent: its ancestors were, quite literally, grave robbers and adventurers. A century and a half ago, even serious archaeological excavation was little more than licensed treasure hunting. Everyone, whether archaeologist or treasure hunter, had the same objective—to recover as many valuable objects as possible in the shortest time. Serious archaeologists would not hesitate to use gunpowder to blast their way into a burial chamber or a pyramid. Everything was cast aside in a frantic search for the valuable and spectacular. As a result, most excavations resembled untidy vegetable gardens.

Mummy hunters in Egypt literally waded through piles of discarded coffins to reach their prey. The famous Italian collector Giovanni Belzoni, who worked in Egypt from 1817 to 1820, would crawl hundreds of yards into the rocky hillsides behind Thebes in search of mummies and papyri. Exhausted, he would perch in the darkness for a few minutes on a convenient mummy. Once his perch collapsed in a cloud of smelly dust. "I sank altogether among the broken mummies, with a crash of bones, rags, and wooden cases," he remembered. It was a good quarter of an hour before Belzoni could extricate himself.

Belzoni and his contemporaries were quite open about their efforts to "rob the Egyptians of their papyri." No one thought this either eccentric or wrong. Rather, Belzoni's audiences would be agog as he related his eerie experiences in the dark burial chambers, where, in the flickering lamp light, the mummies seemed almost to converse with one another and the naked Arab workmen, coated in layers of dust, resembled mummies themselves. The audiences would gasp as Belzoni produced pieces of desiccated ancient Egyptians, remarking casually that "mummies are rather unpleasant to swallow."

In general, the nineteenth century was a time of frantic search for ancient sculptures and fine artifacts, whether from Egypt, Greece, Mesopotamia, or the Americas. Everyone wanted items for their collections and no one had any scruples about the means used to dig up their pet acquisitions. All too often we read in their early reports that such and such a find "crumbled to dust" on discovery or that exposure to the open air caused the finds to "dissolve before our very eyes."

One cannot entirely blame Belzoni and his successors. Basically, they were ignorant. No one had ever tried to dig a large archaeological site at all systematically. Even today, the technology of conservation is in relative infancy and modern archaeologists are still at a loss as to how to preserve many delicate finds satisfactorily. Considering the state of the art, it's a miracle that so much is preserved from early excavations. But the archaeological price of filling the British Museum, the Louvre, and other great museums was simply enormous: witness Austen Henry Layard's excavations in

Mesopotamia at ancient Nineveh and Nimrud from 1845 to 1851.

Layard started digging Nimrud with precious little money and absolutely no archaeological experience. He simply tunneled into the huge mounds reputed to be the remains of these ancient cities and went on digging until he hit a fine sculpture or a stone-walled palace room. At Nimrud he was lucky enough to find two palaces. But, as he dug through mud-brick walls and houses, he failed to recognize invaluable inscribed tablets of unbaked clay. To his unskilled eyes, the bricks and tablets were indistinguishable from the brown soil of the mound. Later excavators recovered thousands of these tablets from areas of Nimrud that Layard left untouched. They had developed the skills and techniques to find them.

The deep tunnels that Layard dug along walls or lines of sculptured slabs at least sheltered him from the merciless sun and sweeping winds of the open plains. He would shovel out the contents of each room with dispatch, then sit down to record the intricate details of prancing horsemen and fighting warriors that flickered in the somber shadows. When his trenches were open to the elements, clouds of blinding dust stirred by savage gale-force winds would bombard the workmen. Layard himself would take refuge behind a giant sculpture until the sandstorm subsided. Under the circumstances, it is remarkable that he succeeded in excavating at all.

Austen Henry Layard shifted thousands of tons of soil, discovered nearly two miles of bas-reliefs, and cleared seventy rooms in the Palace of Sennacherib at Kuyunjik alone. Although he did keep some records, he more or less shoveled his way into the past. He tore Nimrud and Nineveh apart and, in the process, wiped out priceless archaeological information—data on daily life and ancient diet, details of houses and storerooms, and, above all, the complex sequence of layers that made up the occupation mounds.

Every Mesopotamian city mound was formed over centuries of occupation through complex processes of rebuilding houses, dumping garbage, and the natural actions of rain and wind. Many years before Layard came to Nineveh, geolo-

gists studying railway cuttings and canal excavations in Europe and America had observed the layered strata of the earth and established the classic principle of superposition. Very simply stated, this means that the lower levels of a succession of geological horizons were laid down earlier than the higher levels. The law of superposition had obvious applications to great city mounds like Nimrud or Nineveh, for every site started as a small settlement on a low ridge. The first occupation levels were soon covered by later settlements built in the same place. A thousand years later, the same city could look down from the top of a high mound of age-old occupation debris. The archaeologist wishing to understand the history of the city would have to dissect this mound layer by layer.

Layard himself was well aware that his mounds had gone through many changes. He knew that many kings had ruled his cities. But his excavation methods were simply too crude to permit him to dig the mounds period by period. One cannot blame Layard. If anything, he was more conscientious than his contemporaries, for he at least wrote popular accounts of his findings.

Many excavations of Layard's time were little more than picnic parties. Wealthy country gentlemen would open Indian burial mounds or Bronze Age earthworks for the sheer fun of it. When the English antiquarian Thomas Wright attended the opening of an ancient burial mound in 1844, he found a large party of interested gentry assembled for the sport. While the workmen opened eight burial mounds, the ladies and gentlemen "continued to spend [their] time, at intervals between digging and picnicking, in games of various descriptions … and in other amusements. The weather was fortunately exquisitely fine." When a sudden shower threatened to drench the party; they took refuge in the trench under a shield of umbrellas. The burial mounds contained "skeletons, more or less entire, with the remains of weapons in iron, bosses of shields, urns, beads, armlets, and occasionally more vessels." All of these finds vanished into the landowner's private collection, which the party inspected after partaking of a "sumptuous repast." This burial-mound dig was in no way exceptional; rather, it was typical of thousands.

The techniques of excavation were still in their infancy when Heinrich Schliemann began work on the great Hissarlik mound, site of ancient Troy. Schliemann, a millionaire, attacked archaeological problems with the same single-minded intensity he applied to business ventures. His wealth gave him the means to work on a truly grand scale, with resident experts and hundreds of workmen. He arrived on the site in 1871 with the vague notion that the mound contained many different settlements. So he set out to dig to bedrock, on a scale that almost beggars description. In 1872, for example, he borrowed a railroad engineer and employed three overseers to direct over a hundred men. They sliced into Hissarlik with a cutting over 230 feet wide that eventually penetrated over 40 feet into the huge mound. The city walls found in the upper-most strata were ruthlessly cleared away as Schliemann dug his way down through the centuries, toward his Homeric city.

Eventually, Schliemann identified the remains of seven cities, one above the other. His excavations exhibited a notable lack of finesse. In his books, he refers to the clearance of entire ancient streets, to the removal of "older walls which I am also having broken through," and to thousands upon thousands of potsherds, ornaments, and other small finds that were shoveled out as thousands of tons of soil were dug out of Hissarlik. At one point, he boasted that he had removed 325,000 cubic yards of soil from ancient Troy.

Schliemann's motto was speed, more speed, and yet still more. When he dug, he cleared an entire landscape. Every day he described his findings in a comprehensive diary, which he eventually published. Unlike many of his contemporaries, Schliemann kept his finds and recorded all of them, not just the spectacular pieces. And, although he has been castigated as little more than a treasure hunter, he in fact undertook the first large-scale dissection of a city mound where, unlike the situation at Nineveh or Nimrud, there were no sculptures to guide the way to ancient structures. As his digging experience increased, Schliemann began to rely more heavily on ex-

pert diggers, who were able to refine his methods drastically.

While Schliemann was working at Troy, German archaeologists had begun a quiet revolution in excavation methods that was to affect both the Troy excavations and many other digs as well. The Austrian archaeologist Alexander Conze dug at the site of Samothrace in Greece between 1873 and 1875. He dug with the help of architects and a photographer, who recorded the progress of the excavations. The Samothrace report was a beautiful production, the first to be illustrated with photographs. Conze's example was not lost on the German Archaeological Institute, which started work at Olympia in 1875. For six winters, Ernst Curtius directed a brilliant campaign of excavations on the site of the original Olympic Games. The Kaiser himself paid for part of the dig. Every find was carefully preserved and housed in a special museum built at the site. No artifacts were exported. Curtius and Wilhelm Dörpfeld worked out every detail of the stratigraphy at Olympia with the aid of new and very precise record-keeping methods. The Olympia excavations set new standards that the ever-energetic Dörpfeld took with him to Troy. In his later years at Hissarlik, Schliemann became what one authority has called "a constitutional monarch among expert ministers." Dörpfeld refined Schliemann's seven cities into the complex history of a mound that, he said, flourished from about 3000–700 B.C., the Homeric city dating from 1500–1000 B.C.

Curtius and Dörpfeld were concerned with the trivial as well as the spectacular. Their excavations were far more meticulous than those of their predecessors, although still crude by modern standards. A retired British general named Augustus Pitt-Rivers revolutionized the art of excavation even further. The general, a formidable personality, spent much of his military career working on the development of army rifles. His experimental research involved him in the history of firearms and the study of different types of primitive artifacts from all over the world. Pitt-Rivers was deeply interested in the evolution of human technology. He became an avid collector of artifacts of all types—masks, shields, weapons,

even canoes. His collections became so large that he donated them to Oxford University, where they are to this day.

In 1880, Pitt-Rivers inherited an enormous estate in southern England, an estate littered with ancient burial sites and earthworks. The general decided to devote the rest of his life to investigation of the sites on his property. He did so with ruthless efficiency, diverting enormous sums from his fortune into leisured excavations that lasted twenty years, until his death in 1901. Pitt-Rivers had a mania for records and detail. "Every detail should be recorded in the manner most conducive to facility of reference," he wrote. "I have endeavored to record the results of these excavations in such a way that the whole of the evidence may be available for those who are concerned to go into it." He had realized a cardinal point: all archaeological excavation is permanent destruction and all objects found in a site have a vital context in time and space that is just as important a piece of information as the find itself.

The learned general was far ahead of his time. He trained archaeological assistants, had "before" and "after" models of his sites constructed, built a special museum to display his finds, and even marked his filled-in trenches with special medallions that said, in effect, "Pitt-Rivers was here." His ideas were revolutionary. Consider some of his basic principles of digging: "No excavation ought to ever be permitted except under the immediate eye of a responsible and trustworthy superintendent." "Superfluous precision may be regarded as a fault on the right side." "Tedious as it may appear to some to dwell on the discovery of odds and ends that have, no doubt, been thrown away by the owners as rubbish... yet it is by the study of such trivial details that archaeology is mainly dependent for determining the date of earthworks."

Hundreds of man-hours went into each of Pitt-Rivers's sumptuous reports. Each was published privately, complete with detailed plans, accurate measurements of every artifact, and precise information on every aspect of the site from pottery to hut foundations, stratigraphy to animal bones. It was to be years before anyone would equal or surpass Pitt-Rivers's painstaking work. He deplored the destruction of earthworks by plowing, laid out picnic grounds for people visiting his museum, and urged his fellow landowners to follow his example. The general was not a particularly endearing gentleman, but his legacy to archaeology is unquestioned. An interesting glimpse into the man comes from a photograph of the excavations which is tersely captioned: "The figure standing at attention in the foreground gives the scale." Evidently Pitt-Rivers was a military man, as well as an archaeologist, to the very end.

Few people followed Pitt-Rivers's example. One could still become an excavator without any training at all, although well-known archaeologists like Wilhelm Dörpfeld and the immortal Egyptologist Flinders Petrie were busy training students to follow in their footsteps. Petrie begged his colleagues to be quit of "the brandy-and-soda young man … of the adventurous speculator. Without the ideal of solid continuous work, certain, accurate, and permanent, archaeology is as futile as any other pursuit." He went on to urge informal attire: "To attempt serious work in pretty suits, shiny leggings or starched collars, would be like mountaineering in evening dress." "It is sickening to see the rate at which everything is being destroyed," he once remarked, "and the little regard paid to preservation."

Some of the better digging that stemmed from Pitt-Rivers's work took place on Roman sites in Britain. Still, to modern eyes, the efforts appear to have been terribly amateurish and the excavators incredibly ill equipped. Young Leonard Woolley, for example, later to become famous for his skilled excavations of royal graves at Ur-of-the-Chaldees in Mesopotamia, found himself in charge of a major Roman excavation without any experience at all or the least idea of how to survey a site or make plans.

The early part of this century also seems to have been a difficult period for female archaeologists. When a little-known archaeologist named J. P. Droop wrote a small manual on excavation in 1915, he spent a lot of time worrying about male/female roles. "I have never seen a trained lady excavator at work," he admitted. "Of a mixed dig, however, I

have seen something, and it is an experiment that I would be reluctant to try again." His reasons were twofold. "In the first place, there are the proprieties." Excavators should respect the etiquette and mores of the countries they are working in. Droop's other reasons were more personal. It seems that, in his experience, the "charm" of ladies vanishes during an excavation, for the dig lays on its mixed participants "a bond of closer daily intercourse than is conceivable." Droop found this irritating. "The ordinary male at least cannot stand it," he added. He cited the strain of "self-restraint in moments of stress, moments that will occur on the best regulated dig, when you want to say just what you think without translation, which before ladies, whatever their feelings about it, cannot be done." Droop was never to know of the key roles played by twentieth-century women in major archaeological excavations the world over.

Nevertheless, there were a handful of women who carried out important work in the field long before female excavators became commonplace. One pioneer was the English novelist Amelia Edwards, a Victorian lady in the classic sense of the word, who embarked on a two-month journey up the Nile in 1874. She traveled in genteel company aboard a sailing ship complete with upright piano and proper chaperones. Edwards was horrified by the looting and destruction of Ancient Egyptian sites on every side, at the blatant forgery of antiquities, and the "black-robed, grave men, who always lay in wait ready to sell you anything." Nevertheless, she was entranced by the Pyramids, the Temple of Karnak, and Abu Simbel, by the columns of ancient temples which she compared to groves of redwood trees. Her *Thousand Miles Up the Nile* (1877) is one of the classics of early archaeological travel and still bears reading today. Edwards devoted the rest of her life to lecturing and writing about the destruction in Egypt and was instrumental in the founding of the Egypt Exploration Society, which works in the Nile Valley to this day.

Harriet Boyd Hawes, a Smith graduate who met Amelia Edwards while in college, was even more remarkable. In 1897, she traveled to Athens to study archaeology, one of the first women to do

so. Archaeology soon took a back seat to nursing when Turkey declared war on Greece. For months, Hawes cared for wounded Greek soldiers within sound of artillery barrages, developing a passion for humanitarian causes that guided much of her life. Much to her surprise, she won a fellowship at the American School in Athens from Yale University, but was not allowed to excavate, this being considered a male domain. The British were more encouraging and she went over to Crete, where she combed the countryside for archaeological sites on the back of a mule. Her persistence was rewarded and she became the first woman to excavate a Minoan town. Hawes's monograph on Gournia is one of the classics of early Mediterranean archaeology. Not that Harriet did much more fieldwork, for she threw herself into humanitarian work among Serb soldiers in Corfu and served as a ward aid in American hospitals in France during World War I. But she opened doors into the narrow archaeological world for many talented women that followed in her footsteps.

There were other talented women pioneers, too, among them the redoubtable Gertrude Bell, who became an expert desert traveler and founded the Iraq Museum; Gertrude Caton-Thompson, who discovered what were then the earliest farmers in the world in Egypt's Fayum in the 1920s; and Dorothy Garrod, the first woman Professor of Archaeology anywhere in Europe, who excavated the Stone Age caves on Mount Carmel in the Levant in the 1930s. For the most part, they worked on shoestring budgets and often with few companions. But the discoveries they made contributed to the revolution in archaeological methods that took hold after World War I, in the hands of several capable excavators. Indeed the lax standards of Pitt-Rivers's contemporaries and successors were assaulted by archaeologists of the 1920s and 1930s. "There is no right way of digging but there are many wrong ones," wrote one of Pitt-Rivers's most avid disciples—Mortimer Wheeler. Wheeler, who was ten years old when Pitt-Rivers died, came to archaeology through the good offices of Arthur Evans, discoverer of the ancient palace of King Minos on Crete. Wheeler spent his lifetime digging large sites with meticulous precision and training new generations of archaeologists in methods that owed their inspiration to the Victorian general.

Wheeler worked first on Roman forts, then on the famous Iron Age fortress at Maiden Castle in southern Britain. From archaeological evidence, he was able to reconstruct a blow-by-blow account of the Roman storming of that fort. After a distinguished military career in World War II, Wheeler was asked to head up the Archaeological Survey of India. With characteristic and flamboyant energy, he took up the task of organizing archaeology out of chaos. He found Roman imported pottery in southern India and dug deeply into the ancient city mounds of Harappa and Mohenjo-daro in the Indus Valley. There he sketched a fascinating picture of a long-extinct Indian civilization that had traded with Mesopotamia and developed its own distinctive, and still undeciphered, script. Mortimer Wheeler's excavations were, quite simply, meticulous, and the results remarkable. Most modern excavations build on the basic principles that he and Pitt-Rivers, as well as a handful of other pioneers, set out.

"The archaeologist is not digging up things, he is digging up people," Wheeler would begin. Good excavation takes imagination, an ability to understand what one is digging up. According to Wheeler, people who do not have this kind of imagination should collect bus tickets instead of digging. He believed the key to excavation was accurate observation and recording of occupation levels and architectural features, of the layout of burials and minute artifacts. The relationship between different objects in the ground can tell one much about the behavior of their makers, he taught his students. Wheeler's excavations were models of tidiness, with straight walls and carefully swept trenches to make the tasks of observation and discovery more precise. The observation of superimposed layers and the features and artifacts in them would give one an accurate chronology to work with, an essential framework for studying the numerous pot fragments and other finds from the dig. He pointed out

how buildings should be dissected with great care, so that the foundations could be related to the underlying, dated strata and the contents isolated from those in other parts of the site. The burials Wheeler found were exposed bone by bone and carefully photographed in position before removal.

All of Wheeler's excavations were carefully designed not only to find artifacts but to answer specific questions about chronology or other matters. These questions were formulated in advance or as the dig was in progress. The staff of the excavation was organized into a hierarchy of specialists, led by the director himself, whose task was to "cultivate a scrupulous accuracy and completeness in the observation and record of his factual evidence." Wheeler's ideal director had "the combined virtues of the scholar and the man of action," an ability to achieve accuracy "not for accuracy's sake, but as a basis for using his imagination to interpret his finds." "Archaeology," wrote Wheeler, "is primarily a fact-finding discipline." But, he would always add, we have to dig sites as a means to an end, the end being the understanding of humanity's complex and changing relationship with its environment.

Schliemann dug up the past of Troy. He and many other early archaeologists taught us that archaeological sites contain many treasures. Curtius, Dörpfeld, Pitt-Rivers, and Wheeler developed techniques for recording the contents of each site in meticulous detail. And Wheeler himself threw down the gauntlet to his successors—he challenged them to apply these recording methods to such complex problems as "estimating the density and social structure of populations." His words were prophetic, for that is what leading archaeologists are now trying to achieve.

Mortimer Wheeler died in 1976 after witnessing a revolution in digging methods all over the world, a revolution whose impact is still being felt. His students and their students, as well as those of other pioneering archaeologists, have refined his methods even further. Some idea of the complexity of a modern excavation can be gained by a brief look at the investigation of an ancient site at Olduvai Gorge in Tanzania. The site dates to about 1.75 million years ago.

"Archaeology," wrote British archaeologist Stuart Piggott some years ago, "is the science of rubbish." And rubbish is precisely what Louis and Mary Leakey had to dissect when they excavated the scatters of bones and stone artifacts in the lowest levels of Olduvai Gorge. All that remained were small scatters of discarded animal bones, stone tools, and waste chips, lying in irregular concentrations on the very land surfaces ancient people once trod. Often the scatter of artifacts and bones was only a few inches thick and was sealed under dozens of feet of sterile sand and lake clay. How old were these scatters? What activities took place there? Could any information on prehistoric diet and food-getting methods be obtained from the scatters? These and many other questions came to mind as the Leakeys began clearing these small but complicated sites. They had no doubt as to the importance of their excavations: these were probably among the earliest traces of human behavior in the world. To avoid damaging any human fossils and to prevent disturbance of the artifacts from their original positions, only the most delicate methods could be used.

Each scatter lay within a major geological horizon of Olduvai Gorge, one that the Leakeys knew dated to the earliest millennia of the human experience. But dating samples had to be obtained, that is, lumps of lava that could be dated by laboratory tests for their radioactive content. These samples had to come from the scatters themselves, from lava fragments that had actually been carried to the site by those who had lived there. The Leakeys had no choice: they knew they must excavate each entire site, plot all the objects on them, and obtain dating samples from among the finds in the scatter.

One site yielded the famous skull of *Zinjanthropus* in 1959.... Mary Leakey originally found a portion of the fossil outcropping from the lower lake beds of the Gorge. A small excavation was immediately undertaken at the site of this discovery to aid both in the removal of the precious skull and in establishing the exact level from which the fossil came. The immediate surroundings of the skull were sifted carefully in case additional fragments had already fallen down the slope on which it was found. The trial excavation yielded broken animal bones, some rodent fragments, and a few stone tools that lay in place near the skull. There seemed a strong possibility that the skull was directly associated with the tools—indeed, its owner might have made them.

It was seven months before Mary Leakey could return to the site, for the skull had been found at the very end of the 1959 season. When the time came for larger-scale excavations, she did not attack the site at once. Her task was to establish the precise position of the artifact scatter in the Olduvai geological strata. To determine this, she dug a six-foot trial trench in steps through the entire forty feet of the geological bed the skull had come from, right down to bedrock. She found that the scatter was halfway up the bed.

Once the stratigraphical position of the fossil skull was established, Mary Leakey set out to determine the extent of the scatter itself. The workmen removed the sterile over-burden of lake bed from the area around the trial trench. This unproductive soil was removed with picks and shovels in rough levels. When they reached a whitish-yellow volcanic-ash zone that Mary Leakey knew directly overlay the precious scatter, they stepped aside. The trench was now divided into four-foot-wide strips that were worked one by one with great care. Skilled workers carefully pared away the volcanic ash to within a few inches of the underlying artifacts and bones. Sometimes bones and other finds protruded through into the ash. So dry was the soil that the excavators had to dampen it before removal to guard against damaging valuable fossils underneath.

The scatter proved to be about a foot thick. With great care, Mary Leakey worked each strip of the trench from one side of the floor to the other. Whenever possible, every find was cleared from the surrounding soil with dental probes and small paintbrushes. Every find of any size, whether a stone tool or an animal bone, was marked with black or white ink and plotted on the floor plan before being lifted. A complete photographic record of the site was maintained as well. Once the

larger finds had been removed, the soil was wet- or dry-sifted through one-sixteenth-inch screens so that even the tiniest stone chips and bone fragments were recovered for laboratory analysis. As a result of this painstaking excavation, the position of every significant find on the site was known to within an inch or less. What a contrast to Belzoni's burial chambers or Layard's palaces!

The man-hours expended on the *Zinjanthropus* site were well worth the expense. The amount of detail about early human lifeways that came from the *Zinjanthropus* floor was truly astonishing, all of it the result of meticulous excavation. In addition to the dating samples gathered—which proved the site to be 1.75 million years old—the Leakeys obtained data on the dimensions and layout of one of the earliest archaeological sites in the world. Mary Leakey found and took apart a concentration of stone tools and flakes and over a thousand broken bone fragments covering an area twenty-one feet by fifteen feet near the spot where *Zinjanthropus* was found. This central zone was separated from another concentration of bones by a less densely covered area that she felt might have been the site of a crude shelter. We know that the inhabitants used crude stone choppers and many flakes in the preparation of food and the butchering of small animals. They smashed the limb bones of antelope and zebra and broke open the skulls to remove the brain. But large scavengers like hyenas visited the site as well and chewed up some of the freshly broken bones—presumably after the inhabitants left. None of this information could have been obtained without rigorous excavation techniques. The Leakeys literally drained the site of information....

Archaeology has come a long way since Leonard Woolley performed miracles with plaster at Ur. Today, it is a sophisticated science that calls on experts from dozens of academic disciplines. It owes much to the natural and physical sciences, to revolutionary dating techniques ... that enable us to date 2.5-million-year-old archaeological sites or tiny fragments of a wooden spear shaft extracted from the socket of a bronze spearhead used three thousand years ago. Computers enable archaeologists to ma-

nipulate vast data bases of artifacts and food remains, to plot intricate jigsaw puzzles of waterlogged timbers that once formed a prehistoric house. We can trace the sources of volcanic rock used to make mirrors in three-thousand-year-old Mexican villages, establish whether stone workers making tools in a Belgian hunting camp ten thousand years ago were left- or right-handed. Using minute pollen grains, we can reconstruct the landscape around twenty-thousand-year-old Stone Age winter camps. Thousands of bison bones from an ancient mass kill on the American Plains can be reassembled so precisely that we know exactly how bison hunters of eight thousand years ago butchered their prey.

But the greatest advances of all have not been in the field or the laboratory, where all the hi-tech wizardry of archaeology comes into play. They have been in the ways in which we think of archaeology and plan our research. Much early archaeology was designed to recover as many spectacular objects as possible. This is what Layard strove for at Nimrud and Nineveh, and Schliemann at Hissarlik. Today's archaeology has three much more sophisticated goals: to construct the culture history of the past, to reconstruct ancient lifeways, the ways in which people made their living, and, most important of all, to explain how and why ancient human cultures changed through prehistoric times. This is where the most important advances in archaeology have been made—in seeking to explain why humans took up farming and abandoned hunting and gathering, or what caused people to congregate in cities, develop writing, and establish a literate civilization. Studying such topics has involved the development of sophisticated theoretical models for explaining and interpreting the past, models that owe much to evolutionary and ecological theory. Science now realizes that archaeology is about the only discipline that enables us to study human biological and cultural evolution over long periods of time. The development of the tools to do so ranks among the greatest scientific triumphs of this century. Not that archaeology is confined to such topics, for in recent years there has been an explosion of interest in such issues as gender roles in ancient societies, and in such fascinating problems as social inequality in the past. One of the great fascinations of modern archaeology is its sheer range and diversity that accommodates archaeologists who study everything from foraging camps that are millions of years old to Mayan cities and abandoned railroad stations from the Industrial Revolution.

....[T]here is a tremendous satisfaction and excitement in searching out the past. Even today, most talented archaeologists, at one time or another, feel they are in touch with the people they are studying. They seem to have an instinct for discovery, to know where to search and dig, and a sense of identity with their subjects. This sense seems to have been highly developed in Louis Leakey, Heinrich Schliemann, and Howard Carter. Carter experienced an almost eerie bond with Tutankhamun. He summed it up well when he wrote: "I stood in the presence of a king who reigned three thousand years ago." One suspects Carter was not speaking strictly figuratively: he felt he *really had*. Sometimes, as I have stood gazing over a long-deserted prehistoric settlement, silent on a cool evening as the sun casts long shadows over earthworks and eroding occupation deposits, I have experienced a sudden collapse of time. The site comes to life: thatched huts rise from the ground, scented wood smoke ascends in the evening still, dogs bark and children laugh in play. Outside their huts, old men sit and gossip quietly for a brief evening hour. Then, just as quickly, the image recedes and the village once again becomes a deserted archive of archaeological information, a silent complex of mud-hut foundations, dusty pot fragments, and broken food bones. For a moment, the ancient inhabitants of that village sprang to life, shedding their cloaks of anonymity to reach out across the millennia. Heady emotions, perhaps, but, for a moment, one understands why archaeology is so much more than just a set of techniques and tools for digging up the past.

Distinguished Lecture in Archeology: Communication and the Future of American Archaeology

What follows is the revised text of the Distinguished Lecture in Archeology, presented at the 95th Annual Meeting of the American Anthropological Association, held in San Francisco, California, November, 1996.

Jeremy A. Sabloff

University of Pennsylvania Museum of Archaeology and Anthropology Philadelphia, PA 19104

I offer these remarks with somewhat ambivalent feelings. While it is an honor indeed to be asked to give the Archaeology Division's Distinguished Lecture, I nevertheless must admit that it is a daunting challenge. I have looked at many of the superb Distinguished Lectures that have been presented to you in recent years and subsequently published in the *American Anthropologist* and am very impressed with what our colleagues have had to say. Most of the recent talks have focused on aspects of the ongoing debates on modern archaeological theory and methods. I certainly could have continued this tradition, because, as many of you know, I have strong feelings about this topic. However, I decided to pursue a different, more general tack, which I hope you will agree is of equal importance.

In a few short years, we will be entering a new millennium. Will American archaeology survive in the twenty-first century? Of course it will. But will it continue to thrive in the new millennium? The answer to this question is a more guarded "yes." There are various causes for concern about the future health of archaeology. I would like to examine one of these concerns and offer some suggestions as to how this concern might be eased.

My theme will be archaeologists' communication with the public—or lack thereof—and, more specifically, the relevance of archaeology to non-professionals. In thinking about this theme, which has been a particular interest and concern of mine, it struck me how one of my favorite cartoons provided an important insight into the whole question of archaeological communication. I know that many of you have your office doors or bulletin boards festooned with a host of "Calvin and Hobbes," "Shoe," "Bloom County," "Doonesbury," or "Far Side" drawings that unerringly seem to pinpoint many of life's enduring paradoxes and problems. In particular, the "Far Side" cartoons by Gary Larson, who is now lamentably in early retirement like several of our master cartoonists, often resonate well with archaeologists' sensibilities. This cartoon, while not specifically targeting archaeologists or cultural anthropologists, as Larson often did pinpoint a central concern of my discussion.

While archaeologists may think they are talking clearly to the public, what the latter often hears, I believe, is "blah, blah, blah, *tomb,* blah, blah, blah *sacrifice,* blah, blah, blah, arrowhead."

I will argue that the field of American archaeology, despite some significant progress in the past decade, is still failing to effectively tell the public about how modern anthropological archaeology functions and about the huge gains archaeologists have made in understanding the development of ancient cultures through time and space.

More than 25 years ago, John Fritz and Fred Plog ended their article on "The Nature of Archaeological Explanation" (1970:412) with the famous assertion that "We suggest that unless archaeologists find ways to make their research increasingly relevant to the modern world, the modern world will find itself increasingly capable of getting along without archaeologists." Although Fritz and Plog had a very particular definition of relevance in mind relating to the development of laws of culture change, as did Fritz in his important article on "Relevance, Archaeology, and Subsistence Theory" (1973), if one adopts a broader view of the term *relevance,* then the thrust of their statement is just as important today—if not more so—than it was in 1970.

How can this be true? Archaeology appears to be thriving, if one counts number of jobs, money spent on archaeological field research, course enrollments, publications, and public fascination with the subject as measured in media coverage. But is the public interest, or, better yet, the public's interest, being served properly and satisfied in a productive and responsible fashion? With some important exceptions, I unfortunately would answer "no." Why do I think this to be the case?

In the nineteenth century, archaeology played an important public and intellectual role in the fledgling United States. Books concerned wholly or in part with archaeology were widely read and, as Richard Ford has indicated clearly in his article on "Archeology Serving Humanity" (1973), archaeology played an important part in overthrowing the then-dominant Biblical view of human development in favor of Darwinian evolutionary theory. Empirical archaeological research, which excited public interest and was closely followed by the public, was able to provide data that indicated that human activities had considerable antiquity and that archaeological studies of the past could throw considerable light on the development of the modern world.

As is the case in most disciplines, as archaeology became increasingly professionalized throughout the nineteenth century and as academic archaeology emerged in the late-nineteenth and early-twentieth centuries, the communications gap between professionals and the public grew apace. This gap was accentuated because amateurs had always played an important part in the archaeological enterprise. As late as the 1930s, before academic archaeology really burgeoned, the gap between most amateurs and professionals was still readily bridgeable, I believe. The first article in *American Antiquity,* for example, was written by an amateur, and, as I have discussed in detail elsewhere, the founders of the journal hoped that it "would provide a forum for communication between these two groups" (Sabloff 1985:228). However, even a quick look today at *American Antiquity* will indicate that those earlier hopes have been dashed. It may be a terrific journal for professionals, but much of it would be nearly incomprehensible to non-professionals, except perhaps to the most devoted amateurs.

In 1924, Alfred Vincent Kidder published his landmark book *An Introduction to the Study of Southwestern Archaeology.* This highly readable volume both made key advances in scholarly understanding of the ancient Southwest and was completely accessible to the general public. As Gordon Willey (1967:299) has stated: "It is a rarity in that it introduces systematics to a field previously unsystematized, and, at the same time, it is vitally alive and unpedantic.... He wrote a book that was romantic but not ridiculous, scrupulously close to the facts but not a boring recital of them." How many regional archaeological syntheses could have that said of them today? Happily, the answer is not "none," and there is some evidence of a positive trend in the publication of more popularly oriented regional and site syntheses (see, for instance, Kolata 1993; Plog 1997; or Schele and Freidel 1990, among others). Marcus and Flannery's (1996) recent book on Zapotec civilization is a superb example of how such accessible writing can be combined with a clear, theoretically sophisticated approach, as well.

Kidder also was deeply concerned about the relevance of archaeology to the contemporary world and was not shy about expressing his belief that archaeology could and should play an important social role in the modern world (a view which is paralleled today by some post-processual [e.g., Hodder et al. 1995] and feminist [e.g., Spector 1993] concerns with humanizing archaeological narratives). Kidder's views were most clearly expressed by him at a 1940 symposium at the American Philosophical Society on "Characteristics of American Culture and Its Place in General Culture." As Richard Woodbury (1973:171) notes: "Kidder presented one of his most eloquent pleas for the importance of the anthropological understanding of the past through the techniques of archaeology." Kidder (1940:528), for example, states: "it is good for an archaeologist to be forced to take stock, to survey his field, to attempt to show what bearing his delvings into the past may have upon our judgement of present day life; and what service, if any, he renders the community beyond filling the cases of museums and supplying material for the rotogravure sections of the Sunday papers." Lamentably, his prescription for the practitioners of archaeology has not been well filled in the past half century.

The professionalization of archaeology over the course of this century obviously has had innumerable benefits. In the most positive sense, the discipline has little resemblance to the archaeology of 100 years ago. With all the advances in method, theory, and culture historical knowledge, archaeologists are now in a position to make important and useful statements about cultural adaptation and development that should have broad intellectual appeal. Ironically, though, one aspect of the professionalization of the discipline, what can be termed the academization of archaeology, is working against such broad dissemination of current advances in archaeological understanding of cultures of the past. The key factor, I am convinced, is that since World War II, and especially in the past few decades as archaeology rapidly expanded as an academic subject in universities and colleges throughout this country, the competition for university jobs and the institutional pressures to publish in quantity, in general, and in peer review journals, in particular, has led in part to the academic devaluation of popular writing and communication with the general public. Such activities just don't count or, even worse, count against you.

In addition, I believe that it is possible that some archaeologists, in their desire to prove the rigor and scientific standing of the discipline within the academy and among their non-anthropological colleagues and university administrators, have rejected or denigrated popular writing because it might somehow taint archaeology with a nonscientific "softness" from which they would like to distance the field.

If popular writing is frowned upon by some academics, then popularization in other media, such as television, can be treated even more derisively by these scholars, and consequently too few archaeologists venture into these waters. Why should the best known "archaeologist" to the public be an unrepentant looter like Indiana Jones? Is he the role model we want for our profession? When I turn on the television to watch a show with archaeological content, why should I be more than likely to see Leonard Nimoy and the repeated use of the term *mysterious?* It should be professional archaeologists routinely helping to write and perhaps even hosting many of the archaeology shows on television, not just—at best—popular science writers and Hollywood actors. In sum, I strongly feel that we need more accessible writing, television shows, videos, CD-ROMs, and the like with archaeologists heavily involved in all these enterprises.

Forty years ago, Geoffrey Bibby, in his best-selling book *The Testimony of the Spade,* wrote in his foreword (1956:vii):

> It has long been customary to start any book that can be included under the comprehensive heading of "popular science" with an apology from the author to his fellow scientists for his desertion of the icy uplands of the research literature for the supposedly lower and supposedly lush fields of popular representation. This is not an apology, and it is not directed to archaeologists. In our day, when the research literature of one branch of knowledge has become all but incomprehensible to a researcher in another branch, and when the latest advances within any science can revolutionize—or end—our lives within a decade, the task of interpreting every science in language

that can be understood by workers in other fields is no longer—if it ever was—a slightly disreputable sideline, but a first-priority duty.

Bibby was making a point that is similar to one made years ago by C. P. Snow (1959) that scholars in different disciplines do not read or are unable to read each others' works, but should! However, I believe that Bibby's argument can easily be expanded to include the lay public, which should be able to readily find out what archaeologists are doing. If they are interested in the subject, and they have no accessible professionally written sources to turn to—like *The Testimony of the Spade*—is it any surprise that they turn to highly speculative, non-professional sources? Unfortunately, Bibby's wise call has gone relatively unheeded. Where are all the *Testimony of the Spades* of this generation, or even the *Gods, Graves, and Scholars* (Ceram 1951)?

But even encouraging communication between archaeologists and the general public is not sufficient, I believe, to dispel the lack of popular understanding about the modern archaeological enterprise and the potential importance of archaeological knowledge. With all the problems that the world faces today, the conflicts and ethnic strife, the innumerable threats to the environment, and the inadequacy of food supplies in the face of rising populations, there never has been a more propitious time for archaeology's new insights into the nature of human development and diversity in time and space to be appreciated by people in all walks of life. In order for better communication to have a useful impact, I believe that the profession has to heed Fritz and Plog's call and strive to be relevant. Moreover, we should pursue relevance in both the general and specific senses of the term. In its broadest sense, *relevance* is "to the purpose; pertinent," according to *The American College Dictionary*, while in its more narrow definition, relevance according to *The Oxford English Dictionary*, means "pertinency to important current issues."

All things being equal, archaeology could be justified on the basis of its inherent interest. But all things are rarely equal, and therefore archaeological activities and their relevance to today's world do need justification. To what is archaeology pertinent? In the general sense, archaeology's main claim to relevance is its revelation of the richness of human experience through the study and understanding of the development of past cultures over the globe. Among the goals of such study is to foster awareness and respect of other cultures and their achievements. Archaeology can make itself relevant—pertinent—by helping its audiences appreciate past cultures and their accomplishments.

Why should we actively seek to fulfill such a goal? I firmly believe in the lessons of history. By appreciating the nature of cultures both past and present, their uniqueness and their similarities, their development, and their adaptive successes and failures, we have a priceless opportunity to better grapple with the future than is possible without such knowledge. For example, as many of you are aware, I have long argued that new understandings of the decline of Classic Maya civilization in the southern Maya lowlands in the eighth century A.D. can shed important light on the ability of the ancient Maya to sustain a complex civilization in a tropical rain-forest environment for over a millennium and the reasons why this highly successful adapta-

tion ultimately failed (see Sabloff 1990). The potential implications for today's world are profound.

This form of striving for relevance is powerful and should have great appeal to the public, but it is not necessarily sufficient in terms of outreach goals for general audiences. Archaeology also needs to attempt to be relevant, where possible, in the narrower sense, too. As some of our colleagues in the Maya area, for instance, begin to take the new archaeological insights about sustainable agriculture and the potential for demographic growth and begin to directly apply them to modern situations, then archaeology clearly is becoming pertinent "to important current issues" (see, for example, Rice and Rice 1984).

In relation to this latter goal, I would argue that we need more "action archaeology," a term first coined by Maxine Klehidienst and Patty Jo Watson (1956) more than four decades ago (in the same year that *Testimony of the Spade* first appeared), but which I use in a more general way to convey the meaning of archaeology working *for* living communities, not just *in* them. One compelling example of such action archaeology is the field research of my colleague Clark Erickson, who has identified the remains of raised field agriculture in the Bolivian Amazon and has been studying the raised fields and other earthworks on the ground. He has been able to show that there was a complex culture in this area in Precolumbian times. Erickson also is working with local peasants in his field study area to show them how Precolumbian farmers successfully intensified their agricultural production and to indicate how the ancient raised field and irrigation techniques might be adapted to the modern situation so as to improve the current economic picture (see Erickson 1998). This is just one example of many that could be cited, including the close collaboration between archaeologists and Native American groups in, for example, the innovative research of my colleague Robert Preucel (1998) at Cochiti Pueblo, or in organizations like the Zuni Archaeological Project (see Anyon and Ferguson 1995), in the many pathbreaking modern garbage projects initiated by William L. Rathje and his colleagues (Rathje and Murphy 1992), in the thoughtful archaeological/environmental development project initiated by Anabel Ford and her collaborators at El Pilar in Belize and Guatemala (Ford 1998), or in cooperative projects between archaeologists and members of the local communities in locations such as Labrador or Belize that have been reported on by Stephen Loring and Marilyn Masson in recent Archeology Division sections of the *AAA Newsletter* (October and November 1996). However, we need many more examples of such work. They should be the rule, not the exception.

This kind of work in archaeology parallels the continued growth of action anthropology among our cultural colleagues. The potential for collaboration among archaeologists and cultural anthropologists in this regard, as advocated, for example, by Anne Pybum and Richard Wilk (1995), is quite strong. Explorations of the possibilities of such cooperation should be particularly appropriate and of great importance to the Archeology Division of the American Anthropological Association, which I know is interested in integrating archaeology within a general anthropological focus, and I urge the Division to pursue such an endeavor. Applied anthropology in its action form need not—and should not—be restricted to cultural anthropology.

It is depressing to note that the academic trend away from public communication appears to be increasing just as public interest in archaeology seems to be reaching new heights. Whatever the reasons for this growing interest, and clearly there are many potential reasons that could be and have been cited, including a turn to the past in times of current uncertainties, New Age ideological trends, or the growing accessibility of archaeological remains through travel, television, and video, there is no doubt that there is an audience out there that is thirsting for information about the past. But it does not appear that this interest is being well served, given the ratio of off-the-wall publications to responsible ones that one can find in any bookstore. I have written elsewhere (Sabloff 1982:7) that "Unfortunately, one of the prices we must pay for the privilege of sharing a free marketplace of ideas is the possibility that some writers will write unfounded speculation, some publishers will publish them, some bookstores will sell them, and some media will sensationalize them. In this way, unfounded speculations become widely spread among the general population of interested readers." I went on to suggest that "Perhaps the best solution to this problem is to help readers to become aware of the standards of scientific research so that scientific approaches can be better appreciated and pseudoscientific approaches can be read critically" (p. 7).

In order for this solution to work, however, archaeologists need to compete effectively in this free market. Why must we always run into the most outrageous pseudo-archaeology books (what Stephen Williams [1991] has termed "fantastic archaeology") in such visible places as airport news shops? I simply refuse to believe that among the large pool of professional archaeological writing talent that there aren't some of our colleagues who can write books that can replace *Chariots of the Gods?* (Von Däniken 1970). If we abandon much of the field of popular writing to the fringe, we should not be surprised at all that the public often fails to appreciate the significance of what we do. So what? Why does it matter if many archaeologists don't value public communication and much of the public lacks an understanding of archaeology and what archaeologists do and accomplish? There are two principal answers to this question, I believe. First, I strongly feel that we have a moral responsibility to educate the public about what we do. Good science and public education not only are compatible but should go hand in hand. The overwhelming majority of us, whether in the academic, government or business world, receive at least some public support in our work. I believe that we have a responsibility to give back to the public that provides us with grants, or contracts, or jobs. We need to share with them our excitement in our work and our insights into how peoples of the past lived and how our understandings of the past can inform us about the present and future; and we need to share all this in ways that everyone from young schoolchildren to committed amateur archaeologists can understand and appreciate.

Moreover, the better the public understands and appreciates what we do, what we know, and how we come to know it, the better it can assess the uses and—unfortunately—the abuses of archaeology, especially in political contexts. In this age of exploding ethnic conflicts, a public that has been educated to understand the nature of archaeological research and is thus able to cast a critical eye on how archaeological findings are used in modern political arenas clearly is preferable to people who lack such understanding. On a global scale, the use of archaeological myths in some of the former Soviet republics by various ethnic groups to justify repression of others is just one example—unfortunately!—of many kinds of abuses of archaeological data that could be cited (see Kohl and Fawcett 1995).

Second, there are eminently practical reasons for emphasizing and valuing public communication. Namely—and obviously—it is in our enlightened self-interest! As governmental, academic, and corporate budgets grow tighter and tighter, we are increasingly vying with innumerable groups and people, many with very compelling causes and needs, for extremely competitive dollars. If we don't make our case to the public about the significance of our work, then, in Fritz and Plog's (1970) words, we will surely find our public increasingly capable of getting along without us. How many of our representatives in Congress or in state legislatures really understand what archaeologists do and what they can contribute to the modern world? How many of them get letters from constituents extolling the virtues of the archaeological enterprise and urging them to support archaeological research both financially and through legislation? Unless we educate and work with our many publics, we are certain to find our sources of support, many of which have been taken for granted in recent years, rapidly drying up.

Let's turn our attention from the general problem to potential solutions. How can American archaeologists rectify the situation just described and particularly promote more popular writing by professional scholars? One answer is deceptively simple: we need to change our value system and our reward system within the academy. Just as Margaret Mead and other great anthropological popularizers have been sneered at by some cultural anthropologists, so colleagues like Brian Fagan, who has done so much to reach out to general readers (see, for example, Fagan 1977, 1984, 1987, 1991, and 1995, among many others), are often subject to similar snide comments. We need to celebrate those who successfully communicate with the public, not revile them. Ideally, we should have our leading scholars writing for the public, not only for their colleagues. Some might argue that popular writing would be a waste of their time. To the contrary, I would maintain that such writing is part of our collective academic responsibility. Who better to explain what is on the cutting edge of archaeological research than the field's leading practitioners? Moreover, we need to develop a significant number of our own Stephen Jay Goulds or Stephen Hawkings, not just a few.

Why do some scholars look down at archaeologists who are perceived as popularizers? There are probably a host of reasons, but one of them definitely is pure jealousy. Some archaeologists are jealous of their colleagues who successfully write popular books and articles because of the latter's writing skills. They also are jealous, I believe, of the visibility that popular communication brings those who enter this arena, and they are jealous of the monetary rewards that sometimes accompany popular success. But since such jealousy is not socially acceptable, it tends to be displaced into negative comments on the scholarly abilities of the popularizers.

Not only do we need to change our value system so that public communication is perceived in a positive light, more particularly, we need to change the academic evaluation and reward system for archaeologists (and others!), so that it gives suitable recognition to popular writing and public outreach. Clearly, these activities also can be counted as public service. But they further merit scholarly recognition. I also would include the curation of museum exhibits in this regard, especially ones that include catalogs or CD-ROMs that are accessible to broad audiences. Effective writing for general audiences requires excellent control of the appropriate theoretical, methodological, and substantive literature and the ability to comprehend and articulate clearly the core issues of the archaeology of an area, time period, or problem, and therefore should be subject to the same kind of qualitative academic assessment that ideally goes on today in any academic tenure, promotion, or hiring procedure. However, such a development would go against the current pernicious trend that features such aspects as counting peer-review articles and use of citation indices. I strongly believe that the growing reliance on numbers of peer-review articles and the denigration of both popular and non-peer-review writing needs to be reversed. As in so many areas of life, quantity is being substituted for quality, while the measurement of quality becomes increasingly problematic. As the former editor of a major peer-review journal, as well as the editor of many multi-author volumes, I can assure you that the quality of chapters in edited books—often discounted as non-peer-reviewed writings—can be and frequently are of as high or higher quality than peer-reviewed articles. However, many faculty and administrators appear to be looking for formulae that shortchange the qualitative evaluation of research and writing, no matter what form of publication. The whole academic system of evaluation for hiring, tenure, promotion, and salary raises needs to be rethought. In my opinion it is headed in the wrong direction, and the growing trend away from qualitative evaluation is especially worrisome.

As a call to action, in order to encourage popular writing among academics, particularly those with tenure, all of us need to lobby university administrators, department chairs, and colleagues about the value and importance of written communication with audiences beyond the academy. Academics should be evaluated on their popular as well as their purely academic writings. Clearly, what is needed is a balance between original research and popular communication. In sum, evaluations should be qualitative, not quantitative.

Concerning non-academic archaeologists, we need to raise the perceived value of general publications and public outreach in the cultural resource management arm of the profession and work toward having public reporting be routinely included in scopes of work of as many cultural resource management contracts as is feasible. In some areas, fortunately, such as in the National Parks Service or in some Colonial archaeological settings, such outreach already is valued. Positive examples like this need to be professionally publicized and supported.

I would be remiss if I didn't point out that there clearly is a huge irony here. The academic world obviously is becoming increasingly market-oriented with various institutions vying for perceived "stars" in their fields with escalating offers of high salaries, less teaching, better labs, more research funds, and so on, and most academics not only are caught up in this system but have bought into it. At the same time, those scholars who are most successful in the larger marketplace of popular ideas and the popular media and who make dollars by selling to popular audiences are frequently discounted and denigrated by the self-perceived "true scholars," who often have totally bought into the broad academic market economy and are busy playing this narrower market game!

To conclude, I hope that I have been able to stimulate some thought about what might appear to be a very simple problem but which in reality is quite complicated. In order to fulfill what I believe is one of archaeology's major missions, that of public education, we need to make some significant changes in our professional modes of operation. The Archeology Division can form a common cause with many other units of the American Anthropological Association to realize this goal. This is a four-field problem with four-field solutions! The Society for American Archaeology has just endorsed public education and outreach as one of the eight principles of archaeological ethics. This Division can also play a key role in such endeavors by working within the American Anthropological Association and using its influence to help change the emphases of our professional lives and the reward systems within which we work. To reiterate, I strongly believe that we must change our professional value system so that public outreach in all forms, but especially popular writing, is viewed and supported in highly positive terms. We need to make this change. There are signs that the pendulum of general communication in the field of American archaeology is starting to swing in a positive direction. Let us all work to push it much further!

I am sure that we all have heard the clarion call to the American public—"will you help me to build a bridge the twenty-first century"—many, many times. It is my belief that, unfortunately, the bridge to the twenty-first century will be a shaky one indeed for archaeology and anthropology—perhaps even the proverbial bridge to nowhere!— unless we tackle the communication problem with the same energy and vigor with which we routinely debate the contentious issues of contemporary archaeological theory that past lecturers to this group have delineated for you. The fruits of our research and analyses have great potential relevance for the public at large. The huge, exciting strides in understanding the past that anthropological archaeology has made in recent years need to be brought to the public's attention both for our sakes and theirs.

NOTES

Acknowledgments. I am honored that I was asked to deliver the Archeology Division's 1996 Distinguished Lecture and grateful to the Archeology Division for its kind invitation to deliver this important talk. I wish to acknowledge the growing list of colleagues, only a few of which have been cited above, who have accepted the crucial challenge of writing for general public. May your numbers multiply! I also wish thank Paula L. W. Sabloff, Joyce Marcus, and the reviewer for this journal for their many insightful and helpful comments and suggestions, only some of which I have been able to take advantage of, that have certainly improved the quality of paper.

REFERENCES CITED

Anyon, Roger, and T. J. Ferguson 1995 Cultural Resources Management at the Pueblo of Zuni, N.M., U.S.A. Antiquity 69 (266):913–930.

Bibby, Geoffrey 1956 The Testimony of the Spade. New York: Alfred A. Knopf.

Ceram, C. W. 1951 Gods, Graves, and Scholars: The Story of Archaeology. New York: Alfred A. Knopf.

Erickson, Clark L. 1998 Applied Archaeology and Rural Development: Archaeology's Potential Contribution to the Future. *In* Crossing Currents: Continuity and Change in Latin America. M. Whiteford and S. Whiteford, eds. Pp. 34–45. Upper Saddle, NJ: Prentice-Hall.

Fagan, Brian M. 1977 Elusive Treasure: The Story of Early Archaeologists in the Americas. New York: Scribners. 1984 The Aztecs. New York: W. H. Freeman. 1987 The Great Journey: The Peopling of Ancient America. London: Thames and Hudson. 1991 Kingdoms of Gold, Kingdoms of Jade: The Americas before Columbus. London: Thames and Hudson. 1995 Time Detectives: How Archaeologists Use Technology to Recapture the Past. New York: Simon and Schuster.

Ford, Anabel, ed. 1998 The Future of El Pilar: The Integrated Research and Development Plan for the El Pilar Archaeological Reserve for Flora and Fauna, Belize-Guatemala. Department of State Publication 10507, Bureau of Oceans. and International Environmental and Scientific Affairs, Washington, DC.

Ford, Richard I. 1973 Archeology Serving Humanity. *In* Research and Theory in Current Archeology. Charles L. Redman, ed. Pp. 83–94. New York: John Wiley.

Fritz, John M. 1973 Relevance, Archeology, and Subsistence Theory. *In* Research and Theory in Current Archaeology. Charles L. Redman, ed. Pp. 59–82. New York: John Wiley.

Fritz, John M., and Fred Plog 1970 The Nature of Archaeological Explanation. American Antiquity 35:405–12.

Hodder, Ian, Michael Shanks, Alexandra Alexandri, Victor Buchli, John Carman, Jonathan Last, and Gavin Lucas, eds. 1995 Interpreting Archaeology: Finding Meaning in the Past. New York: Routledge.

Kidder, Alfred V. 1924 An Introduction to the Study of Southwestern Archaeology, with a Preliminary Account of the Excavations at Pecos. Papers of the Southwestern Expedition, No. 1. Published for the Department of Archaeology, Phillips Academy, Andover. New Haven, CT: Yale University Press. 1940 Looking Backward. Proceedings of the American Philosophical Society 83:527–537.

Kleindienst, Maxine R., and Patty Jo Watson 1956 'Action Archaeology': The Archaeological Inventory of a Living Community. Anthropology Tomorrow 5:75–78.

Kohl, Philip L., and Clare Fawcett, eds. 1995 Nationalism, Politics, and the Practice of Archaeology. Cambridge: Cambridge University Press.

Kolata, Alan L. 1993 The Tiwanaku: Portrait of an Andean Civilization. Cambridge: Blackwell.

Marcus, Joyce, and Kent V. Flannery 1996 Zapotec Civilization: How Urban Society Evolved in Mexico's Oaxaca Valley. New York: Thames and Hudson.

Plog, Stephen 1997 Ancient Peoples of the American Southwest. London: Thames and Hudson.

Preucel, Robert W. 1998 The Kotyiti Research Project: Report of the 1996 Field Season. Report submitted to the Pueblo of Cochiti and the USDA Forest Service, Santa Fe National Forest, Santa Fe, NM.

Pyburn, Anne, and Richard Wilk 1995 Responsible Archaeology Is Applied Anthropology. *In* Ethics in American Archaeology: Challenges for the 1990s. Mark J. Lynott and Alison Wylie, eds. Pp. 71–76. Washington, DC: Society for American Archaeology.

Rathje, William L., and Cullen Murphy 1992 Rubbish!: The Archaeology of Garbage. New York: HarperCollins.

Rice, Don S., and Prudence M. Rice 1984 Lessons from the Maya. Latin American Research Review 19(3):7–34.

Sabloff, Jeremy A. 1982 Introduction. *In* Archaeology: Myth and Reality. Jeremy A. Sabloff, ed. Pp. 1–26. Readings from Scientific American. San Francisco: W. H. Freeman. 1985 American Antiquity's First Fifty Years: An Introductory Comment. American Antiquity 50:228–236. 1990: The New Archaeology and the Ancient Maya. A Scientific American Library Book. New York: W. H. Freeman.

Schele, Linda, and David A. Freidel 1990 A Forest of Kings: The Untold Story of the Ancient Maya. New York: Morrow.

Snow, C. P. 1959 The Two Cultures and the Scientific Revolution. Cambridge: Cambridge University Press.

Spector, Janet 1993 What This Awl Means: Feminist Archaeology at a Wahpeton Dakota Village. St. Paul: Minnesota Historical Society Press.

Von Däniken, Erich 1970 Chariots of the Gods? New York: G. P. Putnam's Sons.

Willey, Gordon R. 1967 Alfred Vincent Kidder, 1885–1963. *In* Biographical Memoirs, vol. 39. Published for the National Academy of Sciences. New York: Columbia University Press.

Williams, Stephen 1991 Fantastic Archaeology: The Wild Side of North American Prehistory. Philadelphia: University of Pennsylvania Press.

Woodbury, Richard B. 1973 Alfred V. Kidder. New York Columbia University Press.

First Lady of Amazonia

Betty Meggers is a strong-willed octogenarian with immovable beliefs about ancient jungle cultures

by COLLEEN P. POPSON

LIKE A HAPPY EAGLE GUARDING HER YOUNG, eighty-one-year-old archaeologist Betty Meggers hovers protectively over her beliefs about ancient Amazonia that have been unceasingly criticized for half a century.

Beginning in the 1940s, Meggers and her late husband, Clifford Evans, were the first archaeologists to take a close look at how ancient Amazonians lived. Their groundbreaking 1952 monograph, *Archeological Investigations at the Mouth of the Amazon,* concluded, based on their research and that of colleagues in the soil and biological sciences, that Amazonia's tropical rain forest could never have supported long-term complex societies, or chiefdoms.

Despite the couple's trailblazing efforts, detractors began lining up soon after the monograph was published. Among the most outspoken was the late Donald Lathrap, a University of Illinois professor who conducted excavations in upper Amazonia (Peru) in the 1950s. Using ceramic evidence, Lathrap argued that Amazonia could and did support complex societies with advanced technology. Further, he claimed, these societies developed in central Amazonia and spread out along the Amazon River's tributaries. "Though archaeological research is relatively recent," Lathrap wrote in *The Upper Amazon,* "it is clear on the basis of work already accomplished that large communities and complex and varied ceramics are at least as old in the tropical forests of the Amazon Basin as they are in the Highland [the Andes] or on the Coast of Peru." This set the tone of a polemic that would become increasingly bitter over the next half century.

Meggers has put up a game fight over the years, and the fact that Lathrap's ideas are still referred to as "revisionist" today demonstrates the staying power of her scholarship. While Lathrap's students and others labor in the rain forest looking for further evidence to prove her wrong, Meggers pores over data in her office, ten hours a day, seven days a week, seeking more evidence that she is right.

"ARE YOU SURE YOU WANT TO DO THAT?" was a common refrain when I told archaeologists of my plan to interview Meggers. "Betty is a highly partisan person," said Richard Burger, an Andeanist at Yale University. "She tends to be generous with friends and harsh with enemies." My curiosity was piqued.

Meggers finds me in a crowd of dinosaur-dazzled kids on the first floor of the Smithsonian's National Museum of Natural History in Washington, where she has been a research associate since 1954. She guides me to her office through a labyrinth of halls typical of many old museums, past large boxes full of ancient pottery, stone knives, and human bones. Meggers is a slight five-foot-two with bright white hair curled into youthful rolls and a shy smile that breaks into laughter when she lets her guard down. Conversation skips quickly over pleasantries and soon focuses on research. Almost right away, she asks me if I've seen one or another of the "outrageous" claims about Amazonia supporting large, complex populations.

Such claims tend to spur tempestuous rows with Meggers. One of the worst occurred with the 1991 publication of University of Illinois archaeologist Anna Roosevelt's *Moundbuilders of the Amazon,* which attacked the scholarship of Meggers and her late husband while arguing the case for highly advanced chiefdoms. Meggers' response was characteristically blunt: "The uncritical acceptance of Roosevelt's revolutionary characterizations of the environment and prehistory of Amazonia and of her defamatory remarks impels me, as her only surviving victim, to assume the unwelcome task of rebuttal," she wrote in the journal *The Review of Archae-*

ology. "Given the scale of the delusion she has perpetrated and the prestige of the deluded, I feel akin to the child in the fairy tale who announced to the assembled subjects: 'the emperor has no clothes!' "

Roosevelt denies making defamatory remarks about Meggers and insists her criticism was professional. "People coming out with their dissertations are always going to have their own ideas," she says. "You don't have to take it as a huge insult."

Though the claims opponents like Roosevelt make clearly irritate Meggers, they also seem to sharpen her determination to prove her point. "What I can't understand is why it has become so fashionable not to show any data!" she says during an interview in her third-floor office, into which she and Evans first moved in the 1950s. Cluttered with cabinets and bookshelves overflowing with notebooks, maps, charts, and photographs, it could do with an excavation of its own. Though far from her beloved tropics, Meggers improvises. A large plant brought from Guyana looms over her desk from a nearby bookshelf, and two stuffed macaws hang from the ceiling.

Since Evans' death following a heart attack in 1981, Meggers has had to push even harder to publish and defend the work the two did together. "It has been very difficult," she says, "you know, by myself, and not having time enough to do all the work that needs to be done." A painting of Evans hangs behind her office door, the last thing she sees before going home. The room is heavy with his absence, and he is constantly invoked in her use of the collective "we."

A native of Washington, D.C., Meggers can't remember exactly when she was drawn to archaeology. Her physicist father, an archaeology enthusiast, often took the family to Native American sites, like Serpent Mound in Ohio, on their way to visit relatives in Wisconsin. Meggers got her first Smithsonian gig at the age of 16, volunteering to mend pots excavated from Pueblo Bonito, an Anasazi village in New Mexico.

In 1943, Meggers earned a bachelor's degree in anthropology from the University of Pennsylvania. Her eye was on a career in museum work. That changed when she began studying for a master's degree at the University of Michigan. There, she met archaeologist Leslie White, a scholar whose theories of cultural evolution would help revolutionize the way people studies archaeology. According to White, all cultures fell along a continuum of complexity based on technological advancement; the stage of development past societies had achieved could be traced through the artifacts archaeologists collected. White's theories were complemented by the equally revolutionary idea of cultural ecology, a theory focused on the way societies adapt to their natural environment.

Up until then, archaeologists had been collecting pottery and stone tools and categorizing them without asking what the artifacts could say about how societies subsisted, worshiped, interacted with their neighbors

and their environment, and—most importantly—changed over time. "Boy, that changed my life," recalls Meggers, referring to her studies with White. "I'd been memorizing all these unconnected facts about different groups and their material culture, but he put them all in context. I was fascinated."

It was also at Michigan that Meggers studied ceramics collected in the 1870s from Marajó, an island at the mouth of the Amazon on the north coast of Brazil that would become a major focus of her life's work. Because the only publications about the ceramics were in Portuguese, she taught herself the language and published a report—her first scientific article—in 1945.

That same year Meggers began study for her Ph.D. at Columbia University. While there, she met Evans, who had worked on excavations in Peru and the southwest United States and had recently gotten out of the Army. Meggers' work still revolved around collections from Marajó, and she knew additional fieldwork would be needed to make sense of it. "Our goal was to establish the degree of complexity, the duration of the culture, its possible origin, and the reason for its disappearance," says Meggers.

The idea of going to a place that was relatively unexplored excited both Meggers and Evans. The two were married in 1946 and about a year later were on their way to Brazil to gather data for their dissertations, the first of dozens of trips over the next half century.

THE EUROPEANS WHO PLIED THE AMAZON in the sixteenth century reported dense communities of Indians living along its banks. The Spanish friar Gaspar de Carvajal wrote in his account of a trip down the Amazon, "One village was not half a league away from another, and… inland from the river, at a distance of two leagues, more or less, there could be seen some very large cities that glistened in white, and besides this the land is as good, as fertile, and as normal in appearance as our Spain…. We saw some very large provinces and settlements… with hills and valleys thickly populated."

Four centuries later, Meggers and Evans would cover much of the same territory as these early explorers to see if archaeological evidence bore out the claims of large, dense settlements. They navigated tributaries throughout Brazil, Guyana, Venezuela, and Ecuador. Meggers did most of the analysis and the writing; Evans was responsible for logistics and excavation. "It was great," recalls Meggers. "Cliff and I complemented each other. I was more interested in theory, and he was great at technology."

Meggers' love of the rain forest and the fondness with which she remembers her time there are infectious. "Going to Amazonia in the 40s and 50s was wonderful," she says. "Now it's all changed. You see bulldozers and roads all over the place. When we went, we were totally isolated. We traveled by every means of transportation available, from oxen and horses to dugout canoes, you name it. And going through the forest, there was an Indian village here and one there and everything else was unchanged. Along the Upper Essequibo tributary, we met the WaiWai, an indigenous group that still dressed in feathers and glass beads. Other groups in the interior would hunt and fish for us. We ate agouti and paca [large rodents] and turtle eggs, crocodile and all kinds of fish. And armadillo, which is really good. There were no phones. We were lucky we didn't have any accidents or emergencies. It was great."

On Marajó, Meggers and Evans found mounds and more sophisticated pottery that seemed to have appeared in the area fully developed. To make sense of these traits, the two turned to cultural evolution and ecology. "Soil studies indicated that early Amazonians couldn't have engaged in permanent or intensive agriculture," says Meggers. "Fertile soil is just not there and it's never been any other way." There had to be other ways to explain how these anomalous settlements had arisen in this limiting environment. Meggers argues that the mounds and ceramics represent an intrusion at about A.D. 500 by advanced groups from the Andes. The culture's decline, concurrent with a major drought around the first millennium A.D., was evidence that such groups could not be sustained there.

By contrast, Roosevelt's excavations of multiple levels of occupation on Marajó led her to conclude that complex groups lived there for more than a millennium. "it wasn't a flash in the pan at all!" she says. She also claims that evidence of complex culture has been found in other parts of Amazonia and that early pottery dates refute Meggers' idea that any complexity represents intrusions from the Andes. "We don't need to derive cultural innovations like mounds and early pottery from other areas," says Roosevelt. "There were many adaptations, and the environment wasn't as tyrannical as everybody says. Everywhere people look now in Amazonia they're finding something complex."

A similar debate is simmering between Meggers and other Amazonianists, who argue that besides the large sites, mounds, and public architecture they've found, there are vast areas of "black earth," highly fertile soil that some say signifies intensive agriculture and complex culture because it was created by continuous human intervention. Geologist William Woods of Southern Illinois University even suggests in a recent *Science* article that the depth of artifacts and the extent of black earth at one site where an American team is working indicate it could have sustained "about 200,000 to 400,000 people a few centuries before the Spanish came… a population on the same order of Tenochtitlán [the great Aztec capital]."

"Now this is just outrageous," Meggers laughs, sweeping her hand across the article, again amazed that such extreme statements are being published. "I guess the less evidence you have the more exciting your ideas are. But people are buying this! So here I am saying, 'Wait a

minute!' The floodplain where these soils are found is subject to too much uncertainty to sustain long-term cultivation or settlement."

Meggers also objects to theorists who contend Amazonia is an "anthropogenic forest," one manipulated so completely by human hands that it owes is present form to them. Proponents of the idea cite evidence of intensive agriculture in the ancient past: cutting and burning down huge portions of forest, building or draining expansive fields, and carving irrigation canals. The concept of an anthropogenic forest—which implies that there is no part of Amazonia that has not been altered by human presence—flies in the face of traditional conservationist concepts of the Amazon as a pristine, environmental utopia.

To Meggers, the idea of an anthropogenic forest is pure hyperbole. Utter the words and she'll lure you through lectures from shamanism to pollen cores to ecology. "We know that people have interacted with their environment forever," she says. "That's nothing new. But the ecosystem depends on interactions by all kinds of animals, not just humans. Amazonia is not an anthropogenic forest any more than it is a forest made by the primates or the tapirs or any of the other animals that move things around. Look at what elephants or beavers do to a landscape. To act as if only humans are having an impact is anthropocentric." Meggers fears archaeologists are providing a bogus scientific rational to developers: because humans have manipulated the forest for centuries, further exploitation won't be harmful.

Iᴀ ɴᴏᴛ ʙᴇʟᴏᴠᴇᴅ ʙʏ ᴀʟʟ ᴀᴛ ʜᴏᴍᴇ, Meggers is widely respected among archaeologists in Latin America. Early on, she and Evans collaborated with local scientists, who didn't publish often in English or in North American journals. They also trained South American archaeologists in excavation and ceramic analysis and met with them regularly to compare results—a tradition that Meggers continues to this day. With money inherited from Evans' family and without children to support, the two were dedicated to funding the work of hundreds of Latin American archaeologists, providing journals and translations of publications to their institutions, and helping to give their work exposure in North America. "I'm not all at interested in supporting Latinos, that is, people who have left their country," says Meggers. "I only support people who are staying and fighting to make archaeology better at home. I appreciate the difficult circumstances under which most of them are working, and I'll do anything I can to help them spread the word about their research." In part because of this commitment, Meggers has received honorary doctorates from universities in Argentina, Ecuador, and Brazil, and additional honors from Chile, Peru, Ecuador, and Venezuela, "all of which I greatly appreciate," she says.

Transpacific Contact?

FOR THE PAST 50 YEARS, Betty Meggers has argued that the pottery she excavated on Marajó, or any pottery excavated in the Americas for that matter, originated in Japan. In the 1950s, she and her husband, Clifford Evans, visited the site of Valdivia on the coast of Ecuador to look at some very early ceramics. Eventually dated to 400 B.C., they bore a remarkable resemblance to those of Japan's Jomon culture for the same period. "You have this long evolution of pottery in Japan," says Meggers. "Then the same pottery shows up out of nowhere on the coast of Ecuador. When people from Japan introduced the pottery, the people in Valdivia decided it was useful. The early pottery in other parts of South America are later derivatives from this core."

Most archaeologists working in South America are not convinced by the similarities in the ceramics. "There are several earlier ceramic finds in northwestern South America and elsewhere in the Americas," says Warren DeBoer of Queens College, "so Valdivian priority is lost. What is needed is a demonstration that a specific Jomon pottery source, with tightly fixed chronology, can be tied to early Valdivian ceramics. An ensemble of traits is not sufficient."

Further, such ideas still carry the negative connotation of diffusionism, implying that natives of the Americas weren't capable of developing advanced technology in their own, a position many archaeologists are loathe to endorse. Still, Meggers continues to search for more evidence and makes no apologies, suggesting the sensitivity to diffusionism is unfounded. "Well, it makes no sense at all," she says. "What makes us dominant on the planet is that we've been able to borrow from one another and improve, so that not everyone has to invent everything independently. That people refuse to look at these connections… Well, I find it contrary to what one expects from scholarly pursuits."

MEGGERS HAS MUCH DATA LEFT to publish and continues to find collaborators to carry on her research. Meanwhile, her sheer persistence and gutsiness is much admired by colleagues here at home, even by her critics. "I give her credit for standing alone against quite a number of others and not backing down," says Robert Carneiro, curator of South American ethnology at the American Museum of Natural History and one of the first to disagree with Meggers and Evans' theories. Scott Raymond, former Lathrap student and professor at the University of Calgary, says, "It's important to know that there is always someone out there who is going to really give your research a thorough critical examination and who will be skeptical of whatever you publish." Richard Burger adds: "She put environment on the table and forced people to pay attention and argue about it, and that's a positive thing. Regardless of whether you agree with her interpretations of it, it's worth debating."

But Meggers wants more than to encourage debate. She wants to be right. "I tell you, I just get so frustrated when I can't seem to connect with anybody," she says. "I start wondering if I'm misguided, but then the biologists and climatologists agree with me and the data fit, and I know, I just can't be wrong."

COLLEEN P. POPSON *is associate editor of* ARCHAEOLOGY. *For further reading visit www.archaeology.org.*

Archaeology's Perilous Pleasures

An eminent historian reflects on some uses and misuses of the past.

by David Lowenthal

More than any other scholarly calling, archaeology surfs the crest of our obsession with heritage. Cults of bygone times and relics are omnipresent. Links with personal and communal legacies extend the desirable past from great monuments to humble shrines, from relics of architecture and art to remains of everyday folklife, from state and church archives to records of neighborhood groups and family life. Harking back to the most remote and forward to the most recent times, we embrace every epoch from the Palaeolithic to Elvis Presley.

The civic landscape reflects these burgeoning concerns. Themed museums and historic sites proliferate; history and genealogy multiply their devotees; historic preservation becomes a bellwether for urban renewal. Tragedy is hallowed along with triumph; today's ancestral past is as much mourned as cheered. Empathy with medieval serfs, dispossessed indigenes, African slaves, and Holocaust victims haunts popular consciousness. And in most of these backward-looking ventures, archaeology plays a unparalleled role.

What accounts for the discipline's new-found salience? Archaeology has long capitalized on public fascination with death and treasure, but its current popularity stems, I suggest, from three further attributes specific to the field. One is archaeology's unique focus on the remotest epochs of human existence, imbued with an allure of exotic, uncanny secrets hidden in the mists of time. A second is archaeology's concern with tangible remains, lending it an immediacy and credibility unique among the hu-

man sciences. The third is archaeology's patent attachment to pressing issues of identity and possession—of post-imperial hegemony and of ethnic cleansing, the retention or restitution of land and bones and artifact—that embroil First and Third World states, mainstream and minority people.

These three realms of discourse—antiquity, tangibility, and present-day relevance—are not, to be sure, confined to archaeology alone. While astronomy and paleontology claim concern with still more remote antiquity, art and architecture with material artifacts, public history and social science with present politics, archaeology alone uniquely embodies and exemplifies all three realms. Each promises potent new avenues for archaeological advances; each also portends grave risks for archaeological theory and practice. Let me spell out some of these promises and perils.

First, antiquity. Archaeology is not limited to humanity's deep past, but is closely aligned with it in the public and in most practitioners' eyes. Ancient remains arouse widespread awe; hardly a day passes without some rumored find that stirs us in proportion to its purported antiquity. By antiquity I mean not chronological date but time relative to context; no less thrilling than the cosmically ancient is the more recent calendar age of a species, a tribe, a morpheme, or a sacred text. Finds dauntingly antique are mesmeric: a speck of possibly fossilized primordial organic Mars, single-celled eukaryotes and photosynthetic bacteria

2.7 billion years old, Mesozoic pines hidden over many millennia in New South Wales, the frozen body of a neolithic Alpine shepherd, the fragmentary adjurations of first-century Essene scribes near the Dead Sea, turf-wall traces of early Viking sojourns at L'Anse aux Meadows, Newfoundland.

Admiration of the ancient stems from the feeling that priority confers entitlement. We associate primacy with coming first, priority with being best. The first-born is traditionally blessed; first come, first served. The possession of land and chattels, rights to rulership and to guidance, are almost universally accorded to firstcomers, oldest offspring, original discoverers, those who precede others. The first to find a cure or a continent, to detect hidden treasure, to walk on the moon, or to cry "Bingo!" inherits fame or fortune; no one remembers who came next.

What is prior offers prestige and title; primordial origins connote divine aims and attributes; things indigenous are deeply rooted; long persistence betokens stability. Beginnings lost in the mists of time attest the community's primordiality and hence its worth. Ancient origins, especially those predating written evidence, secure pride and fidelity to traditional values. Descendants of indigenes claim lands by dint of primordial occupance. No wonder Canadian Inuit and Indians favor such terms as First Peoples and First Nations. The mantle of prior occupance makes their entitlement morally unassailable. No claims are more potent than "This belongs to us because we were here first."

It is tempting for governments and civic organizations to exploit the popularity of ancientness and origins. But for archaeologists it carries severe risks. One is that temporal primacy explains much less than it seems to do. The earliest sources of self, of society, of the species promise to reveal our place in the scheme of things. "Here is where time began," proclaims an advertisement from the Israel Ministry of Tourism; "Here it was all born," says the Prague Mozart Foundation of central European musical culture. "This is who we are because this is how and where we began." We are apt to assume that to find how and when something began is to understand it completely, but this is sheer fancy. Origins explain little.

Pinpointing "how and where we began" is grand heritage rhetoric but poor history. "Archaeologists and the media all want to know what the oldest site is," said Australia's premier archaeologist John Mulvaney in a recent interview. "That's the wrong question. It's more important to work out what the people were doing—what sort of society they had." Pinpointing the oldest is often only a semantic quibble, for beginnings depend on how we define what has begun. Tracing change and continuity from a before to an after tells history more fruitfully than does finding and dating an event without antecedent. Claims of precedence and primordiality moreover cause immense grief. Obsession with ancient subjugation exacerbates national, religious, and ethnic strife all over the globe. Ulster Catholic recall of William of Orange, Serb memories of the fourth-century Battle of Kosovo immure the present in outworn shibboleths.

But no evidence, historical or archaeological, can ever settle such contests. To rivals who claim an older past, chauvinists often retort that that kind of past doesn't count. Thus, some French repudiated Lucy, then the world's oldest found hominid, as an alien African. And Greeks, besotted by any trace of Philip of Macedon, dismiss English prehistory as irrelevant. So what if Stonehenge is older than the Acropolis? Greeks know their history goes back two and a half millennia, while the English had no "real" history before 1066.

In fact, ancient priority embodies no inherent merit; it merely lends comfort to those persuaded that they alone incarnate some uniquely ancestral essence. There is no intrinsic virtue in having been the first occupants, the first exploiters, the first to stamp culture on the face of nature, or lineal descendants of any of these. All ancestries, foreign as well as domestic, are equally aboriginal. Millennia of global history entitle migrants no less than stay-at-homes to the legacies of myriad restlessly migratory, continually intermixed ancestors.

Tangibility is the second archaeological trait I find alike enticing and troublesome. The very term "fieldwork" typically suggests unearthing treasures of high value, beauty, and historical significance. More than any written record, the earthy substance of sites and artifacts lends them a compelling immediacy, makes them convincingly real. Archaeological finds around the Mediterranean, from Pompeii to Paestum and the pyramids, have brought classical, biblical, and Pharaonic history newly alive to millions. And sites such as Ireland's Tara, Spain's Numantia, and France's Alésia figure as precious national icons of identity.

Locales and remnants of ancient grief and glory have long been prime foci of tourist pilgrimage. But today we treasure ancient sites and relics for other reasons than our forebears did. Two centuries ago, the attrition of monuments induced elegiac reflections on the brevity of life and the evanescence of power. "Look on my works, ye Mighty, and despair," pronounced Shelley's Ozymandias. Today mordant meditation is passé; we cry havoc at physical decay and seek to conserve at all costs.

What explains this mounting concern to see and to save relics of antiquity? Partly it is their heightened visibility. Electronic and other media replace verbal messages with visual images. Vivid depictions of nature and culture display the whole sweep of planetary history to mass audiences as never before. And archaeology, more than any other calling, inspired spectacular presentations from coffee-table picture-books to television programs.

Ostensible truth is a powerful spur to the popularity of the tangible. Never mind that faking is everywhere rife; the sheer solid existence of an artifact or a site compellingly attests its authenticity. The very materiality of archaeology's stock-in-trade conveys a conviction absent from mere tales or texts. Telling the truth about the past is the supreme archaeological cachet, whether or not realized in practice. Indeed, curators and site interpreters eager to claim they are showing history as it really was, warts and all, sanctify their enterprise as "archaeologically correct."

From Petrarch to Freud, archaeological analogies have captivated scholars seeking truth in history and memory. Renaissance devotees of antiquity resurrected both buried artifacts and buried texts; they compared restoring classical learning with rescuing physical relics. "Deciphering historical knowledge under the visual or verbal surfaces," in the American historian Thomas Green's phrase, "the reader divines a buried stratum as a visitor to Rome divines the subterranean foundations of a temple."

Four centuries later the same metaphor fuelled psychoanalytic recovery of memory. Freud repeatedly equated psychoanalysis with prehistoric excavation: "unearthing" unconscious memories, "digging" to find representative "traces," he likened himself to Schliemann quarrying another Troy. He thought analysts even more fortunate than archaeologists, whose significant evidence may well have been destroyed, whereas for excavators of memory "all of the essentials are preserved; even things that seem completely forgotten are present." Unlike the analyst, moreover, the archaeologist could not check his constructs with some surviving Trojan or Babylonian.

An oft-cited claim of the archaeological enterprise, superior truth is perhaps its most powerful appeal. Material evidence is held to provide a healthy corrective to the biases of written history based on scribal records confined to a small cadre of privileged and prejudiced elites. The past these elites recounted largely ignored or trivialized the role of women, children, manual workers, non-whites, non-Europeans—most of the human race. Properly interpreted, tangible remains reveal the true history of this heretofore silent majority—people without history, in anthropologist Eric Wolf's phrase. For, unlike words, things do not lie. "Archaeology has preempted the written record," proclaims this journal's editor (ARCHAEOLOGY, September/October 1998), "with discoveries that illumine the actual rather than the imagined past."

Yet these claims are deeply flawed. Its visible, tangible character makes archaeological evidence uniquely gripping, but by the same token incomplete and deficient. From material remains alone we can merely speculate about past minds, hearts, and memories; only recorded words, whether feigned or sincere, reveal nuances of consciousness and intention, forethought and hindsight. Devotees of cognitive archaeology have not yet extracted traces of thought from relics. Not only are relics mute; they are also static. Whereas a past recalled and recorded can convey a dynamic sweep through time, tangible survivals in general yield isolated moments, not a diachronic palimpsest.

That material evidence gives archaeology a special claim to indubitable truth is likewise delusive. Tangibility lends credence to physical relics. Here we are, they seem to say; you can see us, even touch us; why doubt the reality of your senses? But sense impressions are notoriously fickle. And the data that relics convey are elusive and slippery.

Undue faith in sensory evidence, especially at monumental sites, disserves archaeology's claim to objective truth. The powerful impress of vivid ancient locales privileges erroneous myth over historical evidence. Josephus's tale of mass suicide at Masada is known to be an invented compage of classical lore, disproved by history and archaeology alike. But the enduring salience of the site induces the viewer to experience Masada as a transcendent reality.

Evidence from structures and objects is deficient in other respects as well. One is their relative longevity. Nothing material lasts forever; the best-husbanded relics ultimately expire. More than textual evidence, the material past risks being misinterpreted owing to differential decay. Because things built and made for elites almost always outlast everyman's goods and chattels, material remnants are bound to warp how the past is viewed and understood.

Recent efforts to depict eighteenth-century colonial Williamsburg more comprehensively, including the presence and lifestyles of its many slaves, shows how disparities in tangible remains subvert historical neutrality and perhaps even reinforce historical bias. Much of what belonged to Williamsburg's elite endures and has been exhaustively inventoried. But of the slaves—more than half the population—virtually nothing material survives. To depict slave life, replica huts had to be furnished with generic bedding, utensils, clothing. The incongruity is flagrant—and bizarre. The elite appear inactual, contextualized, explicit detail; the faceless, unprovenanced slaves are generalized, undifferentiated. No contrivance can redress the gross imbalance of what survives in the archaeological record.

Archaeology's third special claim is its relevance to current social and political issues. For a discipline ostensibly about the past, and notably about prehistory, archaeology is strikingly enmeshed in passions and prejudices of the present. Beyond most who delve into bygone eras, archaeologists seem aware—even happily aware, that the past is no longer a "foreign country," as British novelist L. P. Hartley termed it 50 years ago, but rather is part and parcel of the present; what they dissect and disclose is ever freshly reborn. No wonder archaeologists become prominent in politics: they often exemplify national feeling, especially in newly ex-colonial and otherwise beleaguered countries.

That many archaeologists are willing and able to confront salient current issues head-on is just as well. They have little choice but to do so; the present refuses to let them alone. Far more than other disciplines whose remit is the past—history, paleontology, geology—archaeology must reckon with current conflicts of property, heritage, law, and stewardship. When not totally banned, fieldwork in foreign lands, even in one's own, now requires endless negotiations over land rights, labor forces, ethnic and racial interests, disposal of spoils. National sentiment and professional ethics fetter archaeological modes of data disclosure, conversation, infrastructure, training, and long-term accountability.

What archaeologists do and how they are viewed has momentous, perhaps fateful, import for icons of national identity, tribal claims to indemnity, artifact restitution, site pillaging and looting, the faking of relics, the smuggling of art and antiquities. These activities also seal the future viability of their own profession. It is rightly said that archaeology often seems less a science than a vendetta. Meanwhile, their manifest immersion in present-day concerns privileges archaeologists in the public eye. They are often looked to—save by treasure-hunters and collectors—as zealous, disinterested guardians of the public cultural heritage against malevolent private greed, corporate neglect, and selfish chauvinism. Some appear in the public eye as champions of fidelity of context, against collectors' site-destructive avarice. Atoning for callous and ethnocentric precursors, archaeologists today embrace minority rights, indigenous restorations, and self-denying bans of every stripe.

These commitments, in large measure unavoidable, are laudable in principle, but they are also costly and hazardous. They drain time and effort, funding and esprit de corps. They demand of archaeologists a level of high-mindedness that is often neither attainable nor credible to outsiders. And they sometimes willy nilly feed, rather than allay, chauvinist and acquisitive appetites and the warping of history that archaeology genuinely deplores. Archaeologists, of course, are not immune to pressures to conform to national, ethnic, and personal agendas and priorities. What excavator can wholly ignore government or tribal behests now for urgent effort, now for discreet delay, pleas here for a blind eye, there for forceful intervention? With the myth of the selfless academic today exploded, to assume a stance of scientific objectivity is to invite public antipathy. Elsewhere, as the Harvard anthropologist Michael's Herzfeld's *A Place in History* (1991) showed for Rethemnos, Crete, the very term "archaeologist" becomes a byword for officious, bureaucratic meddling in local community affairs.

Excavations are famously the pawns of personal ambitions and nationalist goals. Almost everywhere, archaeologists have sought to justify the ethnic, racial, linguistic, religious, and cultural bases of their state or people. Many if not most digs reflect entrepreneurial hubris; even refuse sites become icons of collective identity. Of Schliemann's obsession with finding Homer's Troy and his wholesale removal of layers that did not fit his Trojan image, the American writer Neil Asher Silberman concludes that "archaeology was not the handmaiden of history, it was the delivery boy of myth." Few German archaeologists hesitated to document the ancient Teutonic sites and artifacts that Nazi prestige demanded, nor Soviet scholars to counter German ethnogenetic expansion with a contrived inflation of Slavic antiquities.

When 1980s excavation pointed to the Japanese imperial family's probable Korean ancestry, archaeologists swiftly sealed the tombs to safeguard the legend of unbroken descent from the sun goddess. Little wonder, for prewar archaeologists had been dismissed, even arrested, for questioning the imperial myth. The Romanian dictator Nikolai Ceausescu lauded prehistorians for validating his country's claims: "with every excavation, the archeologists are bringing to light more evidence, proving that it is here, in this land…that the bones of the forefathers of our forefathers' forefathers are to be found."

In America, too, what gets excavated and how reflects not just scholarly aims but partisan and professional heritage needs. Some archaeologists are importuned to certify tribal sages in legal preceedings, testifying that this or that people came first and kept collective faith making them one with present-day descendants; others are paid to deny such claims. Those who take on worthy causes may succumb to presentist fallacies, attributing present modes of thought and action to folk of the past. For example, archaeologists who re-examined seventeenth-century Narragansett Indian remains in a Rhode Island cemetery in the 1980s concluded that skeletal postures and grave goods proved resistance to white assimilation. Their concurrence with current minority virtues pleased present-day Narragansetts, for continuity of tribal identity with likeminded ancestors gained them tribal pride and Federal privileges. But it ignored or denied a known ethnohistory and archaeology that, according to the American archaeologist Michael Nassaney, attested past racial and cultural synthesis. Empathy may not have been the sole reason for positing past solidarity and cohesion; only an explanation congenial to the tribe enabled archaeologists to maintain access to the site.

Education, information, and other heritage benefits of archaeology here and there outweigh the interests of private—personal, tribal, national—possessors and claimants. But if broader stewardship ideals have begun to actuate some public policy, they are still far from being translated into widespread behavior. Routinely distorted for nationalist aims, the archaeology of the Caucasus—opposing Azeri and Armenian views of the genesis of the carved stone crosses in Azerbaijan—has in this decade fuelled one of the former Soviet Union's bloodiest conflicts. As long as national and ethnic rivalries endure, the past will continue to be perverted for political purposes. Disparities of wealth and stakeholding in much of the world will long preclude any consensus that excavation is for mainly scholarly purposes. As long as impoverished folk in heritage-rich lands have to sell antiquities to feed their children—and perhaps to school them to behave otherwise—there will be no halt to looting and destruction.

We like to suppose our age of enlightened codes of ethics and reforms of practice vouch for an archaeology today that is on the whole more highminded, socially responsible, and intellectually reputable than before. But the nineteenth-century archaeologist who catered to nationalist bias, the curator who rejoiced in acquiring mummies because they would be safer in the British Museum than in any tomb in Egypt, the explorer who purloined tribal African treasures, the consular official who bribed looters of Chinese antiquities, were generally acting in accord with ethical standards we now condemn.

Yet, as I suggest above, certain other preconceptions inherited from these less enlightened times still endure in the archaeological profession. Devotion to priority, to tangibility, and to contemporary relevance have brought the discipline many genuine benefits. Archaeology, however, would benefit from acknowledging the harm as well as the good that such devotion has wrought. It might enable archaeologists to face up more frankly to often justified public doubts about the rectitude of the discipline.

David Lowenthal, professor emeritus of geography at University College London and visiting professor of Heritage Studies at St Mary's University College, Strawberry Hill, is an occasional lecturer at London University's Institute of Archaeology and Cambridge University's Department of Archaeology. With Peter Gathercole he edited *The Politics of the Past* in the *One World Archaeology Series* (Routledge, London 1994). He is the author of *The Past is a Foreign Country* (1985) and *The Heritage Crusade and the Spoils of History* (1997), both *Cambridge University Press*. His *George Perkins Marsh, Prophet of Conservation* was published in April by the University of Washington Press.

Reprinted with permission from *Archaeology* magazine, Vol. 53, No. 2, March/April 2000, pp. 62–66. © 2000 by the Archaeological Institute of America.

The Travails and Tedium of Conflict-Zone Fieldwork

Lori A Allen

The Israeli occupation has placed the entire city of Ramallah under curfew. For more than a month, I, along with every one else, have been forbidden from leaving my house. Two million residents of other West Bank towns also have been stuck at home. Even being outside when curfew is supposedly lifted entails danger, as evidenced by the numerous Palestinian civilians who have been killed and injured while going to market or school during this latest Israeli reoccupation.

Needless to say, this has made *field*work, at least in any normal sense, impossible. True, the curfew in Ramallah was lifted from 2 to 6 pm a few days ago. But those four hours barely allowed enough time for residents to stop up on supplies; giving interviews to foreign academics was not high up on their priority lists. Nor was conducting interviews high up on mine.

The Israeli occupation of the West Bank and Gaza, and the Palestinian *intifada,* or uprising, against it has been steadily intensifying throughout my year-and-a-half of field research. I came with a plan to examine the role of "pain and suffering" in Palestinian nationalism. But unexpected issues have presented themselves as well. Foremost among these is the political salience of the routinization of violence.

Sitting for days in one's house under curfew is intolerably boring. Seeing yet another story on the news of yet another Palestinian activist assassinated by an Israeli attack helicopter—by its very repetition—has become tedious. And while the grief of more than 1,500 Palestinians killed and tens of thousands injured by Israeli settlers and soldiers is intense, leaving almost no Palestinian family unaffected, it too has become routine.

My research has revealed that nationalist fervor in Palestine views with apathy and exhaustion caused by such political exigencies. Even when Israeli tanks were shelling civilian neighborhoods, when the almost daily

assassinations of Palestinian politician's and activists were steadily raising the stakes of the conflict, when the death toll on both sides surpassed what anyone expected, the most common response was, "This is normal. We're used to it." People marched in demonstrations and martyr funerals by the thousands. But these nationalist displays were not inspired so much by political conviction or overwhelming emotion, as they had become, for many, tedious; a duty; habit.

COMMENTARY

Despite this atmosphere of world-weariness, in which everyone describes themselves as *zahqaneen* (fed up), physical forms of resistance continued. The question of how extraordinary violence and victimization becomes routine, and yet, at the same time, some people maintain the kind of motivation it takes to confront armed troops with rocks, or to blow up themselves to kill others, has become central to my investigation.

Going Native in a Conflict Zone

Persistence and adaptation are explicit elements of Palestinian resistance. They are involved in a conflict over territory in which physical presence and refusal to flee is a key element of their arsenal against colonial occupation. In 1948, 700,000 Palestinians fled during the war that resulted in the establishment of the Israeli state. Many Palestinians argue that leaving now could spell the end of their national aspirations. Most are convinced that they can outlast their occupiers, and the Israelis will blink first. Palestinians, they argue, are used to suffering, and can endure more hardships. So staying put and refusing to submit to the intimidations and dangers of military occupation is a political act. But most Palestinians also have gotten used to insecurity, fear and grief because they have no choice. They have nowhere else to go.

But I do. Aside from times of complete curfew and closure, I can leave whenever I want. That I am in a position to act as a witness, to go deeper than the hordes of journalists hounding this small country can do in their brief visits to the hot spots, gives me and other researchers a sense of responsibility, and makes leaving a complicated issue.

I have wondered about the extent to which I have "gone native" in my willingness to continue living in such conditions, conditions which are sometimes dangerous, and always exasperating. Surely it is naturally human, even if in culturally specific ways, to adapt to one's surroundings. My own adaptation, and that which I have observed in others, adds evidence to the critique of some anthropological treatment of ethnic conflicts which argued that violence reduces individuals and societies to states of prelinguistic, existential chaos. To the contrary, it is clear that people manage to create meanings and methods of coping even when such conditions defy the imagination of outsiders.

Today I rushed inside shortly after noon. The sound of the soldiers shouting out the reimposition of curfew three hours earlier than anyone expected was accompanied by window rattling sound-bombs and cars careening wildly through the streets as people rushed to get home. "This is your last warning!" a soldier screamed, waving his gun, as people ran, children carrying school books, moms with their hands full of kids and groceries.

Palestinians know they are living in extraordinary circumstances. People are exhausted and depressed. But those kids running away from the soldiers still are reading their schoolbooks, moms still are managing their households, and many people work from home. It is this normalization of violence, and of victimization, that allows people to persist and resist. As Sartre wrote of another context, "If colonialism was a system … then resistance began to feel systematic too."

Lori A Allen is a graduate student at the U of Chicago; she currently is conducting research on nationalism and the politics of suffering in Palestine.

Annals of Archaeology

All the King's Sons

The biggest archeological find in Egypt since King Tut's tomb is also the most unusual: it may explain the fate of most of Ramesses II's fifty-two sons, New Kingdom funerary practices, and pharaonic sex. What does it feel like to be the first person to enter such a place in three thousand years?

By Douglas Preston

On February 2, 1995, at ten in the morning, the archeologist Kent R. Weeks found himself a hundred feet inside a mountain in Egypt's Valley of the Kings, on his belly in the dust of a tomb. He was crawling toward a long-buried doorway that no one had entered for at least thirty-one hundred years. There were two people with him, a graduate student and an Egyptian workman; among them they had one flashlight.

To get through the doorway, Weeks had to remove his hard hat and force his large frame under the lintel with his toes and fingers. He expected to enter a small, plain room marking the end of the tomb. Instead, he found himself in a vast corridor, half full of debris, with doorways lining either side and marching off into the darkness. "When I looked around with the flashlight," Weeks recalled later, "we realized that the corridor was tremendous. I didn't know *what* to think." The air was dead, with a temperature in excess of a hundred degrees and a humidity of one hundred per cent. Weeks, whose glasses had immediately steamed up, was finding it hard to breathe. With every movement, clouds of powder arose, and turned into mud on the skin.

The three people explored the corridor, stooping, and sometimes crawling over piles of rock that had fallen from the ceiling. Weeks counted twenty doorways lining the hundred-foot hallway,

some opening into whole suites of rooms with vaulted ceilings carved out of the solid rock of the mountain. At the corridor's end, the feeble flashlight beam revealed a statue of Osiris, the god of resurrection: he was wearing a crown and holding crossed flails and sceptres; his body was bound like that of a mummy. In front of Osiris, the corridor came to a T, branching into two transverse passageways, each of them eighty feet long and ending in what looked like a descending staircase blocked with debris. Weeks counted thirty-two additional rooms off those two corridors.

The tomb was of an entirely new type, never seen by archeologists before. "The architecture didn't fit any known pattern," Weeks told me. "And it was so *big*. I just couldn't make sense of it." The largest pharaonic tombs in the Valley contain ten or fifteen rooms at most. This one had at least sixty-seven—the total making it not only the biggest tomb in the Valley but possibly the biggest in all Egypt. Most tombs in the Valley of the Kings follow a standard architectural plan—a series of consecutive chambers and corridors like a string of boxcars shot at an angle into the bedrock, and ending with the burial vault. This tomb, with its T shape, had a warren of side chambers, suites, and descending passageways. Weeks knew from earlier excavations that the tomb was the resting place for at least four sons of Ramesses II, the pha-

raoh also known as Ramesses the Great—and, traditionally, as simply Pharaoh in the Book of Exodus. Because of the tomb's size and complexity, Weeks had to consider the possibility that it was a catacomb for as many as fifty of Ramesses' fifty-two sons—the first example of a royal family mausoleum in ancient Egypt.

Weeks had discovered the tomb's entrance eight years earlier, after the Egyptian government announced plans to widen the entrance to the Valley to create a bus turnaround at the end of an asphalt road. From reading old maps and reports, he had recalled that the entrance to a lost tomb lay in the area that was to be paved over. Napoleon's expedition to Egypt had noted a tomb there, and a rather feckless Englishman named James Burton had crawled partway inside it in 1825. A few years later, the archeologist Sir John Gardner Wilkinson had given it the designation KV5, for Kings' Valley Tomb No. 5, when he numbered eighteen tombs there. Howard Carter—the archeologist who discovered King Tutankhamun's tomb in 1922, two hundred feet farther on—dug two feet in, decided that KV5's entrance looked unimportant, and used it as a dumping ground for debris from his other excavations, thus burying it under ten feet of stone and dirt. The location of the tomb's entrance was quickly forgotten.

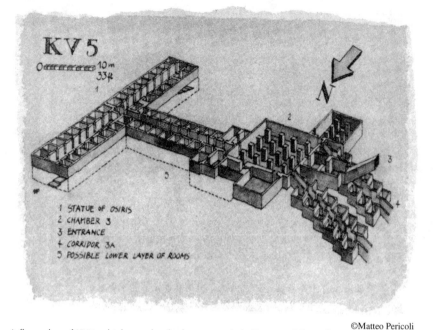

©Matteo Pericoli

A floor plan of KV5, which may be the largest tomb in Egypt and the only royal mausoleum. Ramesses II, the master builder of Thebes, now rests in the Cairo Museum

Egyptian Museum of Antiquities, Cairo

It took about ten days of channelling through Carter's heaps of debris for Weeks and his men to find the ancient doorway of KV5, and it proved to be directly across the path from the tomb of Ramesses the Great. The entrance lay at the edge of the asphalt road, about ten feet below grade and behind the rickety booths of T-shirt venders and fake-scarab-beetle sellers.

Plans for the bus turnaround were cancelled, and, over a period of seven years, Weeks and his workmen cleared half of the first two chambers and briefly explored a third one. The tomb was packed from floor to ceiling with dirt and rocks that had been washed in by flash floods. He uncovered finely carved reliefs on the walls, which showed Ramesses presenting various sons to the gods, with their names and titles recorded in hieroglyphics. When he reached floor level, he found thousands of objects: pieces of faience jewelry, fragments of furniture, a wooden fist from a coffin, human and animal bones, mummified body parts, chunks of sarcophagi, and fragments of the canopic jars used to hold the mummified organs of the deceased—all detritus left by ancient tomb robbers.

The third chamber was anything but modest. It was about sixty feet square, one of the largest rooms in the Valley, and was supported by sixteen massive stone pillars arranged in four rows. Debris filled the room to within about two feet of the ceiling, allowing just enough space for Weeks to wriggle around. At the back of the chamber, in the axis of the tomb, Weeks noticed an almost buried doorway. Still believing that the tomb was like others in the Valley, he assumed that the doorway merely led to a small, dead-end annex, so he didn't bother with it for several years—not until last February, when he decided to have a look.

Immediately after the discovery, Weeks went back to a four-dollar-a-night pension he shared with his wife, Susan, in the mud village of Gezira Bairat, showered off the tomb dust, and took a motorboat across the Nile to the small city of Luxor. He faxed a short message to Cairo, three hundred miles downriver. It was directed to his major financial supporter, Bruce Ludwig, who was attending a board meeting at the American University in Cairo, where Weeks is a professor. It read, simply, "Have made wonderful discovery in Valley of the Kings. Await your arrival."

Ludwig instantly recognized the significance of the fax and the inside joke it represented: it was a close paraphrase of the telegram that Howard Carter had sent to the Earl of Carnarvon, his financial supporter, when he discovered Tutankhamun's tomb. Ludwig booked a flight to Luxor.

"That night, the enormousness of the discovery began to sink in," Weeks recalled. At about two o'clock in the morning, he turned to his wife and said, "Susan, I think our lives have changed forever."

The discovery was announced jointly by Egypt's Supreme Council of Antiquities, which oversees all archeological work in the country, and the American University in Cairo, under whose aegis Weeks was working. It became the biggest archeological story of the decade, making the front page of the Times and the cover of Time. Television reporters descended on the site. Weeks had to shut down the tomb to make the talk-show circuit. The London newspapers had a field day: the Daily Mail headlined its story "PHARAOH'S 50 SONS IN MUMMY OF ALL TOMBS," and one tabloid informed its readers that texts in the tomb gave a date for the Second Coming and the end of the world, and also revealed cures for AIDS and cancer.

The media also wondered whether the tomb would prove that Ramesses II was indeed the pharaoh referred to in Exodus. The speculation centered on Amun-her-khopshef, Ramesses' firstborn son, whose name is prominent on KV5's wall. According to the Bible, in order to force Egypt to free the Hebrews from bondage the Lord visited a number of disasters on the land, including the killing of all firstborn Egyptians from the pharaoh's son on down. Some scholars believe that if Amun-her-khopshef's remains are found it may be possible to show at what age and how he died.

Book publishers and Hollywood producers showed great interest in Weeks's story. He didn't respond at first, dismissing inquiries with a wave of the hand. "It's all *kalam fadi*," he said, using the Arabic phrase for empty talk. Eventually, however, so many offers poured in that he engaged an agent at William Morris to handle them; a book proposal will be submitted to publishers later this month.

In the fall, Weeks and his crew decided to impose a partial media blackout on the excavation site—the only way they could get any work done, they felt—but they agreed to let me accompany them near the end of the digging season. Just before I arrived, in mid-November, two mysterious descending corridors, with dozens of new chambers, unexpectedly came to light, and I had the good fortune to be the only journalist to see them.

The Valley of the Kings was the burial ground for the pharaohs of the New Kingdom, the last glorious period of Egyptian history. It began around 1550 B.C., when the Egyptians expelled the foreign Hyksos rulers from Lower Egypt and reëstablished a vast empire, stretching across the Middle East to Syria. It lasted half a millennium. Sixty years before Ramesses, the pharaoh Akhenaten overthrew much of the Egyptian religion and decreed that thenceforth Egyptians should worship only one god—Light, whose visible symbol was Aten, the disk of the sun. Akhenaten's

revolution came to a halt at his death. Ramesses represented the culmination of the return to tradition. He was an exceedingly conservative man, who saw himself as the guardian of the ancient customs, and he was particularly zealous in erasing the heretic pharaoh's name from his temples and stelae, a task begun by his father, Seti I. Because Ramesses disliked innovation, his monuments were notable not for their architectural brilliance but for their monstrous size. The New Kingdom began a slow decline following his rule, and finally sputtered to an end with Ramesses XI, the last pharaoh buried in the Valley of the Kings.

The discovery of KV5 will eventually open for us a marvellous window on this period. We know almost nothing about the offspring of the New Kingdom pharaohs or what roles they played. After each eldest prince ascended the throne, the younger sons disappeared so abruptly from the record that it was once thought they were routinely executed. The burial chambers' hieroglyphics, if they still survive, may give us an invaluable account of each son's life and accomplishments. There is a remote possibility—it was suggested to me by the secretary-general of the Supreme Council of Antiquities, Professor Abdel-Halim Nur el-Din, who is an authority on women in ancient Egypt—that Ramesses' daughters might be buried in KV5 as well. (Weeks thinks the possibility highly unlikely.) Before Weeks is done, he will probably find sarcophagi, pieces of funerary offerings, identifiable pieces of mummies, and many items with hieroglyphics on them. The tomb will add a new chapter to our understanding of Egyptian funerary traditions. And there is always a possibility of finding an intact chamber packed with treasure.

Ramesses the Great's reign lasted an unprecedented sixty-seven years, from 1279 to 1213 B.C. He covered the Nile Valley from Nubia to the delta with magnificent temples, statuary, and stelae, which are some of the grandest monuments the world has ever seen. Among his projects were the enormous forecourt at Luxor Temple; the Ramesseum; the cliffside temples of Abu Simbel; the great Hall of Columns at Karnak; and the city of Pi-Ramesse. The two "vast and

trunkless legs of stone" with a "shattered visage" in Shelley's poem "Ozymandias" were those of Ramesses—fragments of the largest statue in pharaonic history. Ramesses outlived twelve of his heirs, dying in his early nineties. The thirteenth crown prince, Merneptah, became pharaoh only in his sixties.

By the time Ramesses ascended the throne, at twenty-five, he had fathered perhaps ten sons and as many daughters. His father had started him out with a harem while he was still a teenager, and he had two principal wives, Nefertari and Istnofret. He later added several Hittite princesses to his harem, and probably his sister and two daughters. It is still debated whether the incestuous marriage of the pharaohs were merely ceremonial or actually consummated. If identifiable remains of Ramesses' sons are found in KV5, it is conceivable that DNA testing might resolve this vexing question.

In most pharaonic monuments we find little about wives and children, but Ramesses showed an unusual affection for his family, extolling the accomplishments of his sons and listing their names on numerous temple walls. All over Egypt, he commissioned statues of Nefertari (not to be confused with the more famous Nefertiti, who was Akhenaten's wife), "for whose sake the very sun does shine." When she died, in Year 24 of his reign, Ramesses interred her in the most beautiful tomb yet discovered in the Valley of the Queens, just south of the Valley of the Kings. The tomb survived intact, and its incised and painted walls are nearly as fresh as the day they were fashioned. The rendering of Nefertari's face and figure perhaps speaks most eloquently of Ramesses' love for her. She is shown making her afterlife journey dressed in a diaphanous linen gown, with her slender figure emerging beneath the gossamer fabric. Her face was painted using the technique of chiaroscuro—perhaps the first known example in the history of art of a human face being treated as a three-dimensional volume. The Getty Conservation Institute recently spent millions restoring the tomb. The Getty recommended that access to the tomb be restricted, in order to preserve it, but the Egyptian government has opened it to tourists, at thirty-five dollars a head.

The design of royal tombs was so fixed by tradition that they had no architect, at least as we use that term today. The tombs were laid out and chiselled from ceiling to floor, resulting in ceiling dimensions that are precise and floor dimensions that can vary considerably. All the rooms and corridors in a typical royal tomb had names, many of which we still do not fully understand: the First God's Passage, Hall of Hindering, Sanctuaries in Which the Gods Repose. The burial chamber was often called the House of Gold. Some tombs had a Hall of Truth, whose murals showed the pharaoh's heart being weighed in judgment by Osiris, with the loathsome god Ammut squatting nearby, waiting to devour it if it was found wanting. Many of the reliefs were so formulaic that they were probably taken from copybooks. Yet even within this rigid tradition breathtaking flights of creativity and artistic expression can be found.

Most of the tombs in the Valley were never finished: they took decades to cut, and the plans usually called for something more elaborate than the pharaoh could achieve during his rule. As a result, the burial of the pharaoh was often a panicky, ad-hoc affair, with various rooms in the tomb being adapted for other purposes, and decorations and texts painted in haste or omitted completely. (Some of the most beautiful inscriptions were those painted swiftly; they have a spontaneity and freshness of line rivalling Japanese calligraphy.)

From the time of Ramesses II on, the tombs were not hidden: their great doorways, which were made of wood, could be opened. It is likely that the front rooms of many tombs were regularly visited by priests to make offerings. This may have been particularly true of KV5, where the many side chambers perhaps served such a purpose. The burial chambers containing treasure, however, were always sealed.

Despite all the monuments and inscriptions that Ramesses left us, it is still difficult to bridge the gap of thirty-one hundred years and see Ramesses as a person. One thing we do know: the standard image of the pharaoh, embodied in

Shelley's "frown, and wrinkled lip, and sneer of cold command," is a misconception. One of the finest works from Ramesses' reign is a statue of the young king now in the Museo Egizio, in Turin. The expression on his face is at once compassionate and other-worldly, not unlike that of a Giotto Madonna; his head is slightly bowed, as if to acknowledge his role as both leader and servant. This is not the face of a tyrant-pharaoh who press-ganged his people into building monuments to his greater glory. Rather, it is the portrait of a ruler who had his subjects' interests at heart, and this is precisely what the archeological and historical records suggest about Ramesses. Most of the Egyptians who labored on the pharaoh's monuments did so proudly and were, by and large, well compensated. There is a lovely stela on which Ramesses boasts about how much he has given his workers, "so that they work for me with their full hearts." Dorothea Arnold, the head curator of the Egyptian Department at the Metropolitan Museum, told me, "The pharaoh was *believed* in. As to whether he was beloved, that is beside the point: he was *necessary*. He was life itself. He represented everything good. Without him there would be nothing."

Final proof of the essential humanity of the pharaonic system is that it survived for more than three thousand years. (When Ramesses ascended the throne, the pyramids at Giza were already thirteen hundred years old.) Egypt produced one of the most stable cultural and religious traditions the world has ever seen.

V ery little lives in the Valley of the Kings now. It is a wilderness of stone and light—a silent, roofless sepulchre. Rainfall averages a quarter inch per year, and one of the hottest natural air temperatures on earth was recorded in the surrounding mountains. And yet the Valley is a surprisingly intimate place. Most of the tombs lie within a mere forty acres, and the screen of cliffs gives the area a feeling of privacy. Dusty paths and sun-bleached, misspelled signs add a pleasant, ramshackle air.

The Valley lies on the outskirts of the ancient city of Thebes, now in ruins. In a six-mile stretch of riverbank around the city, there are as many temples, palaces, and monuments as anywhere else on earth, and the hills are so pockmarked with the yawning pits and doorways of ancient tombs that they resemble a First World War battlefield. It is dangerous to walk or ride anywhere alone. Howard Carter discovered an important tomb when the horse he was riding broke through and fell into it. Recently, a Canadian woman fell into a tomb while hiking and fractured her leg; no one could hear her screams, and she spent the days leading up to her death writing postcards. One archeologist had to clear a tomb that contained a dead cow and twenty-one dead dogs that had gone in to eat it.

Almost all the tombs lying open have been pillaged. A papyrus now in Italy records the trial of someone who robbed KV5 itself in 1150 B.C. The robber confessed under torture to plundering the tomb of Ramesses the Great and then going "across the path" to rob the tomb of his sons. Ancient plunderers often vandalized the tombs they robbed, possibly in an attempt to destroy the magic that supposedly protected them. They smashed everything, levered open sarcophagi, ripped apart mummies to get at the jewelry hidden in the wrappings, and sometimes threw objects against the walls with such force that they left dents and smudges of pure gold.

Nobody is sure why this particular valley, three hundred miles up the Nile from the pyramids, was chosen as the final resting place of the New Kingdom pharaohs. Egyptologists theorize that the sacred pyramidal shape of el-Qurn, the mountain at the head of the Valley of the Kings, may have been one factor. Another was clearly security: the Valley is essentially a small box canyon carved out of the barren heart of a desert mountain range; it has only one entrance, through a narrow gorge, and the surrounding cliffs echo and magnify any sounds of human activity, such as the tapping of a robber's pick on stone.

Contrary to popular belief, the tombs in the Valley are not marked with curses. King Tut's curse was invented by Arthur Weigall, an Egyptologist and journalist at the *Daily Mail,* who was furious that Carnarvon had given the London *Times* the exclusive on the discovery. Royal tombs did not need curses to protect them. Priests guarded the Valley night and day, and thieves knew exactly what awaited them if they were caught: no curse could compete with the fear of being impaled alive. "There are a few curses on some private tombs and in some legal documents," James Allen, an Egyptologist with the Metropolitan Museum, told me. "The most extreme I know of is on a legal document of the Ramesside Period. It reads, 'As for the one who will violate it, he shall be seized for Amun-Ra. He shall be for the flame of Sekhmet. He is an enemy of Osiris, lord of Abydos, and so is his son, for ever and ever. May donkeys fuck him, may donkeys fuck his wife, may his wife fuck his son.'"

Some scholars today, looking back over the past two hundred years of archeological activity, think a curse might have been a good idea: most of the archeology done in the Valley has been indistinguishable from looting. Until the nineteen-sixties, those who had concessions to excavate there were allowed to keep a percentage of the spoils as "payment" for their work. In the fever of the treasure hunt, tombs were emptied without anyone bothering to photograph the objects found or to record their positions in situ, or even to note which tomb they came from. Items that had no market value were trashed. Wilkinson, the man who gave the tombs their numbers, burned three-thousand-year-old wooden coffins and artifacts to heat his house. Murals and reliefs were chopped out of walls. At dinner parties, the American lawyer Theodore M. Davis, who financed many digs in the Valley, used to tear up necklaces woven of ancient flowers and fabric to show how strong they were after three thousand years in a tomb. Pyramids were blasted open with explosives, and one tomb door was bashed in with a battering ram. Even Carter never published a proper scientific report on Tut's tomb. It is only in the last twenty-five years that real archeology has come to Egypt, and KV5 will be one of the first tombs in the Valley of the Kings to be entirely excavated and documented according to proper archeological techniques.

Fortunately, other great archeological projects remain to be carried out with the new techniques. The Theban Necropolis is believed to contain between four thousand and five thousand tombs, of which only four hundred have been given numbers. More than half of the royal tombs in the Valley of the Kings have not been fully excavated, and of these only five have been properly documented. There are mysterious blocked passageways, hollow floors, chambers packed with debris, and caved-in rooms. King Tut's was by no means the last undiscovered pharaonic tomb in Egypt. In the New Kingdom alone, the tombs of Amosis, Amenhotep I, Tuthmosis II, and Ramesses VIII have never been identified. The site of the burial ground for the pharaohs of the entire Twenty-first Dynasty is unknown. And the richness and size of KV5 offer the tantalizing suggestion that other princely tombs of its kind are lying undiscovered beneath the Egyptian sands; Ramesses would surely not have been the only pharaoh to bury his sons in such style.

W ork at KV5 in the fall season proceeds from six-thirty in the morning until one-thirty in the afternoon. Every day, to get to KV5 from my hotel in Luxor, I cross the Nile on the public ferry, riding with a great mass of fellaheen—men carrying goats slung around their necks, children lugging sacks of eggplants, old men squatting in their djellabas and smoking cigarettes or eating *leb* nuts— while the ancient diesel boat wheezes and blubs across the river. I am usually on the river in time to catch the sun rising over the shattered columns of Luxor Temple, along the riverbank. The Nile is still magical—crowded with feluccas, lined with date palms, and bearing on its current many clumps of blooming water hyacinths.

The ferry empties its crowds into a chaos of taxis, camels, donkeys, children begging for baksheesh, and hopeful guides greeting every tourist with a hearty "Welcome to Egypt!" In contrast to the grand hotels and boulevards of Luxor, the west bank consists of clusters of mud villages scattered among impossibly green fields of cane and clover, where the air is heavy with smoke and the droning prayers of the muezzin. Disembarkation is followed by a harrowing high-speed taxi ride to the Valley, the driver weaving past donkey carts and herds of goats, his sweaty fist pounding the horn.

On the first day of my visit, I find Kent Weeks sitting in a green canvas tent at the entrance to KV5 and trying to fit together pieces of a human skull. It is a cool Saturday morning in November. From the outside, KV5 looks like all the other tombs— a mere doorway in a hillside. Workmen in a bucket brigade are passing baskets filled with dirt out of the tomb's entrance and dumping them in a nearby pile, on which two men are squatting and sifting through the debris with small gardening tools. "Hmm," Weeks says, still fiddling with the skull. "I had this together a moment ago. You'll have to wait for our expert. He can put it together just like that." He snaps his fingers.

"Whose skull is it?"

"One of Ramesses' sons, I hope. The brown staining on it—here—shows that it might have come from a mummified body. We'll eventually do DNA comparisons with Ramesses and other members of his family."

Relaxing in the tent, Weeks does not cut the dapper, pugnacious figure of a Howard Carter, nor does he resemble the sickly, elegant Lord Carnarvon in waistcoat and watch chain. But because he is the first person to have made a major discovery in the Valley of the Kings since Carter, he is surely in their class. At fifty-four, he is handsome and fit, his ruddy face peering at the world through thick square glasses from underneath a Tilley hat. His once crisp shirt and khakis look like hell after an hour in the tomb's stifling atmosphere, and his Timberland shoes have reached a state of indescribable lividity from tomb dust.

Weeks has the smug air of a man who is doing the most interesting thing he could possibly do in life. He launches into his subject with such enthusiasm that one's first impulse is to flee. But as he settles back in his rickety chair with the skull in one hand and a glass of *yansoon* tea in the other, and yarns on about lost tombs, crazy Egyptologists, graver-obbers, jackal-headed gods, mummies, secret passageways, and the mysteries of the Underworld, you begin to succumb. His conversation is laced with obscene sallies delivered with a schoolboy's relish, and you can tell he has not been to any gender-sensitivity training seminars. He can be disconcertingly blunt. He characterized one archeologist as "ineffectual, ridiculously inept, and a wonderful source of comic relief," another as "a raving psychopath," and a third as "a dork, totally off the wall." When I asked if KV5 would prove that Ramesses was the Biblical Pharaoh, he responded with irritation: "I can almost guarantee you that we will *not* find anything in KV5 bearing on the Exodus question. All the speculation in the press assumed there *was* an exodus and that it was described accurately in the Bible. I don't believe it. There may have been Israelites in Egypt, but I sincerely doubt Exodus is an exact account of what occurred. At least I *hope* it wasn't—with the Lord striking down the firstborn of Egypt and turning the rivers to blood."

His is a rarefied profession: there are only about four hundred Egyptologists in the world, and only a fraction of them are archeologists. (Most are art historians and philologists.) Egyptology is a difficult profession to break into; in a good year, there might be two job openings in the United States. It is the kind of field where the untimely death of a tenured figure sets the photocopying machines running all night.

"From the age of eight, I had no doubt: I wanted to be an Egyptologist," Weeks told me. His parents—one a policeman, the other a medical librarian—did not try to steer him into a sensible profession, and a string of teachers encouraged his interest. When Weeks was in high school, in Longview, Washington, he met the Egyptologist Ahmed Fakhry in Seattle, and Fakhry was so charmed by the young man that he invited him to lunch and mapped out his college career.

In 1963, Weeks's senior year at the University of Washington, one of the most important events in the history of Egyptology took place. Because of the construction of the High Dam at Aswan,

the rising waters of the Nile began to flood Nubia; they would soon inundate countless archeological sites, including the incomparable temples of Abu Simbel. UNESCO and the Egyptian and Sudanese governments issued an international plea for help. Weeks immediately wrote to William Kelly Simpson, a prominent Egyptologist at Yale who was helping to coördinate the salvage project, and offered his services. He received plane tickets by return mail.

"The farthest I'd been away from home was Disneyland, and here I was going to Nubia," Weeks said. "The work had to be done fast: the lake waters were already rising. I got there and suddenly found myself being told, 'Take these eighty workmen and go dig that ancient village.' The nearest settlement was Wadi Halfa, ninety miles away. The first words of Arabic I learned were 'Dig no deeper' and 'Carry the baskets faster.' "

Weeks thereafter made a number of trips to Nubia, and just before he set out on one of them he invited along as artist a young woman he had met near the mummy case at the University of Washington museum—Susan Howe, a solemn college senior with red hair and a deadpan sense of humor.

"We lived on the river on an old rat-infested dahabeah," Susan told me. "My first night on the Nile, we were anchored directly in front of Abu Simbel, parked right in front of Ramesses' knees. It was all lit up, because work was going on day and night." An emergency labor force was cutting the temple into enormous blocks and reassembling it on higher ground. "After five months, the beer ran out, the cigarettes ran out, the water was really hot, the temperature was a hundred and fifteen degrees in the shade, and there were terrible windstorms. My parents were just *desperate* to know when I was coming home. But I thought, Ah! This is the life! It was so romantic. The workmen sang songs and clapped every morning when we arrived. So we wrote home and gave our parents ten days' notice that we were going to get married."

They have now been married twenty-nine years. Susan is the artist and illustrator for many of Kent's projects, and has also worked for other archeologists in Egypt. She spends much of her day in

front of KV5, in the green tent, wearing a scarf and peach-colored Keds, while she makes precise scale drawings of pottery and artifacts. In her spare time, she wanders around Gezira Bairat, painting exquisite watercolors of doorways and donkeys.

Weeks eventually returned to Washington to get his M.A., and in 1971 he received a Ph.D. from Yale; his dissertation dealt with ancient Egyptian anatomical terminology. He landed a plum job as a curator in the Metropolitan Museum's Egyptian Department. Two years later, bored by museum work, he quit and went back to Egypt, and was shortly offered the directorship of Chicago House, the University of Chicago's research center in Luxor. The Weekses have two children, whom they reared partly in Egypt, sending them to a local Luxor school. After four years at Chicago House, Weeks took a professorship at Berkeley, but again the lure of Egypt was too strong. In 1987, he renounced tenure at Berkeley, took a large pay cut, and went back to Egypt as a professor of Egyptology at the American University in Cairo, where he has been ever since.

While in Nubia, Weeks excavated an ancient working-class cemetery, pulling some seven thousand naturally desiccated bodies out of the ground. In a study of diet and health, he and a professor of orthodontics named James Harris X-rayed many of these bodies. Then Weeks and Harris persuaded the Egyptian government to allow them to X-ray the mummies of the pharaohs, by way of comparison. A team of physicians, orthodontists, and pathologists studied the royal X-rays, hoping to determine such things as age at death, cause of death, diet, and medical problems. They learned that there was surprisingly little difference between the two classes in diet and health.

One finding caused an uproar among Egyptologists. The medical team had been able to determine ages at death for most of the pharaohs, and in some cases these starkly contradicted the standard chronologies of the Egyptologists. The mystery was eventually solved when the team consulted additional ancient papyri, which told how, in the late New Kingdom, the high priests realized that many of the tombs in the Valley of the Kings had been robbed. To prevent further desecration, they gathered up almost all the royal mummies (missing only King Tut) and reburied them in two caches, both of which were discovered intact in the nineteenth century. "What we think happened is that the priests let the name dockets with some of the mummies fall off and put them back wrong," Weeks told me. It is also possible that the mixup occurred when the mummies were moved down the river to Cairo in the nineteenth century.

The team members analyzed the craniofacial characteristics of each mummy and figured out which ones looked most like which others. (Most of the pharaohs were related.) By combining these findings with age-at-death information, they were able to restore six of the mummies' proper names.

Weeks' second project led directly to the discovery of KV5. In 1979, he began mapping the entire Theban Necropolis. After an overview, he started with the Valley of the Kings. No such map had ever been done before. (That explains how KV5 came to be found and then lost several times in its history.) The Theban Mapping Project is to include the topography of the Valley and the three-dimensional placement of each tomb within the rock. The data are being computerized, and eventually Weeks will re-create the Valley on CD-s, which will allow a person to "fly" into any tomb and view in detail the murals and reliefs on its walls and ceilings.

Some Egyptologists I spoke with consider the mapping of the Theban Necropolis to be the most important archeological project in Egypt, KV5 notwithstanding. A map of the Valley of the Kings is desperately needed. Some tombs are deteriorating rapidly, with murals cracking and falling to the floors, and ceilings, too, collapsing. Damage has been done by the opening of the tombs to outside air. (When Carter opened King Tut's tomb, he could actually hear "strange rustling, murmuring, whispering sounds" of objects as the new air began its insidious work of destruction. In other tombs, wooden objects turned into "cigar-ash.") Greek, Roman, and early European tourists explored the

tombs with burning torches—and even lived in some tombs—leaving an oily soot on the paintings. Rapid changes in temperature and humidity generated by the daily influx of modern-day tourists have caused even greater damage, some of it catastrophic.

The gravest danger of all comes from flooding. Most of the tombs are now wide open. Modern alterations in the topography, such as the raising of the valley floor in order to build paths for the tourists, have created a highway directing floodwaters straight into the mouths of the tombs. A brief rain in November of 1994 generated a small flash flood that tore through the Valley at thirty miles an hour and damaged several tombs. It burst into the tomb of Bay, a vizier of the New Kingdom, with such force that it churned through the decorated chambers and completely ruined them. Layers of debris in KV5 indicate that a major flash flood occurs about once every three hundred years. If such a flood occurred tomorrow, the Valley of the Kings could be largely destroyed.

There is no master plan for preserving the Valley. The most basic element in such a plan is the completion of Weeks's map. Only then can preservationists monitor changes in the tombs and begin channelling and redirecting floodwaters. For this reason, some archeologists privately panicked when Weeks found KV5. "When I first heard about it," one told me, "I thought, Oh my God, that's it, Kent will never finish the mapping project."

Weeks promises that KV5 will not interfere with the Theban Mapping Project. "Having found the tomb, we've got an obligation to leave it in a good, stable, safe condition," he says. "And we have an obligation to publish. Public interest in KV5 has actually increased funding for the Theban Mapping Project."

At 9 A.M., the workmen laboring in KV5—there are forty-two of them—begin to file out and perch in groups on the hillside, to eat a breakfast of bread, tomatoes, green onions, and a foul cheese called *misht*. Weeks rises from his chair, nods to me, and asks, "Are you ready?"

We descend a new wooden staircase into the mountain and enter Chamber 1, where we exchange our sun hats for hard hats. The room is small and only half cleared. Visible tendrils of humid, dusty air waft in from the dim recesses of the tomb. The first impression I have of the tomb is one of shocking devastation. The ceilings are shot through with cracks, and in places they have caved in, dropping automobile-size pieces of rock. A forest of screw jacks and timbers holds up what is left, and many of the cracks are plastered with "tell-tales"—small seals that show if any more movement of the rock occurs.

The reliefs in Chamber 1 are barely visible, a mere palimpsest of what were once superbly carved and painted scenes of Ramesses and his sons adoring the gods, and panels of hieroglyphics. Most of the damage here was the result of a leaky sewer pipe that was laid over the tomb about forty years ago from an old rest house in the Valley. The leak caused salt crystals to grow and eat away the limestone walls. Here and there, however, one can still see traces of the original paint.

The decorations on the walls of the first two rooms show various sons being presented to the gods by Ramesses, in the classic Egyptian pose: head in profile, shoulders in frontal view, and torso in three-quarters view. There are also reliefs of tables laden with offerings of food for the gods, and hieroglyphic texts spelling out the names and titles of several sons and including the royal cartouche of Ramesses.

A doorway from Chamber 2 opens into Chamber 3—the Pillared Hall. It is filled with dirt and rock almost to the ceiling, giving one a simultaneous impression of grandeur and claustrophobia. Two narrow channels have been cut through the debris to allow for the passage of the workmen. Many of the pillars are split and shattered, and only fragments of decorations remain—a few hieroglyphic characters, an upraised arm, part of a leg. Crazed light from several randomly placed bulbs throws shadows around the room.

I follow Weeks down one of the channels. "This room is in such dangerous condition that we decided not to clear it," he says. "We call this channel the Mubarak trench. It was dug so that President Mubarak could visit the tomb without having to creep around on his hands and knees." He laughs.

When we are halfway across the room, he points out the words "James Burton 1825" smoked on the ceiling with the flame of a candle: it represents the Englishman's farthest point of penetration. Not far away is another graffito—this one in hieratic, the cursive form of hieroglyphic writing. It reads "Year 19"—the nineteenth year of Ramesses' reign. "This date gives us a *terminus ante quem* for the presence of Ramesses' workmen in this chamber," Weeks says.

He stops at one of the massive pillars. "And here's a mystery," he says, "Fifteen of the pillars in this room were cut from the native rock, but this one is a fake. The rock was carefully cut away—you can see chisel marks on the ceiling—and then the pillar was rebuilt out of stone and plastered to look like the others. Why?" He gives the pillar a sly pat. "Was something very large moved in here?"

I follow Weeks to the end of the trench—the site of the doorway that he crawled through in February. The door has been cleared, and we descend a short wooden staircase to the bottom of the great central corridor. It is illuminated by a string of naked light bulbs, which cast a yellow glow through a pall of dust. The many doors lining both sides of the corridor are still blocked with debris, and the stone floor is covered with an inch of dust.

At the far end of the corridor, a hundred feet away, stands the mummiform statue of Osiris. It is carved from the native rock, and only its face is missing. Lit from below, the statue casts a dramatic shadow on the ceiling. I try to take notes, but my glasses have fogged up, and sweat is dripping onto my notebook, making the ink run off the page. I can only stand and blink.

Nothing in twenty years of writing about archeology has prepared me for this great wrecked corridor chiselled out of the living rock, with rows of shattered doorways opening into darkness, and ending in the faceless mummy of Osiris. I feel like a trespasser, a voyeur, grazing

into the sacred precincts of the dead. As I stare at the walls, patterns and lines begin to emerge from the shattered stone: ghostly figures and faint hieroglyphics; animal-headed gods performing mysterious rites. Through doorways I catch glimpses of more rooms and more doorways beyond. There is a presence of death in this wrecked tomb that goes beyond those who were buried here; it is the death of a civilization.

With most of the texts on the walls destroyed or still buried under debris, it is not yet possible to determine what function was served by the dozens of side chambers. Weeks feels it likely, however, that they were *not* burial chambers, because the doorways are too narrow to admit a sarcophagus. Instead, he speculates they were chapels where the Theban priests could make offerings to the dead sons. Because the tomb departs so radically from the standard design, it is impossible even to speculate what the mysterious Pillared Hall or many of the other antechambers were for.

Weeks proudly displays some reliefs on the walls, tracing with his hand the figure of Isis and her husband, Osiris, and pointing out the ibis-headed god Thoth. "Ah!" he cries. "And here is a *wonderful* figure of Anubis and Hathor!" Anubis is the jackal-headed god of mummification, and Hathor a goddess associates with the Theban Necropolis. These were scenes to help guide Ramesses' sons through the rituals, spells, and incantations that would insure them a safe journey through the realm of death. The reliefs are exceedingly difficult to see; Susan Weeks told me later that she has sometimes had to stare at a wall for long periods—days, even—before she could pick out the shadow of a design. She is now in the process of copying these fragmentary reliefs on Mylar film, to help experts who will attempt to reconstruct the entire wall sequence and its accompanying test, and so reveal to us the purpose of the room or the corridor. KV5 will only yield up its secrets slowly, and with great effort.

"Here's Ramesses and one of his sons," Weeks says, indicating two figures standing hand in hand. "But, alas, the name is gone. Very disappointing!" He charges off down the corridor, raising

a trail of dust, and comes to a halt at the statue of Osiris, poking his glasses back up his sweating nose. "Look at this. Spectacular! A three-dimensional statue of Osiris is very rare. Most tombs depict him painted only. We dug around the base here trying to find the face, but instead we found a lovely offering of nineteen clay figs."

He makes a ninety-degree turn down the left transverse corridor, snaking around a cave-in. The corridor runs level for some distance and then plunges down a double staircase with a ramp in the middle, cut from the bedrock, and ends in a wall of bedrock. Along the sides of this corridor we have passed sixteen more partly blocked doors.

"Now, here is something new," Weeks says. "You're the first outsider to see this. I hoped that this staircase would lead to the burial chambers. This kind of ramp was usually built to slide the sarcophagi down. But look! The corridor just ends in a blank wall. Why in the world would they build a staircase and ramp going nowhere? So I decided to clear the two lowest side chambers. We just finished last week."

He ushers me into one of the rooms. There is no light; the room is large and very hot.

"They were empty," Weeks says.

"Too bad."

"Take a look at this floor."

"Nice." Floors do not particularly excite me.

"It happens to be the finest plastered floor in the Valley of the Kings. They went to enormous trouble with this floor, laying down three coats of plaster at different times, in different colors. Why?" He pauses. "Now stamp on the floor."

I thump the floor. There is a hollow reverberation that shakes not only the floor but the entire room. "Oh, my God, there's something underneath there!" I exclaim.

"*Maybe,*" Weeks says, a large smile gathering on his face. "Who knows? It could be a natural cavity or crack, or it might be a passageway to a lower level."

"You mean there might be sealed burial chambers below?"

Weeks smiles again. "Let's not get ahead of ourselves. Next June, we'll drill some test holes and do it properly."

We scramble back to the Osiris statue.

"Now I'm going to take you to our latest discovery," Weeks says. "This is intriguing. *Very* fascinating."

We make our way through several turns back to the Pillared Hall. Weeks leads me down the other trench, which ends at the southwest corner of the hall. Here, earlier in the month, the workmen discovered a buried doorway that opened onto a steep descending passageway, again packed solid with debris. The workmen have now cleared the passageway down some sixty feet, exposing twelve more side chambers, and are still at work.

We pause at the top of the newly excavated passageway. A dozen screw jacks with timbers hold up its cracked ceiling. The men have finished breakfast and are back at work, one man picking away at the wall of debris at the bottom of the passageway while another scoops the debris into a basket made out of old tires. A line of workmen then pass the basket up the corridor and out of the tomb.

"I've called this passageway 3A," Weeks says. He drops his voice. "The incredible thing is that this corridor is heading toward the tomb of Ramesses himself. If it connects, that will be extraordinary. No two tombs were ever deliberately connected. This tomb just gets curiouser and curiouser."

Ramesses' tomb, lying a hundred feet across the Valley, was also wrecked by flooding and is now being excavated by a French team. "I would dearly love to surprise them," Weeks says. "To pop out one day and say *'Bonjour! C'est moi!'* I'd love to beat the French into their own tomb."

I follow him down the newly discovered corridor, slipping and sliding on the pitched floor. "Of course," he shouts over his shoulder, "the sons might also be buried *underneath* their father! We clearly haven't found the burial chambers yet, and it is my profound hope that one way or another this passageway will take us there."

We come to the end, where the workmen are picking away at the massive wall of dirt that blocks the passage. The forty-two men can remove about nine tons of dirt a day.

At the bottom, Weeks introduces me to a tall, handsome Egyptian with a black mustache and wearing a baseball cap on backward. "This is Muhammad Mahmud," Weeks says. "One of the senior workmen."

I shake his hand. "What do you hope to find down here?"

"Something very nice, *inshallah*."

"What's in these side rooms?" I ask Weeks. All the doorways are blocked with dirt.

Weeks shrugs. "We haven't been in those rooms yet."

"Would it be possible… " I start to ask.

He grins. "You mean, would you like to be the first human being in three thousand years to enter a chamber in an ancient Egyptian tomb? Maybe Saturday."

As we are leaving the tomb, I am struck by the amount of work still unfinished. Weeks has managed to dig out only three rooms completely and clear eight others partway—leaving more than eighty rooms entirely untouched. What treasures lie under five or ten feet of debris in those rooms is anyone's guess. It will take from six to ten more years to clear and stabilize the tomb, and then many more years to publish the findings from it. As we emerge from the darkness, Weeks says, "I know what I'll be doing for the rest of my life."

One morning, I find a pudgy, bearded man sitting in the green tent and examining, Hamlet-like, the now assembled skull. He is the paleontologist Elwyn Simons, who has spent decades searching the sands of the Faiyum for primate ancestors of human beings. Susan Weeks once worked for him, and now he is a close friend of the couple, dropping in on occasion to look over bones from the tomb. Kent and Susan are both present, waiting to hear his opinions about the skull's sex. (Only DNA testing can confirm whether it's an actual son of Ramesses, of course.)

Simons rotates the skull, pursing his lips. "Probably a male, because it has fairly pronounced brow ridges," he says. "This"—he points to a hole punched in the top of the cranium—"was made post mortem. You can tell because the edges are sharp and there are no suppressed fractures."

Simons laughs, and sets the skull down. "You can grind this up and put it in your soup, Kent."

When the laughter has died down, I venture that I didn't get the joke.

"In the Middle ages, people filled bottles with powdered mummies and sold it as medicine," Simons explains.

"Or mummies were burned to power the railroad," Weeks adds. "I don't know how many miles you get per mummy, do you, Elwyn?"

While talk of mummies proceeds, a worker brings a tray of tea. Susan Weeks takes the skull away and puts another bone in front of Simons.

"That's the scapula of an artiodactyl. Probably a cow. The camel hadn't reached Egypt by the Nineteenth Dynasty."

The next item is a tooth.

"Artiodactyl again," he says, sipping his tea. "Goat or gazelle."

The identification process goes on.

The many animal bones found in KV5 were probably from offerings for the dead: valley tombs often contained sacrificed bulls, mummified baboons, birds, and cats, as well as steaks and veal chops.

Suddenly, Muhammad appears at the mouth of the tomb. "Please, Dr. Kent," he says, and starts telling Weeks in Arabic that the workers have uncovered something for him to see. Weeks motions for me to follow him into the dim interior. We put on our hard hats and duck through the first chambers into Corridor 3A. A beautiful set of carved limestone steps has appeared where I saw only rubble a few days before. Weeks kneels and brushes the dirt away, excited about the fine workmanship.

Muhammad and Weeks go to inspect another area of the tomb, where fragments of painted and carved plaster are being uncovered. I stay to watch the workmen digging in 3A. After a while, they forget I am there and begin singing, handing the baskets up the long corridor, their bare feet white with dust. A dark hole begins to appear between the top of the debris and the ceiling. It looks as if one could crawl inside and perhaps look farther down the corridor.

"May I take a look in there?" I ask.

One of the workmen hoists me up the wall of dirt, and I lie on my stomach and wriggle into the gap. I recall that archeologists sometimes sent small boys into tombs through holes just like this.

Unfortunately, I am not a small boy, and in my eagerness I find myself thoroughly wedged. It is pitch-black, and I wonder why I thought this would be exciting.

"Pull me out!" I yell.

The Egyptians heave on my legs, and I come sliding down with a shower of dirt. After the laughter subsides, a skinny man named Nubie crawls into the hole. In a moment, he is back out, feet first. He cannot see anything; they need to dig more.

The workmen redouble their efforts, laughing, joking, and singing. Working in KV5 is a coveted job in the surrounding villages; Weeks pays his workmen four hundred Egyptian pounds a month (about a hundred and twenty-five dollars), four times what a junior inspector of antiquities makes and perhaps three times the average monthly income of an Egyptian family. Weeks is well liked by his Egyptian workers, and is constantly bombarded with dinner invitations from even his poorest laborers. While I was there, I attended three of these dinners. The flow of food was limitless, and the conversation competed with the bellowing of a water buffalo in an adjacent room or the braying of a donkey tethered at the door.

After the hole has been widened a bit, Nubie goes up again with a light and comes back down. There is great disappointment: it looks as though the passageway might come to an end. Another step is exposed in the staircase, along with a great deal of broken pottery. Weeks returns and examines the hole himself, without comment.

As the week goes by, more of Corridor 3A is cleared, foot by foot. The staircase in 3A levels out to a finely made floor, more evidence that the corridor merely ends in a small chamber. On Wednesday, however, Weeks emerges from the tomb smiling. "Come," he says.

The hole in 3A has now been enlarged to about two feet in diameter. I scramble up the dirt and peer inside with a light, choking on the dust. As before, the chiselled ceiling comes to an abrupt end, but below it lies what looks like a shattered door lintel.

"It's got to be a door," Weeks says, excited. "I'm afraid we're going to have to halt for the season at that doorway. We'll break through next June."

Later, outdoors, I find myself coughing up flecks of mud.

"Tomb cough," Weeks says cheerfully.

On Thursday morning, Weeks is away on business, and I go down into the tomb with Susan. At the bottom of 3A, we stop to watch Ahmed Mahmud Hassan, the chief supervisor of the crew, sorting through some loose dirt at floor level. Suddenly, he straightens up, holding a perfect alabaster statuette of a mummy.

"Madame," he says, holding it out.

Susan begins to laugh. "Ahmed, that's beautiful. Did you get that at one of the souvenir stalls?"

"No," he says. "I just found it." He points to the spot. "Here."

She turns to me. "They once put a rubber cobra in here. Everyone was terrified, and Muhammad began beating it with a rock."

"Madame," Ahmed says. "Look, please." By now, he is laughing, too.

"I see it," Susan says. "I hope it wasn't too expensive."

"Madame, please."

Susan takes it, and there is a sudden silence. "It's real," she says quietly.

"This is what I was telling Madame," Ahmed says, still laughing.

Susan slowly turns it over in her hands. "It's beautiful. Let's take it outside."

In the sunlight, the statuette glows. The head and shoulders still have clear traces of black paint, and the eyes look slightly crossed. It is an *ushabti,* a statuette that was buried only with the dead, meant to spare the deceased toil in the afterlife: whenever the deceased was called upon to do work, he would send the *ushabti* in his place.

That morning, the workmen also find in 3A a chunk of stone. Weeks hefts it. "This is very important," he says.

"How?"

"It's a piece of a sidewall of a sarcophagus that probably held one of Ramesses' sons. It's made out of serpentine, a valuable stone in ancient Egypt." He pulls out a tape measure and marks off the thickness of the rim. "It's eight-point-five centimetres, which, doubled, gives seventeen centimetres. Add to that the width of an average pair of human shoulders, and perhaps an inner coffin,

and you could not have fitted this sarcophagus through any door to any of the sixty side chambers in that tomb." He pauses. "So, you see, this piece of stone is one more piece of evidence that we have yet to find the burial chambers."

Setting the stone down with a thud on a specimen mat, he dabs his forehead. He proceeds to lay out a theory about KV5. Ramesses had an accomplished son named Khaemwaset, who became the high priest of an important cult that worshipped a god represented by a sacred bull. In Year 16, Khaemwaset began construction of the Serapeum, a vast catacomb for the bulls, in Saqqara. The original design of the Serapeum is the only one that remotely resembles KV5's layout, and it might have been started around the same time. In the Serapeum, there are two levels: an upper level of offering chapels and a lower level for burials. "But," Weeks adds, throwing open his arms, "until we find the burial chambers it's *all* speculation."

On Friday, Bruce Ludwig arrives—a great bear of a man with white hair and a white beard. Dressed like an explorer, he is lugging a backpack full of French wine for the team.

Unlike Lord Carnarvon and other wealthy patrons who funded digs in the Valley of the Kings, Ludwig is a self-made man. His father owned a grocery store in South Dakota called Ludwig's Superette. Bruce Ludwig made his money in California real estate and is now a partner in a firm managing four billion dollars in pension funds. He has been supporting Weeks and the Theban Mapping Project for twelve years.

Over the past three, he has sunk a good deal of his own money into the project and has raised much more among his friends. Nevertheless, the cost of excavation continually threatens to outstrip the funds at hand. "The thing is, it doesn't take a Rockefeller or a Getty to be involved," he told me over a bottle of Château Lynch-Bages. "What I like to do is show other successful people that it won't cost a fortune and that it's just hugely rewarding. Buildings crumble and fall down, but when you put something in the books, it's there forever."

Ludwig's long-term support paid off last February, when he became one of the first people to crawl into the recesses of KV5. There may be better moments to come. "When I discover that door covered with unbroken Nineteenth Dynasty seals," Weeks told me, joking, "you bet I'll hold off until Bruce can get here."

Saturday, the workers' taxi picks the Weekses and me up before sunrise and then winds through a number of small villages, collecting workers as it goes along.

The season is drawing to a close, and Susan and Kent Weeks are both subdued. In the last few weeks, the probable number of rooms in the tomb has increased from sixty-seven to ninety-two, with no end in sight. Everyone is frustrated at having to lock up the tomb now, leaving the doorway at the bottom of 3A sealed, the plaster floor unplumbed, the burial chambers still not found, and so many rooms unexcavated.

Weeks plans to tour the United States lecturing and raising more funds. He estimates that he will need a quarter of a million dollars per year for the indefinite future in order to do the job right.

As we drive alongside sugarcane fields, the sun boils up over the Nile Valley through a screen of palms, burning into the mists lying on the fields. We pass a man driving a donkey cart loaded with tires, and whizz by the Colossi of Memnon, two enormous wrecked statues standing alone in a farmer's field. The taxi begins the climb to a village once famous for tomb robbing, some of whose younger residents now work for Weeks. The houses are completely surrounded by the black pits of tombs. The fragrant smell of dung fires drifts through the rocky streets.

Along the way, I talk with Ahmed, the chief supervisor. A young man with a handsome, aristocratic face, who comes from a prominent family in Gezira Bairat, he has worked for Weeks for about eight years. I ask him how he feels about working in the tomb.

Ahmed thinks for a moment, then says, "I forget myself in this tomb. It is so vast inside."

"How so?"

"I feel at home there. I know this thing. I can't express the feeling, but it's not so strange for me to be in this tomb. I feel something in there about myself. I am descended from these people who built this tomb. I can feel their blood is in me."

When we arrive in the Valley of the Kings, an inspector unlocks the metal gate in front of the tomb, and the workers file in, with Weeks leading the way. I wait outside to watch the sunrise. The tourists have not yet arrived, and if you screen out some signs you can imagine the Valley as it might have appeared when the pharaohs were buried here three thousand years ago. (The venders and rest house were moved last year.) As dawn strikes el-Qurn and invades the upper reaches of the canyon walls, a soft, peach-colored lights fills the air. The encircling cliffs lock out the sounds of the world; the black doorways of the tombs are like dead eyes staring out; and one of the guard huts of the ancient priests can still be seen perched at the cliff edge. The whole Valley becomes a slowly changing play of light and color, mountain and sky, unfolding in absolute stillness. I am given a brief, shivery insight into the sacredness of this landscape.

At seven, the tourists begin to arrive, and the spell is dispersed. The Valley rumbles to life with the grinding of diesel engines, the frantic expostulations of venders, and the shouting of guides leading groups of tourists. KV5 is the first tomb in the Valley, and the tourists begin gathering at the rope, pointing and taking pictures, while the guides impart the most preposterous misinformation about the tomb: that Ramesses had four hundred sons by only two wives, that there are eight hundred rooms in the tomb, that the greedy Americans are digging for gold but won't find any. Two thousand tourists a day stand outside the entrance to KV5.

I go inside and find Weeks in 3A, supervising the placement of more screw jacks and timbers. When he has finished, he turns to me. "You ready?" He points to the lowest room in 3A. "This looks like a good one for you to explore."

One of the workmen clears away a hole at the top of the blocked door for me to crawl through, and then Muhammad gives me a leg up. I shove a caged light bulb into the hold ahead of me and wriggle through. I can barely fit.

In a moment, I am inside. I sit up and look around, the light throwing my distorted shadow against the wall. There is three feet of space between the top of the debris and the ceiling, just enough for me to crawl around on my hands and knees. The room is about nine feet square, the walls finely chiselled from the bedrock. Coils of dust drift past the light. The air is just breathable.

I run my finders along the ancient chisel marks, which are as fresh as if they were made yesterday, and I think of workmen who carved out this room, three millennia ago. Their only source of light would have been the dim illumination from wicks burning in a bowl of oil salted to reduce smoke. There was no way to tell the passage of time in the tomb: the wicks were cut to last eight hours, and when they guttered it meant that the day's work was done. The tombs were carved from the ceiling downward, the workers whacking off flakes of limestone with flint choppers, and then finishing the walls and ceilings with copper chisels and sandstone abrasive. Crouching in the hot stone chamber, I suddenly get a powerful sense of the enormous religious faith of the Egyptians. Nothing less could have motivated an entire society to pound these tombs out of rock.

Much of the Egyptian religion remains a mystery to us. It is full of contradictions, inexplicable rituals, and impenetrable texts. Amid the complexity, one simple fact stands out: it was a great human bargain with death. Almost everything that ancient Egypt has left us—the pyramids, the tombs, the temples—represents an attempt to overcome that awful mystery at the center of all our lives.

A shout brings me back to my senses.

"Find anything?" Weeks calls out.

"The room's empty," I say. "There's nothing in here but dust."

UNIT 2
Problem Oriented Archaeology

Unit Selections

Key Points to Consider

- Explain the causes of primitive warfare. Is warfare endemic to the human species?

- Who is the "Iceman"? What archaeological evidence?

- Compare the major theories as to when modern humans migrated to the New World. Please cite the archaeological evidence.

- What is NAGPRA? Please give some examples from archaeology.

- What new methods have been used by archaeologist to show that people began cultivating crops before they embraced full-scales farming? Cite examples.

- What is the archaeological evidence for human cannibalism? How widespread is it?

- What role did women play in hunting and gathering in Ice Age Europe? How does this run contrary to what was thought?

- What does ethnoarchaeology tell us about women as tool-makers in the Ice Age? Cite the archaeological evidence.

- Human female menopause cannot be dug up by archaeologists. However, how do archaeologists make highly probably theories about its evolution?

- What is a garbologist? What kind of archaeology do they do? Cite examples.

- What does the excavation of present hunter-gather peoples tell us about their past? Cite the example of the Bushmen.

 **Links: www.dushkin.com/online/**
These sites are annotated in the World Wide Web pages.

Archaeology Links (NC)
http://www.arch.dcr.state.nc.us/links.htm#stuff

Archaeology Magazine
http://www.archaeology.org

What are the goals of archaeology? What kinds of things motivate well-educated people to go out and dig square holes in the ground and sift through their diggings like flour for a cake? How do they know where to dig? What are they looking for? What do they do with the things they find? Let us drop in on an archaeology class at Metropolis University.

"Good afternoon, class, I'm Dr. Penny Pittmeyer. Welcome to Introductory Archaeology. Excuse me, young lady. Yes, you in the back, wearing the pith helmet. I don't think you'll need to bring that shovel to class this semester. We aren't going to be doing any digging."

A moan like that of an audience that had just heard a bad pun sounded throughout the classroom. Eyes bugged out, foreheads receded, sweat formed on brow ridges, and mouths formed into alphabet-soup at this pronouncement.

"That's right, no digging. You are here to learn about archaeology."

"But archaeology is digging. So what are we going to do all semester? Sheesh!" protested a thin young man with stern, steel granny glasses and a straight, scraggly beard, wearing a stained old blue work shirt and low slung 501's with an old, solid, and finely tooled leather belt and scuffed cowboy boots. A scratched trowel jutted from his right back pocket where the seam was half torn away.

Dr. Pittmeyer calmly surveyed the class and quietly repeated, "You are here to learn about archaeology." In a husky, compelling voice, she went on. "Archaeology is not digging, nor is it just about Egyptian ruins or lost civilizations. It's a science. First you have to learn the basics of that science. Digging is just a technique. Digging comes later. Digging comes after you know why you are going to dig."

"No Egyptian ruins," a plaintive echo resonated through the still classroom.

"You can have your ruins later. Take a class in Egyptian archaeology—fine, fine! But this class is the prerequisite to all those other classes. I hate to be the one to tell you this, people, but there ain't no Indiana Jones! I would have found him by now if there were." Dr. Pittmeyer said this with a slightly lopsided smile. But a veiled look in her light eyes sent an "uh-oh" that the students felt somewhere deep in their guts. They knew that the woman had something to teach them. And teach them she would!

Dr. Pittmeyer half sat on the old desk at the front of the classroom. Leaning one elbow on the podium to her right, she picked up a tall, red, opaque glass, and took a long and satisfying drink from it. Behind her large-framed black glasses, her eyes brightened noticeably. She wiped away an invisible mustache from her upper lip and settled onto the desk, holding the red glass in her left hand and letting it sway slightly as she unhurriedly looked over the students. Her left eyebrow rose unconsciously. The quiet lengthened so that the students filling out the Day-Glo-orange drop cards stopped writing, conscious of the now-loud silence in the room.

"O.K! LET'S GO!" Dr. Pittmeyer said with a snap like a whip singing over their heads. The startled students went straight-backed in unison.

"Archaeology is a science, ladies and gentlemen. It's part of the larger science of anthropology. The goals of both are to understand and predict human behavior. Let's start by looking at an area or subfield of archaeology that we may designate as problem-oriented archaeology. Humans evolved in Africa, Asia, and Europe, or what we refer to as the Old World."

Dr. Pittmeyer simultaneously turned out the lights and clicked on an overhead projector and wrote rapidly with a harshly bright purple pen in a hieroglyphic scrawl. Dangling from her neck was a microphone that was plugged into a speaker that was then plugged back into the overhead projector which in turn was plugged into an old, cracked socket, the single electric outlet offered by the ancient high-ceilinged asbestos-filled room.

Doubtful students suddenly felt compelled to take notes in the dim light provided by the irregularities of old-fashioned thick blinds that did not quite close completely.

"In the New World, in the Americas, from Alaska down to the tip of Tierra del Fuego, people did not live here until about 11,000 years ago. Whereas people have been living in the Old World for 200,000 years or more. People in the sense of Homo sapiens.

"So what took them so long to get here?" a perplexed female voice asked.

"Please let me point out that your question contains a very telling assumption. You said what took them so long to get here. The question is moot because these early peoples were not try-ing to get here. We're talking about the Paleolithic. People were migratory. They hunted and collected their food every day. They followed their food resources usually in seasonal patterns that moved them around but within fairly local areas. So it is a non-question. Let me explain, please.

"In archaeology, you have to ask the right questions before you can get any useful answers. That is why archaeologists dig—not to make discoveries, but to answer questions. Now here's what I want you to do. Go home and try to think yourself back into the Paleolithic. It's 35,000 years ago, and mostly you hang out with your family and other close relatives. You get your food and shelter on a daily basis, and you have some free time, too. Everyone cooperates to survive. The point is that wherever you are, you are there. There is no place to try to get to. There is no notion of private property or ownership of land. Nobody needs to conquer anybody. There are no cities, no freeways, no clocks, no rush. Think about it. It's a concept of life without measurements or urgencies."

"But they must have been pretty stupid back that long ago!" the young man with the beard, now nibbling his trowel, protested.

"Please think about that assumption! No, these were people just like you and me. If they were here today, they probably could program their VCRs. These were people with many skills and accomplishments. They met their needs as we meet ours. But they had something we might envy. They were already there no matter where they were! There's a lot to be learned from our prehistoric ancestors.

"But, frankly, tomorrow's another day." Alone in the classroom, Dr. Penny Pittmeyer finished her soda and allowed her eyes to glaze over as the forgotten Day-Glo-orange drop cards fluttered to the floor. She stared far back in time where she saw intelligent people living a simple life in peace… or so she hoped.

Prehistory *of* Warfare

Humans have been at each others' throats since the dawn of the species.

by STEVEN A. LEBLANC

IN THE EARLY 1970s, working in the El Morro Valley of west-central New Mexico, I encountered the remains of seven large prehistoric pueblos that had once housed upwards of a thousand people each. Surrounded by two-story-high walls, the villages were perched on steep-sided mesas, suggesting that their inhabitants built them with defense in mind. At the time, the possibility that warfare occurred among the Anasazi was of little interest to me and my colleagues. Rather, we were trying to figure out what the people in these 700-year-old communities farmed and hunted, the impact of climate change, and the nature of their social systems—not the possibility of violent conflict.

One of these pueblos, it turned out, had been burned to the ground; its people had clearly fled for their lives. Pottery and valuables had been left on the floors, and bushels of burned corn still lay in the storerooms. We eventually determined that this site had been abandoned, and that immediately afterward a fortress had been built nearby. Something catastrophic had occurred at this ancient Anasazi settlement, and the survivors had almost immediately, and at great speed, set about to prevent it from happening again.

Thirty years ago, archaeologists were certainly aware that violent, organized conflicts occurred in the prehistoric cultures they studied, but they considered these incidents almost irrelevant to our understanding of past events and people. Today, some of my colleagues are realizing that the evidence I helped uncover in the El Morro Valley is indicative warfare endemic throughout the entire Southwest, with its attendant massacres, population decline, and area abandonments that forever changed the Anasazi way of life.

When excavating eight-millennia-old farm villages in southeastern Turkey in 1970, I initially marveled how similar modern villages were to ancient ones, which were occupied at a time when an abundance of plants and animals made warfare quite unnecessary. Or so I thought. I knew we had discovered some plaster sling missiles (one of our workmen showed me how shepherds used slings to hurl stones at predators threatening their sheep). Such missiles were found at many of these sites, often in great quantities, and were clearly not intended for protecting flocks of sheep; they were exactly the same size and shape as later Greek and Roman sling stones used for warfare.

The so-called "donut stones" we had uncovered at these sites were assumed to be weights for digging sticks, presumably threaded on a pole to make it heavier for digging holes to plant crops. I failed to note how much they resembled the round stone heads attached to wooden clubs—maces—used in many places of the world exclusively for fighting and still used ceremonially to signify power. Thirty years ago, I was holding mace heads and sling missiles in my hands, unaware of their use as weapons of war.

We now know that defensive walls once ringed many villages of this era, as they did the Anasazi settlements. Rooms were massed together behind solid outside walls and were entered from the roof. Other sites had mud brick defensive walls, some with elaborately defended gates. Furthermore, many of these villages had been burned to the ground, their inhabitants massacred, as indicated by nearby mass graves.

Certainly for those civilizations that kept written records or had descriptive narrative art traditions, warfare is so clearly present that no one can deny it. Think of Homer's *Iliad* or the Vedas of South India, or scenes of prisoner sacrifice on Moche pottery. There is no reason to think that warfare played any less of a role in prehistoric societies for which we have no such records, whether they be hunter-gatherers or farmers. But most scholars studying these cultures still are not seeing it. They should assume warfare occurred among the people they study, just as they assume religion and art were a normal part of human culture. Then they could ask more interesting questions, such as: What form did warfare take? Can warfare explain some of the material found in the archaeological record? What were people fighting over and why did the conflicts end?

Today, some scholars know me as Dr. Warfare. To them, I have the annoying habit of asking un-politic questions about their research. I am the one who asks why the houses at a particular site were jammed so close together and many catastrophically burned. When I suggest that the houses were crowded behind defensive walls that were not found because no one was looking for them, I am not terribly appreciated. And I don't win any popularity contests when I suggest that twenty-mile-wide zones with no sites in them imply no-man's lands—clear evidence for warfare—to archaeologists who have explained a region's history without mention of conflict.

Scholars should assume warfare occurred among the people they study, just as they assume religion was a normal part of human culture. Then they would ask more interesting questions, such as: What form did warfare take? Why did people start and stop fighting?

Virtually all the basic textbooks on archaeology ignore the prevalence or significance of past warfare, which is usually not discussed until the formation of state-level civilizations such as ancient Sumer. Most texts either assume or actually state that for most of human history there was an abundance of available resources. There was no resource stress, and people had the means to control population, though how they accomplished this is never explained. The one archaeologist who has most explicitly railed against this hidden but pervasive attitude is Lawrence Keeley of the University of Illinois, who studies the earliest farmers in Western Europe. He has fund ample evidence of warfare as farmers spread west, yet most of his colleagues still believe the expansion was peaceful and his evidence a minor aberration, as seen in the various papers in Barry Cunliffe's *The Oxford Illustrated Prehistory of Europe* (1994) or Douglas Price's *Europe's First Farmers* (2000). Keeley contends that "prehistorians have increasingly pacified the past," presuming peace or thinking up every possible alternative explanation for the evidence they cannot ignore. In his *War Before Civilization* (1996) he accused archaeologists of being in denial on the subject.

Witness archaeologist Lisa Valkenier suggesting in 1997 that hilltop constructions along the Peruvian coast are significant because peaks are sacred in Andean cosmology. Their enclosing walls and narrow guarded entries may have more to do with restricting access to the *huacas,* or sacred shrines, on top of the hills than protecting defenders and barring entry to any potential attackers. How else but by empathy can one formulate such an interpretation in an area with a long defensive wall and hundreds of defensively located fortresses, some still containing piles of sling missiles ready to be used; where a common artistic motif is the parading and execution of defeated enemies; where hundreds were sacrificed; and where there is ample evidence of conquest, no-man's lands, specialized weapons, and so on?

A talk I gave at the Mesa Verde National Park last summer, in which I pointed out that the over 700-year-old cliff dwellings were built in response to warfare, raised the hackles of National Park Service personnel unwilling to accept anything but the peaceful Anasazi message peddled by their superiors. In fact, in the classic book *Indians of Mesa Verde,* published in 1961 by the park service, author Don Watson first describes the Mesa Verde people as "peaceful farming Indians," and admits that the cliff dwellings had a defensive aspect, but since he had already decided that the inhabitants were peaceful, the threat must have been from a new enemy—marauding nomadic Indians. This, in spite of the fact that there is ample evidence of Southwestern warfare for more than a thousand years before the cliff dwellings were built, and there is no evidence for the intrusion of nomadic peoples at this time.

Of the hundreds of research projects in the Southwest, only one—led by Jonathan Haas and Winifred Creamer of the Field Museum and Northern Illinois University, respectively—deliberately set out to research prehistoric warfare. They demonstrated quite convincingly that the Arizona cliff dwellings of the Tsegi Canyon area (known best for Betatakin and Kiet Siel ruins) were defensive, and their locations were not selected for ideology or because they were breezier and cooler in summer and warmer in the winter, as was previously argued by almost all Southwestern archaeologists.

For most prehistoric cultures, one has to piece together the evidence for warfare from artifactual bits and pieces. Most human history involved foragers, and so they are particularly relevant. They too were not peaceful. We know from ethnography that the Inuit (Eskimo) and Australian Aborigines engaged in warfare. We've also discovered remains of prehistoric bone armor in the Arctic, and skeletal evidence of deadly blows to the head are well documented among the prehistoric Aborigines. Surprising to some is the skeletal evidence for warfare in prehistoric California, once thought of as a land of peaceful acorn gatherers. The prehistoric people who lived in southern Californian had the highest incident of warfare deaths known anywhere in the world. Thirty percent of a large sample of males dating to the first centuries A.D. had wounds or died violent deaths. About half that number of women had similar histories. When we remember that not all warfare deaths leave skeletal evidence, this is a staggering number.

There was nothing unique about the farmers of the Southwest. From the Neolithic farmers of the Middle East and Europe to the New Guinea highlanders in the twentieth century, tribally organized farmers probably had the most intense warfare of any type of society. Early villages in China, the Yucatán, present-day Pakistan, and Micronesia were well fortified. Ancient farmers in coastal Peru had plenty of forts. All Polynesian societies had warfare, from the smallest islands like Tikopia, to Tahiti, New Zealand (more than four thousand prehistoric forts), and Hawaii. No-man's lands separated farming settlements in Okinawa, Oaxaca, and the southeastern United States. Such societies took trophy heads and cannibalized their enemies. Their skeletal remains show ample evidence of violent deaths. All well-studied prehistoric farming societies had warfare. They may have had intervals of peace, but over the span of hundreds of years there is plenty of evidence for real, deadly warfare.

When farmers initially took over the world, they did so as warriors, grabbing land as they spread out from the Levant through the Middle East into Europe, or from South China down through Southeast Asia. Later complex societies like the Maya, the Inca, the Sumerians, and the Hawaiians were no less belligerent. Here, conflict took on a new dimension. Fortresses, defensive walls hundreds of miles long, and weapons and armor expertly crafted by specialists all gave the warfare of these societies a heightened visibility.

Demonstrating the prevalence of warfare is not an end in itself. It is only the first step in understanding why there was so much of it, why it was "rational" for everyone to engage in it all the time. I believe the question of warfare links to the availability of resources.

There is a danger in making too much of the increased visibility of warfare we see in these complex societies. This is especially true for societies with writing. When there are no texts, it is easy to see no warfare. But the opposite is true. As soon as societies can write, they write about warfare. It is not a case of literate societies having warfare for the first time, but their being able to write about what had been going on for a long time. Also, many of these literate societies link to European civilization in one way or another, and so this raises the specter of Europeans being warlike and spreading war to inherently peaceful people elsewhere, a patently false but prevalent notion. Viewing warfare from their perspective of literate societies tells us nothing about the thousands of years of human societies that were not civilizations—that is, almost all of human history. So we must not rely too much on the small time slice represented by literate societies if we want to understand warfare in the past.

The Maya were once considered a peaceful society led by scholarly priests. That all changed when the texts written by their leaders could be read, revealing a long history of warfare and conquest. Most Mayanists now accept that there was warfare, but many still resist dealing with its scale or implications. Was there population growth that resulted in resource depletion, as throughout the rest of the world? We would expect the Maya to have been fighting each other over valuable farmlands as a consequence, but Mayanist Linda Schele concluded in 1984 that "I do not think it [warfare] was territorial for the most part,"

this even though texts discuss conquest, and fortifications are present at sites like El Mirador, Calakmul, Tikal, Yaxuná, Uxmal, and many others from all time periods. Why fortify them, if no one wanted to capture them?

Today, more Maya archaeologists are looking at warfare in a systematic way, by mapping defensive features, finding images of destruction, and dating these events. A new breed of younger scholars is finding evidence of warfare throughout the Maya past. Where are the no-man's lands that almost always open up between competing states because they are too dangerous to live in? Warfare must have been intimately involved in the development of Maya civilization, and resource stress must have been widespread.

Demonstrating the prevalence of warfare is not an end in itself. It is only the first step in understanding why there was so much, why it was "rational" for everyone to engage in it all the time. I believe the question of warfare links to the availability of resources.

During the 1960s, I lived in Western Samoa as a Peace Corps volunteer on what seemed to be an idyllic South Pacific Island—exactly like those painted by Paul Gauguin. Breadfruit and coconut groves grew all around my village, and I resided in a thatched-roof house with no walls beneath a giant mango tree. If ever there was a Garden of Eden, this was it. I lived with a family headed by an extremely intelligent elderly chief named Sila. One day, Sila happened to mention that the island's trees did not bear fruit as they had when he was a child. He attributed the decline to the possibility that the presence of radio transmissions had affected production, since Western Samoa (now known as Samoa) had its own radio station by then. I suggested that what had changed was not that there was less fruit but that there were more mouths to feed. Upon reflection, Sila decided I was probably right. Being an astute manager, he was already taking the precaution of expanding his farm plots into some of the last remaining farmable land on the island, at considerable cost and effort, to ensure adequate food for his growing family. Sila was aware of his escalating provisioning problems but was not quite able to grasp the overall demographic situation. Why was this?

The simple answer is that the rate of population change in our small Samoan village was so gradual that during an adult life span growth was not dramatic enough to be fully comprehended. The same thing happens to us all the time. Communities grow and change composition, and often only after the process is well advanced do we recognize just how significant the changes have been—and we have the benefit of historic documents, old photographs, long life spans, and government census surveys. All human societies can grow substantially over time, and all did whenever resources permitted. The change may seem small in one person's lifetime, but over a couple of hundred years, populations can and do double, triple, or quadruple in size.

The consequences of these changes become evident only when there is a crisis. The same can be said for environmental changes. The forests of Central America were being denuded and encroached upon for many years, but it took Hurricane Mitch, which ravaged most of the region in late October 1998, to produce the dramatic flooding and devastation that fully demonstrated the magnitude of the problem: too many people cutting down the forest and farming steep hillsides to survive. The natural environment is resilient and at the same time delicate, as modern society keeps finding out. And it was just so in the past.

> From foragers to farmers to more complex societies, when people no longer have resource stress they stop fighting. When climate greatly improves, warfare declines. The great towns of Chaco Canyon were built during an extended warm–and peaceful–period.

These observations about Mother Nature are incompatible with popular myths about peaceful people living in ecological balance with nature in the past. A peaceful past is possible only if you live in ecological balance. If you live in a Garden of Eden surrounded by plenty, why fight? By this logic, warfare is a sure thing when natural resources run dry. If someone as smart as Sila couldn't perceive population growth, and if humans all over Earth continue to degrade their environments, could people living in the past have been any different?

A study by Canadian social scientists Christina Mesquida and Neil Wiener has shown that the greater the proportion of a society is composed of unmarried young men, the greater the likelihood of war. Why such a correlation? It is not because the young men are not married; it is because they cannot get married. They are too poor to support wives and families. The idea that poverty breeds war is far from original. The reason poverty exists has remained the same since the beginning of time: humans have invariably overexploited their resources because they have always outgrown them.

There is another lesson from past warfare. It stops. From foragers to farmers, to more complex societies, when people no longer have resource stress they stop fighting. When the climate greatly improves, warfare declines. For example, in a variety of places the medieval warm interval of ca. 900–1100 improved farming conditions. The great towns of Chaco Canyon were built at this time, and it was the time of archaeologist Stephen Lekson's *Pax Chaco*—the longest period of peace in the Southwest. It is no accident that the era of Gothic cathedrals was a response to similar climate improvement. Another surprising fact is that the amount of warfare has declined over time. If we count the proportion of a society that died from warfare, and not the size of the armies, as the true measure of warfare, then we find that foragers and farmers have much higher death rates—often approaching 25 percent of the men—than more recent complex societies. No complex society, including modern states, ever approached this level of warfare.

If warfare has ultimately been a constant battle over scarce resources, then solving the resource problem will enable us to become better at ridding ourselves of conflict.

There have been several great "revolutions" in human history: control of fire, the acquisition of speech, the agricultural revolution, the development of complex societies. One of the most recent, the Industrial Revolution, has lowered the birth rate and increased available resources. History shows that peoples with strong animosities stop fighting after adequate resources are established and the benefits of cooperation recognized. The Hopi today are some of the most peaceful people on earth, yet their history is filled with warfare. The Gebusi of lowland New Guinea, the African !Kung Bushmen, the Mbuti Pygmies of central Africa, the Sanpoi and their neighbors of the southern Columbia River, and the Sirionno of Amazonia are all peoples who are noted for being peaceful, yet archaeology and historical accounts provide ample evidence of past warfare. Sometimes things changed in a generation; at other times it took longer. Adequate food and opportunity does not instantly translate into peace, but it will, given time.

The fact that it can take several generations or longer to establish peace between warring factions is little comfort for those engaged in the world's present conflicts. Add to this a recent change in the decision-making process that leads to war. In most traditional societies, be they forager bands, tribal farmers, or even complex chiefdoms, no individual held enough power to start a war on his own. A consensus was needed; pros and cons were carefully weighed and hotheads were not tolerated. The risks to all were too great. Moreover, failure of leadership was quickly recognized, and poor leaders were replaced. No Hitler or Saddam Hussein would have been tolerated. Past wars were necessary for survival, and therefore were rational; too often today this is not the case. We cannot go back to forager-band-type consensus, but the world must work harder at keeping single individuals from gaining the power to start wars. We know from archaeology that the amount of warfare has declined markedly over the course of human history and that peace can prevail under the right circumstances. In spite of the conflict we see around us, we are doing better, and there is less warfare in the world today than there ever has been. Ending it may be a slow process, but we are making headway.

©2003 by STEVEN A. LEBLANC. *Portions of this article were taken from his book* Constant Battles, *published in April 2003 by St. Martin's Press. LeBlanc is director of collections at Harvard University's Peabody Museum of Archaeology and Ethnology. For further reading visit www.archaeology.org.*

The Iceman Reconsidered

Where was the Iceman's home and what was he doing at the high mountain pass where he died? Painstaking research—especially of plant remains found with the body—contradicts many of the initial speculations

By James H. Dickson, Klaus Oeggl and Linda L. Handley

On a clear day in September 1991 a couple hiking along a high ridge in the Alps came upon a corpse melting out of the ice. When they returned to the mountain hut where they were staying, they alerted the authorities, who assumed the body was one of the missing climbers lost every year in the crevasses that crisscross the glaciers of the region. But after the remains were delivered to nearby Innsbruck, Austria, Konrad Spindler, an archaeologist from the University there, ascertained that the corpse was prehistoric. The victim, a male, had died several thousand years ago. Spindler and other scientists deduced that his body and belongings had been preserved in the ice until a fall of dust from the Sahara and an unusually warm spell combined to melt the ice, exposing his head, back and shoulders.

No well-preserved bodies had ever been found in Europe from this period, the Neolithic, or New Stone Age. The Iceman is much older than the Iron Age men from the Danish peat bogs and older even than the Egyptian royal mummies. Almost as astounding was the presence of a complete set of clothes and a variety of gear.

In the ensuing excitement over the discovery, the press and researchers offered many speculations about the ancient man. Spindler hypothesized

THE ICEMAN was discovered in a rocky hollow high in the Alps, in the zone of perennial snow and ice. Pressure from the overlying ice had removed a piece of the scalp. His corpse lay draped over a boulder. Contrary to earlier assumptions, evidence indicates it had floated into that position during previous thaws.

an elaborate disaster theory. He proposed that the man had fled to safety in the mountains after being injured in a fight at his home village. It was autumn, Spindler went on, and the man was a shepherd who sought refuge in the high pastures where he took his herds in summer. Hurt and in a state of exhaustion, he fell asleep and died on the boulder on which he was found five millennia later. The beautiful preservation of the body, according to this account, was the result of a fall of snow that protected the corpse from scavengers, followed by rapid freeze-drying.

Because the uniqueness of the discovery had not been immediately evident, the corpse was torn from the ice in a way that destroyed much archaeological information and damaged the body itself. A more thorough archaeological excavation of the site took place in the summer of 1992 and produced much valuable evidence, including an abundance or organic material (seeds, leaves, wood, mosses). This material added greatly to the plant remains, especially mosses, already washed from the clothes during the conservation process. Now, after a decade of labor-intensive research by us and other scientists on these plant remains and on samples taken from the Iceman's intestines, some hard facts are revising those first, sketchily formed impressions and replacing them with a more substantiated story.

Ötzi had been WARMLY DRESSED in leggings, loincloth and jacket made of the hide of deer and goat, and a cape made of grass and bast.

Who Was He?

THE HIKERS HAD DISCOVERED the body at 3,210 meters above sea level in the Ötztal Alps, which led to the popular humanizing nickname Ötzi. A mere 92 meters south of the Austrian-Italian border, the shallow, rocky hollow that sheltered the body is near the pass called Hauslabjoch between Italy's Schnalstal (Val Senales in Italian) and the Ventertal in Austria [*see map on the next page*]. Ötzi lay in an awkward position, draped prone over a boulder, his left arm sticking out to the right, and his right hand trapped under a large stone. His gear and clothing, also frozen or partially frozen in the ice, were scattered around him, some items as far as several meters away. Radiocarbon dates from three different laboratories made both on plant remains found with the body and on samples of Ötzi's tissues and gear all confirm that he lived about 5,300 years ago.

Certain other features of Ötzi were relatively easy to discover as well. At 159 centimeters (5'2.5"), he was a small man, as many men in Schnalstal vicinity are today. Bone studies show he was 46 years old, an advanced age for people of his time. DNA analysis indicates his origin in central-northern Europe, which may seem obvious, but it differentiates him from Mediterranean people, whose lands lie not too far distant to the south.

In an unusual congenital anomaly, his 12th ribs are missing. His seventh and eighth left ribs had been broken and had healed in his lifetime. According to Peter Vanezis of the University of Glasgow, his right rib cage is deformed and there are possible fractures of the third and fourth ribs. These changes happened after he died, as did a fracture of the left arm. That these breakages occurred after death is among the considerable evidence that casts doubt on the early disaster theory. So does the finding that an area of missing scalp was caused by pressure, not by a blow or decay.

Holding aside the unanswered questions concerning Ötzi' death and whether it was violent or not, several sound reasons suggest that he had not been in the best of health when he died. Although most of his epidermis (the outer layer of the skin), hair and fingernails are gone, probably having decayed as a result of exposure to water during occasional thaws, his remains still offer something of a health record for modern investigators. Examination of the only one of his fingernails to have been found revealed three Beau's lines, which develop when the nails stop growing and then start again. These lines show that he had been very ill three times in the last six months of his life and that the final episode, about two months before his death, was the most serious and lasted at least two weeks. Horst Aspöck of the University of Vienna found that he had an infestation of the intestinal parasite whipworm, which can cause debilitating diarrhea and even dysentery, although we do not know how bad his infestation was.

Overview/A New Look at an Ancient Man

The most current research indicates that the Iceman:

- May have lived near where Juval Castle now stands in southern Tyrol (Italy)
- Ate a varied diet of primitive wheat, other plants and meat
- Was 46 years old and had not been in the best of health
- Died in the spring, not in the autumn as previously thought
- May have been killed by being shot in the back with an arrow
- Did not expire on the boulder where he was found, as was believed, but floated into position there during occasional thaws

---

Moreover, many simple, charcoal-dust tattoos are visible on the layer of skin under the missing epidermis. These marks were certainly not decorative and were probably therapeutic. Several are on or close to Chinese acupuncture points and at places where he could have suffered from arthritis—the lower spine, right knee and ankle. This coincidence has led to claims of treatment by acupuncture. Yet, according to Vanezis and Franco Tagliaro of the University of Rome, x-rays show little if any sign of arthritis.

The little toe of his left foot reveals evidence of frostbite. Ötzi's teeth are very worn, a reflection of his age and diet. Remains of two human fleas were found in his clothes. No lice were seen, but because his epidermis had been shed, any lice may have been lost.

What Was His Gear Like?

TURNING TO ÖTZI'S clothing and gear, scientists have learned not only about Ötzi himself but about the community in which he lived. The items are a testament of how intimately his people knew the rocks, fungi, plants and animals in their immediate surroundings. And we can see that they also knew how to obtain resources from farther afield, such as flint and copper ore. This knowledge ensured that Ötzi was extremely well equipped, each object fashioned from the material best suited to its purpose.

He had been warmly dressed in three layers of clothing—leggings, loincloth and jacket made of the hide of deer and goat, and a cape made of grass and bast, the long, tough fibers from the bark of the linden tree. His hat was bearskin, and his shoes, which were insulated with grass, had bearskin soles and goatskin uppers

He had carried a copper ax and a dagger of flint from near Lake Garda, about 150 kilometers to the south. The handle of the dagger was ash wood, a material still used for handles today because it does not splinter easily. His unfinished longbow was carved from yew, the best wood for such a purpose because of its great tensile strength. The famous English longbows used to defeat the

THE ROUTE THE ICEMAN MAY HAVE TAKEN

THE AREA WHERE the Iceman was found (*red circle*) straddles the frontier between Austria and Italy. At first thought to lie in Austria, the body was taken to Innsbruck. Later, however, authorities determined that the site falls just over the border in Italy, where the Iceman now resides in a specially prepared museum at Bolzano. Based mainly on botanical remains preserved with the body, the authors speculate that the Iceman's last journey (*red line*) may have been from the area near Juval Castle through the Schnalstal and finally the steep climb up the Tisental (*profile below*). Dickson and his fellow fieldworkers have surveyed this region for the 80 species of mosses and liverworts found with the Iceman and extracted from the sand and gravel in the hollow; only about 20 of the species grow around the site now. The moss found in largest amount adhering to the clothing is *Neckera complanata* (*green circles indicate where it grows today*). The greatest concentration of this moss and the presence of many of the other plants found with the Iceman occur to the south of the site, at Juval Castle, where there is archaeological evidence of a prehistoric settlement. This spot may have been his home.

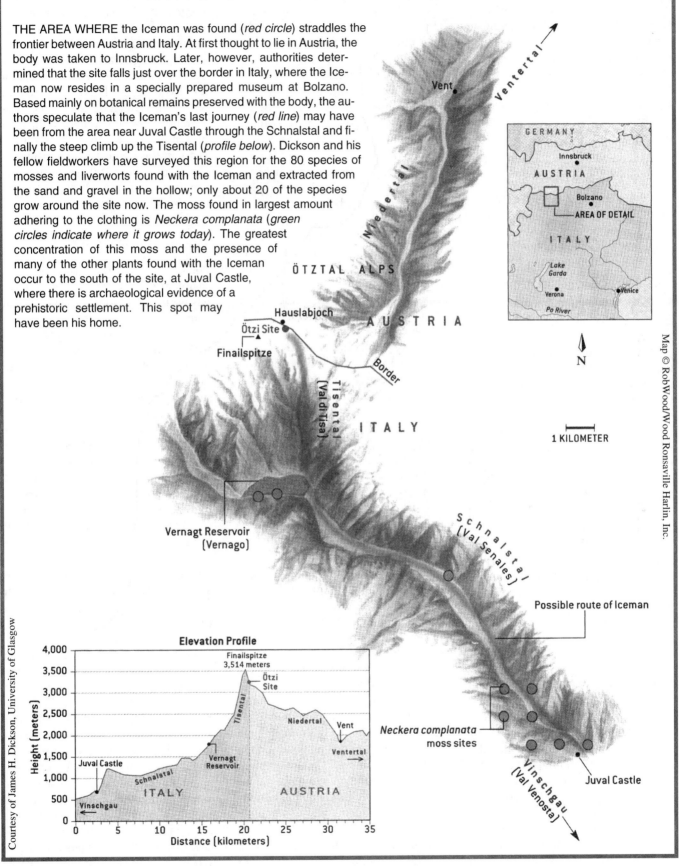

Map © RobWood/Wood Ronsaville Harlin, Inc.

Courtesy of James H. Dickson, University of Glasgow

French at Agincourt some 4,000 years later were made of yew. A hide quiver contained 14 arrows, only two of which had feathers and flint arrowheads attached, but these two were broken. Thirteen of the arrow shafts were made of wayfaring tree, which produces long, straight, rigid stems of suitable diameter; one was partly of wayfaring tree and partly of dogwood.

On hide thongs, he carried two pierced pieces of BIRCH BRACKET FUNGUS, known to contain pharmacologically active compounds.

A belted pouch contained a tinder kit, which held a bracket fungus that grows on trees, known as the true tinder fungus, and iron pyrites and flints for making sparks. A small tool for sharpening the flints was also found with the body. On hide thongs, Ötzi carried two pierced pieces of birch bracket fungus; it is known to contain pharmacologically active compounds (triterpens) and so may have been used medicinally. There were also the fragments of a net, the frame of a backpack, and two containers made of birch bark; one held both charcoal and leaves of Norway maple—perhaps it originally transported embers wrapped in the leaves.

Where Was He From?

IN THIS PART OF THE ALPS, the valleys run north and south between towering ranges of mountains. Thus, the question of Ötzi's homeland resolves itself into north versus south rather than east versus west. The botanical evidence points to the south. A Neolithic site has been discovered at Juval, a medieval castle at the southern end of the Schnalstal, more than 2,000 meters lower but only 15 kilo-

meters from the hollow as the crow flies. Archaeologists have not excavated the site in modern times, and there has been no radiocarbon dating, but Juval is the nearest place to the hollow where a number of the flowering plants and mosses associated with Ötzi now grow. We have no reason to suppose that they did not grow there in prehistoric times, and so perhaps that is the very place where Ötzi lived.

When his clothes were conserved, the washing revealed many plant fragments, including a mass of the large woodland moss *Neckera complanata*. This moss and others he had carried grow to the north and to the south of where he was found, but the southern sources are much closer. *N. complanata* grows in some abundance near Juval. Wolfgang Hofbauer of the Fraunhofer Institute for Building Physics in Valley, Germany, has discovered that this moss grows, in more moderate amounts, at Vernagt (Vernago), just 1,450 meters lower than the site and only five kilometers away. And most recently, Alexandra Schmidl of the University of Innsbruck Botanical Institute discovered small leaf fragments of the moss *Anomodon viticulosus* in samples taken from the stomach. This woodland moss grows with *N. complanata* in lowermost Schnalstal.

If Juval was not his home, signs of Neolithic occupation at other locations in the immediately adjacent Vinschgau (Val Venosta), the valley of the River Etsch (Adige), offer other possibilities. In contrast, to the north, the nearest known Stone Age settlements are many tens of kilometers away, and we are not aware of any Neolithic settlements in the Ventertal or elsewhere in the Ötztal. If Ötzi's home was indeed in lowermost Schnalstal or in Vinschgau, then his community lived in a region of mild, short, largely snow-free winters, especially so if the climate was then slightly warmer.

Investigations by Wolfgang Müller of the Australian National

University of the isotopic composition of the Iceman's tooth enamel suggest that he had grown up in one area but spent the last several decades of his life in a different place. Investigating stable isotopes and trace elements, Jurian Hoogewerff of the Institute of Food Research in Norwich, England, and other researchers have claimed that Ötzi probably spent most of his final years in the Ventertal or nearby valleys to the north. If these deductions can be substantiated, they are intriguing developments.

What Did He Eat?

THE ONGOING STUDIES of the plant remains in samples taken from the digestive tract provide direct evidence of some of Ötzi's last meals. One of us (Oeggl) has detected bran of the primitive wheat called einkorn, so fine that it may well have been ground into flour for baking bread rather than having been made into a gruel. Microscopic debris of as yet unidentified types shows that he had eaten other plants as well. And Franco Rollo and his team at the University of Camerino in Italy, in their DNA studies of food residues in the intestines, have recognized both red deer and alpine ibex (wild goat). Splinters of ibex neck bones were also discovered close to Ötzi's body. A solitary but whole sloe lay near the corpse as well. Sloes are small, bitter, plumlike fruit, and Ötzi may have been carrying dried sloes as provisions.

Several types of moss were recovered from the digestive tract. There is virtually no evidence that humans have ever eaten mosses, certainly not as a staple of their diet. But 5,000 and more years ago no materials were manufactured for wrapping, packing, stuffing or wiping. Mosses were highly convenient for such purposes, as many archaeological discoveries across Europe have revealed: various mosses in Viking and medieval cesspits were clearly used as toilet paper. Had Ötzi's provisions been wrapped in moss, that would neatly explain, as an accidental ingestion, the several leaves and leaf fragments of *N. complanata* recovered from the samples taken from the gut.

Analyzing archaeological remains of bone and hair for their abundances of the stable isotopes of carbon and nitrogen (carbon 13 and nitrogen 15) can provide information about a person's diet. Nitrogen 15 can reveal the extent to which the individual relied on animal or plant protein. Carbon 13 can indicate the type of food plant the person ate and whether seafood or terrestrial carbon was an important part of the diet.

The isotopic data agree with the other evidence that Ötzi ate a mixed diet of plants and animals. He obtained about 30 percent of his dietary nitrogen from animal protein and the rest from plants. This value is consistent with those found in hunter-gatherer tribes living today. The data also indicate that seafood was probably not a component of his diet, a finding that makes sense because of the great distance to the sea.

What Was He Doing There?

TO THIS DAY, in what may be an ancient custom, shepherds take their flocks from the Schnalstal up to high pastures in the Ötztal in June and bring them down again in September. The body was found near one of the traditional routes, which is why early theories held that he was a shepherd. Nothing about his clothing or equipment, however, proves that he had done such work. No wool was on or around his person, no dead collie by his feet, no crook in his hand. Some support for the shepherd hypothesis comes from the grass and bast cape, which has modern parallels in garments worn by shepherds in the Balkans, but that alone is not conclusive; for all we know, it was standard dress for travelers at that time.

Analysis of the few strands of Ötzi's hair that survived reveals very high values of both arsenic and copper. The published explanation (also given independently on television) was that he had taken part in the smelting of copper. But Geoffrey Grime of the University of Surrey in England now considers that these exceptional levels may have resulted from the action of metal-fixing bacteria after Ötzi died and that the copper was *on*, not *in*, the hair. Further support for the possibility of copper having attached itself to the hair after death comes from the presence of the moss *Mielichhoferia elongata*, called copper moss, which spreads preferentially on copper-bearing rocks. It has been found growing at the site by one of us (Dickson) and, independently, by Ronald D. Porley of the U.K. government agency English Nature.

Another hypothesis is that Ötzi was a hunter of alpine ibex; the longbow and quiver of arrows may support this notion. If, however, he had been actively engaged in hunting at the time of his death, why is the bow unfinished and unstrung and all but two of the arrows without heads and feathers and those two broken?

Other early ideas about Ötzi are that he was an outlaw, a trader of flint, a shaman or a warrior. None of these has any solid basis, unless the pieces of bracket fungus he was carrying had medicinal or spiritual use for a shaman.

How Did He Die?

IN JULY 2001 Paul Gostner and Eduard Egarter Vigl of the Regional Hospital of Bolzano in Italy announced that x-rays had revealed an arrowhead in Ötzi's back under the left shoulder. This assertion has led to numerous statements in the media that Ötzi was murdered and to claims from Gostner and Egarter Vigl that it is "now proven that Ötzi did not die a natural death, nor due to exhaustion or frostbite alone." Although three-dimensional reconstructions of the object, which is 27 millimeters long and 18 millimeters wide, exist, requests by Vanezis and Tagliaro for the object to be removed to show convincingly that it is an arrowhead are still unanswered. Furthermore, it must be removed in a way that makes clear what fatal damage it might have done.

The arrowhead need not have caused death. Many people stay alive after foreign objects such as bullets have entered their bodies. A notable archaeological example is the Cascade spear point in the right pelvis of the famous Kennewick Man in North America; it had been there long enough for the bone to begin healing around it.

Even more recently, in a statement to the media, Egarter Vigl has reported that Ötzi's right hand reveals a deep stab wound. No scientific publication of this finding has been made yet.

At What Time of Year?

INITIAL REPORTS PLACED the season of death in autumn. The presence of the sloe, which ripens in late summer, near the body and small pieces of grain in Ötzi's clothing, presumed to have lodged there during harvest threshing, formed the basis for these reports. But strong botanical evidence now indicates that Ötzi died in late spring or early summer. Studies by Oeggl of a tiny sample of food residue from Ötzi's colon have revealed the presence of the pollen of a small tree called hop hornbeam. Strikingly, much of that pollen has retained its cellular contents, which normally decay swiftly. This means that Ötzi might have ingested airborne pollen or drunk water containing freshly shed pollen shortly before he died. The hop hornbeam, which grows up to about 1,200 meters above sea level in the Schnalstal, flowers only in late spring and early summer.

As for the sloe found near his body, if Ötzi had been carrying sloes dried like prunes, the drying could have taken place some time before his journey. Small bits of grain also keep indefinitely, and a few scraps could have been carried inadvertently in his clothes for a long period.

What We Know

MORE THAN 10 YEARS after the discovery of the oldest, best-preserved human body, interpretations about who he was and how he came to rest in a rocky hollow high in the Alps have changed greatly. Just as important, we see that much careful research still needs to be done. The studies of the plant remains-the pollen, seeds, mosses and fungi found both inside and outside the body-have already disclosed a surprising number of Ötzi's secrets. We are aware of his omnivorous diet, his intimate knowledge of his surroundings, his southern domicile, his age and state of health, the season of his death, and something of his environment. Perhaps one of the most surprising reinterpretations is that Ötzi did not die on the boulder on which he was found. Rather he had floated there during one of the temporary thaws known to have occurred over the past 5,000 years. The positioning of the body, with the left arm stuck out awkwardly to the right and the right hand trapped under a stone, and the missing epidermis both suggest this conclusion. So does the fact that some of his belongings lay several meters distant, as if they had floated away from the body.

But we do not know and may never know what reason Ötzi had for being at a great altitude in the Alps. And we may never understand exactly how he died. An autopsy would be too destructive to be carried out. In the absence of this kind of proof, we cannot completely exclude the possibility that perhaps Ötzi died elsewhere and was carried to the hollow where the hikers found him 5,000 years later.

THE AUTHORS *JIM DICKSON, KLAUS OEGGL* and *LINDA HANDLEY* share an interest in the plants that the Tyrolean Iceman may have used in his daily life. Dickson, professor of archaeobotany and plant systematics at the University of Glasgow, is recipient of the Neill Medal of the Royal Society of Edinburgh. He has written more than 150 papers and five books, including *Plants and People in Ancient Scotland* (Tempus Publishing, 2000), which he co-authored with his late wife, Camilla. Oeggl is professor of botany at the University of Innsbruck in Austria. He is an expert in archaeobotany and co-editor of the book *The Iceman and His Natural Environment* (Springer-Verlag, 2000). Handley, an ecophysiologist at the Scottish Crop Research Institute in Invergowrie, near Dundee, Scotland, specializes in the study of stable isotopes of carbon and nitrogen in plants and soils.

IN THE BEGINNING WAS THE WORD

The Bible is at the core of Western civilization, writes BRIAN BETHUNE,
and the assault on the history in it still has repercussions

THE OPENING of the Gospel of John is the perfect expression of the Bible's crucial role in Western civilization. The Hebrew scriptures, known as the Tanakh to Jews and the Old Testament to Christians, are at the heart of both religions. The great Biblical themes—man's relationship with God, atonement and forgiveness, the call to ethical and social responsibility, the absolute worth of the individual—have formed the essential Western way of seeing the human condition, as much for non-believers as for the faithful. In the 16th century, biblical translations became the very engine of national languages, especially in Germany and England. For centuries the King James Bible of 1611 was the English-speaking world's basic text, the book from which people learned to read and think, their major source of images, metaphors and collected wisdom.

One of the Bible's deepest implants in the Western mind comes from its self-definition as a work of history, a narrative that plots events and God's plans along a skein of time. History is purposeful, according to the scriptures, not an endless and meaningless cycle. Since the Bible began to be shaped about 2,500 years ago, the West has never lost touch with it, as it did with the works of classical antiquity in the Dark Ages. The distilled thought of an ancient Near Eastern culture has never seemed foreign, but rather the most familiar source of intellectual, moral and spiritual ideas available to us. We have always been, and still remain, the people of *that* book.

Nor is the Bible's influence restricted to our cultural DNA—to art and music, law codes and political theory. Prime among its decisive, on-the-ground effects is the survival of Judaism and the Jewish people over 2,000 years of dispersal and persecution—one of the most astounding survival stories in human history. Without the Bible, there could have been no Judaism, and none of its profound influence on Western civilization. No Holocaust. No Zionism.

No Israel.

But what if the word is not to be trusted? And not just some parts, the ones that modern Christians and Jews—fundamentalists and the Orthodox aside—have already repudiated. The clearly mythical account of creation in six days, for one, or the miraculous touches in later accounts, like the parting of the Red Sea or the tumbling walls of Jericho.

FAITH AND HISTORY

The major Christian traditions—Orthodox, Protestant and Roman Catholic—all incorporate the Jewish Bible, known as the Tanakh, within their Old Testaments. The Tanakh's opening nine books—Genesis, Exodus, Leviticus, Numbers, Deuteronomy, Joshua, Judges, Samuel and Kings—give the history of the Children of Israel. It takes them from their mythic origins to the Babylonian Captivity that began in 586 BCE, an event within the living memory of the men—or, possibly, the individual religious genius—who stitched together the story of the Chosen People and their demanding God.

No, now it's the *whole thing*, historically speaking. The exodus from Egypt, the conquest of the Promised Land, even the glorious united monarchy of David and Solomon—all are derided as fiction by revisionist academics known as minimalists. Textual scholars for the most part, they have deconstructed the Bible to fragments while casting a baleful outsider's eye on a century of Near Eastern archaeology. Once conducted by religious scholars who examined their discoveries in the light of the Bible, archaeology is now carried out by secular experts who view scripture in the light of their findings. And what they're digging up offers a startlingly new picture of ancient Israel.

They are hotly denounced by more traditional scholars, often known as maximalists. And in the context of the Mideast crisis, where everything to do with land is already violently charged, it was inevitable that a dispute over Biblical history would be thoroughly politicized. Archaeology has "always favoured dominant interests," notes University of Toronto professor Timothy Harrison. In Israel it's been state business from the start. The Palestinian Authority, hard pressed to deliver even basic services to its people, has set up its own archaeology department. And many devout settlers in the West Bank—the epicentre of the Israeli-Palestinian struggle—assert their right to live in Arab territory on scripture.

There's no room in this quarrel for academic civility. Rival scholars have gone for one another like 'a pack of feral canines.'

In Hebron, the Biblical site of the tombs of the patriarchs, some 450 Jews live in a tightly guarded enclave in the midst of 150,000 Arabs. After 12 Israeli troops and three Palestinian gunmen died on Nov. 15 in the city's latest violent clash, settler—and history teacher—Meir Menachem said it was the Arabs who should leave. Hebron, he said, "is more ours than Tel Aviv, this is the land of the Bible." Even in North America, dismissing some of Christianity's and Judaism's dearest religious beliefs can start a firestorm, as Rabbi David Wolpe of Sinai Temple Synagogue in Los Angeles discovered last year, when he told his congregation that new discoveries show the exodus never happened. He was deluged by virulent e-mail, and Orthodox rabbis took out a half-page ad in the *Los Angeles Times* in protest.

It's no surprise that the more radical revisionists claim traditional scholarship, in its search for the never-never land of Ancient Israel, consciously or unconsciously acts to validate Israeli claims to Palestinian land and to erase Palestinian history. Nor is it astonishing that opponents should accuse the minimalists of flirting with anti-Semitism. There's no room in this quarrel for academic civility. Rival scholars have instead gone for one another like "a pack of feral canines," in the apt phrase of Queen's University historian Donald Akenson. Charges of forgery and evidence suppression are common. In 1993 a fragment of inscribed stone was discovered at Tel Dan and dated to the mid-9th century BCE. The fractured wording makes reference to a king of Israel and his then ally, a king of "the House of David." It is the first ever extra-Biblical mention of David. And although it proves little more than the fact that kings of Judah claimed descent from David at an early date, it was still considered a major coup for the maximalist cause. Minimalists didn't hesitate to call it

a forgery—"one guy wrote the stone had been cut by a circular saw," marvels U of T's Harrison.

In a similar vein, University of Copenhagen minimalist Thomas Thompson once wrote that archaeologist William Dever and his team had destroyed chronologically inconvenient evidence at one Israelite site. Dever, a distinguished and courtly professor at the University of Arizona, simply rolls his eyes when asked about the accusation. A leading maximalist, Dever is equally scathing about Thompson and his associates. "A lot of revisionists are simply ill-educated, renegade ex-fundamentalists who went from one literalism to another," says Dever, an adult convert to reform Judaism whose father was a fundamentalist preacher. "And they've let themselves be kidnapped by Palestinian extremists who say, 'No Ancient Israel, no legitimate modern Israel.' They've encouraged the translation of their books into Arabic, even though Arab intellectuals read English. Why do you think they want to be read on the Arab street?"

The minimalists met with sympathy at first. Much of the older model of scripture-supportive scholarship was a house of cards waiting to fall. It's been 250 years since scholars noticed there seemed to be two strands of narrative running from the very start of Genesis. One referred to the Almighty as Elohim or God, the other as Yahweh or Lord. The former thinks highly of Israel, the northern and larger of the two Israelite kingdoms that eventually arose, while the latter favours the smaller southern realm of Judah. Later, more than 20 other sources were postulated to cover material that didn't seem to come from the first two—a remarkable development, given that every last one of them is purely theoretical.

Growing awareness of Bible sources meant a new appreciation of when it was compiled. Passages that favour the southern realm—like Genesis 49:8, where Jacob sets his son Judah as king over his 11 brothers, founders of the other Israelite tribes—could only have been written after they had become a reality. Most scholars push that date of composition to the 7th century BCE or later. For one thing, the patriarchal narratives—the stories about Abraham, Isaac and Jacob—make constant mention of caravans of camels, an animal not widely used as a beast of burden before then. That means that well over a millennium of Biblical narrative is drawn from oral sources: epic sagas, folk tales, hymns, poetry, even puns and jokes. Little of it is a reliable guide to what actually happened, and the only confirmation is what excavations provide.

Holy Land archaeology began in the 19th century, and long remained the domain of religious scholars. They came to the Near East seeking support for their beliefs. As the French Dominican Roland de Vaux noted, "if the historical faith of Israel is not founded in history, such faith is erroneous, and therefore, our faith is also." Those early archaeologists thought they were able to place Abraham within a period of urban collapse and a migration of pastoral easterners at about 2100 BCE, just when the Bible

ALONG A SKEIN OF TIME Academic convention now calls the years since Christ's birth Common Era or CE and the years before it BCE or Before Common Era; the Bible's opening history books cover a vast span of the latter, some 3,400 years from creation to 586 BCE

BIBLE STORY	The Genesis account; Abraham, a nomad with whom God makes the Covenant, goes west to Canaan from Mesopotamia	Abraham's son Isaac and grandson Jacob, father of the 12 tribes of Israel; famine drives Jacob and his sons from Canaan to the Nile delta.	Moses leads the exodus, bringing the Israelites out of slavery in Egypt and through 40 years in the desert; Joshua conquers the Promised Land	Age of the Judges and of the powerful united monarchy of David and Solomon; the realm fractures into Israel and Judah	The shifting wars and alliances of the independent Israelite kingdoms; Israel eventually destroyed by Assyria, Judah by Babylon
ARCHAEOLOGICAL ERA	**Early Bronze Age 3500-2000 BCE**	**Middle Bronze 2000-1550 BCE**	**Late Bronze Age 1550-1150 BCE**	**Iron Age I 1150-900 BCE**	**Iron Age II 900-586 BCE**
EXTRA-BIBLICAL EVIDENCE	No trace of large-scale migration from east, or of socio-economic conditions that would match Biblical narrative (camels not used as beasts of burden until much later)	Evidence of migration from Canaan to Egypt in times of drought, and of sometimes violent reaction, but no trace of Israelites in extensive Egyptian records	Only Egyptian mention of Israelites (about 1210 BCE) says Israel already in Canaan; considerable evidence of peaceful, indigenous emergence in the central highlands	Israelites becoming ethnically distinct—digs show avoidance of pork; no trace of David or Solomon; population in north--Jerusalem only a tiny village	Israel and Judah appear in written evidence; Tel Dan stele refers to "House of David;" foreign accounts record fall of Israel in 722 BCE, Judah in 586 BCE

THE BLESSING OF JACOB, SCHOOL OF RAPHAEL SCALA/ ART RESOURCE, N.Y.; MOSES' JOURNEY TO EGYPT, PIETRO PERUGINO SCALA/ ART RESOURCE, N.Y.; JUDGEMENT OF SOLOMON (LEFT HALF), BY GIAMGATTISTA TIEPOLO ALINARI/ ART RESOURCE, N.Y.

said he lived. But subsequent excavations showed the eastern influx didn't actually take place. Attempts to move the patriarchs to other eras produced the same unhappy results. Today even maximalists like Dever have given up hope of establishing Abraham, Isaac or Jacob as credible historical figures.

For the exodus from slavery in Egypt—the very heart of Judaism celebrated each Passover (and familiar to millions of Christians, if only from Charlton Heston's portrayal of Moses in *The Ten Commandments*)—scholars relied on little more than faith dressed as reasonable presumptions. Many, however inadvertently, simply demonstrated the hold the Exodus story had on their imaginations. "Moses was beyond the power of the human mind to invent," British historian Paul Johnson confidently asserted as late as 1987. Something real must lie behind a story so vividly told, so long entrenched. And besides, adds Hershel Shanks, editor of the prominent *Biblical Archaeological Review*, no one can prove it didn't happen. Absence of evidence, runs the well-worn historian's mantra, is not evidence of absence.

But what an absence. Decades of searching the Sinai Peninsula for any trace of 40 years of Israelite wandering has turned up nothing, not a skeleton or campsite, from the period in question—even though archaeologists have found far older and sketchier remains in the Sinai. Scholars now agree that the exodus—if it happened—had to have occurred in the 13th century BCE, which also turns out to have been an era of strong Egyptian border control, complete with records of who was coming and going. As for the traces of ruined Canaanite cities attributed to the Israelite conquest described in the Book of Joshua, the destruction turns out to have occurred at other times.

The settlement surveys show the bulk of the wealth and population to have been in the north— Jerusalem was only a tiny village

So where did the Israelites come from? For they were surely there, in some form, almost as early as Exodus suggests. That much is known from a two-metre tall stele (an inscribed stone) that the Egyptian Pharaoh Merneptah erected about 1210 BCE to commemorate his military victories in Libya and Canaan. A single line provides the oldest known written evidence of Israel's existence—"Israel is laid waste, its seed is not." The answer to the puzzle of who these Israelites were and how they arose in Canaan had to wait for another generation of secular archaeologists, and for the Six Day War of 1967.

The children of Israel were always a people of the central highlands. Many lived in what is now the occupied West Bank. Until the war it was terra incognita for Israeli archaeologists, both because they were concentrating their efforts on a fruitless search for Joshua's victories on the coastal plain, and because the land was under Jordanian control. After 1967 they began large-scale settlement surveys in the newly opened Palestinian lands. The results were stunning.

Archaeologists found that the central highlands, which had been sparsely inhabited in the Bronze Age, experienced a population explosion. In the century or so of economic and social collapse that led up to the transition from Bronze to Iron Age at about 1150 BCE, peoples were on the move all around the eastern Mediterranean. And about the time the Philistines colonized the coast, high-

A LAND OF MULTIPLE NAMES

What's in a name? The power to name is the power to impose a version of events, just as a dispute over defining the past is "invariably a struggle for power and control in the present." The phrase is from Keith Whitelam, a British scholar who attempted to impose his version of Biblical history with the very title of his book, *The Invention of Ancient Israel: The Silencing of Palestinian History*. For centuries the Western world called the land of milk and honey the Holy Land, but in modern times, Westerners have tended to stick to geographical terms. We call the general area the Near East or, more commonly, the Mideast, in opposition to the Far East of China and Japan. But Mideast is a term that merely seems geographical and neutral—Asia's western edge is only in the "middle" of anything when viewed through *our* cultural lens, as a central hinge in an Islamic zone extending from Morocco to Pakistan.

As for the land of the Bible itself, that sliver of territory between the Mediterranean Sea and the Jordan River, almost everyone—at least until the establishment of modern Israel in 1948—has preferred Palestine, a name that derives from the Philistines who colonized the coast 3,200 years ago. Long before that, the land had another name, Canaan, a term used by foreigners and by the inhabitants themselves, who were politically fractured into tiny statelets. Hence the names the Bible gives those—the Perizzites, Jebusites, Gathazites and others—whom the Israelites encountered there during their conquest of the Promised Land. And just before the Philistines' arrival Canaan also included some kind of "significant socioethnic entity," in one academic's rather desperate description, called Israel.

That much is known from an inscribed Egyptian stone from about 1210 BCE. What kind of entity is uncertain, as is how it evolved into the two later Israelite kingdoms of Israel and Judah. (The latter is the source of the modern terms Judaism and Jew, as well as Judea, the name many Israelis Use for the southern West Bank; the northern part of the occupied territory is often called Samaria, the name of one of Ancient Israel's capital cities.) But regardless of what Israel was 3,200 years ago, it was undeniably there.

So too were others, then and now, even if contemporary Palestinians cannot match the *recorded* thread linking Israeli to Israelite. In fact, although the name Palestine dates back to ancient times, its inhabitants did not refer to themselves as Palestinians until recently. That's a development that has paralleled Zionism, and one that enrages some hawkish Israelis, who prefer to see their antagonists as Arabs indistinguishable from Jordanians or Syrians, people who could and should simply fade into neighbouring nations.

But it's not shared ethnicity, language or religious faith that creates a people—or how could there be a Canada? It's shared history that matters, and a century of violent conflict and upheaval has created a Palestinian people living alongside the Iraelis. Their claim to their name is a claim to their land and to their story, a statement that they too have nowhere else to go. —B.B.

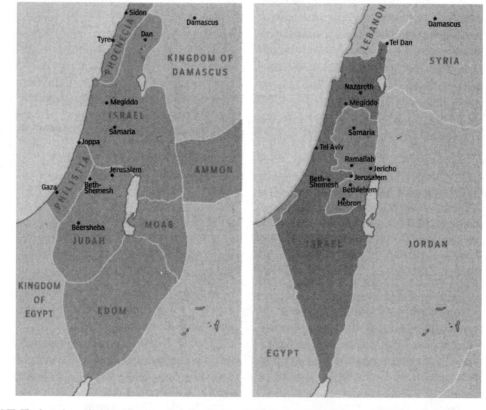

PROMISED LAND The breeders of Ancient and modern Israel are not identical. Much of the central highlands—the heart of the 9th-century BCE kingdoms of Israel and Judah—lie within the occupied Palestinian territories, now also home to some 400,000 Israeli settlers.

TOO PERFECT TO BE TRUE?

As always, it boils down to an act of faith, just as it did from the moment a French scholar noticed the inscription on the side of the 1st-century CE stone ossuary. Faith was required to recognize the implications of the Aramaic phrase "James son of Joseph brother of Jesus," to overlook the lack of commonly accepted archaeological provenance—a Tel Aviv collector bought it from an antiquities dealer 30 years ago for $200; and to announce that this ossuary might, just might, be the first tangible proof of the existence of Jesus. Hundreds of academics, archaeologists, theologians and even statisticians have become involved in an international frenzy over whose bones had been kept in this box. Could they have belonged to James, the brother of Jesus, the leader of Jerusalem's emerging Christian community until he was stoned to death in 62 CE?

And does it matter? For Christians, the discovery of the box, currently on display at the Royal Ontario Museum in Toronto, could be additional proof of something they already believe—the historical existence of Jesus. If it really is James's ossuary, "it is the most significant find in Christian archaeology," says James Beverley, professor of theology and ethics at Toronto's Tyndale Seminary. "It makes Jesus a really present figure in terms of history and not just a shadow figure." Beverley, also a columnist for *Faith Today*," adds that the ossuary will help bring the historical Jesus into the limelight. "He is often obscured by the emphasis on faith," he says. "As if faith shouldn't have concerns about what actually happened."

This sort of single-minded focus on Jesus worries Robert Eisenman. Author of the 1,000-page tome, *James the Brother of Jesus*, he argues that the box is too perfect to be true. (Perhaps someone has been reading his 1997 book—in it, he suggests that the best proof of Jesus would be to establish his relationship with the well-documented James.) "I never needed an ossuary to prove that James was important," says Eisenman. "But now we're going to throw James on the scrap heap of history again. Marginalize him. Treat him as an nonentity and use this to prove Jesus again."

Rev. William Veenstra, the Canadian ministries director for the Christian Reformed Church in North America, finds the debate fascinating but says it doesn't matter whom the box once contained. "Certainly we want to know if it is the true thing or not, because the truth is important," he says. "But it is not going to shake my faith one way or the other." However, for those whose faith isn't rock-solid, and for the simply curious, the discovery may mean a renewed interest in early Christianity. Ed Keall, curator of the James exhibit and head of the ROM's Near Eastern and Asian Civilizations department, is surprised by the attention paid the ossuary and the number of people flocking to see. But he keeps it in perspective. "The lineup for the *Lord of the Rings* exhibit was still longer."

Amy Cameron

land settlements in the interior began to explode in number from 25 to 300. Scholars still quarrel about where these people—the first Israelites—came from. They were Canaanites moving from nomadism to farming, according to Tel Aviv University archaeologist Israel Finkelstein, who has achieved the unique—and dangerously exposed—distinction of being distrusted by both maximalists and minimalists ("I am in the middle," he says, only half-jokingly, "being shot at from both sides").

Merneptah's Israel, at least at the beginning, was close to indistinguishable from its Canaanite neighbours; it used the same pottery (always archaeology's favourite identifier), and even its four-room farmhouses, once thought unique, are found elsewhere. Although Finkelstein raises the ire of the minimalists for ascribing historical value to Biblical books, they cite him approvingly for his dismissal of the united monarchy of David and his son Solomon. For maximalists, that Biblically attested realm, which gathered under one rule all the Israelites between 1005 and 931 BCE, was a major regional force. Solomon, in the Book of Kings, is unmatched for his wisdom and wealth, and a master builder who raised the first temple for Yahweh in Jerusalem, capital of the kingdom. Although misrule by Solomon's son meant the realm would split into the rival states of Israel and Judah, that fleeting moment of power and unity has long been celebrated by Christians and Jews.

In a now-familiar pattern, archaeologists have searched without success for mention of Solomon in contemporary foreign records and for traces of his building program. They thought they found the latter in impressive gates at Megiddo—the site of Biblical Armageddon—and other cities, works mentioned in the Book of Kings. But Finkelstein is having none of it. The settlement surveys show the bulk of the wealth and population to have been in the north—Jerusalem was only a tiny village. It would have been impossible for a southerner like David to have marshalled the resources necessary to conquer Israel. The monumental building was in the north too, and came long after Solomon.

Like Isaac's sons, Jacob and Esau, the two Hebrew realms were thus independent rivals from birth. If David and Solomon lived at all, they were petty hill chieftains whose exploits were wildly exaggerated by their Judean descendants, Finkelstein contends. The whole panoply of Biblical history, in fact, was crafted by the southern religious elite to bolster its claim to rule all the children of Israel after the northern realm was wiped from the map by the Assyrian Empire in 722 BCE. Minimalists applaud, though many think that the compilation was much later. Traditional scholars, though they may have yielded on the patriarchs and the conquest, are adamant on the reality of David's kingdom and the historical facts contained in the books of Samuel and Kings.

How to to bring the debate forward, to get a non-Biblical picture of what the Israelites were doing in the 350 years between Merneptah's stele and the Tel Dan fragment, is now the issue. Like Finkelstein, Dever was among the almost 8,000 participants who went to Toronto in late November for the annual meetings of the Society of Biblical Literature and the American Schools for Oriental Research. Dever's talk on searching for ethnicity in the archaeological record drew a standing-room-only crowd that spilled out into the hallway. Given the Israelites' indigenous origins, everyone is looking for a way to mark their emergence as a distinct people. But the quest for a set of ethnic markers to identify something that mainly exists in the mind—you are who you think you are—and in the sort of soft tissue, like skin, that doesn't survive 3,000 years in the ground, has a certain potential for absurdity. When a woman in the audience asked about circumcision as an Israelite marker, Dever deadpanned, "Sure, but what would the evidence look like?"

But Dever does have one ace in the archaeological hole, a single ethnic marker capable of surviving. Or, to be exact—and in keeping with a debate that is all about absence—a marker that could but shouldn't be there. Pig bones. Considerable effort has gone into attempts to find the one people, in the otherwise swine-friendly Near East, with a prohibition against eating pork. Zvi Lederman and Shlomo Bunimovitz, two archaeologists from Tel Aviv University who attended the ASOR session, have dug for a decade at the Iron Age site of Beth-Shemesh. They're confident in their results. "There's a clear avoidance of pork, and no environmental reason that might have made pig-raising difficult," Lederman says. "Otherwise you can't tell them from the Canaanites."

Bunimovitz and Lederman place the origin of the pork avoidance in the context of Philistine pressure. "Beth-Shemesh was on the border between later Judah and the expanding Philistines," says Lederman. "Group identities form in times of stress, it forces people to set themselves off." That's it? A key and clearly ancient tenet in Jewish religion, ascribed to everything from an early awareness of swine-borne diseases to the deepest spiritual symbolism, originated in a desire to distinguish themselves from the neighbours? An apologetic smile and a shrug from Lederman. "What else is there to say?"

The short answer is, more than the minimalists assert and less than the maximalists hope. Some kind of Israel *was* there by 1200 BCE—that much Pharoah's inscription makes clear—and it was already engaged in the process of self-determination that would later set Jews apart from the rest of the world. Pork avoidance is one marker; another, insufficiently remarked upon, is its very name. There is no scholarly agreement on what the word Israel means. It certainly involves God, and probably also the idea of struggle—"he who fights with God" is a common translation. An ethnic group that invoked a deity in its very name was a new development in the ancient Near East, and a sign that from the very beginning, the children of Israel, having defined themselves by their relationship to God, were on a path that would eventually lead them to monotheism.

What followed the highland settlements—the evolution to sophisticated but small states eventually swallowed by expansionist empires—is still open to debate. The political implications are as fluid. Even William Dever, a friend to Ancient and modern Israel, has voiced doubts over the roots of the violent opposition Orthodox Israelis exhibit towards archaeology. That's supposed to derive from worries over disturbing ancient graves, he notes, but Dever suspects it lies in fear of what might be found out about their origins and traditions. Continued erosion of the Bible's literal historicity cannot help but undermine their claims to West Bank land.

The Bible itself remains, in the midst of a debate that, in some ways, only serves to emphasize its enormous power. The northern kingdom of Israel was literally erased by the Assyrians in 722 BCE, its 10 tribes lost from history to myth. Judah had another 136 years before the Babylonians destroyed their state. But because during that time Judeans hammered out the scriptures on the anvil of their collective experience, their heirs too endure.

Who Were the First Americans?

If your answer was fur-clad mammoth hunters, guess again. The first people to settle the New World may have been fisherfolk and basket weavers

by Sasha Nemecek, *staff writer*

The leaf-shaped spearpoint I'm holding is surprisingly dainty—for a deadly weapon. I let my mind wander, trying to imagine life some 14,700 years ago in the marshes of southern Chile, where this relic was found. The 30 or so people who lived there then, at the creekside campsite now known as Monte Verde, were some of the earliest inhabitants of South America—most likely descendants of people who reached North America by crossing the Bering land bridge from Asia at least 15,000 years ago, perhaps more. Did this roving crew realize they were such pioneers? Or are such musings reserved for people who don't have to worry about where to find their next meal?

My thoughts are interrupted by Tom Dillehay, professor of anthropology at the University of Kentucky and the man who in the 1970s uncovered Monte Verde, the oldest known site of human habitation in the Americas. In a basement classroom on the university's campus, Dillehay has spread out a gallery of artifacts from Monte Verde on the table before me. He directs my attention to a fragment of another spearpoint, which, were it still intact, would be virtually identical to the one I'm holding. "These were probably made by the same person," he says.

The misty images of primitive explorers evaporate, and I suddenly picture a single artisan spending hours, perhaps days, crafting these stone tools, each less than four inches long and half an inch wide. The workmanship is exquisite, even to my untrained eye: the series of tiny notches that form the sharp edges are flawlessly symmetrical. Whoever made these tools was clearly a perfectionist.

The question of when people first reached the Americas has been an ongoing discussion in anthropology and archaeology circles for years. Yet how the first Americans actually lived—how my diligent toolmaker spent his (or her?) days—is only now receiving significant attention. The findings at Monte Verde shattered the previously accepted entry date into the Americas, which had been considered to be around 14,000 years ago. (Because of the significance of this shift in thinking, acceptance of the

Monte Verde site was a slow process; the archaeological community did not endorse Dillehay's analysis until 1997, when a paper on the site was published in the journal *Science.* A handful of scholars still have reservations about the age of the site.)

Excavations under way in the eastern U.S. and throughout South America hint that humans' arrival date may have to be pushed back to as far as 20,000 or even 40,000 years ago. Such discoveries may very well do more than just alter our understanding of how long people have lived in the Americas. With every new artifact, researchers like Dillehay are slowly piecing together more about the day-to-day lives of the early Americans: how they hunted, what plants they ate, how they moved across vast stretches of land—in short, what life was *really* like for those men, women and children who originally settled in the New World.

The canonical view of how humans first reached the Americas can be traced back to 1589, when José de Acosta, a Jesuit missionary to South America, suggested that the original Americans had somehow migrated from Siberia many thousands of years ago. The theory persisted, and by the early part of the 20th century archaeologists had agreed on the identity of the very first Americans. The evidence seemed irrefutable. Archaeological sites dating to approximately 13,000 years ago had turned up all across the landscape; nothing older had yet been found. Moreover, the tools from these sites shared striking similarities, as though the people who created them had a common cultural background and had all moved onto the continent together. Researchers termed these people and their culture "Clovis" (after Clovis, N.M., where the first such artifact was found). Clovis spearpoints, for instance, can be found in Canada, across the U.S. and into Central America.

In certain parts of the U.S., particularly the desert Southwest, these Clovis points are nearly as common as cacti.

Why would the Clovis people have needed so many weapons? Again, the answer seemed clear. They must have been voracious hunters, following their prey—big game animals like the woolly mammoth—across the Bering land bridge around 14,000 or 15,000 years ago, when the ice sheets extending from the North Pole had melted just enough to open a land passageway through Canada. The hunters pursued the animals relentlessly, taking around 1,000 years to spread through North and South America. The emphasis on hunting made sense—this was the Ice Age, after all, and meat from a mammoth or bison provided lots of much needed fat and protein for the entire family. And the fur hides could be fashioned into warm clothes.

"People make the mistake of thinking the Ice Age was cold all the time."

Thomas Lynch, an expert on Clovis culture and director of the Brazos Valley Museum of Natural History in Bryan, Tex., points out another advantage: "The easiest way to get food is by hunting big game, in particular herding animals. And at first, the animals would not be afraid of humans." A quick sweep across the continent fits the pattern as well, Lynch argues, remarking that the hunters would have had to move fast "as the animals got spooked by humans."

The idea that the first Americans were Ice Age hunters has been accepted for decades, filling pages in both textbooks and scientific journals. But researchers have increasingly pointed to holes in the theory. David Meltzer, a professor of anthropology at Southern Methodist University who has studied Clovis culture extensively, suggests that this view of the first settlers is too simplistic, relying as it does on a stereotype that "people worked their way through the continent gnawing on mammoth bones." With closer scrutiny, he says, "this just doesn't hold up."

Meltzer contends that the small bands of 15 to 30 people, typical of nomadic tribes, were essentially always at risk of dying out, either from inbreeding or some sort of catastrophe. Hunting a mammoth was, of course, extremely dangerous, possibly even too perilous for these groups to have relied on it as their sole source of food. So they must have turned to other sources, particularly small game, nuts and berries, and maybe even fish and turtles. Indeed, a few archaeologists have discovered the remains of smaller animals, including deer, rabbits and snakes, at Clovis sites. Unfortunately, though, the technology associated with small-game hunting, fishing and gathering—the wooden tools, nets and baskets—generally don't survive as well as stone artifacts do.

One site in Pennsylvania, however, has yielded just these kinds of remains. James Adovasio, an archaeologist at Mercyhurst College, has spent almost 30 years excavating Meadowcroft Rockshelter southwest of Pittsburgh, where early settlers set up camp at least 12,900 years ago. He has found baskets that he believes would have been used to carry plants or even mussels from the nearby Ohio River. Adovasio has also uncovered parts of snares for catching small game, and bone awls for working textiles and hides.

For much of the past three decades, other archaeologists have disputed Adovasio's interpretation of these finds; even today some question the antiquity of the site, although a recent analysis of the site by an outside researcher may help resolve the issue. "We have found bone needles, and people would say, 'Oh, they used them to sew hides.' But you and I know they would snap!" Adovasio insists. Instead, he argues, these needles must have been for weaving lightweight fabrics made from plant material. "People make the mistake of thinking the Ice Age was cold all the time. They remember the 40,000 Januarys but forget the 40,000 Julys," he laughs.

And just who was sewing clothes for the warmer weather? Adovasio complains that the official mammoth-centric picture of early Americans completely neglects the role of women, children and grandparents. He points to the icon of the Ice Age hunter with his stone spears: "By focusing only on stones, we are ignoring 95 percent of what these people made and what they did." Look at more recent hunter-gatherer societies, he says. Women, children and older people of both sexes supply the vast majority of the food and carry out vital tasks such as making clothes, nets and baskets. Why would the earliest Americans have been any different?

Margaret Jodry, an archaeologist at the Smithsonian Institution, also cautions against overlooking the issue of how families traveled through the New World. Conventional wisdom has the Clovis people walking the entire way. But, Jodry asks, what about Clovis sites that have been found on both sides of a river? "Unless we're suggesting they would swim across" the river every day just to get home, she says incredulously, they must have relied on boats for transportation. "How are you going to swim the Missouri River with Grandma, your wife who's eight months pregnant, your kids and dogs?" Furthermore, she points out, humans had developed watercraft by at least 40,000 years ago, because by then they were in Australia.

Early American boats would have been constructed from animal skins or wood—again, fairly ephemeral substances. But Jodry thinks that archaeologists might be able to find distinct signatures of the boatbuilding process. Based on her observations of construction techniques used by modern indigenous groups of North America, she has proposed archaeological markers—a certain configuration of post holes encircled by stones, for instance—that might represent an ancient workshop for assembling boats.

In response to these novel lines of reasoning, archaeologists are beginning to change how and where they dig. Jodry reports that some colleagues have told her they plan to revisit previously excavated sites, looking for evidence of boats. And finds at Meadowcroft and elsewhere

ARCHAEOLOGY'S DATING GAME

Matching Radiocarbon Dates to the Calendar

The complex question of when people first reached the Americas is further complicated by a problem with dates. Archaeologists generally rely on radio-carbon dating to determine the age of such artifacts as bones, charcoal or wood. But one radiocarbon year isn't always the same as one calendar year.

Radiocarbon dating works because all living things absorb carbon. Specifically, they take up two isotopes: carbon 14 and carbon 12. (Isotopes of an element have the same number of protons inside the atomic nucleus but different numbers of neutrons.) While an animal or plant is alive, the ratio of carbon 14 to carbon 12 in its tissues reflects the ratio present in the atmosphere. Once it dies, the ratio changes.

Carbon 14 is radioactive (but not dangerous) and undergoes radioactive decay; carbon 12 is stable. During a creature's lifetime, processes such as breathing replenish carbon 14. After death, however, the amount drops, and the ratio between carbon 14 and carbon 12 falls as well. Scientists know the rate at which carbon 14 decays, and by assessing how much has been lost compared with carbon 12, they can determine the age of an object.

Notably, the ratio of carbon 14 to carbon 12 in the atmosphere is not constant, which alters the baseline for calibrating dates. To match radiocarbon years to calendar years, researchers have turned to independent timescales based on tree rings, ice cores and uranium-thorium dating.

Unfortunately for scientists studying the peopling of the Americas, the period between 10,000 and 20,000 years ago has been difficult to calibrate. For many years archaeologists simply presented their results in uncorrected radiocarbon years. Recent findings, however, make it easier to adjust dates from this era. All the dates in this article have been calibrated to calendar years (for information on the calibration program, go on-line at www.raha.ox.ac.uk/orau/).

The distinction between radiocarbon years and calendar years is important. A report earlier this year described a 13,000-year-old skeleton found in California and compared it to 12,500-year-old Monte Verde, without mentioning that the former date was in calendar years and the latter, radiocarbon years. Some readers understandably thought that the California skeleton was older than the campsite at Monte Verde. But in calendar years, Monte Verde is 14,700 years old.—*S.N.*

RADIOCARBON	9.6	10.2	11	12	12.7	13.3	14.2	15	15.9	16.8	17.6	18.5	19.3	20
CALENDAR	11	12	13	14	15	16	17	18	19	20	21	22	23	~24

Thousands of Years Ago

RADIOCARBON YEARS before the present *(top)* must be translated into calendar years before the present *(bottom)*. For example, an artifact that is 11,000 radiocarbon years old is actually 13,000 calendar years old.

have prompted archaeologists to hunt for more than just stones and bones. (At Monte Verde, Dillehay found knotted cords that he thinks were used to secure tents made of animal hides; remains of the tents turned up as well.)

But they'll have to change the types of sites they look for, according to Dillehay. "People concentrate on caves and open-air sites," he explains, where preservation of delicate artifacts is unlikely. "If you want to find another Monte Verde"—where a layer of peat from the nearby swamp covered the campsite and prevented oxygen from reaching the remains—"you've got to look where wet sites are preserved," he says.

This newfound emphasis on softer artifacts should help to substantiate the emerging picture of the first Americans as people with an intricate knowledge of their environment, who could not only spear a mammoth once in a while but who also knew how to catch fish, pick the right berries, weave plant fibers into clothes and baskets, and build boats for local travel.

And as researchers cast a wider net for artifacts, they may have to consider a range of explanations for what they find. Texas A&M University archaeologist and Clovis specialist Mike Waters notes that when the archaeological community accepted the 14,700-year-old date for Monte Verde just three years ago, the recognition "jumpstarted the whole debate about Clovis being first." As scholars digest the evidence from Monte Verde, they have been rethinking many long-held ideas on who populated the Americas and when and how they got here. For his part, Waters maintains three working hypotheses: that the Clovis people were in fact the first in the Americas, that there was a smattering of people in North America before Clovis but they left almost no trace or that there was a large pre-Clovis occupation we have yet to identify.

Transportation to the New World is a big topic for debate. If the early Americans did cruise around the continent in canoes and kayaks, might the first settlers have arrived by boat as well? For decades the archaeological community rejected this notion (Ice Age hunters could never have carried all their weapons and leftover mammoth meat in such tiny boats!), but in recent years the idea has gathered more support. One reason for the shift: the nagging problem of just how fast people can make the journey from Alaska to Tierra del Fuego.

Consider Dillehay's 14,700-year-old Monte Verde site. According to the previously accepted timeline, people could have made the journey from Asia on foot no earlier than 15,700 years ago (before this time, the ice sheets extending from the North Pole covered Alaska and Canada completely, making a land passage impossible). If this entry date is correct, the Monte Verde find would indicate that the first settlers had to make the 12,000-mile trip through two continents in only 1,000 years. In archaeological time, that's as fast as Marion Jones.

One way to achieve this pace, however, would be by traveling along the Pacific coastlines of North and South America in boats. Knut Fladmark, a professor of archaeology at Simon Fraser University in Burnaby, B.C., first suggested this possibility in the 1970s and remains an advocate of a coastal entry into the Americas. If people had a reason to keep moving, he says, they could have traversed both continents in 100 years. Fladmark estimates that traveling at a rate of 200 miles a month would have been quite reasonable; the settlers no doubt stopped during winter months and probably stayed in some spots for a generation or so if the local resources were particularly tempting.

Fladmark's theory, though enticing, won't be easy to prove. Rising sea levels from the melting Ice Age glaciers inundated thousands of square miles along the Pacific coasts of both continents. Any early sites near the ocean that were inhabited before 13,000 years ago would now be deep underwater.

Some evidence links the settling of the Americas to the migration of modern humans out of Africa.

Recently a few enterprising researchers have attempted to dredge up artifacts from below the Pacific. In 1997, for example, Daryl Fedje, an archaeologist with Parks Canada (which runs that country's national parks system), led a team that pulled up a small stone tool from 160 feet underwater just off the coast of British Columbia. The single tool, which Fedje estimates to be around 10,200 years old, does establish that people once lived on the now submerged land but reveals little about the culture there.

Excavating underwater sites might turn out to be the only way to prove when humans first arrived on this continent. And for many researchers this is still a very open question, with answers ranging from 15,000 years ago to as far back as 50,000 years ago. When Fladmark first proposed the idea of a coastal migration, the entry date of 14,000 or 15,000 years ago was orthodoxy. But many researchers have since speculated that humans must have been in the Americas for much, much longer.

Which brings me back to my skilled spearpoint designer from Monte Verde. Although his ancestors theoretically could have made it to the southern tip of Chile in just 100 years if they traveled in watercraft, practically speaking, the group wouldn't then have had much time to adapt to the new surroundings.

And for Dillehay, this distinction between theory and reality is crucial: The people living at Monte Verde 14,700 years ago, he says, "knew exactly where they were positioning themselves." They had been in the region long enough to set up camp on prime real estate, within an hour's walk of nearby wetlands, lush with edible plants. The ocean and the Andean foothills were both about a day's walk away. The group had carefully situated itself close to three different environments, all of which provided them with food and supplies.

Dillehay has found desiccated cakes, or "quids," of seaweed that the people sucked on, probably for the high iodine content in the plants (the quids are almost perfect molds of the top of a person's mouth—down to the impressions of molars). And based on the mastodon bones found at the site, Dillehay believes that the Monte Verdeans either killed or scavenged animals trapped in the nearby bogs. He also suspects they used rib bones from the animals as digging sticks to unearth tubers and rhizomes from the surrounding marshes.

Such elaborate knowledge of one's environment does not come quickly; it probably requires several generations at least. Precisely how long the folks at Monte Verde would have needed to gain such an understanding, though, is difficult to estimate. The arrival of modern humans into an unpopulated continent has happened only twice—in Australia and in the Americas—so we have little by way of reference. But Dillehay looks at the issue in a broader context. In places like the Indus Valley and China, it took tens of thousands of years for complex civilizations to arise. He remarks that unless Americans were "the most remarkable people in the world"—setting up the beginnings of civilization in only a couple thousand years—they must have been here for much longer. Dillehay suggests that an arrival time of around 20,000 years ago would have given the first Americans ample time to put down the roots of civilization.

Such an early entry date is bolstered by two other lines of evidence. Linguist Johanna Nichols of the University of California at Berkeley argues that the amazing diversity of languages among Native Americans could have arisen only after humans had been in the New World for at least 20,000 years—possibly even 30,000. Geneticists, including Theodore Schurr of the Southwest Foundation for Biomedical Research in San Antonio, Tex., and Douglas Wallace of Emory University, present a related argument based on genetic diversity. By comparing several DNA markers found in modern Native Americans and modern Siberians, Schurr and Wallace estimate that the ancestors of the former left Siberia for the New World at least 30,000 years ago.

These ancient dates—if they are correct—would have important implications. Experts on human origins believe that behaviorally modern humans left Africa for Europe and Asia around 50,000 or 60,000 years ago. So as archaeologists push back the arrival date of humans in the Americas, they move the peopling of the New World into the larger story of human evolution. As Robson Bonnichsen, director of the Center for the Study of the First Americans at Oregon State University, has written, the occupation of the Americas should be "understood in respect to the process that led to the global expansion of modern humans."

Some evidence links the settling of the Americas to the migration of modern humans out of Africa. In perhaps one of the most startling finds of recent years, Walter Neves of the University of São Paulo determined that the oldest skeleton ever found in the Americas—a 13,500-year-old adult female from southeastern Brazil—resembles Africans and Australian aborigines more than modern Asians or Native Americans. Neves interprets this result (and similar ones from some 50 skulls dated to between 8,900 and 11,600 years old) to mean that non-Mongoloid migrants were among the first in the Americas.

Neves is quick to point out, though, that he does not think these people came directly from Africa or Australia but that they splintered off from the band moving slowly through Asia that eventually went south to Australia. According to the fossil record, Mongoloid groups arrived in South America around 9,000 years ago, where they appear to have replaced the previous population. "I don't have an answer for [what happened]," Neves says. "Maybe war, maybe killing, maybe they were absorbed" by all the intermixing that was surely going on, he suggests.

So it seems the New World has been a melting pot for millennia. Those famous Ice Age hunters no doubt did cross the Bering land bridge at some point and head onto the continent. But they probably were not the first ones to do so, and they most certainly were not the only ones. Thanks to recent archaeological finds, researchers are beginning to figure out what life was like for some of the other people here—the fisherfolk boating along the Pacific coast, the hunter-gatherers living in the temperate forests of North and South America.

In the meantime, investigators can't dig fast enough to keep pace with the rapid shifts in our knowledge of who the first Americans were. Archaeologists are scouring Alaska for remains of early inhabitants; geologists are trying to determine exactly when the glaciers melted enough for settlers to start moving into central Canada and the U.S. Others continue hunting for even earlier signs of Clovis in the U.S. The eastern U.S. is home to several important ongoing excavations: Cactus Hill in Virginia and Topper Site in South Carolina. Preliminary finds at Cactus Hill suggest that a group possibly related to the Clovis people may have lived in the area around 18,000 years ago.

Al Goodyear, an archaeologist at the University of South Carolina, went back to a Clovis site at Topper, near the Savannah River, to see what was underneath (and thus older). The results surprised him: artifacts in the deeper layers at Topper are completely unlike Clovis technology. He has found no Clovis-type spearpoints, only tiny stone blades and scraping tools thought to be associated with the use of wood, bone and antlers.

Goodyear recounts how he "went into a mild state of shock" when he realized just how difficult it would be to explain who these people were. This summer he brought in two experts on determining the age of archaeological sites, Waters of Texas A&M and Tom Stafford of Stafford Research Laboratories in Boulder, Colo., the leading carbon-14 dating facility in the country. The team is still unsure of how old the tools are—as Stafford says, they could be from just 100 years before Clovis—but the analysis continues. Goodyear hopes eventually to excavate in a nearby marshy area, where conditions should be more suited to the preservation of delicate items such as wooden tools or clothing fibers.

Other investigators working at sites in South America, including Dillehay, have described camps that could be as old as 30,000 years. Dillehay himself, however, is cautious about these dates, saying more spots must be found from this era before researchers can be certain these highly contested numbers are correct.

But he has little doubt on another point: that the individuals who lived at Monte Verde and throughout the New World—whenever it was truly new—were part of "one of the most intricate, thrilling and inspiring episodes of the human adventure." In his book *The Settlement of the Americas* (Basic Books, 2000), he describes the expansion into new environments as the "high adventure that gave people a strong sense of mission"—analogous to having our space program continue for thousands of years.

But isn't this sort of self-awareness rather too modern? Wasn't the main adventure for these people trying to stay alive? Dillehay thinks perhaps they had more on their minds. "People pick the same good campsites over and over—rock-shelters, overlooks," he says, so it wouldn't have been strange to see the remains of previous inhabitants. "But there must have been some point when people realized that no one had been there before," he adds. "When they realized, 'We are the first.'"

Who's On First?

There's still no end to the controversy over when and how humans populated the New World.

By Anna Curtenius Roosevelt

A little less than 13,000 years ago, as the Ice Age was drawing to a close, big-game hunters crossed the Bering land bridge from Siberia into the Americas. By 12,000 years ago, they had made their way south from the interior of Alaska through an ice-free corridor to the high plains of North America. Hunting effectively by using spears tipped with fluted, flaked stone points (called Clovis points, after an archaeological site in New Mexico), these Paleoindians decimated the game herds of the plains in less than a thousand years. Some then migrated farther south through the highlands of Central America and the Andes, reaching the tip of South America about 10,000 years ago, just as global warming and rising sea levels marked the end of the Ice Age, or Pleistocene epoch. Only then did people spread to the coasts and big rivers; develop new varieties of triangular, stemmed points; and begin to subsist on small game, fish, shellfish, and wild plants. The game-poor tropical forests remained off-limits until after New World peoples had developed agriculture, about 5,000 years ago.

This attractively simple tale, still enshrined in some textbooks, is unraveling as a result of archaeological evidence accumulated over the past two decades. Nearly seventy years after excavations first revealed the Clovis big game hunting culture, new sites and new dates in both North and South America are challenging Clovis's claim to priority. But a new consensus has not yet emerged. Instead, scholars are engaging in acrimonious public disputes while dramatic press releases with conflicting claims incite the media.

Two new books on the first Americans offer to clarify the picture. One is by Thomas D. Dillehay, the T. Marshall Hahn Jr. Professor of Anthropology at the University of Kentucky, Lexington; the other is by E. James Dixon, the curator of archaeology at the Denver Museum of Natural History. Both books are definitely worth reading, but they require considerable effort and a critical eye. Both use terms and dating criteria inconsistently and contain inaccuracies or out-of date information that will confuse the general reader.

Although the books differ in several respects—for one thing, Dillehay's emphasizes South American discoveries, while Dixon's focuses more on North America and the Clovis sites—both take it for granted that people entered the New World before the rise of Clovis culture. The idea of an earlier migration is not new. For more than thirty years, Alan Bryan and Ruth Gruhn, as well as other archaeologists, have argued that people who lacked projectile points for big-game hunting entered the Americas more than 30,000 years ago. Recurring claims for such early cultures have been based on a handful of sites, along with analyses of Native American linguistic and genetic diversity suggesting that people have lived in the New World for a long time. But with the exception of evidence for the Nenana culture (known from several sites in central Alaska), the data supporting all pre-Clovis cultures have failed to withstand careful scrutiny. C. Vance Haynes and others have shown that the sites in question do not provide a consistent series of early dates that are securely tied to unambiguous evidence of human presence.

Neither Dillehay nor Dixon can marshal a consistent pattern of evidence for an arrival prior to 12,000 years ago. The new claims for pre-Clovis sites are no stronger than the old ones, and the old ones continue to circulate despite their evident flaws. A number of the sites championed by one or both authors—for example, Putu and Bluefish Caves—have no evidence of human presence at an early date. Some, such as Meadowcroft Rockshelter, have questionable dates due to possible contamination, and others, such as Cactus Hill, a new site in Virginia, have inconsistent dates, vague stratigraphy, and inadequate artifact

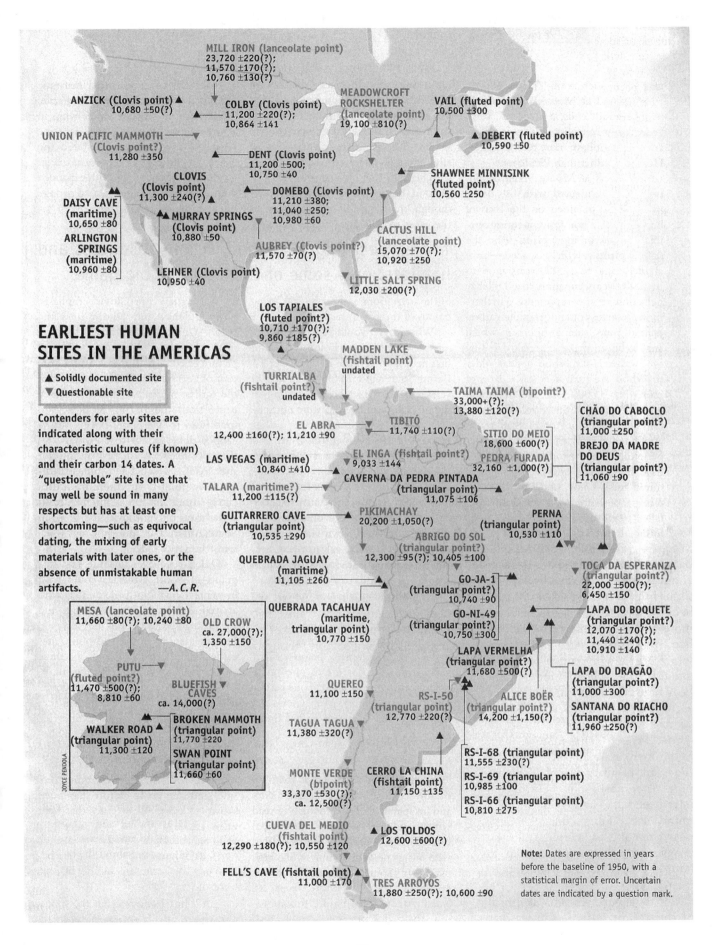

EARLIEST HUMAN SITES IN THE AMERICAS

▲ Solidly documented site
▼ Questionable site

Contenders for early sites are indicated along with their characteristic cultures (if known) and their carbon 14 dates. A "questionable" site is one that may well be sound in many respects but has at least one shortcoming—such as equivocal dating, the mixing of early materials with later ones, or the absence of unmistakable human artifacts. —A.C.R.

MILL IRON (lanceolate point)
23,720 ±220(?);
11,570 ±170(?);
10,760 ±130(?)

ANZICK (Clovis point) ▲
10,680 ±50(?)

COLBY (Clovis point)
11,200 ±220(?);
10,864 ±141

MEADOWCROFT ROCKSHELTER
(lanceolate point)
19,100 ±810(?)

VAIL (fluted point)
10,500 ±300

DEBERT (fluted point)
10,590 ±50

UNION PACIFIC MAMMOTH
(Clovis point?)
11,280 ±350

DENT (Clovis point)
11,200 ±500;
10,750 ±40

SHAWNEE MINNISINK
(fluted point)
10,560 ±250

CLOVIS
(Clovis point)
11,300 ±240(?) ▲

DOMEBO (Clovis point)
11,210 ±380;
11,040 ±250;
10,980 ±60

DAISY CAVE
(maritime)
10,650 ±80

MURRAY SPRINGS
(Clovis point)
10,880 ±50

CACTUS HILL
(lanceolate point)
15,070 ±70(?);
10,920 ±250

ARLINGTON SPRINGS
(maritime)
10,960 ±80

AUBREY (Clovis point?)
11,570 ±70(?)

LEHNER (Clovis point)
10,950 ±40

LITTLE SALT SPRING
12,030 ±200(?)

LOS TAPIALES
(fluted point?)
10,710 ±170(?);
9,860 ±185(?)

MADDEN LAKE
(fishtail point)
undated

TURRIALBA
(fishtail point?)
undated

TAIMA TAIMA (bipoint?)
33,000+(?);
13,880 ±120(?)

CHÃO DO CABOCLO
(triangular point?)
11,000 ±250

EL ABRA
12,400 ±160(?); 11,210 ±90

TIBITÓ
11,740 ±110(?)

SITIO DO MEIO
18,600 ±600(?)

BREJO DA MADRE DO DEUS
(triangular point?)
11,060 ±90

LAS VEGAS (maritime)
10,840 ±410

EL INGA (fishtail point)
9,033 ±144

PEDRA FURADA
32,160 ±1,000(?)

CAVERNA DA PEDRA PINTADA
(triangular point)
11,075 ±106

TALARA (maritime?)
11,200 ±115(?)

PIKIMACHAY
20,200 ±1,050(?)

PERNA
(triangular point)
10,530 ±110

GUITARRERO CAVE
(triangular point)
10,535 ±290

ABRIGO DO SOL
(triangular point?)
12,300 ±95(?); 10,405 ±100

TOCA DA ESPERANZA
(triangular point?)
22,000 ±500(?);
6,450 ±150

QUEBRADA JAGUAY
(maritime)
11,105 ±260

GO-JA-1
(triangular point?)
10,740 ±90

LAPA DO BOQUETE
(triangular point?)
12,070 ±170(?);
11,440 ±240(?);
10,910 ±140

MESA (lanceolate point)
11,660 ±80(?); 10,240 ±80

OLD CROW
ca. 27,000(?);
1,350 ±150

QUEBRADA TACAHUAY
(maritime,
triangular point)
10,770 ±150

GO-NI-49
(triangular point?)
10,750 ±300

LAPA VERMELHA
(triangular point?)
11,680 ±500(?)

LAPA DO DRAGÃO
(triangular point?)
11,000 ±300

PUTU
(fluted point?)
11,470 ±500(?);
8,810 ±60

BLUEFISH CAVES
ca. 14,000(?)

QUEREO
11,100 ±150

RS-I-50
(triangular point)
12,770 ±220(?)

ALICE BOËR
(triangular point?)
14,200 ±1,150(?)

SANTANA DO RIACHO
(triangular point?)
11,960 ±250(?)

BROKEN MAMMOTH
(triangular point)
11,770 ±220

WALKER ROAD
(triangular point)
11,300 ±120

TAGUA TAGUA
11,380 ±320(?)

SWAN POINT
(triangular point)
11,660 ±60

RS-I-68 (triangular point)
11,555 ±230(?)

MONTE VERDE
(bipoint)
33,370 ±530(?);
ca. 12,500(?)

CERRO LA CHINA
(fishtail point)
11,150 ±135

RS-I-69 (triangular point)
10,985 ±100

RS-I-66 (triangular point)
10,810 ±275

CUEVA DEL MEDIO
(fishtail point)
12,290 ±180(?); 10,550 ±120

▲ **LOS TOLDOS**
12,600 ±600(?)

FELL'S CAVE (fishtail point) ▲
11,000 ±170

▼ **TRES ARROYOS**
11,880 ±250(?); 10,600 ±90

Note: Dates are expressed in years before the baseline of 1950, with a statistical margin of error. Uncertain dates are indicated by a question mark.

JOYCE PENDOLA

samples that disqualify them from scientific acceptance, at least for the present. (On the accompanying map, I have indicated which early sites I think do—and which I think do not-meet stringent criteria.)

Even Dillehay's Chilean site of Monte Verde-which he, Dixon, and many others believe to be about 12,500 years old-can be challenged. (After these two books went to press, the magazine *Discovering Archaeology* carried an acerbic article by Stuart Fiedel criticizing the quality of the data.) As Fiedel, Dena Dincauze, Tom Lynch, and I have pointed out, this site presents many problems. Located in boggy terrain along a stream, Monte Verde has discontinuous stratigraphy, suggesting a mixing of strata. Few of the objects unearthed are indisputably tools, and there are no flakes from the manufacture of such tools. Three narrow points found at Monte Verde are tapered at both ends, a "bipoint" form common in established sites in Chile and Peru that have more recent dates—Holocene rather than Pleistocene.

The tools at Monte Verde cannot be firmly connected with the dates, which were obtained on the basis of bog material, not from incontrovertible artifacts or food plants. And the dates are too widely spaced—from about 14,000 to 12,000 years ago—to fit the brief occupation that Dillehay believes the site represents. Furthermore, the site contains possible carbon contaminants, such as bitumen, which are known to make materials dated by the carbon 14 method appear older than they are (two very early dates of more than 33,000 years ago are typical of those recorded for petroleum material such as bitumen). Human traces could be the result of intrusion by later peoples. The mastodons believed to have been killed and eaten could be mired fossil fauna, and the supposed remains of shelters could be snags from fallen trees—similar to natural deposits found elsewhere in the region.

For their part, scholars skeptical of the validity of pre-Clovis sites

typically fail to apply the same rigorous criteria to the Clovis sites they *do* accept. As a consequence, the age of Clovis, which many still claim is the ancestor to all other cultures in the New World, has been exaggerated. It is regularly put at 11,500 or sometimes even 12,000 years old, but no indisputably valid Clovis site has such early carbon 14 dates. (When carbon 14 results are that old, they turn out to be from sites that yield only isolated single dates, dates with a margin of error greater than 300 years, or dates based on carbon that has no certain connection with a human presence.) Even Dixon, despite his preClovis yearnings, perpetuates this exaggeration of Clovis's antiquity.

The earliest migrants used various resources and habitats; only some of them hunted big game.

The inconsistent treatment of dates has given the false impression of a rapid wave of colonization by groups descended from Clovis peoples and has drawn attention away from numerous valid sites that are contemporaneous with Clovis but very different culturally Most archaeologists ignore such sites because they do not have the cachet of being pre-Clovis. For now, though, their age and location provide the most reliable basis for an account of the migrations and ecological adaptations of the first Americans.

What, then, would be a more accurate picture? My conclusion is that the first people to venture into the eastern Bering Strait region, a bit before 12,000 years ago, may have been a group like the Nenana people, who were not specialized big-game hunters but rather foragers of small game, fish, fruits, and nuts. Instead of fluted spear-points they made triangular points that they probably used as knives. During the ensuing thousand years, their descendants penetrated

diverse ecological zones throughout the Americas. Clovis was only one of these descendant cultures and not, therefore, either the earliest in the Americas or a culture that set an adaptive pattern for the hemisphere. None of the other descendant cultures were characterized by specialized big-game hunting.

No one type of environment seems to have been colonized before others, and people did not create one single style of artifact or survive on one particular kind of resource. Most Clovis-age peoples in the far north lacked fluted points; they used microblade tools (small blades struck off a prepared core) to hunt and gather a variety of resources. Even the Clovis fluted point (with its shallow channel on one or both sides and its parallel edges), which spread widely in the interior continental United States, is conclusively associated with big-game hunting only in the high plains. In South America, by about 11,000 years ago, specialized maritime foragers had already settled the Pacific coast, guanaco hunters were living in the southern grasslands, and riverine tropical-forest foragers inhabited the eastern lowlands. The peoples of the far south used fishtail points with expanded stems, and the forest and coastal peoples used triangular points, often with tapered stems.

With their pre-Clovis emphasis, both Dillehay and Dixon miss the broad significance of these sites, and neither manages to sketch a coherent picture of colonization that fits the pattern of current data. Dixon argues that the earliest migrants followed a coastal route from the Bering Strait region southward to Tierra del Fuego, yet he cannot demonstrate that coastal sites were occupied any earlier than interior sites. As Ted Goebel and John Erlandson have pointed out, there are no securely dated maritime sites in North America as old as Clovis, and those in South America are the same age as interior sites, not older.

Dillehay believes that the first migrants in South America could have been pre-Clovis big-game hunters who arrived at least 15,000 years ago and used fishtail projectile points. However, he can identify no fishtail-point sites earlier than 11,000 years ago, and these are in the far south, not the north, as would be expected. And, as he admits, few early South American human sites include the bones of now-extinct Ice Age game animals. In addition, Dillehay distinguishes another South American tradition of foragers with only unifacial tools (made by flaking one side), but no such culture has been shown to exist. All the sites that have been adequately sampled and dated yield bifacial as well as unifacial tools.

Both authors try to make sense of the current heated debate about the biological origins of the first Americans, a debate with political and racial overtones. Some archaeologists argue that modern-day Native Americans are significantly different physically from the Paleoindians—and that Paleoindian sites are therefore not subject to the Native American Graves Protection and Repatriation Act (NAGPRA). They suggest that the very first New World peoples were of European origin and that modern-day Native Americans descend principally from later waves of migrants from Asia. The long and narrow prehistoric crania, such as that belonging to Kennewick Man (discovered in Washington State), are taken to be Caucasoid, while Solutrean tools from France are proposed as precursors of Clovis points. However, this cranial shape and the relevant tool traits are found in Asia as well. Citing studies of teeth, Dixon rightly points to maritime northeastern Asia rather than to Europe for the origin of Paleoindians. Dillehay is ambivalent, but gives some credence to claims of Australian or African affinities—such as for a woman's skull found at Lapa Vermelha, Brazil—but these claims are weak on both geographical and chronological grounds.

All modern groups differ significantly from their distant ancestors. With more precise studies, the cultural and biological links of living Native Americans to the Paleoindians are becoming clearer. Although some groups, such as the Umatilla in Washington State, want to prevent future research on Paleoindians, members of other groups, such as the Tlingit, welcome the new information about their predecessors. From my own experience with Paleoindian archaeology, I'd say that present-day Native Americans have much to gain, and nothing to fear, from continuing research.

Anna Curtenius Roosevelt is a professor of anthropology at the University of Illinois, Chicago, and the curator of archaeology at the Field Museum of Natural History.

Reprinted with permission from *Natural History*, July/August 2000, pp. 76-79. © 2000 by the American Museum of Natural History.

The Slow Birth of Agriculture

New methods show that around the world, people began cultivating some crops long before they embraced full-scale farming, and that crop cultivation and village life often did not go hand in hand

Heather Pringle

According to early Greek storytellers, humans owe the ability to cultivate crops to the sudden generosity of a goddess. Legend has it that in a burst of goodwill, Demeter, goddess of crops, bestowed wheat seeds on a trusted priest, who then crisscrossed Earth in a dragon-drawn chariot, sowing the dual blessings of agriculture and civilization.

For decades, archaeologists too regarded the birth of agriculture as a dramatic transformation, dubbed the Neolithic Revolution, that brought cities and civilization in its wake. In this scenario, farming was born after the end of the last Ice Age, around 10,000 years ago, when hunter-gatherers settled in small communities in the Fertile Crescent, a narrow band of land arcing across the Near East. They swiftly learned to produce their own food, sowing cereal grains and breeding better plants. Societies then raised more children to adulthood, enjoyed food surpluses, clustered in villages, and set off down the road to civilization. This novel way of life then diffused across the Old World.

But like many a good story, over time this tale has fallen beneath an onslaught of new data. By employing sensitive new techniques—from sifting through pollen cores to measuring minute shape changes in ancient cereal grains—researchers are building a new picture of agricultural origins. They are pushing back the dates of both plant domestication and animal husbandry around the world, and many now view the switch to an agrarian lifestyle as a long, complex evolution rather than a dramatic revolution.

The latest evidence suggests, for example, that hunter-gatherers in the Near East first cultivated rye fields as early as 13,000 years ago.[*] But for centuries thereafter, they continued to hunt wild game and gather an ever-decreasing range of wild plants, only becoming full-blown farmers living in populous villages by some 8500 B.C. And in some cases, villages appear long before intensive agriculture. "The transition from hunters and gatherers to agriculturalists is not a brief sort of thing," says Bruce Smith, an expert on agricultural origins at the Smithsonian Institution's National Museum of Natural History in Washington, D.C. "It's a long developmental process"—and one that did not necessarily go hand in hand with the emergence of settlements.

Similar stories are emerging in South America, Mesoamerica, North America, and China. Although cultivation may have been born first in the Near East, the latest evidence suggests that people on other continents began to domesticate the plants they lived with—squash on the tropical coast of Ecuador and rice along the marshy banks of the Yangtze in China, for example—as early as 10,000 to 11,000 years ago, thousands of years earlier than was thought and well before the first signs of farming villages in these regions. To many researchers, the timing suggests that worldwide environmental change—climate fluctuations at the end of the Ice Age—may well have prompted cultivation, although they are still pondering exactly how this climate change spurred people around the world to begin planting seeds and reaping their bounty.

CULTIVATING THE GREEN HELL

Perhaps the most dramatic and controversial new discoveries in ancient agriculture have emerged from the sultry lowland rainforests of Central and South America. These forests, with their humid climate, poor soils, and profusion of pests, were long considered an unlikely place for ancient peoples to embark upon the sweaty toil of farming, says Dolores Piperno, an archaeobotanist at the Smithsonian Tropical Research Institution in Balboa, Panama. "If people were going to have a hard time living in [these forests], how were they ever going to develop agriculture there?" she asks. And most research suggested that these forest dwellers were relative latecomers to agriculture, first cultivating crops between 4000 to 5000 years ago.

But tropical forests harbor the wild ancestors of such major food crops as manioc and yams. Back in the 1950s, American cultural geographer Carl Sauer speculated that these regions were early centers of plant domestication, but there was little evidence to support the idea, as the soft fruit and starchy root crops of these regions rapidly rot away in the acid soils. The better preserved evidence found in arid regions, such as seeds from grain crops in the Near East, captured the attention of most archaeologists.

In the early 1980s, however, Piperno and colleague Deborah Pearsall, an archaeobotanist from the University of Missouri, Columbia, began searching the sediments of rainforest sites in Panama and Ecuador for more enduring plant remnants. They focused on phytoliths, microscopic silica bodies that form when plants take up silica from groundwater. As the silica gradually fills plant cells, it assumes their distinctive size and shape. Piperno and Pearsall came up with ways to distinguish phytoliths from wild and domestic species—domestic plants, for example, have larger fruits and seeds, and hence larger cells and phytoliths. Then they set about identifying specimens from early archaeological sites.

This spring, after nearly 20 years of research, the team published its findings in a book entitled *The Origins of Agriculture in the Lowland Neotropics*. In one study, they measured squash phytoliths from a sequence of layers at Vegas Site 80, a coastal site bordering the tropical forest of southwestern Ecuador. From associated shell fragments as well as the carbon trapped inside the phytoliths themselves, they were able to carbon-date the microfossils. A sharp increase in phytolith size indicated that early Ecuadorians had domesticated squash, likely *Cucurbita moschata*, by 10,000 years ago—some 5000 years earlier than some archaeologists thought farming began there. Such timing suggests, she notes, that people in the region began growing their own plants after much local game went extinct at the end of the last Ice Age and tropical forest reclaimed the region. "I think that's the key to the initiation of agriculture here," says Piperno. If this find holds up, the Ecuador squash rivals the oldest accepted evidence of plant domestication in the Americas—the seeds of another squash, *C. pepo*, excavated from an arid Mexican cave and directly dated to 9975 years ago (*Science*, 9 May 1997, pp. 894 and 932).

The phytolith technique is also pushing back the first dates for maize cultivation in the Americas, says Piperno. Phytoliths taken from sediment samples from Aguadulce rock-shelter in central Panama by Piperno and her colleagues and carbon-dated both directly and by analyzing shells from the same strata imply that maize cultivation began there as early as 7700 years ago. That's not only more than 2500 years earlier than expected in a rainforest site, it's also 1500 years earlier than the first dates for maize cultivation anywhere in the

more arid parts of the Americas. Almost certainly, the oldest partially domesticated maize at the site came from somewhere else, because the wild ancestor of corn is known only from a narrow band of land in Mexico. But the squash data raise important questions, says Piperno, about where agriculture first emerged in the Americas. "Clearly tropical forest is in the ball game."

But the community is split over whether to accept the phytolith evidence. Some critics question the dating of the phytoliths themselves, saying that carbon from other sources could have become embedded in the cracks and crevices on the fossil surfaces, skewing the results. Others such as Gayle Fritz, an archaeobotanist at Washington University in St. Louis, point out that the shells and other objects used to support the dates may not be the same age as the phytoliths. "I would be as thrilled as anyone else to push the dates back," says Fritz, "but my advice now is that people should be looking at these as unbelievable."

However, proponents such as Mary Pohl, an archaeologist at Florida State University in Tallahassee, note that the Piperno team typically supports its claims with multiple lines of evidence, so that even if one set of dates is suspect, the body of work makes it clear that some domestication took place startlingly early in the rainforest. "The data seem irrefutable to my mind," she says.

If so, they overturn some basic assumptions about the relationship between village life and agriculture in the tropical forest. For years, says Piperno, researchers believed that the first farmers there lived in villages, like the well-studied Neolithic grain farmers of the Near East. "Because settled village life is just not seen in [this part of the] Americas until 5000 years ago, [researchers thought] that means food production was late too," says Piperno. "But it doesn't work." In her view, farming in the region came long before village life. For thousands of years, she says, "you had slash-and-burn agriculture instead of settled village agriculture."

TAMING WILD RICE

At the same time as early Americans may have been planting their first squash, hunter-gatherers some 16,000 kilometers east along the banks of the Yangtze River were beginning to cultivate wild rice, according to new studies by archaeobotanist

Zhijun Zhao of the Smithsonian Tropical Research Institution and colleagues. Rice, the most important food crop in the world, was long thought to have been cultivated first around 6500 years ago in southern Asia, where the climate is warm enough to support luxuriant stands of wild rice. But in the 1980s, ancient bits of charred rice turned up in a site along the banks of the middle Yangtze River, in the far northern edge of the range of wild rice today. Directly carbon-dated to 8000 years ago, these grains are the oldest known cultivated rice and suggest that the center of rice cultivation was actually farther north.

Now the dates have been pushed back even farther, revealing a long, gradual transition to agriculture, according to work in press in *Antiquity* by Zhao. He has analyzed a sequence of abundant rice phytoliths from a cave called Diaotonghuan in northern Jiangxi Province along the middle Yangtze, which was excavated by Richard MacNeish, research director at the Andover Foundation for Archaeological Research in Massachusetts, and Yan Wenming, a Peking University archaeologist in Beijing.

Radiocarbon dates for the site seemed to have been contaminated by groundwater, so Zhao constructed a relative chronology based on ceramic and stone artifacts of known styles and dates found with the phytoliths. In recent weeks, Zhao has further refined his *Antiquity* chronology as a result of a joint study with Piperno on paleoecological data from lake sediments in the region.

To trace the work of ancient cultivators at the site, he distinguished the phytoliths of wild and domesticated rice by measuring minute differences in the size of a particular type of cell in the seed covering. With this method, which Zhao pioneered with Pearsall, Piperno, and others at the University of Missouri, "we can get a 90% accuracy," he says.

By counting the proportions of wild and domesticated rice fossils, Zhao charted a gradual shift to agriculture. In a layer dated to at least 13,000 years ago, the phytoliths show that hunter-gatherers in the cave were dining on wild rice. But by 12,000 years ago, those meals abruptly ceased—Zhao suspects because the climate became colder and the wild grain, too tender for such conditions, vanished from this region. Studies of the Greenland ice cores have revealed a global cold spell called the Younger Dryas from about 13,000 to 11,500 years ago. Zhao's own studies of phytoliths and pollen in lake sediments from the region reveal that warmth-loving vegetation began retreating from this region around 12,000 years ago.

As the big chill waned, however, rice returned to the region. And people began dabbling in something new around 11,000 years ago—sowing, harvesting, and selectively breeding rice. In a zone at Diaotonghuan littered with sherds from a type of crude pottery found in three other published sites in the region and radiocarbon-dated to between 9000 and 13,000 years ago, Zhao found the first domesticated rice phytoliths—the oldest evidence of rice cultivation in the world. But these early Chinese cultivators were still hunting and gathering, says Zhao. "The cave at that time is full of animal bones—mainly deer and wild pig—and wild plants," he notes. Indeed, it was another 4000 years before domestic rice dominated wild rice to become the dietary staple, about 7000 years ago.

It makes sense that the transition to farming was slow and gradual and not the rapid switch that had been pictured, says MacNeish. "Once you learn to plant the stuff, you must learn to get a surplus and to get the best hybrid to rebreed this thing you're planting," he notes. "And when this begins to happen, then very gradually your population begins going up. You plant a little bit more and a little bit more." At some point, he concludes, the hunter-gatherers at sites like Diaotonghuan were unable to gather enough wild food to support their burgeoning numbers and so had little choice but to embrace farming in earnest.

THE CRADLE OF CIVILIZATION

In the Near East, archaeologists have been studying early agriculture for decades, and it was here that the idea of the Neolithic Revolution was born. Yet even here, it seems there was a long and winding transition to agriculture. And although settled village life appeared early in this region, its precise connection to farming is still obscure.

The latest findings come from Abu Hureyra, a settlement east of Aleppo, Syria, where the inhabitants were at least semisedentary, occupying the site from at least early spring to late autumn, judging from the harvest times of more than 150 plant species identified there to date. Among the plant remains are seeds of cultivated rye, distinguished from wild grains by their plumpness and much larger size.

University College London archaeobotanists Gordon Hillman and Susan Colledge have now dated one of those seeds to some 13,000 years ago, according to unpublished work they presented at a major international workshop in September. If the date is confirmed, this rye will be the oldest domesticated cereal grain in the world.

These dates are nearly a millennium earlier than previous evidence for plant domestication. And the rye is not even the first sign of cultivation at the Abu Hureyra site: Just before the appearance of this domestic grain, the team found a dramatic rise in seed remains from plants that typically grow among crops as weeds. All this occurs some 2500 years before the most widely accepted dates for full-scale agriculture and populous villages in the Near East. Although the semisedentism of the inhabitants fits with earlier ideas, the long time span contradicts ideas of a rapid agricultural "revolution."

The early date for plant domestication in the Near East is not entirely unexpected, says Ofer Bar-Yosef of Harvard University. For example, inhabitants of Ohallo II in what is now Israel had made wild cereal seeds a major part of their diets as early as 17,000 B.C., according to published work by Mordechai Kislev, an archaeobotanist at Bar Ilan University in Ramat-Gan, Israel. Moreover, as close observers of nature, these early foragers were almost certain to have noticed that a seed sown in the ground eventually yielded a plant with yet more seeds. "These people knew their fauna and flora very well," says Bar-Yosef, "and they probably played with planting plants long before they really switched into agriculture."

Just what spurred hunter-gatherers to begin regularly sowing seeds and cultivating fields, however, remains unclear. For several years, many Near Eastern experts have favored the theory that climate change associated with the Younger Dryas was the likely trigger. Bar-Yosef, for example, suggests that inhabitants of the Fertile Crescent first planted cereal fields in order to boost supplies of grain when the Younger Dryas cut drastically into wild harvests. And at Abu Hureyra, Hillman thinks that the drought accompanying the Younger Dryas was a key factor. Before the jump in weeds and the appearance of domestic rye, the inhabitants relied on wild foods as starch staples. Over time, they turned to more and more drought-resistant plants—and even these dwindled in abundance. So "progressive desiccation could

indeed have been the impetus for starch cultivation," says Hillman.

But new dates for the cold spell in the Near East paint a more complex view. At the Netherlands workshop, Uri Baruch, a palynologist at the Israel Antiquities Authority in Jerusalem, and Syze Bottema, a palynologist at the Groningen Institute of Archeology in the Netherlands, announced that they had redated a crucial pollen core at Lake Hula in northern Israel. Their original published estimate put a retreat in the region's deciduous oak forest—due to cool, dry conditions believed to be the local manifestation of the Younger Dryas—starting about 13,500 years ago. But after correcting for contamination by old carbon dissolved in the lake water, they found that the cold spell in the Near East was a bit later, starting around 13,000 years ago and ending around 11,500 years ago.

These dates suggest that farmers of Abu Hureyra may have begun cultivating rye before the Younger Dryas set in, at the very end of the warm, moist interval that preceded it. "The domesticated rye dates and the pollen core don't match up so well at this time," says Mark Blumler, a geographer at the State University of New York, Binghamton.

Moreover, others point out that the clearest evidence for the domestication of grains such as wheat and barley in the Near East comes around 10,500 years ago, after the Younger Dryas had waned and the climate had improved again. By then, says George Willcox, an archaeobotanist at the Institut de Prehistoire Orientale in St-Paul-le-Jeune, France, other factors could have contributed to the transition. Hunter-gatherers in the region, for example, had settled year-round in small villages between 12,300 and 10,500 years ago. There, he says, rising human populations and over-exploitation of wild foods could have driven people to take up farming. "Because people at this time appear to be living in one place," says Willcox, "they could use up all the resources in a particular area."

Putting the evidence from around the world together, a new picture of the origins of agriculture begins to emerge. In the Near East, some villages were born before agriculture and may even have forced its adoption in some cases. But elsewhere—China, North America, and Mesoamerica—plants were cultivated and domesticated by nomadic hunter-gatherers, perhaps to increase their yield during the dramatic climate shifts that accompanied the final phase of the last Ice Age. Either way, it no longer makes sense to suppose a strong causal link between farming and settled village life, Piperno says.

Indeed, in many regions, settled agriculturalists emerged only centuries or millennia after cultivation, if at all. Many ancient peoples simply straddled the middle ground between foraging and farming, creating economies that blended both. "For so long, we've put everybody in black boxes" as farmers or hunter-gatherers, notes Joanna Casey, an archaeologist at the University of South Carolina, Columbia, and a specialist in agricultural origins in western Africa. But mixed cultivation and foraging is not necessarily a step "on the way" to full-scale farming—it was a long-term lifestyle for many groups. "These societies in the middle ground are certainly not failures," says the Smithsonian's Smith. "They are not societies that stum-

bled or stuttered or got frozen developmentally. They're societies that found an excellent long-term solution to their environmental challenges."

Eventually, for reasons still unclear, many of the early domesticators did become true agriculturalists—by 10,500 years ago in the Near East, 7000 years ago in China, and later in the Americas and Africa. And during this transition, human populations did indeed soar, and hamlets became villages. Archaeological sites in the intensively studied Fertile Crescent, for example, increased more than 10-fold in size, from 0.2 hectares to 2.0 to 3.0 hectares, during this period of transition. The combination of settlement and reliable food probably brought about "a longer period of fertility for the now better fed

women," says Bar-Yosef, setting the stage for cities and civilization.

So it seems that the ancient Greek legends got it half right when they told how seeds fell throughout the world, sparking independent centers of domestication on many continents. But cities and civilization did not necessarily arrive at the same time as the seeds. Demeter's priest apparently gave out only one blessing at a time.

---

*All dates are calendar years.

†The Transition From Foraging to Farming in Southwest Asia, Groningen, the Netherlands, 7–11 September.

Heather Pringle is a science writer in Vancouver, British Columbia.

Archaeologists Rediscover Cannibals

At digs around the world, researchers have unearthed strong new evidence that people ate their own kind from the early days of human evolution through recent prehistory

When Arizona State University bio-archaeologist Christy G. Turner II first looked at the jumbled heap of bones from 30 humans in Arizona in 1967, he was convinced that he was looking at the remains of a feast. The bones of these ancient American Indians had cut marks and burns, just like animal bones that had been roasted and stripped of their flesh. "It just struck me that here was a pile of food refuse," says Turner, who proposed in *American Antiquity* in 1970 that these people from Polacca Wash, Arizona, had been the victims of cannibalism.

But his paper was met with "total disbelief," says Turner. "In the 1960s, the new paradigm about Indians was that they were all peaceful and happy. So, to find something like this was the antithesis of the new way we were supposed to be thinking about Indians"—particularly the Anasazi, thought to be the ancestors of living Pueblo Indians. Not only did Turner's proposal fly in the face of conventional wisdom about the Anasazi culture, but it was also at odds with an emerging consensus that earlier claims of cannibalism in the fossil record rested on shaky evidence. Where earlier generations of archaeologists had seen the remains of cannibalistic feasts, current researchers saw bones scarred by ancient burial practices, war, weathering, or scavenging animals.

To Turner, however, the bones from Polacca Wash told a more disturbing tale, and so he set about studying every prehistoric skeleton he could find in the Southwest and Mexico to see if it was an isolated event. Now, 30 years and 15,000 skeletons later, Turner is putting the final

touches on a 1500-page book to be published next year by the University of Utah press in which he says, "Cannibalism was practiced intensively for almost four centuries" in the Four Corners region. The evidence is so strong that Turner says "I would bet a year of my salary on it."

He isn't the only one now betting on cannibalism in prehistory. In the past decade, Turner and other bioarchaeologists have put together a set of clear-cut criteria for distinguishing the marks of cannibalism from other kinds of scars. "The analytical rigor has increased across the board," says paleoanthropologist Tim D. White of the University of California, Berkeley. Armed with the new criteria, archaeologists are finding what they say are strong signs of cannibalism throughout the fossil record. This summer, archaeologists are excavating several sites in Europe where the practice may have occurred among our ancestors, perhaps as early as 800,000 years ago. More recently, our brawny cousins, the Neandertals, may have eaten each other. And this behavior wasn't limited to the distant past—strong new evidence suggests that in addition to the Anasazi, the Aztecs of Mexico and the people of Fiji also ate their own kind in the past 2500 years.

These claims imply a disturbing new view of human history, say Turner and others. Although cannibalism is still relatively rare in the fossil record, it is frequent enough to imply that extreme hunger was not the only driving force. Instead of being an aberration, practiced only by a few prehistoric Donner Parties, killing people for food may have been

standard human behavior—a means of social control, Turner suspects, or a mob response to stress, or a form of infanticide to thin the ranks of neighboring populations.

Not surprisingly, some find these claims hard to stomach: "These people haven't explored all the alternatives," says archaeologist Paul Bahn, author of the *Cambridge Encyclopedia* entry on cannibalism. "There's no question, for example, that all kinds of weird stuff is done to human remains in mortuary practice"—and in warfare. But even the most prominent skeptic of earlier claims of cannibalism, cultural anthropologist William Arens of the State University of New York, Stony Brook, now admits the case is stronger: "I think the procedures are sounder, and there is more evidence for cannibalism than before."

White learned how weak most earlier scholarship on cannibalism was in 1981, when he first came across what he thought might be a relic of the practice—a massive skull of an early human ancestor from a site called Bodo in Ethiopia. When he got his first look at this 600,000-year-old skull on a museum table, White noticed that it had a series of fine, deep cut marks on its cheekbone and inside its eye socket, as if it had been defleshed. To confirm his suspicions, White wanted to compare the marks with a "type collection" for cannibalism—a carefully studied assemblage of bones showing how the signature of cannibalism differs from damage by animal gnawing, trampling, or excavation.

"We were naïve at the time," says White, who was working with archaeol-

PHOTOS BY: C. TURNER/ARIZONA STATE UNIVERSITY

Cannibals house? The Peasco Blanco great house at Chaco Canyon, New Mexico, where some bones bear cut marks (upper left); others were smashed, perhaps to extract marrow.

ogist Nicholas Toth of Indiana University in Bloomington. They learned that although the anthropological literature was full of fantastic tales of cannibalistic feasts among early humans at Zhoukoudian in China, Krapina cave in Croatia, and elsewhere, the evidence was weak—or lost.

Indeed, the weakness of the evidence had already opened the way to a backlash, which was led by Arens. He had deconstructed the fossil and historical record for cannibalism in a book called *The Man-Eating Myth: Anthropology and Anthropophagy* (Oxford, 1979). Except for extremely rare cases of starvation or insanity, Arens said, none of the accounts of cannibalism stood up to scrutiny—not even claims that it took place among living tribes in Papua New Guinea (including the Fore, where cannibalism is thought to explain the spread of the degenerative brain disease kuru). There were no reliable eye witnesses for claims of cannibalism, and the archaeological evidence was circumstantial. "I

didn't deny the existence of cannibalism," he now says, "but I found that there was no good evidence for it. It was bad science."

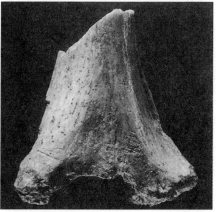

T . D. WHITE/BERKELEY

Unkind cuts. A Neandertal bone from Vindija Cave, Croatia.

Physical anthropologists contributed to the backlash when they raised doubts about what little archaeological evidence there was (*Science,* 20 June 1986, p.

1479). Mary Russell, then at Case Western Reserve University in Cleveland, argued, for example, that cut marks on the bones of 20 Neandertals at Krapina Cave could have been left by Neandertal morticians who were cleaning the bones for secondary burial, and the bones would have been smashed when the roof caved in, for example. In his 1992 review in the *Cambridge Encyclopedia,* Bahn concluded that cannibalism's "very existence in prehistory is hard to swallow."

RISING FROM THE ASHES

But even as some anthropologists gave the ax to Krapina and other notorious cases, a new, more rigorous case for cannibalism in prehistory was emerging, starting in the American Southwest. Turner and his late wife, Jacqueline Turner, had been systematically studying tray after tray of prehistoric bones in museums and private collections in the United States and Mexico. They had identified a pattern of bone processing in several hundred specimens that showed little respect for the dead. "There's no known mortuary practice in the Southwest where the body is dismembered, the head is roasted and dumped into a pit unceremoniously, and other pieces get left all over the floor," says Turner, describing part of the pattern.

White, meanwhile, was identifying other telltale signs. To fill the gap he discovered when he looked for specimens to compare with the Bodo skull, he decided to study in depth one of the bone assemblages the Turners and others had cited. He chose Mancos, a small Anasazi pueblo on the Colorado Plateau from A.D. 1150, where archaeologists had recovered the scattered and broken remains of at least 29 individuals. The project evolved into a landmark book, *Prehistoric Cannibalism at Mancos* (Princeton, 1992). While White still doesn't know why the Bodo skull was defleshed—"it's a black box," he says—he extended the blueprint for identifying cannibalism.

In his book, White describes how he painstakingly sifted through 2106 bone fragments, often using an electron microscope to identify cut marks, burn traces, percussion and anvil damage, disarticulations, and breakages. He reviewed how to distinguish marks left by butchering from those left by animal gnawing, trampling, or other wear and tear. He also proposed a new category of bone damage, which he called "pot polish"—shiny abrasions on bone tips that come from being stirred in pots (an idea he tested by stirring deer bones in a replica of an Anasazi pot). And he outlined how to compare the remains of suspected victims with those of ordinary game animals at other sites to see if they were processed the same way.

When he applied these criteria to the Mancos remains, he concluded that they were the leavings of a feast in which 17 adults and 12 children had their heads cut off, roasted, and broken open on rock anvils. Their long bones were broken—he believes for marrow—and their vertebral bodies were missing, perhaps crushed and boiled for oil. Finally, their bones were dumped, like animal bones.

In their forthcoming book, the Turners describe a remarkably similar pattern

of bone processing in 300 individuals from 40 different bone assemblages in the Four Corners area of the Southwest, dating from A.D. 900 to A.D. 1700. The strongest case, he says, comes from bones unearthed at the Peñasco Blanco great house at Chaco Canyon in New Mexico, which was the highest center of the Anasazi culture and, he argues, the home of cannibals who terrorized victims within 100 miles of Chaco Canyon, where most of the traumatized bones have been excavated. "Whatever drove the Anasazi to eat people, it happened at Chaco," says Turner.

The case for cannibalism among the Anasazi that Turner and White have put together hasn't swayed all the critics. "These folks have a nice package, but I don't think it proves cannibalism," says Museum of New Mexico archaeologist Peter Bullock. "It's still just a theory."

But even critics like Bullock acknowledge that Turner and White's studies, along with work by the University of Colorado, Boulder's, Paolo Villa and colleagues at another recent site, Fontbrégoua Cave in southeastern France (*Science*, 25 July 1986, p. 431), have raised the standards for how to investigate a case of cannibalism. In fact, White's book has become the unofficial guidebook for the field, says physical anthropologist Carmen Pijoan at the Museum of Anthropology in Mexico City, who has done a systematic review of sites in Mexico where human bones were defleshed. In a forthcoming book chapter, she singles out three sites where she applied diagnostic criteria outlined by Turner, White, and Villa to bones from Aztec and other early cultures and concludes that all "three sites, spread over 2000 years of Mexican prehistory, show a pattern of violence, cannibalism, and sacrifice through time."

White's book "is my bible," agrees paleontologist Yolanda Fernandez-Jalvo of the Museum of Natural History in Madrid, who is analyzing bones that may be the oldest example of cannibalism in the fossil record—the remains of at least six individuals who died 800,000 years ago in an ancient cave at Atapuerca in northern Spain.

AGE-OLD PRACTICES

The Spanish fossils have caused considerable excitement because they may represent a new species of human ancestor (*Science,* 30 May, pp. 1331 and 1392). But they also show a pattern familiar from the more recent sites: The bones are highly fragmented and are scored with cut marks, which Fernandez-Jalvo thinks were made when the bodies were decapitated and the bones defleshed. A large femur was also smashed open, perhaps for marrow, says Fernandez-Jalvo, and the whole assemblage had been dumped, like garbage. The treatment was no different from that accorded animal bones at the site. The pattern, says Peter Andrews, a paleoanthropologist at The Natural History Museum, London, is "pretty strong evidence for cannibalism, as opposed to ritual defleshing." He and others note, however, that the small number of individuals at the site and the absence of other sites of similar antiquity to which the bones could be compared leave room for doubt.

A stronger case is emerging at Neandertal sites in Europe, 45,000 to more than 130,000 years old. The new criteria for recognizing cannibalism have not completely vindicated the earlier claims about Krapina Cave, partly because few animal bones are left from the excavation of the site in 1899 to compare with the Neandertal remains. But nearby Vindija Cave, excavated in the 1970s, did yield both animal and human remains. When White and Toth examined the bones recently, they found that both sets showed cut marks, breakage, and disarticulation, and had been dumped on the cave floor. It's the same pattern seen at Krapina, and remarkably similar to that at Mancos, says White, who will publish his conclusions in a forthcoming book with Toth. Marseilles prehistorian Alban DeFleur is finding that Neandertals may also have feasted on their kind in the Moula-Guercy Cave in the Ardeche region of France, where animal and Neandertal bones show similar processing. Taken together, says White, "the evidence from Krapina, Vindija, and Moula is strong."

Not everyone is convinced, however. "White does terrific analysis, but he hasn't proved this is cannibalism," says Bahn. "Frankly, I don't see how he can unless you find a piece of human gut [with human bone or tissue in it]." No matter how close the resemblance to butchered animals, he says, the cut marks and other bone processing could still be the result of mortuary practices. Bullock adds that warfare, not cannibalism, could explain the damage to the bones.

White, however, says such criticism resembles President Clinton's famous claim about marijuana: "Some [although not all] of the Anasazi and Neandertals processed their colleagues. They skinned them, roasted them, cut their muscles off, severed their joints, broke their long bones on anvils with hammerstones, crushed their spongy bones, and put the pieces into pots." Borrowing a line from a review of his book, White says: "To say they didn't eat them is the archaeological equivalent of saying Clinton lit up and didn't inhale."

White's graduate student David De-Gusta adds that he has compared human bones at burial sites in Fiji and at a nearby trash midden from the last 2000 years. The intentionally buried bones were less fragmentary and had no bite marks, burns, percussion pits, or other signs of food processing. The human bones in the trash midden, however, were processed like those of pigs. "This site really challenges the claim that these assemblages of bones are the result of mortuary ritual," says DeGusta.

After 30 years of research, Turner says it is a modern bias to insist that cannibalism isn't part of human nature. Many other species eat their own, and our ancestors may have had their own "good" reasons—whether to terrorize subject peoples, limit their neighbors' offspring, or for religious or medicinal purposes. "Today, the only people who eat other people outside of starving are the crazies," says Turner. "We're dealing with a world view that says this is bad and always has been bad.... But in the past, that view wasn't necessarily the group view. Cannibalism could have been an adaptive strategy. It has to be entertained."

—Ann Gibbons

Reprinted with permission from *Science,* August 1, 1997, pp. 635-637. © 1997 by the American Association for the Advancement of Science.

New Women of the Ice Age

Forget about hapless mates being dragged around by macho mammoth killers. The women of Ice Age Europe, it appears, were not mere cavewives but priestly leaders, clever inventors, and mighty hunters.

By Heather Pringle

THE BLACK VENUS OF DOLNÍ VESTONICE, A SMALL, splintered figurine sensuously fashioned from clay, is an envoy from a forgotten world. It is all soft curves, with breasts like giant pillows beneath a masked face. At nearly 26,000 years old, it ranks among the oldest known portrayals of women, and to generations of researchers, it has served as a powerful—if enigmatic—clue to the sexual politics of the Ice Age.

Excavators unearthed the Black Venus near the Czech village of Dolní Vestonice in 1924, on a hillside among charred, fractured mammoth bones and stone tools. (Despite its nickname, the Black Venus is actually reddish—it owes its name to the ash that covered it when it was found.) Since the mid-nineteenth century, researchers had discovered more than a dozen similar statuettes in caves and open-air sites from France to Russia. All were cradled in layers of earth littered with stone and bone weaponry, ivory jewelry, and the remains of extinct Ice Age animals. All were depicted naked or nearly so. Collectively, they came to be known as Venus figurines, after another ancient bare-breasted statue, the Venus de Milo. Guided at least in part by prevailing sexual stereotypes, experts interpreted the meaning of the figurines freely. The Ice Age camps that spawned this art, they concluded, were once the domain of hardworking male hunters and secluded, pampered women who spent their days in idleness like the harem slaves so popular in nineteenth-century art.

Over the next six decades, Czech archeologists expanded the excavations at Dolní Vestonice, painstakingly combing the site square meter by square meter. By the 1990s they had unearthed thousands of bone, stone, and clay artifacts and had wrested 19 radiocarbon dates from wood charcoal that sprinkled camp floors. And they had shaded and refined their portrait of Ice Age life. Between 29,000 and 25,000 years ago, they concluded, wandering bands had passed the cold months of the year repeatedly at Dolní Vestonice. Armed with short-range spears, the men appeared to have been specialists in hunting tusk-wielding mammoths and other big game, hauling home great mountains

of meat to feed their dependent mates and children. At night men feasted on mammoth steaks, fed their fires with mammoth bone, and fueled their sexual fantasies with tiny figurines of women carved from mammoth ivory and fired from clay. It was the ultimate man's world.

Or was it? Over the past few months, a small team of American archeologists has raised some serious doubts. Amassing critical and previously overlooked evidence from Dolní Vestonice and the neighboring site of Pavlov, Olga Soffer, James Adovasio, and David Hyland now propose that human survival there had little to do with manly men hurling spears at big-game animals. Instead, observes Soffer, one of the world's leading authorities on Ice Age hunters and gatherers and an archeologist at the University of Illinois in Champaign-Urbana, it depended largely on women, plants, and a technique of hunting previously invisible in the archeological evidence—net hunting. "This is not the image we've always had of Upper Paleolithic macho guys out killing animals up close and personal," Soffer explains. "Net hunting is communal, and it involves the labor of children and women. And this has lots of implications."

MANY OF THESE IMPLICATIONS MAKE HER CONservative colleagues cringe because they raise serious questions about the focus of previous studies. European archeologists have long concentrated on analyzing broken stone tools and butchered big-game bones, the most plentiful and best preserved relics of the Upper Paleolithic era (which stretched from 40,000 to 12,000 years ago). From these analyses, researchers have developed theories about how these societies once hunted and gathered food. Most researchers ruled out the possibility of women hunters for biological reasons. Adult females, they reasoned, had to devote themselves to breast-feeding and tending infants. "Human babies have always been immature and dependent," says Soffer. "If women are the people who are always involved with biological reproduction and the rearing of the young, then that is going to constrain their behavior. They have to provision that child. For fathers, provisioning is optional."

To test theories about Upper Paleolithic life, researchers looked to ethnography, the scientific description of modern and historical cultural groups. While the lives of modern hunters do not exactly duplicate those of ancient hunters, they supply valuable clues to universal human behavior. "Modern ethnography cannot be used to clone the past," says Soffer. "But people have always had to solve problems. Nature and social relationships present problems to people. We use ethnography to look for theoretical insights into human behavior, test them with ethnography, and if they work, assume that they represent a universal feature of human behavior."

But when researchers began turning to ethnographic descriptions of hunting societies, they unknowingly relied on a very incomplete literature. Assuming that women in surviving hunting societies were homebodies who simply tended hearths and suckled children, most early male anthropologists spent their time with male informants. Their published ethnographies brim with descriptions of males making spears and harpoons and heaving these weapons at reindeer, walruses, and whales. Seldom do they mention the activities of women. Ethnography, it seemed, supported theories of ancient male big-game hunters. "When they talked about primitive man, it was always 'he,'" says Soffer. "The 'she' was missing."

Recent anthropological research has revealed just how much Soffer's colleagues overlooked. By observing women in the few remaining hunter-gatherer societies and by combing historical accounts of tribal groups more thoroughly, anthropologists have come to realize how critical the female half of the population has always been to survival. Women and children have set snares, laid spring traps, sighted game and participated in animal drives and surrounds—forms of hunting that endangered neither young mothers nor their offspring. They dug starchy roots and collected other plant carbohydrates essential to survival. They even hunted, on occasion, with the projectile points traditionally deemed men's weapons. "I found references to Inuit women carrying bows and arrows, especially the blunt arrows that were used for hunting birds," says Linda Owen, an archeologist at the University of Tübingen in Germany.

The revelations triggered a volley of new research. In North America, Soffer and her team have found tantalizing evidence of the hunting gear often favored by women in historical societies. In Europe, archeobotanists are analyzing Upper Paleolithic hearths for evidence of plant remains probably gathered by women and children, while lithics specialists are poring over stone tools to detect new clues to their uses. And the results are gradually reshaping our understanding of Ice Age society. The famous Venus figurines, say archeologists of the new school, were never intended as male pornography: instead they may have played a key part in Upper Paleolithic rituals that centered on women. And such findings, pointing toward a more important role for Paleolithic women than had previously been assumed, are giving many researchers pause.

Like many of her colleagues, Soffer clearly relishes the emerging picture of Upper Paleolithic life. "I think life back then was a hell of a lot more egalitarian than it was with your later peasant societies," she says. "Of course the Paleolithic women were pulling their own weight." After sifting through Ice Age research for nearly two decades, Soffer brings a new critical approach to the notion—flattering to so many of her male colleagues—of mighty male mammoth hunters. "Very few archeologists are hunters," she notes, so it never occurred to most of them to look into the mechanics of hunting dangerous tusked animals. They just accepted the ideas they'd inherited from past work.

But the details of hunting bothered Soffer. Before the fifth century B.C., no tribal hunters in Asia or Africa had ever dared make their living from slaying elephants; the great beasts were simply too menacing. With the advent of the Iron Age in Africa, the situation changed. New weapons allowed Africans to hunt elephants and trade their ivory with Greeks and Romans. A decade ago, keen to understand how prehistoric bands had slaughtered similar mammoths, Soffer began studying Upper Paleolithic sites on the Russian and Eastern European plains. To her surprise, the famous mammoth bone beds were strewn with cumbersome body parts, such as 220-pound skulls, that sensible hunters would generally abandon. Moreover, the bones exhibited widely differing degrees of weathering, as if they had sat on the ground for varying lengths of time. To Soffer, it looked suspiciously as if Upper Paleolithic hunters had simply camped next to places where the pachyderms had perished naturally—such as water holes or salt licks—and mined the bones for raw materials.

"If one of these Upper Paleolithic guys killed a mammoth, and occasionally they did, they probably didn't stop talking about it for ten years."

Soffer began analyzing data researchers had gathered describing the sex and age ratios of mammoths excavated from four Upper Paleolithic sites. She found many juveniles, a smaller number of adult females, and hardly any males. The distribution mirrored the death pattern other researchers had observed at African water holes, where the weakest animals perished closest to the water and the strongest farther off. "Imagine the worst time of year in Africa, which is the drought season," explains Soffer. "There is no water, and elephants need an enormous amount. The ones in the worst shape—your weakest, your infirm, your young—are going to be tethered to that water before they die. They are in such horrendous shape, they don't have any extra energy to go anywhere. The ones in better shape would wander off slight distances and then keel over farther away. You've got basket cases and you've got ones that can walk 20 feet."

To Soffer, the implications of this study were clear. Upper Paleolithic bands had pitched their camps next to critical resources such as ancient salt licks or water holes. There the men spent more time scavenging bones and ivory from mammoth carcasses then they did risking life and limb by attacking 6,600-pound pachyderms with short-range spears. "If one of these

Upper Paleolithic guys killed a mammoth, and occasionally they did," concedes Soffer dryly, "they probably didn't stop talking about it for ten years."

But if Upper Paleolithic families weren't often tucking into mammoth steaks, what were they hunting and how? Soffer found the first unlikely clue in 1991, while sifting through hundreds of tiny clay fragments recovered from the Upper Paleolithic site of Pavlov, which lies just a short walk from Dolní Vestonice. Under a magnifying lens, Soffer noticed something strange on a few of the fragments: a series of parallel lines impressed on their surfaces. What could have left such a regular pattern? Puzzled, Soffer photographed the pieces, all of which had been unearthed from a zone sprinkled with wood charcoal that was radiocarbon-dated at between 27,000 and 25,000 years ago.

W HEN SHE RETURNED HOME, SOFFER HAD THE film developed. And one night on an impulse, she put on a slide show for a visiting colleague, Jim Adovasio. "We'd run out of cable films," she jokes. Staring at the images projected on Soffer's refrigerator, Adovasio, an archeologist at Mercyhurst College in Pennsylvania and an expert on ancient fiber technology, immediately recognized the impressions of plant fibers. On a few, he could actually discern a pattern of interlacing fibers—weaving.

Without a doubt, he said, he and Soffer were gazing at textiles or basketry. They were the oldest—by nearly 7,000 years—ever found. Just how these pieces of weaving got impressed in clay, he couldn't say. "It may be that a lot of these [materials] were lying around on clay floors," he notes. "When the houses burned, the walked-in images were subsequently left in the clay floors."

Soffer and Adovasio quickly made arrangements to fly back to the Czech Republic. At the Dolní Vestonice branch of the Institute of Archeology, Soffer sorted through nearly 8,400 fired clay pieces, weeding out the rejects. Adovasio made positive clay casts of 90. Back in Pennsylvania, he and his Mercyhurst colleague David Hyland peered at the casts under a zoom stereomicroscope, measuring warps and wefts. Forty-three revealed impressions of basketry and textiles. Some of the latter were as finely woven as a modern linen tablecloth. But as Hyland stared at four of the samples, he noted something potentially more fascinating: impressions of cordage bearing weaver's knots, a technique that joins two lengths of cord and that is commonly used for making nets of secure mesh. It looked like a tiny shred of a net bag, or perhaps a hunting net. Fascinated, Soffer expanded the study. She spent six weeks at the Moravian Museum in Brno, sifting through the remainder of the collections from Dolní Vestonice. Last fall, Adovasio spied the telltale impression of Ice Age mesh on one of the new casts.

The mesh, measuring two inches across, is far too delicate for hunting deer or other large prey. But hunters at Dolní Vestonice could have set nets of this size to capture hefty Ice Age hares, each carrying some six pounds of meat, and other fur-bearers such as arctic fox and red fox. As it turns out, the bones of hares and foxes litter camp floors at Dolní Vestonice and

Pavlov. Indeed, this small game accounts for 46 percent of the individual animals recovered at Pavlov. Soffer, moreover, doesn't rule out the possibility of turning up bits of even larger nets. Accomplished weavers in North America once knotted mesh with which they captured 1,000-pound elk and 300-pound bighorn sheep. "In fact, when game officials have to move sheep out west, it's by nets," she adds. "You throw nets on them and they just lie down. It's a very safe way of hunting."

Illustration by Ron Miller

NETS MADE ICE AGE HUNTING safe enough for entire communities to participate, and they captured everything from hares and foxes to deer and sheep.

In many historical societies, she observes, women played a key part in net hunting since the technique did not call for brute strength nor did it place young mothers in physical peril. Among Australian aborigines, for example, women as well as men knotted the mesh, laboring for as much as two or three years on a fine net. Among native North American groups, they helped lay out their handiwork on poles across a valley floor. Then the entire camp joined forces as beaters. Fanning out across the valley, men, women, and children alike shouted and screamed, flushing out game and driving it in the direction of the net. "Everybody and their mother could participate," says Soffer. "Some people were beating, others were screaming or holding the net. And once you got the net on these animals, they were immobilized. You didn't need brute force. You could club them, hit them any old way."

People seldom returned home empty-handed. Researchers living among the net-hunting Mbuti in the forests of Congo report that they capture game every time they lay out their woven traps, scooping up 50 percent of the animals encountered. "Nets are a far more valued item in their panoply of food-producing things than bows and arrows are," says Adovasio. So lethal are these traps that the Mbuti generally rack up more meat than they can consume, trading the surplus with neighbors. Other net hunters traditionally smoked or dried their catch and stored it for leaner times. Or they polished it off immediately in large ceremonial feasts. The hunters of Dolní Vestonice and Pavlov, says Soffer, probably feasted during ancient rituals. Archeologists unearthed no evidence of food storage pits at either site. But there is much evidence of ceremony. At Dolní Vestonice, for example, many clay figurines appear to have been ritually destroyed in secluded parts of the site.

Soffer doubts that the inhabitants of Dolní Vestonice and Pavlov were the only net makers in Ice Age Europe. Camps stretching from Germany to Russia are littered with a notable abundance of small-game bones, from hares to birds like ptarmigan. And at least some of their inhabitants whittled bone tools that look much like the awls and net spacers favored by historical net makers. Such findings, agree Soffer and Adovasio, reveal just how shaky the most widely accepted reconstructions of Upper Paleolithic life are. "These terribly stilted interpretations," says Adovasio, "with men hunting big animals all the time and the poor females waiting at home for these guys to bring home the bacon—what crap."

Illustration by Ron Miller
ONCE ANIMALS were caught in the nets, hunters could beat them to death with whatever was handy.

In her home outside Munich, Linda Owen finds other faults with this traditional image. Owen, an American born and raised, specializes in the microscopic analysis of stone tools. In her years of work, she often noticed that many of the tools made by hunters who roamed Europe near the end of the Upper Paleolithic era, some 18,000 to 12,000 years ago, resembled pounding stones and other gear for harvesting and processing plants. Were women and children gathering and storing wild plant foods?

Most of her colleagues saw little value in pursuing the question. Indeed, some German archeologists contended that 90 percent of the human diet during the Upper Paleolithic era came from meat. But as Owen began reading nutritional studies, she saw that heavy meat consumption would spell death. To stoke the body's cellular engines, human beings require energy from protein, fat, or carbohydrates. Of these, protein is the least efficient. To burn it, the body must boost its metabolic rate by 10 percent, straining the liver's ability to absorb oxygen. Unlike carnivorous animals, whose digestive and metabolic systems are well adapted to a meat-only diet, humans who consume more than half their calories as lean meat will die from protein poisoning. In Upper Paleolithic times, hunters undoubtedly tried to round out their diets with fat from wild game. But in winter, spring, and early summer, the meat would have been very lean. So how did humans survive?

Owen began sifting for clues through anthropological and historical accounts from subarctic and arctic North America. These environments, she reasoned, are similar to that of Ice Age Europe and pose similar challenges to their inhabitants. Even in the far north, Inuit societies harvested berries for winter storage and gathered other plants for medicines and for fibers. To see if any of the flora that thrived in Upper Paleolithic Europe could be put to similar uses, Owen drew up a list of plants economically important to people living in cold-climate regions of North America and Europe and compared it with a list of species that botanists had identified from pollen trapped in Ice Age sediment cores from southern Germany. Nearly 70 plants were found on both lists. "I came up with just a fantastic list of plants that were available at that time. Among others, there were a number or reeds that are used by the Eskimo and subarctic people in North America for making baskets. There are a lot of plants with edible leaves and stems, and things that were used as drugs and dyes. So the plants were there."

The chief plant collectors in historical societies were undoubtedly women. "It was typically women's work," says Owen. "I did find several comments that the men on hunting expeditions would gather berries or plants for their own meals, but they did not participate in the plant-gathering expeditions. They might go along, but they would be hunting or fishing."

Were Upper Paleolithic women gathering plants? The archeological literature was mostly silent on the subject. Few archeobotanists, Owen found, had ever looked for plant seeds and shreds in Upper Paleolithic camps. Most were convinced such efforts would be futile in sites so ancient. At University College London, however, Owen reached a determined young archeobotanist, Sarah Mason, who had analyzed a small sample of charcoal-like remains from a 26,390-year-old hearth at Dolní Vestonice.

The sample held more than charcoal. Examining it with a scanning electron microscope, Mason and her colleagues found fragments of fleshy plant taproots with distinctive secretory cavities—trademarks of the daisy and aster family, which boasts several species with edible roots. In all likelihood, women at Dolní Vestonice had dug the roots and cooked them into starchy meals. And they had very likely simmered other plant foods too. Mason and her colleagues detected a strange pulverized substance in the charred sample. It looked as if the women had either ground plants into flour and then boiled the results to make gruel or pounded vegetable material into a mush for their babies. Either way, says Soffer, the results are telling. "They're stuffing carbohydrates."

Owen is pursuing the research further. "If you do look," she says, "you can find things." At her urging, colleagues at the University of Tübingen are now analyzing Paleolithic hearths for botanical remains as they unearth them. Already they have turned up more plants, including berries, all clearly preserved after thousands of years. In light of these findings, Owen suggests that it was women, not men, who brought home most of the calories to Upper Paleolithic families. Indeed, she estimates that if Ice Age females collected plants, bird eggs, shellfish, and edible insects, and if they hunted or trapped small game and participated in the hunting of large game—as northern women did in historical times—they most likely contributed 70 percent of the consumed calories.

Illustration by Ron Miller
THE CLAY FIGURINES at Dolní Vestonice may have been used in divination rituals.

Moreover, some women may have enjoyed even greater power, judging from the most contentious relics of Ice Age life: the famous Venus figurines. Excavators have recovered more than 100 of the small statuettes, which were crafted between 29,000 and 23,000 years ago from such enduring materials as bone, stone, antler, ivory, and fired clay. The figurines share a strange blend of abstraction and realism. They bare prominent breasts, for example, but lack nipples. Their bodies are often minutely detailed down to the swaying lines of their backbones and the tiny rolls of flesh—fat folds—beneath their shoulder

blades, but they often lack eyes, mouths, and any facial expression. For years researchers viewed them as a male art form. Early anthropologists, after all, had observed only male hunters carving stone, ivory, and other hard materials. Females were thought to lack the necessary strength. Moreover, reasoned experts, only men would take such loving interest in a woman's body. Struck by the voluptuousness of the small stone, ivory, and clay bodies, some researchers suggested they were Ice Age erotica, intended to be touched and fondled by their male makers. The idea still lingers. In the 1980s, for example, the well-known American paleontologist Dale Guthrie wrote a scholarly article comparing the postures of the figurines with the provocative poses of *Playboy* centerfolds.

But most experts now dismiss such contentions. Owen's careful scouring of ethnographic sources, for example, revealed that women in arctic and subarctic societies did indeed work stone and ivory on occasion. And there is little reason to suggest the figurines figured as male erotica. The Black Venus, for example, seems to have belonged to a secret world of ceremony and ritual far removed from everyday sexual life.

THE EVIDENCE, SAYS SOFFER, LIES IN THE RAW material from which the Black Venus is made. Clay objects sometimes break or explode when fired, a process called thermal-shock fracturing. Studies conducted by Pamela Vandiver of the Smithsonian Institution have demonstrated that the Black Venus and other human and animal figurines recovered from Dolní Vestonice—as well as nearly 2,000 fired ceramic pellets that litter the site—were made from a local clay that is resistant to thermal-shock fracturing. But many of the figurines, including the celebrated Black Venus, bear the distinctive jagged branching splinters created by thermal shock. Intriguingly, the fired clay pellets do not.

Curious, Vandiver decided to replicate the ancient firing process. Her analysis of the small Dolní Vestonice kilns revealed that they had been fired to temperatures around 1450 degrees Fahrenheit—similar to those of an ordinary hearth. So Vandiver set about making figurines of local soil and firing them in a similar earthen kiln, which a local archeological crew had built nearby. To produce thermal shock, she had to place objects larger than half an inch on the hottest part of the fire; moreover, the pieces had to be so wet they barely held their shape.

To Vandiver and Soffer, the experiment—which was repeated several times back at the Smithsonian Institution—suggests that thermal shock was no accident. "Stuff can explode naturally in the kiln," says Soffer, "or you can make it explode. Which was going on at Dolní Vestonice? We toyed with both ideas. Either we're dealing with the most inept potters, people with two left hands, or they are doing it on purpose. And we reject the idea that they were totally inept, because other materials didn't explode. So what are the odds that this would happen only with a very particular category of objects?"

These exploding figurines could well have played a role in rituals, an idea supported by the location of the kilns. They are situated far away from the dwellings, as ritual buildings often are. Although the nature of the ceremonies is not clear, Soffer speculates that they might have served as divination rites for discerning what the future held. "Some stuff is going to explode. Some stuff is not going to explode. It's evocative, like picking petals off a daisy. She loves me, she loves me not."

Moreover, ritualists at Dolní Vestonice could have read significance into the fracturing patterns of the figurines. Many historical cultures, for example, attempted to read the future by a related method called scapulimancy. In North America, Cree ceremonialists often placed the shoulder blade, or scapula, of a desired animal in the center of a lodge. During the ceremonies, cracks began splintering the bone: a few of these fractures leaked droplets of fat. To Cree hunters, this was a sign that they would find game if they journeyed in the direction indicated by the cracks.

Venus figurines from other sites also seem to have been cloaked in ceremony. "They were not just something made to look pretty," says Margherita Mussi, an archeologist at the University of Rome-La Sapienza who studies Upper Paleolithic figurines. Mussi notes that several small statuettes from the Grimaldi Cave carvings of southern Italy, one of the largest troves of Ice Age figurines ever found in Western Europe, were carved from rare materials, which the artists obtained with great difficulty, sometimes through trade or distant travel. The statuettes were laboriously whittled and polished, then rubbed with ocher, a pigment that appears to have had ceremonial significance, suggesting that they could have been reserved for special events like rituals.

The nature of these rites is still unclear. But Mussi is convinced that women took part, and some archeologists believe they stood at the center. One of the clearest clues, says Mussi, lies in a recently rediscovered Grimaldi figurine known as Beauty and the Beast. This greenish yellow serpentine sculpture portrays two arched bodies facing away from each other and joined at the head, shoulders, and lower extremities. One body is that of a Venus figurine. The other is a strange creature that combines the triangular head of a reptile, the pinched waist of a wasp, tiny arms, and horns. "It is clearly not a creature of this world," says Mussi.

The pairing of woman and supernatural beast, adds Mussi, is highly significant. "I believe that these women were related to the capacity of communicating with a different world," she says. "I think they were believed to be the gateway to a different dimension." Possessing powers that far surpassed others in their communities, such women may have formed part of a spiritual elite, rather like the shamans of ancient Siberia. As intermediaries between the real and spirit worlds, Siberian shamans were said to be able to cure illnesses and intercede on behalf of others for hunting success. It is possible that Upper Paleolithic women performed similar services for their followers.

Although the full range of their activities is unlikely ever to be known for certain, there is good reason to believe that Ice Age women played a host of powerful roles—from plant collectors and weavers to hunters and spiritual leaders. And the research that suggests those roles is rapidly changing our mental images of the past. For Soffer and others, these are exciting times. "The data do speak for themselves," she says finally. "They answer the questions we have. But if we don't envision the questions, we're not going to see the data."

HEATHER PRINGLE *lives in Vancouver, British Columbia. "I love how this article overturns the popular image of the role of women in the past," says Pringle, who specializes in writing about archeology. "It was fun to write and a delight to research." Pringle is the author of* In Search of Ancient North America.

WOMAN
THE TOOLMAKER

A day in the life of an Ethiopian woman who scrapes
hides the old-fashioned way.

by STEVEN A. BRANDT *and* KATHRYN WEEDMAN

ON THE EDGE OF THE WESTERN ESCARPMENT of the Ethiopian Rift Valley, we sit in awe, not of the surrounding environment—some of the world's most spectacular scenery—but of an elderly woman deftly manufacturing stone scrapers as she prepares food, answers an inquisitive child, and chats with a neighbor. She smiles at us, amused and honored by our barrage of questions and our filming of her activities.

In our world of electronic and digital gadgetry, it is surprising to meet someone who uses stone tools in their everyday life. Yet, over the past three decades, researchers have identified a handful of ethnic groups in Ethiopia's southern highlands whose artisans live by making stone scrapers and processing animal hides.

In 1995, with colleagues from Ethiopia's Authority for Research and Conservation of Cultural Heritage and the University of Florida, we surveyed the highlands and, much to our surprise, identified hundreds of stone tool makers in ten different ethnic groups.

The Konso, one group we surveyed, grow millet and other crops on terraces and raise livestock that provide the skins for the hide workers. While hide working in virtually all of the other groups is conducted by men who learn from their fathers, among the Konso the hide workers are women, taught by their mothers or other female relatives.

In archaeological writings, scholarly and popular, stone toolmaking has generally been presented as a male activity; *Man the Toolmaker* is the title of one classic work. This is despite the fact that Australian Aboriginal, North American Inuit (Eskimo), and Siberian women, among others, have been reported in recent times to have made flaked-stone artifacts. The Konso hide workers are probably the only women in the world still making stone tools on a regular basis. They provide a unique opportunity for ethnoarchaeology, the study of the material remains of contemporary peoples. In the past two summers, our team returned to study the women hide workers, following them with our notebooks and cameras, and observing them as they went through their daily lives.

One Konso woman we studied is Sokate, a respected and energetic grandmother now in her 70s. Our many questions amuse Sokate, but she is polite and patient with us. When we ask why only 31 of the 119 Konso hide workers are men, she can only laugh and say that hide working has always been women's work.

AFTER AN EARLY MORNING RAIN, Sokate strides through her village's terraced millet fields to the same riverbed in which her mother and grandmother searched for chert, a flakeable stone similar to flint. She uses a digging stick to pry stones loose. After almost an hour, Sokate picks up a small nodule of chert. She places it on a large, flat basalt rock. Lifting another large piece of basalt, she brings it down onto the nodule several times, striking off many pieces. Sokate selects ten of the flakes and places them into the top ruffle of her skirt, folding it into her waistband. She also tucks in three pieces of usable quartz, found with the aid of accompanying children.

Returning home, Sokate is greeted by children, goats, and chickens. She picks up the iron tip of a hoe, and, sitting on a goat hide in front of her house, strikes flakes off a chert nodule she collected earlier. She then picks up a wooden bowl filled with scraper components—wooden handles, used stone scrapers, small, unused flakes—and puts the new chert and quartz flakes in it. Moving to the hearth area in front of her house, she takes a flake from the bowl. Resting the flake directly along the edge of a large basalt block that serves as a hearthstone and an anvil, she strikes the flake's edges with the hoe tip, shaping it into a scraper that will fit into the socket of the wooden handle. Although she has access to iron, Sokate tells us that she prefers using stone because it is sharper, more controllable, and easier to resharpen than iron, or even glass. But not all Konso hide workers share her opinion, and in fact, there are now only 21 of them who still use stone regularly.

She places the handle, passed down to her from her mother, into the ashes of the hearth, warming the acacia tree gum (mastic) that holds the scraper in its socket. When the mastic becomes pliable, Sokate pulls the old, used-up scraper out of the socket, then places the end of the handle back into the ashes. After a few minutes, she takes it out and removes some of the old mastic with a stick. On an earthenware sherd, she mixes fresh resin she collected earlier in the day with ashes and heats it. Winding it onto a stick, she drips it into the socket. Sokate then puts a new scraper into the socket, patting the resin down around it with her index finger, making certain that it is set at the proper 90-degree angle to the haft.

Local farmers and other artisans bring Sokate hides to scrape, paying her with grain or money. The morning she is going to scrape a cow hide, Sokate brushes it with a mixture of water and juice from the enset plant, or false banana. If the hide is too dry, removing the fat from its inner side is difficult. After the hide is saturated, she latches one end of it to a tree or post so the hide is slightly above the ground. Squatting or kneeling, she holds the hide taut with her feet to facilitate scraping it. Then with both hands holding the wooden handle, she scrapes the cow hide in long strokes, using a "pull" motion. Goat hides are laid flat on the ground with Sokate sitting with one leg on top of the hide and the other underneath to keep it taut. She scrapes a got hide with short strokes and a "push" motion away from her body, giving better control of the scraper with the thin goat skin.

Sokate removes the fatty inner layer, shaving off long strips in a rhythmic motion. When the edge of her tool becomes dull, usually after about 60 strokes, she resharpens it. Most of the small chips she removes from the scraper to resharpen it fall into a wooden bowl or gourd. Her barefoot grandchildren periodically dump the sharp chips onto the communal trash pile just outside the village. Sokate uses the scraper until it becomes too dull for scraping and too small to resharpen further. She'll wear out two or three scraping a single cattle hide, one or two for a goat hide.

After Sokate scrapes the hide, she spreads a reddish, oily paste of ground castor beans and pieces of red ocher over it. She then folds the hide over and works the mixture into it. After a few days, the skin is soft. Cow hides are then made into bedding, sandals, straps, belts, and musical instruments, while goat hides are made into bags and (now much more rarely) clothing. During harvest time, the demand for goat hides increases because more bags are

> Many hide-working activities take place in Konso compounds, which are often surrounded by stone walls. A broken pot on the roof indicates the father of a household is a first-born son, a person of higher status.

needed to carry agricultural goods. Sokate then sends her granddaughter to tell the hide's owner that it is ready.

Sokate and the other Ethiopian hide workers say they are proud of their profession, as they play important economic and social roles within their villages. In addition to hide working, they may also be responsible for announcing births, deaths, and meetings, and for performing puberty initiation ceremonies and other ritual activities. Despite the usefulness of their craft and other duties in the community, Konso hide workers and other artisans, such as ironsmiths and potters, have low social status. Farmers hold them in low esteem and consider them polluted, probably because their crafts involve contact with items that are thought to be impure, like the skins of dead animals. They cannot marry outside of their artisan group, usually cannot own land, and are often excluded from political and judicial life.

Clearly, the Konso hide workers are a rich source of information from which we can address a range of questions: Can excavations of abandoned hide worker compounds provide insights into the identification of social inequality and ranking? How and in what social contexts is stone toolmaking learned? Can we differentiate women's activities from men's on the basis of stone tools?

There is a sense of urgency in our work. Many of the hide workers are elderly and have not taught their children their craft; the influx of plastic bags and Western furnishings have greatly reduced demand for their products. And many of the hide workers have abandoned the use of stone in favor of bottle glass: why hike two hours for chert when you can just walk down the road and pick up pieces of glass? We want to complete our study of the Konso hide workers as soon as possible and begin studying other groups in southern Ethiopia whose hide workers are still using flaked stone, for after 2.5 million years of stone tool use and probably more than 100,000 years of scraping hides with stone, humanity's first and longest-lasting cultural tradition is rapidly being lost.

STEVEN A. BRANDT *and* KATHRYN WEEDMAN *are in the department of anthropology at the University of Florida, Gainseville. Their work is supported by funds from the National Science Foundation.*

WHY WOMEN CHANGE

The winners of evolution's race are those who can leave behind the most offspring to carry on their progenitors' genes. So doesn't it seem odd that human females should be hobbled in their prime by menopause?

JARED DIAMOND

Most wild animals remain fertile until they die. So do human males: although some may eventually become less fertile, men in general experience no shutdown of fertility, and indeed there are innumerable well-attested cases of old men, including a 94-year-old, fathering children.

But for women the situation is different. Human females undergo a steep decline in fertility from around the age of 40 and within a decade or so can no longer produce children. While some women continue to have regular menstrual cycles up to the age of 54 or 55, conception after the age of 50 was almost unknown until the recent advent of hormone therapy and artificial fertilization.

Human female menopause thus appears to be an inevitable fact of life, albeit sometimes a painful one. But to an evolutionary biologist, it is a paradoxical aberration in the animal world. The essence of natural selection is that it promotes genes for traits that increase one's number of descendants bearing those genes. How could natural selection possibly result in every female member of a species carrying genes that throttle her ability to leave more descendants? Of course, evolutionary biologists (including me) are not implying that a woman's only proper role is to stay home and care for babies and to forget about other fulfilling experiences. Instead I am using standard evolutionary

reasoning to try to understand how men's and women's bodies came to be the way they are. That reasoning tends to regard menopause as among the most bizarre features of human sexuality. But it is also among the most important. Along with the big brains and upright posture that every text of human evolution emphasizes, I consider menopause to be among the biological traits essential for making us distinctively human—something qualitatively different from, and more than, an ape.

Not everyone agrees with me about the evolutionary importance of human female menopause. Many biologists see no need to discuss it farther, since they don't think it poses an unsolved problem. Their objections are of three types. First, some dismiss it as a result of a recent increase in human expected life span. That increase stems not just from public health measures developed within the last century but possibly also from the rise of agriculture 10,000 years ago, and even more likely from evolutionary changes leading to increased human survival skills within the last 40,000 years.

According to proponents of this view, menopause could not have been a frequent occurrence for most of the several million years of human evolution, because (supposedly) almost no women or men used to survive past the age of 45 or 50. Of course the female reproductive

tract was programmed to shut down by age 50, since it would not have had the opportunity to operate thereafter anyway. The increase in human life span, these critics believe, has occurred much too recently in our evolutionary history for the female reproductive tract to have had time to adjust.

What this view overlooks, however, is that the human male reproductive tract and every other biological function of both women and men continue to function in most people for decades after age 50. If all other biological functions adjusted quickly to our new long life span, why was female reproduction uniquely incapable of doing so?

Furthermore, the claim that in the past few women survived until the age of menopause is based solely on paleodemography, which attempts to estimate age at time of death in ancient skeletons. Those estimates rest on unproven, implausible assumptions, such as that the recovered skeletons represent an unbiased sample of an entire ancient population, or that ancient adult skeletons' age of death can accurately be determined. While there's no question that paleodemographers can distinguish an ancient skeleton of a 10-year-old from that of a 25-year-old, they have never demonstrated that they can distinguish an ancient 40-year-old from a 55-year-old. One can hardly reason by comparison with skeletons of modern people, whose bones surely age at different rates from bones of ancients with different life-styles, diets, and diseases.

A second objection acknowledges that human female menopause may be an ancient phenomenon but denies that it is unique to humans. Many wild animals undergo a decline in fertility with age. Some elderly individuals of many wild mammal and bird species are found to be infertile. Among animals in laboratory cages or zoos, with their lives considerably extended over expected spans in the wild by a gourmet diet, superb medical care, and protection from enemies, many elderly female rhesus monkeys and individuals of several strains of laboratory mice do become infertile. Hence some biologists object that human female menopause is merely part of a widespread phenomenon of animal menopause, not something peculiar to humans.

However, one swallow does not make a summer, nor does one sterile female constitute menopause. Establishing the existence of menopause as a biologically significant phenomenon in the wild requires far more than just coming upon the occasional sterile elderly individual in the wild or observing regular sterility in caged animals with artificially extended life spans. It requires finding a wild animal population in which a substantial proportion of females become sterile and spend a significant fraction of their life spans after the end of their fertility.

The human species does fulfill that definition, but only one wild animal species is known to do so: the short-finned pilot whale. One-quarter of all adult females killed by whalers prove to be post-menopausal, as judged by the condition of their ovaries. Female pilot whales enter menopause at the age of 30 or 40 years, have a mean survival of at least 14 years after menopause, and may live for over 60 years. Menopause as a biologically significant phenomenon is thus not strictly unique to humans, being shared at least with that one species of whale.

But human female menopause remains sufficiently unusual in the animal world that its evolution requires explanation. We certainly did not inherit it from pilot whales, from whose ancestors our own ancestors parted company over 50 million years ago. In fact, we must have evolved it after we separated from the apes just 7 million to 5 million years ago, because we undergo menopause whereas chimps and gorillas appear not to (or at least not regularly).

There is no obvious reason we had to evolve eggs that degenerate by the end of half a century. Eggs of elephants, baleen whales, and tortoises remain viable for at least 60 years.

The third and last objection acknowledges human menopause as an ancient phenomenon that is indeed unusual among animals. But these critics say that we need not seek an explanation for menopause, because the puzzle has already been solved. The solution, they say, is the physiological mechanism of menopause: the senescence and exhaustion of a woman's egg supply, fixed at birth and not added to after birth. An egg is lost at each menstrual cycle. By the time a woman is 50 years old, most of that original egg supply has been depleted. The remaining eggs are half a century old and increasingly unresponsive to hormones.

But there is a fatal counterobjection to this objection. While the objection is not wrong, it is incomplete. Yes, exhaustion and aging of the egg supply are the immediate cause of human menopause, but why did natural selection program women so that their eggs become exhausted or aged in their forties? There is no obvious reason we had to evolve eggs that degenerate by the end of half a century. Eggs of elephants, baleen whales, and tortoises remain viable for at least 60 years. A mutation only slightly altering how eggs degenerate might have sufficed for women to remain fertile until age 60 or 75.

The easy part of the menopause puzzle is identifying the physiological mechanism by which a woman's egg supply becomes depleted or impaired by the time she is around 50 years old. The challenging problem is understanding why we evolved that seemingly self-defeating detail of reproductive physiology. Apparently there was nothing physiologically inevitable about human female menopause, and there was nothing evolutionarily inevitable about it from the perspective of mammals in general. Instead the human female, but not the human male, was programmed by natural selection, at some time within the last few million years, to shut down reproduction prematurely. That premature senescence is all the more surprising because it goes against an overwhelming trend: in other respects, we humans have evolved to age more slowly, not more rapidly, than most other animals.

As a woman ages, she can do more to increase the number of people bearing her genes by devoting herself to her existing children and grandchildren than by producing yet another child.

Any theory of menopause evolution must explain how a woman's apparently counterproductive evolutionary strategy of making fewer babies could actually result in her making more. Evidently, as a woman ages, she can do more to increase the number of people bearing her genes by devoting herself to her existing children, her potential grandchildren, and her other relatives than by producing yet another child.

The evolutionary chain of reasoning rests on several cruel facts. One is that the human child depends on its parents for an extraordinarily long time, longer than in any other animal species. A baby chimpanzee, as soon as it starts to be weaned, begins gathering its own food, mostly with its own hands. (Chimpanzee use of tools, such as fishing for termites with blades of grass or cracking nuts with stones, is of great interest to human scientists but of only limited dietary significance to chimpanzees.) The baby chimpanzee also prepares its food with its own hands. But human hunter-gatherers acquire most food with tools (digging sticks, nets, spears), prepare it with other tools (knives, pounders, huskers), and then cook it in a fire made by still other tools. Furthermore, they use tools to protect themselves against dangerous predators, unlike other prey animals, which use teeth and strong muscles. Making and wielding all those tools are completely beyond the manual dexterity and mental ability of young children. Tool use and toolmaking are transmitted not just by imitation but also by language, which takes over a decade for a child to master.

As a result, human children in most societies do not become capable of economic independence until their teens or twenties. Before that, they remain dependent on their parents, especially on the mother, because mothers tend to provide more child care than do fathers. Parents not only bring food and teach toolmaking but also provide protection and status within the tribe. In traditional societies, early death of either parent endangers a child's life even if the surviving parent remarries, because of possible conflicts with the stepparent's genetic interests. A young orphan who is not adopted has even worse chances of surviving.

Hence a hunter-gatherer mother who already has several children risks losing her genetic investment in them if she does not survive until the youngest is at least a teenager. That's one cruel fact underlying human female menopause. Another is that the birth of each successive child immediately jeopardizes a mother's previous children because the mother risks dying in childbirth. In most other animal species that risk is very low. For example, in one study of 401 rhesus monkey pregnancies, only three mothers died in childbirth. For humans in traditional societies, the risk is much higher and increases with age. Even in affluent twentieth-century Western societies, the risk of dying in childbirth is seven times higher for a mother over the age of 40 than for a 20-year-old. But each new child puts the mother's life at risk not only because of the immediate risk of death in childbirth but also because of

the delayed risk of death related to exhaustion by lactation, carrying a young child, and working harder to feed more mouths.

Infants of older mothers are themselves increasingly unlikely to survive or be healthy, because the risks of abortion, stillbirth, low birth weight, and genetic defects rise as the mother grows older. For instance, the risk of a fetus's carrying the genetic condition known as Down syndrome increases from one in 2,000 births for a mother under 30, one in 300 for a mother between the ages of 35 and 39, and one in 50 for a 43-year-old mother to the grim odds of one in 10 for a mother in her late forties.

Thus, as a woman gets older, she is likely to have accumulated more children, and she has been caring for them longer, so she is putting a bigger investment at risk with each successive pregnancy. But her chances of dying in or after childbirth, and the chances that the infant will die, also increase. In effect, the older mother is risking more for less potential gain. That's one set of factors that would tend to favor human female menopause and that would paradoxically result in a woman's having more surviving children by giving birth to fewer children.

But a hypothetical nonmenopausal older woman who died in childbirth, or while caring for an infant, would thereby be throwing away even more than her investment in her previous children. That is because a woman's children eventually begin producing children of their own, and those children count as part of the woman's prior investment. Especially in traditional societies, a woman's survival is important not only to her children but also to her grandchildren.

That extended role of postmenopausal women has been explored by anthropologists Kristen Hawks, James O'Connell, and Nicholas Blurton Jones, who studied foraging by women of different ages among the Hadza hunter-gatherers of Tanzania. The women who devoted the most time to gathering food (especially roots, honey, and fruit) were postmenopausal women. Those hardworking Hadza grandmothers put in an impressive seven hours per day, compared with a mere three hours for girls

not yet pregnant and four and a half hours for women of childbearing age. As one might expect, foraging returns (measured in pounds of food gathered per hour) increased with age and experience, so that mature women achieved higher returns than teenagers. Interestingly, the grandmothers' returns were still as high as women in their prime. The combination of putting in more foraging hours and maintaining an unchanged foraging efficiency meant that the postmenopausal grandmothers brought in more food per day than women of any of the young groups, even though their large harvests were greatly in excess of their own personal needs and they no longer had dependent young children of their own to feed.

Observations indicated that the Hadza grandmothers were sharing their excess food harvest with close relatives, such as their grandchildren and grown children. As a strategy for transforming food calories into pounds of baby, it's more efficient for an older woman to donate the calories to grandchildren and grown children than to infants of her own, because her fertility decreases with age anyway, while her children are young adults at peak fertility. Naturally, menopausal grandmothers in traditional societies contribute more to their offspring than just food. They also act as baby-sitters for grandchildren, thereby helping their adult children churn out more babies bearing Grandma's genes. And though they work hard for their grandchildren, they're less likely to die as a result of exhaustion than if they were nursing infants as well as caring for them.

But menopause has another virtue, one that has received little attention. That is the importance of old people to their entire tribe in preliterate societies, which means every human society in the world from the time of human origins until the rise of writing in Mesopotamia around 3300 B.C.

A common genetics argument is that natural selection cannot weed out mutations that do not damage people until they are old, because old people are supposedly "postreproductive." I believe that such statements overlook an essential fact distinguishing humans from most animal species. No humans, except hermits, are ever truly postreproductive, in the sense of being unable to aid in the survival and reproduction of other people bearing their genes. Yes, I grant that if any orangutans lived long enough in the wild to become sterile, they would count as postreproductive, since orangutans (other than mothers with one young offspring) tend to be solitary. I also grant that the contributions of very old people to modern literate societies tend to decrease with age. That new phenomenon of modern societies is at the root of the enormous problems that old age now poses, both for the elderly themselves and for the rest of society. But we moderns get most of our information through writing, television, or radio. We find it impossible to conceive of the overwhelming importance of elderly people in preliterate societies as repositories of information and experience.

Here is an example of that role. During my field studies of bird ecology on New Guinea and adjacent southwestern Pacific islands, I live among people who traditionally were without writing, depended on stone tools, and subsisted by farming and fishing supplemented by hunting and gathering. I am constantly asking villagers to tell me the names of local birds, animals, and plants in their language, and to tell me what they know about each species. New Guineans and Pacific islanders possess an enormous fund of biological knowledge, including names for a thousand or more species, plus information about where each species occurs, its behavior, its ecology, and its usefulness to humans. All that information is important because wild plants and animals furnish much of the people's food and all their building materials, medicines, and decorations.

Again and again, when I ask about some rare bird, only the older hunters know the answer, and eventually I ask a question that stumps even them. The hunters reply, "We have to ask the old man [or the old woman]." They take me to a hut where we find an old man or woman, blind with cataracts and toothless, able to eat food only after someone else has chewed it. But that old person is

the tribe's library. Because the society traditionally lacked writing, that old person knows more about the local environment than anyone else and is the sole person with accurate knowledge of events that happened long ago. Out comes the rare bird's name, and a description of it.

Supposedly, natural selection can't weed out mutations that affect only old people, because old people are postreproductive. But no humans, except hermits, are ever truly postreproductive.

The accumulated experience that the elderly remember is important for the whole tribe's survival. In 1976, for instance, I visited Rennell Island, one of the Solomon Islands, lying in the southwestern Pacific's cyclone belt. When I asked about wild fruits and seeds that birds ate, my Rennellese informants named dozens of plant species by Rennell language names, named for each plant species all the bird and bat species that eat its fruit, and said whether the fruit is edible for people. They ranked fruits in three categories: those that people never eat, those that people regularly eat, and those that people eat only in famine times, such as after—and here I kept hearing a Rennell term initially unfamiliar to me—the hungi kengi.

Those words proved to be the Rennell name for the most destructive cyclone to have hit the island in living memory—apparently around 1910, based on people's references to datable events of the European colonial administration. The hungi kengi blew down most of Rennell's forest, destroyed gardens, and drove people to the brink of starvation. Islanders survived by eating fruits of wild plant species that were normally not eaten. But doing so required detailed knowledge about which plants are poisonous, which are not poisonous, and whether and how the poison can be re-

moved by some technique of food preparation.

When I began pestering my middle-aged Rennellese informants with questions about fruit edibility, I was brought into a hut. There, once my eyes had become accustomed to the dim light, I saw the inevitable frail old woman. She was the last living person with direct experience of which plants were found safe and nutritious to eat after the *hungi kengi*, until people's gardens began producing again. The old woman explained that she had been a child not quite of marriageable age at the time of the *hungi kengi*. Since my visit to Rennell was in 1976, and since the cyclone had struck 66 years before, the woman was probably in her early eighties. Her survival after the 1910 cyclone had depended on information remembered by aged survivors of the last big cyclone before the *hungi kengi*. Now her people's ability to survive another cyclone would depend on her own memories, which were fortunately very detailed.

Such anecdotes could be multiplied indefinitely. Traditional human societies face frequent minor risks that threaten a few individuals, and also face rare natural catastrophes or intertribal wars that threaten the lives of everybody in the society. But virtually everyone in a small traditional society is related to one another. Hence old people in a traditional society are essential to the survival not only of their children and grandchildren but also of hundreds of other people who share their genes. In preliterate societies, no one is ever postreproductive.

Any preliterate human societies that included individuals old enough to remember the last *hungi kengi* had a much better chance of surviving the next one than did societies without such old people. The old men were not at risk from childbirth or from exhausting responsibilities of lactation and child care, so they did not evolve protection by menopause. But old women who did not undergo menopause tended to be eliminated from the human gene pool because they remained exposed to the risk of childbirth and the burden of child care. At times of crisis, such as a *hungi kengi*, the prior death of such an older woman also tended to eliminate all the woman's relatives from the gene pool—a huge genetic price to pay just for the dubious privilege of continuing to produce another baby or two against lengthening odds. That's what I see as a major driving force behind the evolution of human female menopause. Similar considerations may have led to the evolution of menopause in female pilot whales. Like us, whales are long-lived, involved in complex social relationships and life-long family ties, and capable of sophisticated communication and learning.

If one were playing God and deciding whether to make older women undergo menopause, one would do a balance sheet, adding up the benefits of menopause in one column for comparison with its costs in another column. The costs of menopause are the potential children of a woman's old age that she forgoes. The potential benefits include avoiding the increased risk of death due to childbirth and parenting at an advanced age, and thereby gaining the benefit of improved survival for one's grandchildren, prior children, and more distant relatives. The sizes of those benefits depend on many details: for example, how large the risk of death is in and after childbirth, how much that risk increases with age, how rapidly fertility decreases with age before menopause, and how rapidly it would continue to decrease in an aging woman who did not undergo menopause. All those factors are bound to differ between societies and are not easy for anthropologists to estimate. But natural selection is a more skilled mathematician because it has had millions of years in which to do the calculation. It concluded that menopause's benefits outweigh its costs, and that women can make more by making less.

Jared Diamond is a contributing editor of DISCOVER, *a professor of physiology at the* UCLA *School of Medicine, a recipient of a MacArthur genius award, and a research associate in ornithology at the American Museum of Natural History. Expanded versions of many of his* DISCOVER *articles appear in his book* The Third Chimpanzee: The Evolution and Future of the Human Animal, *which won Britain's 1992* COPUS *prize for best science book and the Los Angeles Times science book prize.*

From *Discover* magazine, July 1996, pp. 130–137. © 1996 by Jared Diamond. Reproduced with permission of the author.

Yes, Wonderful Things

**William Rathje and
Cullen Murphy**

On a crisp October morning not long ago the sun ascended above the Atlantic Ocean and turned its gaze on a team of young researchers as they swarmed over what may be the largest archaeological site in the world. The mound they occupied covers three thousand acres and in places rises more than 155 feet above a low-lying island. Its mass, estimated at 100 million tons, and its volume, estimated at 2.9 billion cubic feet, make it one of the largest man-made structures in North America. And it is known to be a treasure trove—a Pompeii, a Tikal, a Valley of the Kings—of artifacts from the most advanced civilization the planet has ever seen. Overhead sea gulls cackled and cawed, alighting now and then to peck at an artifact or skeptically observe an archaeologist at work. The surrounding landscape still supported quail and duck, but far more noticeable were the dusty, rumbling wagons and tractors of the New York City Department of Sanitation.

The site was the Fresh Kills landfill, on Staten Island, in New York City, a repository of garbage that, when shut down, in the year 2005, will have reached a height of 505 feet above sea level, making it the highest geographic feature along a fifteen-hundred-mile stretch of the Atlantic seaboard running north from Florida all the way to Maine. One sometimes hears that Fresh Kills will have to be closed when it reaches 505 feet so as not to interfere with the approach of aircraft to Newark Airport, in New Jersey, which lies just across the waterway called Arthur Kill. In reality, though, the 505-foot elevation is the result of a series of calculations designed to maximize the landfill's size while avoiding the creation of grades so steep that roads built upon the landfill can't safely be used.

Fresh Kills was originally a vast marshland, a tidal swamp. Robert Moses's plan

for the area, in 1948, was to dump enough garbage there to fill the marshland up—a process that would take, according to one estimate, until 1968—and then to develop the site, building houses, attracting light industry, and setting aside open space for recreational use. ("The Fresh Kills landfill project," a 1951 report to Mayor Vincent R. Impelliteri observed, "cannot fail to affect constructively a wide area around it. It is at once practical and idealistic.") Something along these lines may yet happen when Fresh Kills is closed. Until then, however, it is the largest active landfill in the world. It is twenty-five times the size of the Great Pyramid of Khufu at Giza, forty times the size of the Temple of the Sun at Teotihuacan. The volume of Fresh Kills is approaching that of the Great Wall of China, and by one estimate will surpass it at some point in the next few years. It is the sheer physical stature of Fresh Kills in the hulking world of landfills that explains why archaeologists were drawn to the place.

To the archaeologists of the University of Arizona's Garbage Project, which is now entering its twentieth year, landfills represent valuable lodes of information that may, when mined and interpreted, produce valuable insights—insights not into the nature of some past society, of course, but into the nature of our own. Garbage is among humanity's most prodigious physical legacies to those who have yet to be born; if we can come to understand our discards, Garbage Project archaeologists argue, then we will better understand the world in which we live. It is this conviction that prompts Garbage Project researchers to look upon the steaming detritus of daily existence with the same quiet excitement displayed by Howard Carter and Lord George Edward Carnarvon at the unpillaged, unopened tomb of Tutankhamun.

"Can you see anything?" Carnarvon asked as Carter thrust a lighted candle through a hole into the gloom of the first antechamber. "Yes," Carter replied. "Wonderful things."

Garbage archaeology can be conducted in several ways. At Fresh Kills the method of excavation involved a mobile derrick and a thirteen-hundred-pound bucket auger, the latter of which would be sunk into various parts of the landfill to retrieve samples of garbage from selected strata. At 6:15 a.m. Buddy Kellett of the company Kellett's Well Boring, Inc., which had assisted with several previous Garbage Project landfill digs, drove one of the company's trucks, with derrick and auger collapsed for travel, straight up the steep slope of one of the landfill mounds. Two-thirds of the way up, the Garbage Project crew directed Kellett to a small patch of level ground. Four hydraulic posts were deployed from the stationary vehicle, extending outward to keep it safely moored. Now the derrick was raised. It supported a long metal rod that in turn housed two other metal rods; the apparatus, when pulled to its full length, like a telescope, was capable of penetrating the landfill to a depth of ninety-seven feet—enough at this particular spot to go clear through its bottom and into the original marsh that Fresh Kills had been (or into what was left of it). At the end of the rods was the auger, a large bucket made of high-tension steel: four feet high, three feet in diameter, and open at the bottom like a cookie cutter, with six graphite-and-steel teeth around the bottom's circumference. The bucket would spin at about thirty revolutions per minute and with such force that virtually nothing could impede its descent. At a Garbage Project excavation in Sunnyvale, California, in 1988, one of the first things the bucket hit in the cover dirt a few feet below the surface of the Sunnyvale Landfill was the skeleton of a car. The bucket's teeth snapped the axle, and drilled on.

The digging at Fresh Kills began. Down the whirring bucket plunged. Moments later it returned with a gasp, laden with garbage that, when released, spewed a thin vapor into the chill autumnal air. The smell was pungent, somewhere between sweet and disagreeable. Kellett's rig operator, David Spillers, did his job with the relaxation that comes of familiarity, seemingly oblivious to the harsh grindings and sharp clanks. The rest of the archaeological crew, wearing cloth aprons and heavy rubber gloves, went about their duties with practiced efficiency and considerable speed. They were veteran members of the Garbage Project's A-Team—its landfill-excavating arm—and had been through it all before.

Again a bucketful of garbage rose out of the ground. As soon as it was dumped Masakazu Tani, at the time a Japanese graduate student in anthropology at the University of Arizona (his Ph.D. thesis, recently completed, involves identifying activity areas in ancient sites on the basis of distributions of litter), plunged a thermometer into the warm mass. "Forty-three degrees centigrade," Tani called out. The temperature (equivalent to 109.4 degrees Fahrenheit) was duly logged. The garbage was then given a brusque preliminary examination to determine its generic source and, if possible, its date of origin. In this case the presence of telltale domestic items, and of legible newspapers, made both tasks easy. Gavin Archer, another anthropologist and a research associate of the Garbage Project, made a notation in the running log that he would keep all day long: "Household, circa 1977." Before the next sample was pulled up Douglas Wilson, an anthropologist who specializes in household hazardous waste, stepped up to the auger hole and played out a weighted tape measure, eventually calling out, "Thirty-five feet." As a safety precaution, Wilson, like any other crew member working close to the sunken shaft on depth-measure duty, wore a leather harness tethered to a nearby vehicle. The esophagus created by the bucket auger was just large enough to accept a human being, and anyone slipping untethered a story or two into this narrow, oxygen- starved cavity would die of asphyxiation before any rescue could be attempted.

Most of the bucketfuls of garbage received no more attention than did the load labeled "Household, circa 1977." Some basic data were recorded for tracking purposes, and the garbage was left on a quickly

accumulating backdirt pile. But as each of what would finally be fourteen wells grew deeper and deeper, at regular intervals (either every five or every ten feet) samples were taken and preserved for full-dress analysis. On those occasions Wilson Hughes, the methodical and serenely ursine co-director and field supervisor of the Garbage Project, and the man responsible for day-to-day logistics at the Fresh Kills dig, would call out to the bucket operator over the noise of the engine: "We'll take the next bucket." Then Hughes and Wilson would race toward the rig in a running crouch, like medics toward a helicopter, a plywood sampling board between them. Running in behind came a team of microbiologists and civil engineers assembled from the University of Oklahoma, the University of Wisconsin, and Procter & Gamble's environmental laboratory. They brought with them a variety of containers and sealing devices to preserve samples in an oxygen-free environment—an environment that would allow colonies of the anaerobic bacteria that cause most of the biodegradation in landfills (to the extent that biodegradation occurs) to survive for later analysis. Behind the biologists and engineers came other Garbage Project personnel with an assortment of wire mesh screens and saw horses.

Within seconds of the bucket's removal from the ground, the operator maneuvered it directly over the sampling board, and released the contents. The pile was attacked first by Phillip Zack, a civil engineering student from the University of Wisconsin, who, as the temperature was being recorded, directed portions of the material into a variety of airtight conveyances. Then other members of the team moved in—the people who would shovel the steaming refuse atop the wire mesh; the people who would sort and bag whatever didn't go through the mesh; the people who would pour into bags or cannisters or jars whatever did go through the mesh; the people who would label everything for the trip either back to Tucson and the Garbage Project's holding bins or to the laboratories of the various microbiologists. (The shortest trip was to the trailer-laboratory that Procter & Gamble scientists had driven from Cincinnati and parked at the edge of the landfill.) The whole sample-collection process, from dumping to sorting to storing, took no more than twelve minutes. During the Fresh Kills dig it was repeated forty- four times at various places and various depths.

As morning edged toward afternoon the bucket auger began to near the limits of its

reach in one of the wells. Down through the first thirty-five feet, a depth that in this well would date back to around 1984, the landfill had been relatively dry. Food waste and yard waste—hot dogs, bread, and grass clippings, for example—were fairly well preserved. Newspapers remained intact and easy to read, their lurid headlines ("Woman Butchered-Ex-Hubby Held") calling to mind a handful of yesterday's tragedies. Beyond thirty-five feet, however, the landfill became increasingly wet, the garbage increasingly unidentifiable. At sixty feet, a stratum in this well containing garbage from the 1940s and 1950s, the bucket grabbed a sample and pulled it toward the surface. The Garbage Project team ran forward with their equipment, positioning themselves underneath. The bucket rose majestically as the operator sat at the controls, shouting something over the noise. As near as anyone can reconstruct it now, he was saying, "You boys might want to back off some, 'cause if this wind hits that bucket...." The operator broke off because the wind did hit that bucket, and the material inside—a gray slime, redolent of putrefaction—thoroughly showered the crew. It would be an exaggeration to suggest that the victims were elated by this development, but their curiosity was certainly piqued, because on only one previous excavation had slime like this turned up in a landfill. What was the stuff made of? How had it come to be? What did its existence mean? The crew members doggedly collected all the usual samples, plus a few extra bottles of slime for special study. Then they cleaned themselves off.

It would be a blessing if it were possible to study garbage in the abstract, to study garbage without having to handle it physically.* But that is not possible. Garbage is not mathematics. To understand garbage you have to touch it, to feel it, to sort it, to smell it. You have to pick through hundreds of tons of it, counting and weighing all the daily newspapers, the telephone books; the soiled diapers, the foam clamshells that once briefly held hamburgers, the lipstick cylinders coated with grease, the medicine vials still encasing brightly colored pills, the empty bottles of scotch, the half-full cans of paint and muddy turpentine, the forsaken toys, the cigarette butts. You have to sort and weigh and measure the volume of all the organic matter, the discards from thousands of plates: the noodles and the Cheerios and the tortillas; the pieces of pet food that have made their own gravy; the hardened jelly doughnuts, bleeding from their side wounds; the half-eaten bananas, mostly still within their peels, black and incomparably sweet in the embrace of final decay. You have to confront sticky green mountains of yard waste, and slippery brown hills of potato peels, and brittle ossuaries of chicken bones and T-bones. And then, finally, there are the "fines," the vast connecting mixture of tiny bits of paper, metal, glass, plastic, dirt, grit, and former nutrients that suffuses every landfill like a kind of grainy lymph. To understand garbage you need thick gloves and a mask and some booster shots. But the yield in knowledge—about people and their behavior as well as about garbage itself—offsets the grim working conditions.

To an archaeologist, ancient garbage pits or garbage mounds, which can usually be located within a short distance from any ruin, are always among the happiest of finds, for they contain in concentrated form the artifacts and comestibles and remnants of behavior of the people who used them. While every archaeologist dreams of discovering spectacular objects, the bread-and-butter work of archaeology involves the most common and routine kinds of discards. It is not entirely fanciful to define archaeology as the discipline that tries to understand old garbage, and to learn from that garbage something about ancient societies and ancient behaviors. The eminent archaeologist Emil Haury once wrote of the aboriginal garbage heaps of the American Southwest: "Whichever way one views the mounds—as garbage piles to avoid, or as symbols of a way of life—they nevertheless are features more productive of information than any others." When the British archaeologist Sir Leonard Woolley, in 1916, first climbed to the top of the ancient city of Carchemish, on the Euphrates River near the modern-day Turkish-Syrian border, he moistened his index finger and held it in the air. Satisfied, he scanned the region due south of the city—that is, downwind—pausing to draw on his map the location of any mounds he saw. A trench dug through the largest of these mounds revealed it to be the garbage dump Woolley was certain it was, and the exposed strata helped establish the chronological sequence for the Carchemish site as a whole. Archaeologists have been picking through ancient garbage ever since archaeology became a profession, more than a century ago, and they will no doubt go on doing so as long as garbage is produced.

Several basic points about garbage need to be emphasized at the outset. First, the creation of garbage is an unequivocal sign of a human presence. From Styrofoam cups along a roadway and urine bags on the moon there is an uninterrupted chain of garbage that reaches back more than two million years to the first "waste flake" knocked off in the knapping of the first stone tool. That the distant past often seems misty and dim is precisely because our earliest ancestors left so little garbage behind. An appreciation of the accomplishments of the first hominids became possible only after they began making stone tools, the debris from the production of which, along with the discarded tools themselves, are now probed for their secrets with electron microscopes and displayed in museums not as garbage but as "artifacts." These artifacts serve as markers—increasingly frequent and informative markers—of how our forebears coped with the evolving physical and social world. Human beings are mere placeholders in time, like zeros in a long number; their garbage seems to have more staying power, and a power to inform across the millennia that complements (and often substitutes for) that of the written word. The profligate habits of our own country and our own time—the sheer volume of the garbage that we create and must dispose of—will make our society an open book. The question is: Would we ourselves recognize our story when it is told, or will our garbage tell tales about us that we as yet do not suspect?

That brings up a second matter: If our garbage, in the eyes of the future, is destined to hold a key to the past, then surely it already holds a key to the present. This may be an obvious point, but it is one whose implications were not pursued by scholars until relatively recently. Each of us throws away dozens of items every day. All of these items are relics of specific human activities—relics no different in their inherent nature from many of those that traditional archaeologists work with (though they are, to be sure, a bit fresher). Taken as a whole the garbage of the United States, from its 93 million households and 1.5 million retail outlets and from all of its schools, hospitals, government offices, and other public facilities, is a mirror of American society. Of course, the problem with the mirror garbage offers is that, when encountered in a garbage can, dump, or landfill, it is a broken one: our civilization is reflected in billions of fragments that may reveal little in and of themselves. Fitting some of the pieces back together requires painstaking effort—effort that a small number of archaeologists and natural scientists have only just begun to apply.

A third point about garbage is that it is not an assertion but a physical fact—and thus may sometimes serve as a useful corrective. Human beings have over the centuries left many accounts describing their lives and civilizations. Many of these are little more than self-aggrandizing advertisements. The remains of the tombs, temples, and palaces of the elite are filled with personal histories as recorded by admiring relatives and fawning retainers. More such information is carved into obelisks and stelae, gouged into clay tablets, painted or printed on papyrus and paper. Historians are understandably drawn to written evidence of this kind, but garbage has often served as a kind of tattle-tale, setting the record straight.

It had long been known, for example, that French as well as Spanish forts had been erected along the coast of South Carolina during the sixteenth century, and various mounds and depressions have survived into our own time to testify to their whereabouts. Ever since the mid-nineteenth century a site on the tip of Parris Island, South Carolina, has been familiarly known as the site of a French outpost, built in 1562, that is spelled variously in old documents as Charlesfort, Charlesforte, and Charles Forte. In 1925, the Huguenot Society of South Carolina successfully lobbied Congress to erect a monument commemorating the building of Charlesfort. Subsequently, people in nearby Beaufort took up the Charlesfort theme, giving French names to streets, restaurants, and housing developments. Gift shops sold kitschy touristiana with a distinctly Gallic flavor. Those restaurants and gift shops found themselves in an awkward position when, in 1957, as a result of an analysis of discarded matter discovered at Charlesfort, a National Park Service historian, Albert Manucy, suggested that the site was of Spanish origin. Excavations begun in 1979 by the archaeologist Stanley South, which turned up such items as discarded Spanish olive jars and broken majolica pottery from Seville, confirmed Manucy's view: "Charlesfort," South established, was actually Fort San Marcos, a Spanish installation built in 1577 to protect a Spanish town named Santa Elena. (Both the fort and the town had been abandoned after only a few years.)

Garbage, then, represents physical fact, not mythology. It underscores a point that can not be too greatly emphasized: Our private worlds consist essentially of two realities—mental reality, which encompasses beliefs, attitudes, and ideas, and material reality, which is the picture embodied in the physical record. The study of garbage reminds us that it is a rare person in whom mental and material realities completely coincide. Indeed, for the most part, the pair exist in a state of tension, if not open conflict.

Americans have always wondered, sometimes with buoyant playfulness, what their countrymen in the far future will make of Americans "now." In 1952, in a monograph he first circulated privately among colleagues and eventually published in *The Journal of Irreproducible Results,* the eminent anthropologist and linguist Joseph H. Greenberg—the man who would one day sort the roughly one thousand known Native American languages into three broad language families—imagined the unearthing of the so-called "violence texts" during an excavation of the Brooklyn Dodgers' Ebbets Field in the year A.D. 2026; what interpretation, he wondered, would be given to such newspaper reports as "Yanks Slaughter Indians" and "Reese made a sacrifice in the infield"? In 1979 the artist and writer David Macaulay published *Motel of the Mysteries,* an archaeological site-report setting forth the conclusions reached by a team of excavators in the year A.D. 4022 who have unearthed a motel dating back to 1985 (the year, Macaulay wrote, in which "an accidental reduction in postal rates on a substance called third- and fourth-class mail literally buried the North Americans under tons of brochures, fliers, and small containers called FREE"). Included in the report are illustrations of an archaeologist modeling a toilet seat, toothbrushes, and a drain stopper (or, as Macaulay describes them, "the Sacred Collar … the magnificent 'plasticus' ear ornaments, and the exquisite silver chain and pendant"), all assumed to be items of ritual or personal regalia. In 1982 an exhibit was mounted in New York City called "Splendors of the Sohites"—a vast display of artifacts, including "funerary vessels" (faded, dusky soda bottles) and "hermaphrodite amulets" (discarded pop-top rings), found in the SoHo section of Manhattan and dating from the Archaic Period (A.D. 1950–1961), the Classical Period (1962–1975), and the Decadent Period (1976–c.1980).

Greenberg, Macaulay, and the organizers of the Sohites exhibition all meant to have some fun, but there is an uneasy undercurrent to their work, and it is embodied in the question: What are we to make of ourselves? The Garbage Project, conceived in 1971, and officially established at the University of Arizona in 1973, was an attempt to come up with a new way of providing serious answers. It aimed to apply *real* archaeology to this very question; to see if it would be possible to investigate human behavior "from the back end," as it were. This scholarly endeavor has come to be known as garbology, and practitioners of garbology are known as garbologists. The printed citation (dated 1975) in the *Oxford English Dictionary* for the meaning of "garbology" as used here associates the term with the Garbage Project.

In the years since its founding the Garbage Project's staff members have processed more than 250,000 pounds of garbage, some of it from landfills but most of it fresh out of garbage cans in selected neighborhoods. All of this garbage has been sorted, coded, and catalogued—every piece, from bottles of furniture polish and egg-shaped pantyhose packaging to worn and shredded clothing, crumpled bubble-gum wrappers, and the full range of kitchen waste. A unique database has been built up from these cast-offs, covering virtually every aspect of American life: drinking habits, attitudes toward red meat, trends in the use of convenience foods, the strange ways in which consumers respond to shortages, the use of contraceptives, and hundreds of other matters.[*]

The antecedents of the Garbage Project in the world of scholarship and elsewhere are few but various. Some are undeniably dubious. The examination of fresh refuse is, of course, as old as the human species—just watch anyone who happens upon an old campsite, or a neighbor scavenging at a dump for spare parts or furniture. The first systematic study of the components of America's garbage dates to the early 1900s and the work of the civil engineers Rudolph Hering (in New York) and Samuel A. Greeley (in Chicago), who by 1921 had gathered enough information from enough cities to compile *Collection and Disposal of Municipal Refuse,* the first textbook on urban trash management. In academe, not much happened after that for quite some time. Out in the field, however, civil engineers and solid-waste managers did now and again sort and weigh fresh garbage as it stood in transit between its source and destination, but their categories were usually simple: paper, glass, metal. No one sorted garbage into detailed categories relating to particular consumer discard patterns. No one, for example, kept track of

phenomena as specific as the number of beer cans thrown away versus the number of beer bottles, or the number of orange-juice cans thrown away versus the number of pounds of freshly squeezed oranges, or the amount of candy thrown away in the week after Halloween versus the amount thrown away in the week after Valentine's Day. And no one ever dug into the final resting places of most of America's garbage: dumps (where garbage is left in the open) and sanitary landfills (where fresh garbage is covered every night with six to eight inches of soil).

Even as America's city managers over the years oversaw—and sometimes desperately attempted to cope with—the disposal of ever-increasing amounts of garbage, the study of garbage itself took several odd detours—one into the world of the military, another into the world of celebrity-watching, and a third into the world of law enforcement.

The military's foray into garbology occurred in 1941, when two enlisted men, Horace Schwerin and Phalen Golden, were forced to discontinue a survey they were conducting among new recruits about which aspects of Army life the recruits most disliked. (Conducting polls of military personnel was, they had learned, against regulations.) Schwerin and Golden had already discovered, however, that the low quality of the food was the most frequently heard complaint, and they resolved to look into this one matter with an investigation that could not be considered a poll. What Schwerin and Golden did was to station observers in mess halls to record the types of food that were most commonly wasted and the volume of waste by type of food. The result, after 2.4 million man-meals had been observed, was a textbook example of how garbage studies can produce not only behavioral insights but also practical benefits. Schwerin and Golden discovered that 20 percent of the food prepared for Army mess halls was eventually thrown away, and that one reason for this was simply excess preparation. Here are some more of their findings, as summarized in a wartime article that appeared in the *The Saturday Evening Post:*

> Soldiers ate more if they were allowed to smoke in the mess hall. They ate more if they went promptly to table instead of waiting on line outside—perhaps because the food became cold. They ate more if they fell to on their own initiative instead of by command. They cared little for soups, and 65 percent of the kale and

nearly as much of the spinach went into the garbage can. Favorite desserts were cakes and cookies, canned fruit, fruit salad, and gelatin. They ate ice cream in almost any amount that was served to them.

"That, sergeant, is an excellent piece of work," General George C. Marshall, the Army chief of staff, told Horace Schwerin after hearing a report by Schwerin on the research findings. The Army adopted many of Schwerin and Golden's recommendations, and began saving some 2.5 million pounds of food a day. It is perhaps not surprising to learn that until joining the Army Horace Schwerin had been in market research, and, among other things, had helped CBS to perfect a device for measuring audience reaction to radio shows.

The origins of an ephemeral branch of garbage studies focused on celebrities—"peeping-Tom" garbology, one might call it—seem to lie in the work of A. J. Weberman. Weberman was a gonzo journalist and yippie whose interest in the songs of Bob Dylan, and obsession with their interpretation, in 1970 prompted him to begin stealing the garbage from the cans left out in front of Dylan's Greenwich Village brownstone on MacDougal Street. Weberman didn't find much—some soiled Pampers, some old newspapers, some fast-food packaging from a nearby Blimpie Base, a shopping list with the word vanilla spelled "vanella." He did, however, stumble into a brief but highly publicized career. This self-proclaimed "garbage guerrilla" quickly moved on to Neil Simon's garbage (it included a half-eaten bagel, scraps of lox, the Sunday Times), Muhammad Ali's (an empty can of Luck's collard greens, and empty roach bomb), and Abbie Hoffman's (a summons for hitchhiking, an unused can of deodorant, an estimate of the cost for the printing of Steal This Book, and the telephone numbers of Jack Anderson and Kate Millet). Weberman revealed many of his findings in an article in Esquire in 1971. It was antics such as his that inspired a prior meaning of the term "garbology," one very different from the definition established today.

Weberman's work inspired other garbage guerrillas. In January of 1975, the Detroit Free Press Sunday magazine reported on the findings from its raids on the garbage of several city notables, including the mayor, the head of the city council, the leader of a right-wing group, a food columnist, a disk jockey, and a prominent psychiatrist. Nothing much was discovered that

might be deemed out of the ordinary, save for some of the contents of the garbage taken from a local Hare Krishna temple: a price tag from an Oleg Cassini garment, for example, and four ticket stubs from the Bel-Aire Drive-In Theater, which at the time was showing Horrible House on the Hill and The Night God Screamed. Six months after the Free Press exposé, a reporter for the National Enquirer, Jay Gourley, drove up to 3018 Dumbarton Avenue, N.W., in Washington, D.C., and threw the five garbage bags in front of Secretary of State Henry A. Kissinger's house into the trunk of his car. Secret Service agents swiftly blocked Gourley's departure, but after a day of questioning allowed him to proceed, the garbage still in the trunk. Among Gourley's finds: a crumpled piece of paper with a dog's teeth marks on it, upon which was written the work schedules of the Secret Service agents assigned to guard the Secretary; empty bottles of Seconal and Maalox; and a shopping list, calling for a case of Jack Daniel's, a case of Ezra Brooks bourbon, and a case of Cabin Still bourbon. Gourley later returned most of the garbage to the Kissingers—minus, he told reporters, "several dozen interesting things."

After the Kissinger episode curiosity about the garbage of celebrities seems to have abated. In 1977 the National Enquirer sent a reporter to poke through the garbage of President Jimmy Carter's press secretary, Jody Powell. The reporter found so little of interest that the tabloid decided not to publish a story. In 1980 Secret Service agents apprehended A. J. Weberman as he attempted to abduct former President Richard Nixon's garbage from behind an apartment building in Manhattan. Weberman was released, without the garbage.

The third detour taken by garbage studies involves police work. Over the years, law enforcement agents looking for evidence in criminal cases have also been more-than-occasional students of garbage; the Federal Bureau of Investigation in particular has spent considerable time poring over the household trash of people in whom it maintains a professional interest. ("We take it on a case-by-case basis," an FBI spokesman says.) One of the biggest criminal cases involving garbage began in 1975 and involved Joseph "Joe Bananas" Bonanno, Sr., a resident of Tucson at the time and a man with alleged ties to organized crime that were believed to date back to the days of Al Capone. For a period of three years officers of the Arizona Drug Control District collected Bonanno's trash

just before the regular pickup, replacing it with "fake" Bonanno garbage. (Local garbagemen were not employed in the operation because some of them had received anonymous threats after assisting law enforcement agencies in an earlier venture.) The haul in evidence was beyond anyone's expectations: Bonanno had apparently kept detailed records of his various transactions, mostly in Sicilian. Although Bonanno had torn up each sheet of paper into tiny pieces, forensic specialists with the Drug Control District, like archaeologists reconstructing ceramic bowls from potsherds, managed to reassemble many of the documents and with the help of the FBI got them translated. In 1980 Bonanno was found guilty of having interfered with a federal grand jury investigation into the business operations of his two sons and a nephew. He was eventually sent to jail.

Unlike law-enforcement officers or garbage guerrillas, the archaeologists of the Garbage Project are not interested in the contents of any particular individual's garbage can. Indeed, it is almost always the case that a given person's garbage is at once largely anonymous and unimaginably humdrum. Garbage most usefully comes alive when it can be viewed in the context of broad patterns, for it is mainly in patterns that the links between artifacts and behaviors can be discerned.

The seed from which the Garbage Project grew was an anthropology class conducted at the University of Arizona in 1971 that was designed to teach principles of archaeological methodology. The University of Arizona has long occupied a venerable place in the annals of American archaeology and, not surprisingly, the pursuit of archaeology there to this day is carried on in serious and innovative ways. The class in question was one in which students undertook independent projects aimed precisely at showing links between various kinds of artifacts and various kinds of behavior. For example, one student, Sharon Thomas, decided to look into the relationship between a familiar motor function ("the diffusion pattern of ketchup over hamburgers") and a person's appearance, as manifested in clothing. Thomas took up a position at "seven different hamburger dispensaries" and, as people came in to eat, labeled them "neat" or "sloppy" according to a set of criteria relating to the way they dressed. Then she recorded how each of the fifty-seven patrons she studied—the ones who ordered hamburgers—

poured ketchup over their food. She discovered that sloppy people were far more likely than neat people to put ketchup on in blobs, sometimes even stirring it with their fingers. Neat people, in contrast, tended to apply the ketchup in patterns: circles, spirals, and crisscrosses. One person (a young male neatly dressed in a body shirt, flared pants, and patent-leather Oxfords) wrote with ketchup what appeared to be initials.

Two of the student investigations, conducted independently by Frank Ariza and Kelly Allen, led directly to the Garbage Project. Ariza and Allen, wanting to explore the divergence between (or correlation of) mental stereotypes and physical realities, collected garbage from two households in an affluent part of Tucson and compared it to garbage from two households in a poor and, as it happens, Mexican-American part of town. The rich and poor families, each student found, ate about the same amount of steak and hamburger, and drank about the same amount of milk. But the poor families, they learned, bought more expensive child-education items. They also bought more household cleansers. What did such findings mean? Obviously the sample—involving only four households in all—was too small for the results even to be acknowledged as representative, let alone to provide hints as to what lay behind them. However, the general nature of the research effort itself—comparing garbage samples in order to gauge behavior (and, what is more, gauging behavior unobtrusively, thereby avoiding one of the great biases inherent in much social science)—seemed to hold great promise.

A year later, in 1972, university students, under professorial direction, began borrowing samples of household garbage from different areas of Tucson, and sorting it in a lot behind a dormitory. The Garbage Project was under way. In 1973, the Garbage Project entered into an arrangement with the City of Tucson, whereby the Sanitation Division, four days a week, delivered five to eight randomly selected household pickups from designated census tracts to an analysis site that the Division set aside for the Project's sorters at a maintenance yard. (Wilson Hughes, who as mentioned earlier is the Garbage Project's co-director, was one of the first undergraduate garbage sorters.) In 1984 operations were moved to an enclosure where many of the university's dumpsters are parked, across the street from Arizona Stadium.

The excavation of landfills would come much later in the Garbage Project's history,

when to its focus on issues of garbage and human behavior it added a focus on issues of garbage management. The advantage in the initial years of sorting fresh garbage over excavating landfills was a basic but important one: In landfills it is often quite difficult and in many cases impossible to get some idea, demographically speaking, of the kind of neighborhood from which any particular piece of garbage has come. The value of landfill studies is therefore limited to advancing our understanding of garbage in the aggregate. With fresh garbage, on the other hand, one can have demographic precision down to the level of a few city blocks, by directing pickups to specific census districts and cross-tabulating the findings with census data.

Needless to say, deciding just which characteristics of the collected garbage to pay attention to posed a conceptual challenge, one that was met by Wilson Hughes, who devised the "protocol" that is used by the Garbage Project to this day. Items found in garbage are sorted into one of 150 specific coded categories that can in turn be clustered into larger categories representing food (fresh food versus prepared, health food versus junk food), drugs, personal and household sanitation products, amusement-related or educational materials, communications-related materials, pet-related materials, yard-related materials, and hazardous materials. For each item the following information is recorded on a standardized form: the date on which it was collected; the census tract from which it came; the item code (for example, 001, which would be the code for "Beef"); the item's type (for example, "chuck"); its original weight or volume (in this case, derived from the packaging); its cost (also from the packaging); material composition of container; brand (if applicable); and the weight of any discarded food (if applicable). The information garnered over the years from many thousands of such forms, filled out in pursuit of a wide variety of research objectives, constitutes the Garbage Project's database. It has all been computerized and amounts to some two million lines of data drawn from some fifteen thousand household-refuse samples. The aim here has been not only to approach garbage with specific questions to answer or hypotheses to prove but also to amass sufficient quantities of information, in a systematic and open-minded way, so that with the data on hand Garbage Project researchers would be able to answer any future questions or evaluate any future hypotheses that might arise. In 1972 gar-

bage was, after all, still terra incognita, and the first job to be done was akin to that undertaken by the explorers Lewis and Clark.

From the outset the Garbage Project has had to confront the legal and ethical issues its research involves: Was collecting and sorting someone's household garbage an unjustifiable invasion of privacy? This very question has over the years been argued repeatedly in the courts. The Fourth Amendment unequivocally guarantees Americans protection from unreasonable search and seizure. Joseph Bonanno, Sr., tried to invoke the Fourth Amendment to prevent his garbage from being used as evidence. But garbage placed in a garbage can in a public thoroughfare, where it awaits removal by impersonal refuse collectors, and where it may be picked over by scavengers looking for aluminum cans, by curious children or neighbors, and by the refuse collectors themselves (some of whom do a thriving trade in old appliances, large and small), is usually considered by the courts to have been abandoned. Therefore, the examination of the garbage by outside parties cannot be a violation of a constitutional right. In the Bonanno case, U.S. District Court Judge William Ingram ruled that investigating garbage for evidence of a crime may carry a "stench," but was not illegal. In 1988, in *California v. Greenwood,* the U.S. Supreme Court ruled by a margin of six to two that the police were entitled to conduct a warrantless search of a suspected drug dealer's garbage—a search that led to drug paraphernalia, which led in turn to warrants, arrests, and convictions. As Justice Byron White has written, "The police cannot reasonably be expected to avert their eyes from evidence of criminal activity that could have been observed by any member of the public."

Legal issues aside, the Garbage Project has taken pains to ensure that those whose garbage comes under scrutiny remain anonymous. Before obtaining garbage for study, the Project provides guarantees to communities and their garbage collectors that nothing of a personal nature will be examined and that no names or addresses or other personal information will be recorded. The Project also stipulates that all of the garbage collected (except aluminum cans, which are recycled) will be returned to the community for normal disposal.

As noted, the Garbage Project has now been sorting and evaluating garbage, with scientific rigor, for two decades. The Project has proved durable because its findings have supplied a fresh perspective on what we know—and what we think we know—about certain aspects of our lives. Medical researchers, for example, have long made it their business to question people about their eating habits in order to uncover relationships between patterns of diet and patterns of disease. These researchers have also long suspected that people—honest, well-meaning people—may often be providing information about quantities and types and even brands of food and drink consumed that is not entirely accurate. People can't readily say whether they trimmed 3.3 ounces or 5.4 ounces of fat off the last steak they ate, and they probably don't remember whether they had four, five, or seven beers in the previous week, or two eggs or three. The average person just isn't paying attention. Are there certain patterns in the way in which people wrongly "self-report" their dietary habits? Yes, there are, and Garbage Project studies have identified many of them.

Garbage archaeologists also know how much edible food is thrown away; what percentage of newspapers, cans, bottles, and other items aren't recycled; how loyal we are to brandname products and which have earned the greatest loyalty; and how much household hazardous waste is carted off to landfills and incinerators. From several truckloads of garbage and a few pieces of ancillary data—most importantly, the length of time over which the garbage was collected—the Garbage Project staff can reconstruct the community from which it came with a degree of accuracy that the Census Bureau might in some neighborhoods be unable to match.

Garbage also exposes the routine perversity of human ways. Garbage archaeologists have learned, for example, that the volume of garbage that Americans produce expands to fill the number of receptacles that are available to put it in. They have learned that we waste more of what is in short supply than of what is plentiful; that attempts by individuals to restrict consumption of certain foodstuffs are often counterbalanced by extra and inadvertent consumption of those same foodstuffs in hidden form; and that while a person's memory of what he has eaten and drunk in a given week is inevitably wide of the mark, his guess as to what a family member or even neighbor has eaten and drunk usually turns out to be more perceptive.

Some of the Garbage Project's research has prompted unusual forays into arcane aspects of popular culture. Consider the matter of those "amulets" worn by the Sohites—that is, the once-familiar detachable pop-top pull tab. Pull tabs first became important to the Garbage Project during a study of household recycling practices, conducted on behalf of the federal Environmental Protection Agency during the mid-1970s. The question arose: If a bag of household garbage contained no aluminum cans, did that mean that the household didn't dispose of any cans or that it had recycled its cans? Finding a way to answer that question was essential if a neighborhoods's recycling rate was to be accurately determined. Pull tabs turned out to hold the key. A quick study revealed that most people did not drop pull tabs into the cans from which they had been wrenched; rather, the vast majority of people threw the tabs into the trash. If empty cans were stored separately for recycling, the pull tabs still went out to the curb with the rest of the garbage. A garbage sample that contained several pull tabs but no aluminum cans was a good bet to have come from a household that recycled.

All this counting of pull tabs prompted a surprising discovery one day by a student: Pull tabs were not all alike. Their configuration and even color depended on what kind of beverage they were associated with and where the beverage had been canned. Armed with this knowledge, Garbage Project researchers constructed an elaborate typology of pull tabs, enabling investigators to tease out data about beverage consumption—say, beer versus soda, Michelob versus Schlitz—even from samples of garbage that contained not a single can. Detachable pull tabs are no longer widely used in beverage cans, but the pull-tab typology remains useful even now. Among other things, in the absence of such evidence of chronology as a newspaper's dateline, pull tabs can reliably help to fix the dates of strata in a landfill. In archaeological parlance objects like these that have been widely diffused over a short period of time, and then abruptly disappear, are known as horizon markers.

The unique "punch-top" on Coors beer cans, for example, was used only between March of 1974 and June of 1977. (It was abandoned because some customers complained that they cut their thumbs pushing the holes open.) In landfills around the country, wherever Coors beer cans were discarded, punch-top cans not only identify strata associated with a narrow band of dates but also separate two epochs one from another. One might think of punch-tops playfully as the garbage equivalent of

the famous iridium layer found in sediment toward the end of the Cretaceous Era, marking the moment (proponents of the theory believe) when a giant meteor crashed into the planet Earth, exterminating the dinosaurs.

All told, the Garbage Project has conducted nine full-scale excavations of municipal landfills in the United States and two smaller excavations associated with special projects. In the fall of 1991 it also excavated four sites in Canada, the data from which remains largely unanalyzed (and is not reflected in this book). The logistics of the landfill excavations are complex, and they have been overseen in all cases by Wilson Hughes. What is involved? Permission must be obtained from a raft of local officials and union leaders; indemnification notices must be provided to assure local authorities that the Garbage Project carries sufficient insurance against injury; local universities must be scoured for a supply of students to supplement the Garbage Project team; in many cases construction permits, of all things, must be obtained in advance of digging. There is also the whole matter of transportation, not only of personnel but also of large amounts of equipment. And there is the matter of personal accommodation and equipment storage. The time available for excavation is always limited, sometimes extremely so; the research program must be compressed to fit it, and the staff must be "tasked" accordingly. When the excavation has been completed the samples need to be packed and shipped—frequently on ice—back to headquarters or to specialized laboratories. All archaeologists will tell you that field work is mostly laborious, not glamorous; a landfill excavation is archaeology of the laborious kind.

For all the difficulties they present, the Garbage Project's landfill digs have acquired an increasing timeliness and relevance as concerns about solid-waste disposal have grown. Even as the Garbage Project has trained considerable attention on garbage as an analytical tool it has also taken up the problem of garbage itself— garbage as a problem, garbage as symbolized by *Mobro 4000,* the so-called "garbage barge," which sailed from Islip, Long Island, on March 22, 1987, and spent the next fifty-five days plying the seas in search of a place to deposit its 3,168 tons of cargo. Strange though it may seem, although more than 70 percent of America's household and commercial garbage ends up in landfills, very little reliable data existed until recently as to a landfill's contents and biological dynamics. Much of the conventional wisdom about garbage disposal consists of assertions that turn out, upon investigation, to be simplistic or misleading: among them, the assertion that, as trash, plastic, foam, and fast-food packaging are causes for great concern, that biodegradable items are always more desirable than nonbiodegradable ones, that on a per capita basis the nation's households are generating a lot more garbage than they used to, and that we're physically running out of places to put landfills.

This is not to say that garbage isn't a problem in need of serious attention. It is. But if they are to succeed, plans of action must be based on garbage realities. The most critical part of the garbage problem in America is that our notions about the creation and disposal of garbage are often riddled with myth. There are few other subjects of public significance on which popular and official opinion is so consistently misinformed....

Gaps—large gaps—remain in our knowledge of garbage, and of how human behavior relates to it, and of how best to deal with it. But a lighted candle has at least been seized and thrust inside the antechamber.

---

*A note on terminology. Several words for the things we throw away—"garbage," "trash," "refuse," "rubbish"—are used synonymously in casual speech but in fact have different meanings. *Trash* refers specifically to discards that are at least theoretically "dry"—newspapers, boxes, cans, and so on. *Garbage* refers technically to "wet" discards—food remains, yard waste, and offal. *Refuse* is an inclusive term for both the wet discards and the dry. *Rubbish* is even more inclusive: It refers to all refuse plus construction and demolition debris. The distinction between wet and dry garbage was important in the days when cities slopped garbage to pigs, and needed to have the wet material separated from the dry; it eventually became irrelevant, but may see a revival if the idea of composting food and yard waste catches on. We will frequently use "garbage" in this book to refer to the totality of human discards because it is the word used most naturally in ordinary speech. The word is etymologically obscure, though it probably derives from Anglo-French, and its earliest associations have to do with working in the kitchen.

*A question that always comes up is: What about garbage disposers? Garbage disposers are obviously capable of skewing the data in certain garbage categories, and Garbage Project researchers can employ a variety of techniques to compensate for the bias that garbage disposers introduce. Studies were conducted at the very outset of the Garbage Project to determine the discard differential between households with and without disposers, and one eventual result was a set of correction factors for various kinds of garbage (primarily food), broken down by subtype. As a general rule of thumb, households with disposers end up discarding in their trash about half the amount of food waste and food debris as households without disposers. It should be noted, however, that the fact that disposers have ground up some portion of a household's garbage often has little relevance to the larger issues the Garbage Project is trying to address. It means, for example, not that the Garbage Project's findings about the extent of food waste are invalid, but merely that its estimates are conservative.

From *Rubbish! The Archaeology of Garbage* by William Rathje and Cullen Murphy, (HarperCollins 1992), Chapter 1, pp. 3–29. © 1992 by William Rathje and Cullen Murphy. Reprinted by permission of the authors.

BUSHMEN

John Yellen

I followed Dau, kept his slim brown back directly in front of me, as we broke suddenly free from the dense Kalahari bush and crossed through the low wire fence that separated Botswana from Namibia to the West. For that moment while Dau held the smooth wires apart for me, we were out in the open, in the full hot light of the sun and then we entered the shadows, the tangled thickets of arrow grass and thorn bush and mongongo trees once again. As soon as the bush began to close in around us again, I quickly became disoriented, Dau's back my only reference point.

Even then, in that first month of 1968, while my desert boots retained their luster, I knew enough to walk behind, not next to Dau. I had expected the Kalahari Desert to be bare open sand. I had imagined myself looking out over vast stretches that swept across to the horizon. But to my surprise, I found that the dunes were covered with trees and that during the rains the grasses grew high over my head. The bare sand, where I could see it, was littered with leaves, and over these the living trees and brush threw a dappled pattern of sunlight and shade. To look in the far distance and maintain a sense of direction, to narrow my focus and pick a way between the acacia bushes and their thorns, and then to look down, just in front of my feet to search out menacing shapes, was too much for me. Already, in that first month, the Bushmen had shown me a puff adder coiled motionless by the base of an acacia tree, but not until Cumsa the Hunter came up close to it, ready to strike it with his spear, could I finally see what all those hands were pointing at.

As Dau walked, I tried to follow his lead. To my discomfort I knew that many of these bushes had thorns—the Kalahari cloaks itself in thorns—some hidden close to the ground just high enough to rake across my ankles and draw blood when I pushed through, others long and straight and white so they reflected the sun. That morning, just before the border fence, my concentration had lagged and I found myself entangled in wait-a-bit thorns that curved backwards up the branch. So I stopped and this short, brown-skinned Bushman pushed me gently backwards to release the tension, then worked the branch, thorn by thorn from my shirt and my skin.

In the mid-1960s, the South African government had decided to accurately survey the Botswana border, mark it with five-strand fence, and cut a thin firebreak on either side. At intervals they constructed survey towers, strange skeletal affairs, like oil drilling rigs, their tops poking well above the highest mongongo trees. It was to one of these that Dau led me across the border, through the midday sun. Although he would not climb it himself, since it was a white man's tower, he assumed I would. I followed his finger, his chain of logic as I started rather hesitantly up the rusted rungs. I cleared the arrow grass, the acacia bushes, finally the broad leafy crowns of the mongongo nut trees. Just short of the top I stopped and sat, hooked my feet beneath the rung below, and wrapped my arms around the metal edges of the sides.

For a month now I had copied the maps—the lines and the circles the !Kung tribesmen had drawn with their fingers in the sand. I had listened and tried to transcribe names of those places, so unintelligible with their clicks, their rising and falling tones. I had walked with Dau and the others to some of those places, to small camps near ephemeral water holes, but on the ground it was too confusing, the changes in altitude and vegetation too subtle, the sun too nearly overhead to provide any sense of where I was or from where I had come.

For the first time from the tower, I could see an order to the landscape. From up there on the tower, I could see that long thin border scar, could trace it off to the horizon to both the north and south. But beyond that, no evidence, not the slightest sign of a human hand. The Bushmen camps were too few in number, too small and well-hidden in the grass and bush to be visible from here. Likewise, the camp where we anthropologists lived, off to the east at the Dobe waterhole, that also was too small to see.

As Dau had intended, from my perch on that tower I learned a lot. At least now I could use the dunes, the shallow valleys, to know whether I was walking east and west or north and south.

In those first years with the Dobe Bushmen, I did gain at least a partial understanding of that land. And I

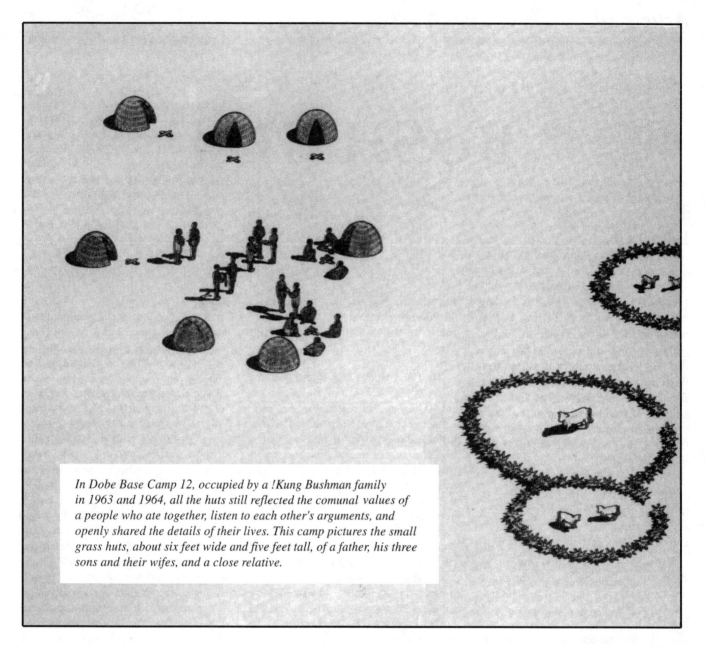

In Dobe Base Camp 12, occupied by a !Kung Bushman family in 1963 and 1964, all the huts still reflected the comunal values of a people who ate together, listen to each other's arguments, and openly shared the details of their lives. This camp pictures the small grass huts, about six feet wide and five feet tall, of a father, his three sons and their wifes, and a close relative.

learned to recognize many of those places, the ones that rate no name at all but are marked only by events— brief, ephemeral happenings that leave no mark on the land. I learned to walk with the Bushmen back from a hunt or a trip for honey or spear-shaft wood and listen. They talked, chattered almost constantly, decorating the bus, these no-name places as they went, putting ornaments of experience on them: "See that tree there, John? That's where we stopped, my brother and I, long before he was married, when he killed a kudu, a big female. We stopped under that tree, hung the meat up there

and rested in the shade. But the flies were so bad, the biting flies, that we couldn't stay for long."

It took me a long time to realize that this chatter was not chatter at all, to understand that those remarks were gifts, a private map shared only among a few, an overlay crammed with fine, spidery writing on top of the base map with its named waterholes and large valleys, a map for friends to read. Dau would see a porcupine burrow, tiny, hidden in the vastness of the bush. And at night he could sit by the fire and move the others from point to point across the landscape to that small opening in the ground.

But as an archeologist, I had a task to do—to name those places and to discover what life had been like there in the past. "This place has a name now," I told Dau when I went back in 1976. Not the chicken camp, because when I was there I kept 15 chickens, or the cobra camp, for the cobra we killed one morning among the nesting hens, but Dobe Base Camp 18. Eighteen because it's the eighteenth of these old abandoned camps I've followed you to in the last three days. See? That's what goes into this ledger, this fat bound book in waterproof ballpoint ink. We could get a reflector in here—a big piece of tin like some

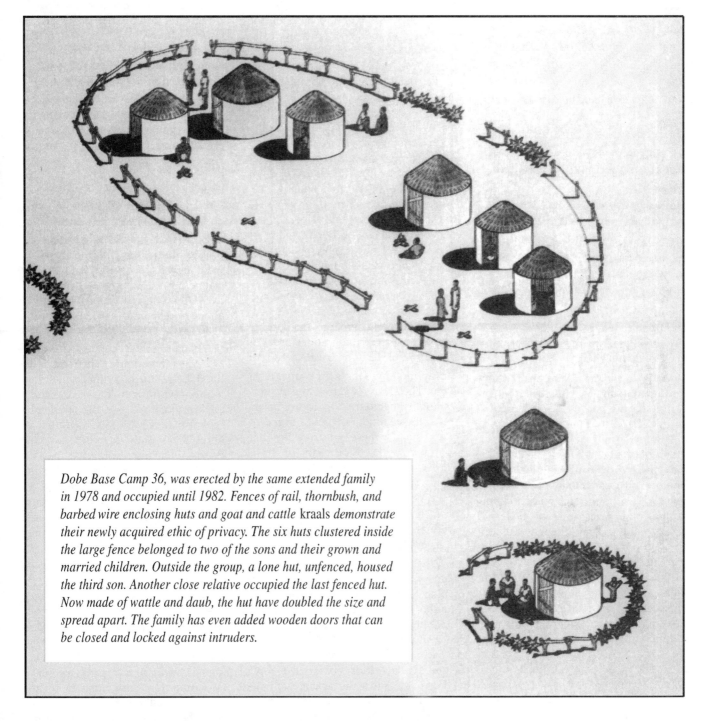

Dobe Base Camp 36, was erected by the same extended family in 1978 and occupied until 1982. Fences of rail, thornbush, and barbed wire enclosing huts and goat and cattle kraals *demonstrate their newly acquired ethic of privacy. The six huts clustered inside the large fence belonged to two of the sons and their grown and married children. Outside the group, a lone hut, unfenced, housed the third son. Another close relative occupied the last fenced hut. Now made of wattle and daub, the hut have doubled the size and spread apart. The family has even added wooden doors that can be closed and locked against intruders.*

metal off a roof and get some satellite or a plane to photograph it. We could tell just where it is then, could mark it on one of those large aerial maps down to the nearest meter if we wanted.

We came back to these camps, these abandoned places on the ground, not once but month after month for the better part of a year. Not just Dau and myself but a whole crew of us, eight Bushmen and I, to

dig, to look down into the ground. We started before the sun was too high up in the sky, and later Dau and I sat in the shade sipping thick, rich tea. I asked questions and he talked.

"One day when I was living here, I shot a kudu: an adult female. Hit it with one arrow in the flank. But it went too far and we never found it. Then another day my brother hit a wildebeest, another adult female and that one we

got. We carried it back to camp here and ate it."

"What other meat did you eat here, Dau?"

"One, no two, steenbok, it was."

1948: 28 years ago by my counting was when Dau, his brothers, his family were here. How could he remember the detail? This man sat in the shade and recalled trivial events that have repeated themselves in more or less the

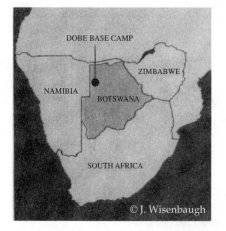
© J. Wisenbaugh

same way at so many places over the last three decades.

We dug day after day in the old camps —and found what Dau said we should. Bones, decomposing, but still identifiable: bones of wildebeest and steenbok among the charcoal and mongongo nut shells.

We dug our squares, sifting through the sand for bones. And when I dumped the bones, the odd ostrich eggshell bead, the other bits and pieces out onto the bridge table to sort, so much of what my eyes and ears told me was confirmed in this most tangible form. If excavation in one square revealed the bones of a wildebeest or kudi or other large antelope, then the others would contain them as well. In an environment as unpredictable as the Kalahari, where the game was hard to find and the probability of failure high, survival depended on sharing, on spreading the risk. And the bones, distributed almost evenly around the individual family hearths confirmed that. What also impressed me was how little else other than the bones there was. Most archeological sites contain a broad range of debris. But in those years the Bushmen owned so little. Two spears or wooden digging sticks or strings of ostrich eggshell beads were of no more use than one. Better to share, to give away meat or extra belongings and through such gifts create a web of debts, of obligations that some day would be repaid. In 1948, even in 1965, to accumulate material goods made no sense.

When it was hot, which was most of the year, I arranged the bridge table and two chairs in a patch of nearby shade. We sat there with the bound black and red ledger and dumped the bones in a heap in the center of the table, then sorted them out. I did the easy stuff, separated out the turtle shells, the bird bones, set each in a small pile around the table's edge. Dau did the harder part, separated the steenbok from the duiker, the wildebeest from kudu, held small splintered bone fragments and turned them over and over in his hands. We went through the piles then, one by one, moved each in its turn to the center of the table, sorted them into finer categories, body part by body part, bone by bone. Cryptic notes, bits of data that accumulated page by page. The bones with their sand and grit were transformed into numbers in rows and columns, classes and subclasses which would, I hoped, emerge from some computer to reveal a grander order, a design, an underlying truth.

Taphonomy: That's the proper term for it. The study of burial and preservation. Archeologists dig lots of bones out of the ground, not just from recent places such as these but from sites that span the millions of years of mankind's existence. On the basis of the bones, we try to learn about those ancient people. We try to reconstruct their diet, figure out how the animals were hunted, how they were killed, butchered, and shared.

What appealed to me about the Dobe situation, why I followed Dau, walked out his youth and his early manhood back and forth around the waterhole was the neat, almost laboratory situation Dobe offered. A natural experiment. I could go to a modern camp, collect those discarded food bones even before the jackals and hyenas had gotten to them, examine and count them, watch the pattern emerge. What happened then to the bones after they'd been trampled, picked over, rained on, lain in the ground for five years? Five years ago? Dobe Base Camp 21, 1971. I could go there, dig up a sample and find out.

What went on farther and farther back in time? Is there a pattern? Try eight years ago. 1968, DBC 18. We could go there to the cobra camp and see. Thirty-four years ago? The camp where Tsaa with the beautiful wife was born. One can watch, can see how things fall apart, can make graphs, curves, shoot them back, watch them arc backwards beyond Dau, beyond Dau's father, back into the true archeological past.

We dug our way through the DBCs, back into the early 1940s, listening day after day to the South African soap operas on the short-wave radio, and our consumption of plastic bags went down and down. Slim pickings in the bone department. And the bones we did find tended to be rotten: They fragmented, fell apart in the sieve.

So we left the 1940s, collapsed the bridge table and the folding chairs and went to that site that played such a crucial role for anthropologists: DBC 12, the 1963 camp where those old myths about hunters and gatherers came up against the hard rock of truth.

They built this camp just after Richard Lee, the pioneer, arrived. They lived there through the winter and hunted warthog with spears and a pack of dogs so good they remember each by name to this day. Richard lived there with them. He watched them—what they did, what they ate, weighed food on his small scale slung with a rope from an acacia tree. He weighed people, sat in camp day after day with his notebook and his wristwatch and scale. He recorded times: when each person left camp in the morning, when each returned for the day.

In this small remnant group, one of the last in the world still living by hunting and gathering, it should be possible, he believed, to see a reflection, a faint glimmer of the distant universal past of all humanity, a common condition that had continued for millions and millions of years. He went there because of that and for that reason, later on, the rest of us followed him.

What he found in that desert camp, that dry, hard land, set the anthropological world back on its collective ear. What his scale and his wristwatch and his systematic scribbles showed was that we were fooled, that we had it all wrong. To be a hunter and gatherer wasn't that bad after all. They didn't work that hard, even in this land of thorns: For an adult, it came to less time than a nine-to-five office worker puts in on the job. They lived a long time, too, didn't wear out and die young but old-looking, as we had always thought. Even in this camp, the camp with the good hunting dogs, it was plants, not meat, which provided the staff of life. Women walked through the nut groves and collected nuts with their toes, dug in the molapos and sang to each other through the bush. Unlike the game, which spooked so easily and followed the unpredictable rains, the nuts, roots, and berries were dependable, there in plenty, there for the picking. Another distinguished anthropologist, Marshall Sahlins, termed those DBC 12 people "the original affluent society"—something quite different from the traditional conception of hunting and gathering as a mean, hard existence half a step ahead of starvation and doom.

Over the years that name has held—but life in the Kalahari has changed. That kind of camp, with all the bones and mongongo nuts and dogs, is no more.

By the mid-1970s, things were different at Dobe. Diane Gelburd, another of the anthropologists out there then, only needed to look around her to see how the Bushman lifestyle had changed from the way Richard recorded it, from how Sahlins described it. But what had changed the people at DBC 12 who believed that property should be commonly held and shared? What had altered their system of values? That same winter Diane decided to find out.

She devised a simple measure of acculturation that used pictures cut from magazines: an airplane, a sewing machine, a gold mine in South Africa. (Almost no one got the gold mine right.) That was the most enjoyable part of the study. They all liked to look at pictures, to guess.

Then she turned from what people knew to what they believed. She wanted to rank them along a scale, from traditional to acculturated. So again she asked questions:

"Will your children be tattooed?"

To women: "If you were having a difficult childbirth and a white doctor were there, would you ask for assistance?"

To men: "If someone asked you for permission to marry your daughter would you demand (the traditional) bride service?"

Another question so stereotyped that in our own society one would be too embarrassed to ask it: "Would you let your child marry someone from another tribe—a Tswana or a Herero—a white person?"

First knowledge, then belief, and finally material culture. She did the less sensitive questions first. "Do you have a field?" What do you grow? What kind of animals do you have? How many of what?" Then came the hard part: She needed to see what people actually owned. I tagged along with her one day and remember the whispers inside one dark mud hut. Trunks were unlocked and hurriedly unpacked away from the entrance to shield them from sight. A blanket spread out on a trunk revealed the secret wealth that belied their statements: "Me? I have nothing." In the semidarkness she made her inventory. Then the trunks were hastily repacked and relocked with relief.

She went through the data, looked at those lists of belongings, itemized them in computer printouts. Here's a man who still hunts. The printout shows it. He has a bow and quiver and arrows on which the poison is kept fresh. He has a spear and snares for birds. He has a small steenbok skin bag, a traditional carryall that rests neatly under his arm.

He also has 19 goats and two donkeys, bought from the Herero or Tswana, who now get Dobe Bushmen to help plant their fields and herd their cows. They pay in livestock, hand-me-down clothing, blankets, and sometimes cash. He has three large metal trunks crammed full: One is packed to the top with shoes, shirts, and pants, most well-worn. He has two large linen mosquito nets, 10 tin cups, and a metal file. He has ropes of beads: strand upon strand—over 200 in all, pounds of small colored glass beads made in Czechoslovakia that I had bought in Johannesburg years earlier. He has four large iron pots and a five-gallon plastic jerry can. He has a plow, a gift form the anthropologists. He has a bridle and bit, light blankets, a large

tin basin. He has six pieces of silverware, a mirror and hairbrush, two billycans. His wife and his children together couldn't carry all that. The trunks are too heavy and too large for one person to carry so you would have to have two people for each. What about the plow, those heavy iron pots? Quite a job to carry those through bush, through the thick thorns.

But here is the surprising part. Talk to that man. Read the printout. See what he knows, what he believes. It isn't surprising that he speaks the Herero language and Setswana fluently or that he has worked for the Herero, the anthropologists. Nothing startling there. A budding Dobe capitalist. But then comes the shock: He espouses the traditional values.

"Bushmen share things, John. We share things and depend on each other, help each other out. That's what makes us different from the black people."

But the same person, his back to the door, opens his trunks, unlocks them one by one, lays out the blankets, the beads, then quickly closes each before he opens the next.

Multiply that. Make a whole village of people like that, and you can see the cumulative effect: You can actually measure it. As time goes on, as people come to own more possessions; the huts move farther and farther apart.

In the old days a camp was cosy, intimate and close. You could sit there by one fire and look into the other grass huts, see what the other people were doing, what they were making or eating. You heard the conversations, the arguments and banter.

We ask them why the new pattern?

Says Dau: "It's because of the livestock that we put our huts this way. They can eat the grass from the roofs and the sides of our houses. So we have to build fences to keep them away and to do that, you must have room between the huts."

I look up from the fire, glance around the camp, say nothing. No fences there. Not a single one around any of the huts, although I concede that one day they probably will build them. But why construct a lot of separate small fences, one around each hut? Why not clump the huts together the way they did in the old days and make a single large fence around the lot? Certainly a more efficient approach. Why worry about fences now in any case? The only exposed grass is on the roofs, protected by straight mud walls and nothing short of an elephant or giraffe could eat it.

Xashe's answer is different. Another brief reply. An attempt to dispose of the subject politely but quickly. "It's fire, John. That's what we're worried about. If we put our houses too close together, if one catches fire, the others will burn as well. We don't want one fire to burn all our houses down. That's why we build them so far apart."

But why worry about fire now? What about in the old days when the huts were so close, cheek by jowl? Why is it that when the huts were really vulnerable, when they were built entirely of dried grass, you didn't worry about fires then?

You read Diane's interviews and look at those lists of how much people own. You see those shielded mud huts with doors spaced, so far apart. You also listen to the people you like and trust. People who always have been honest with you. You hear their explanations and realize the evasions are not for you but for themselves. You see things they can't. But nothing can be done. It would be ludicrous to tell these brothers: "Don't you see, my friends, the lack of concordance between your values and the changing reality of your world?"

Now, years after the DBC study, I sit with data spread out before me and it is so clear. Richard's camp in 1963: just grass huts, a hearth in front of each. Huts and hearths in a circle, nothing more. 1968: more of the same. The following year though the first *kraal* appears, just a small thorn enclosure, some acacia bushes cut and dragged haphazardly together for their first few goats. It's set apart way out behind the circle of huts. On one goes, from plot to plot, following the pattern from year to year. The huts change from grass to mud. They become larger, more solidly built. Goats, a few at first, then more of them. So you build a fence around your house to keep them away from the grass

roofs. The *kraals* grow larger, move in closer to be incorporated finally into the circle of huts itself. The huts become spaced farther and farther apart, seemingly repelled over time, one from the next. People, families move farther apart.

The bones tell the same story. 1947: All the bones from wild animals, game caught in snares or shot with poisoned arrows—game taken from the bush. By 1964 a few goat bones, a cow bone or two, but not many. Less than 20 percent of the total. Look then at the early 1970s and watch the line on the graph climb slowly upwards—by 1976 over 80 percent from domesticated stock.

But what explains the shattering of this society? Why is this hunting and gathering way of life, so resilient in the face of uncertainty, falling apart? It hasn't been a direct force—a war, the ravages of disease. It is the internal conflicts, the tensions, the inconsistencies, the impossibility of reconciling such different views of the world.

At Dobe it is happening to them all together. All of the huts have moved farther apart in lockstep, which makes it harder for them to see how incompatible the old system is with the new. But Rakudu, a Bushman who lived at the Mahopa waterhole eight miles down the valley from Dobe, was a step ahead of the rest. He experienced, before the rest of them, their collective fate.

When I was at the Cobra Camp in 1969, Rakudu lived down near Mahopa, off on his own, a mile or so away from the pastoral Herero villages. He had two hats and a very deep bass voice, both so strange, so out of place in a Bushman. He was a comical sort of man with the hats and that voice and a large Adam's apple that bobbed up and down.

The one hat must have been a leftover from the German-Herero wars because no one in Botswana wore a hat like that—a real pith helmet with a solid top and rounded brim. It had been cared for over the years because, although soiled and faded, it still retained the original strap that tucks beneath the chin. The second hat was also unique—a World War I aviator's hat, one of those leather sacks that fits tightly over the head and buckles un-

der the chin. Only the goggles were missing.

I should have seen then how out of place the ownership of two hats was in that hunter-gatherer world. Give two hats like that to any of the others and one would have been given away on the spot. A month or two later, the other would become a gift as well. Moving goods as gifts and favors along that chain of human ties. That was the way to maintain those links, to keep them strong.

When I went to Rakudu's village and realized what he was up to, I could see that he was one of a kind. The mud-walled huts in his village made it look like a Herero village—not a grass hut in sight. And when I came, Rakudu pulled out a hand-carved wood and leather chair and set it in the shade. This village was different from any of the Bushman camps I had seen. Mud huts set out in a circle, real clay storage bins to hold the corn—not platforms in a tree—and *kraals* for lots of goats and donkeys. He had a large field, too, several years before the first one appeared at Dobe.

Why shouldn't Bushmen do it—build their own villages, model their subsistence after the Herero? To plant a field, to tend goats, to build mud-walled houses like that was not hard to do. Work for the Herero a while and get an axe, accumulate the nucleus of a herd, buy or borrow the seeds. That year the rains were long and heavy. The sand held the water and the crickets and the birds didn't come. So the harvest was good, and I could sit there in the carved chair and look at Rakudu's herd of goats and their young ones and admire him for his industry, for what he had done.

Only a year later I saw him and his eldest son just outside the Cobra Camp. I went over and sat in the sand and listened to the negotiations for the marriage Rakudu was trying to arrange. His son's most recent wife had run away, and Rakudu was discussing a union between his son and Dau the Elder's oldest daughter who was just approaching marriageable age. They talked about names and Dau the Elder explained why the marriage couldn't take place. It was clear that the objection was trivial, that he was making an excuse. Even I could see that his explanation was a face-saving gesture to make the refusal easier for all of them.

Later I asked Dau the Elder why he did it. It seemed like a good deal to me. "Rakudu has all that wealth, those goats and field. I'd think that you would be anxious to be linked with a family like that. Look at all you have to gain. Is the son difficult? Did he beat his last wife?"

"She left because she was embarrassed. The wife before her ran away for the same reason and so did the younger brother's wife," he said. "Both brothers treated their wives well. The problem wasn't that. It was when the wives' relatives came. That's when it became so hard for the women because Rakudu and his sons are such stingy men. They wouldn't give anything away, wouldn't share anything with them. Rakudu has a big herd just like the Herero, and he wouldn't kill goats for them to eat."

Not the way Bushmen should act toward relatives, not by the traditional value system at least. Sharing, the most deeply held Bushman belief, and that man with the two hats wouldn't go along. Herero are different. You can't expect them to act properly, to show what is only common decency; you must take them as they are. But someone like Rakudu, a Bushman, should know better than that. So the wives walked out and left for good.

But Rakudu understood what was happening, how he was trapped—and he tried to respond. If you can't kill too many goats from the herd that has become essential to you, perhaps you can find something else of value to give away. Rakudu thought he had an answer.

He raised tobacco in one section of his field. Tobacco, a plant not really adapted to a place like the northern Kalahari, has to be weeded, watered by hand, and paid special care. Rakudu did that and for one year at least harvested a tobacco crop.

Bushmen crave tobacco and Rakudu hoped he had found a solution—that they would accept tobacco in place of goats, in place of mealie meal. A good try. Perhaps the only one open to him. But, as it turned out, not good enough. Rakudu's son could not find a wife.

Ironic that a culture can die yet not a single person perish. A sense of identity, of a shared set of rules, of participation in a single destiny binds individuals together into a tribe or cultural group. Let that survive long enough, let the participants pass this sense through enough generations, one to the next, create enough debris, and they will find their way into the archeological record, into the study of cultures remembered only by their traces left on the land.

Rakudu bought out. He, his wife, and his two sons sold their goats for cash, took the money and walked west, across the border scar that the South Africans had cut, through the smooth fence wire and down the hard calcrete road beyond. They became wards of the Afrikaaners, were lost to their own culture, let their fate pass into hands other than their own. At Chum kwe, the mission station across the border 34 miles to the west, they were given numbers and the right to stand in line with the others and have mealie meal and other of life's physical essentials handed out to them. As wards of the state, that became their right. When the problems, the contradictions of your life are insoluble, a paternalistic hand provides one easy out.

Dau stayed at Dobe. Drive there today and you can find his mud-walled hut just by the waterhole. But he understands: He has married off his daughter, his first-born girl to a wealthy Chum kwe man who drives a tractor—an old man, more than twice her age, and by traditional Bushmen standards not an appropriate match. Given the chance, one by one, the others will do the same.

John Yellen, director of the anthropology program at the National Science Foundation, has returned to the Kalahari four times since 1968.

UNIT 3
Techniques in Archaeology

Unit Selections

Key Points to Consider

- How has photography been useful to archaeology? What kinds of new camera techniques have improved the quality of the results? Give an example of a site where this technique was used.

- What kind of advances have been made in techniques to date archaeological sites in the last 50 years or so? Discuss the use of laser technology, nuclear physics, and computers.

- How has DNA been used to help date archaeological materials? Please explain.

- What kinds of techniques have archaeologists been able to borrow from space technology? How are remote sensing devices from satellites circling the earth used to locate archaeological sites?

- How can a wasp's nest possibly be used to date archaeological sites? Explain this technique of optical luminescence. This technique can go back in time around 17,000 years. How?

- What have archaeologists been able to borrow from physical anthropologists in terms of dating techniques? Give examples.

- How is forensics used in archaeology?

- Who was "Nursing Home Man"? How did forensic anthropologists date his life and suspicious death? How can this technique be applied to solving present day murders?

- How can such techniques as a gas chromatograph/mass spectrometer be used to identify and date archaeological materials? Give an example of this using a prehistoric unglazed piece of pottery.

- Why is archaeological surveying, just walking around looking at a site, still one of the best techniques available in archaeology? Please explain.

DUSHKIN ONLINE **Links: www.dushkin.com/online/**
These sites are annotated in the World Wide Web pages.

American Anthropologist
http://www.aaanet.org
Ancient Economies II
http://www.angelfire.com/ms/ancecon/
NOVA Online/Pyramids—The Inside Story
http://www.pbs.org/wgbh/nova/pyramid/

Archaeology has evolved significantly from being an exercise in separating the remains of past human behavior from the "dirt". And as such, archaeology in turn employs a diversified group of highly sophisticated techniques. Digging in itself has gone through its own evolution of techniques ranging from the wild thrashings of Heinrich Schielmann to the obsessive military precision of Sir Mortimer Wheeler.

Archaeology continues to expand the use of a multidisciplinary approach and is therefore incorporating more techniques that will prove to enlighten us about our human past.

The most well known technique to be developed in archaeology was radiocarbon dating. This provides archaeologists with one of their most valuable means of establishing the age of archaeological materials. This technique was developed by W. F. Libby at UCLA in 1949. This new technique was a major revolution. It has enabled archaeologists for the first time (in all of history and prehistory!) to have an empirical means of determining the age of archaeological sites in terms of absolute years. This dating technique is based on the principle of radioactive decay in which unstable radioactive isotopes transform into stable elements at a constant rate. In order to fine-tune accuracy, dates are presented with a standard statistical margin of error. Great care is taken with respect to any factors that may skew the results of materials being dated. Radiocarbon dating is limited to the dating of organic materials and is not able to date such things as stone tools. It can date materials as far back as 100,000 years or more. As the technique is perfected, it will be able to date organic matter of even earlier times. The word "present" was designated to be 1950 A.D. Now of course, we can add another 53 years to this date.

The state of preservation of archaeological materials is dependent upon many variables. These include the original material of the artifact and the conditions of the site in which it is preserved. For example, a nineteenth-century adobe mission in the Mojave desert in California may be so weathered as to be unrecognizable. This is due to the fact that extreme temperatures, varying from very hot to very cold, typical of a low desert climate, tend to rapidly destroy any kind of matter. On the other hand, consistently wet or consistently dry conditions tend to preserve organic matter in a relatively pristine state for long periods of time. The preservation of human remains is therefore very good in bogs, such as in Denmark, or in coastal deserts of Peru. At these sites the conditions are constantly moist in Denmark. In the coastal deserts of Peru the conditions remain dry. Therefore archaeological material may be preserved for many thousands of years.

Since the discovery of radiocarbon dating, numerous other techniques have been invented that have their applications to ar-chaeology to further clarify dates, preservation, and in general, add to the ability of archaeologists to do cultural historical reconstruction.

Discussed in this section are some of the extraordinary applications of such varied hard sciences as nuclear physics, laser technology, and computers. We can now describe sites in terms of time-space systemics and virtual reality in a way that exceeds recent science-fiction fantasies.

Remote sensing devices from outer space allow sites to be reconstructed without invasive excavation. New, cleverly devised radiometric techniques are being developed to suit specific conditions to date archaeological remains by association. The use of wasp's nests is one such example.

Archaeologists sometimes rely on the use of forensic specialists to present images of the past that we could never before see. Used in conjunction with the exponential knowledge rapidly developing from DNA analysis, our images from the past are focused into a detail comparable to a digital camera.

Unglazed cooking pots have been tested to yield information on prehistoric diets through molecular analysis.

Yet, the simple time-tested technique of archaeological surveying still helps reconstruct sites, again without invasive excavation. The future of archaeology will increasingly depend on techniques to maximize preservation of sites and minimize archaeological excavation. Archaeological excavation, for all its good intents and purposes, destroys archaeological sites as fully as pot hunting or parking lots.

Camera Bodies

EUGENE F LALLY

My first photograph in 1942 was taken with a Kodak Brownie Box camera that my grandmother in Boston gave me when I was eight years old. It was love at first sight when that picture appeared like an apparition in the developer tray.

We had only grainy black and white film available and lenses of poor quality, and prints developed in our own make-shift darkrooms turned brown after a few years. I have seen great innovations since then, even helped create some, but nothing like the fast pace currently set by digital photography.

The improvements in photography the past few years are making it easier for anthropologists to record work in the field and indoors for cataloguing and publishing. Using less equipment, resulting in a lighter camera bag, you now can bring home better photographs. Simplifying the job of recording images lets you spend more time on the basics of your work.

Camera Bodies

The advent of digital cameras permits innovations to be discussed for film camera bodies as well as new digital bodies, which employ a light-sensing array or chip that takes the place of film. The term "camera body" is used to isolate the workings of the camera, less its lens. Quality camera bodies are purchased separate from the lens. Digital bodies are improving rapidly, and when coupled with image-processing software, eventually will surpass film cameras in many aspects.

Features in 35 mm single-lens-reflex camera bodies and support equipment have improved to the level that the use of larger-format, bulkier and more costly camera bodies rarely is needed. Automatic exposure and focus control have made 35 mm film and digital cameras dependable and easy-to-use tools. Programmable modes in camera bodies allow computer chips to solve special situations automatically by turning one dial. The camera determines the optimum shutter speed/aperture combination for overall exposure based on subject type, including: portrait, landscape, hyperfocal, silhouette, action, close-up, etc. For example, in "landscape" mode, the depth-of-field (sharpness from close-up distance to infinity), is optimized by automatic focus and shutter speed/aperture setting selections, depending on the film speed used and lighting conditions.

Automatic exposure control has gone a long way to assure correct exposures even for hard-to-please transparency films. Top-of-the-line camera bodies divide the image into many segments for exposure evaluation. Light values, contrast and scene content of each segment instantly are compared to a large database of photos as the shutter button is being compressed in certain brand camera body's memory, so as to determine the best overall exposure based on past results of similar scenes.

Photos shown with this article were taken in the Taos Pueblo, NM. No tripods were allowed, so a handheld camera was required. Slow-speed color transparency film was selected to preserve the rich color tones of the Pueblo.

Taos Pottery on Wall #0104-R10-33V

The images required depth-of-field from several feet in front of the camera to infinity. This was provided by the body's automatic capabilities when set for "hyperfocal" mode. Quality images could have been obtained if a tripod was permitted and all made manually, but this would have required some thought and set-up time.

While the manual efforts are challenging and fun to figure out, they do take your mind off your anthropology work. The above features, available in both film and digital top-of-the-line camera bodies, produce photographs in the field of excellent quality in less time with less equipment.

Taos Pueblo/Oven #0104-R10-8H

Eugene F Lally is a photo archaeologist. He graduated as an electrical engineer in Boston, and then went to California in 1957 to pioneer in the space business. Lally became Jet Propulsion Laboratory's planetary mission conceptual designer, all the while immersed in every element of photography, including the Mt Palomar 200-inch telescope. He has developed camera innovations, consults camera companies, teaches photography workshops, exhibits Southwest Indian Pueblo photos in museums and magazines, lectures, and writes. To learn more about his experience and work, visit www.lallyphotography.com.

High-Tech "Digging"

Fifty years of technological innovation has revolutionized the practice of archaeology.

by Chris Scarre

Archaeology is the study of people, of past human societies. For many, this simple and obvious fact makes the subject a humanity or social science and distinguishes it sharply from hard sciences such as physics or chemistry. Yet modern archaeology uses a wide range of scientific aids, and a great deal of what we discover about the past comes directly from the application of technology. Here as much as anywhere, the last 50 years have seen enormous changes. Archaeology has benefited from the growing computerization of society; advances in nuclear physics, like electron microscopes and particle accelerators; and the development of laser technology used in sophisticated and highly accurate surveying equipment. Meanwhile, DNA analysis is opening up possibilities for studying relationships among people buried in ancient cemeteries, detecting the arrival of immigrant groups, and more. This, in turn, links directly with ideas of ethnicity and identity, among the hottest topics in politics today. It is all part of the great transformation of archaeology from an amateur pursuit with relatively few salaried full-timers to a highly professional discipline employing thousands of university-trained specialists. Men and women in white coats, toiling away in their laboratories, have become as important as rugged fieldworkers slogging away under the hot sun.

Today's rugged fieldworkers, however, slog away rather differently than did their predecessors 50 years ago. At my own excavation of a Neolithic burial mound at Prissé-la-Charrière in western France, the picks, shovels, and trowels haven't changed much. We still cart earth away in wheelbarrows and pile it neatly beyond the edges of the site. But when we lay out the trenches, we use an electronic distance meter (EDM), which automatically records distances, directions, and heights by laser beam and then sends them to a computer. Before deciding where to dig, we carry a fluxgate gradiometer (a type of magnetometer) over the site to detect tiny variations in the magnetic sensitivity of deposits. The results are downloaded onto an onsite computer to produce a diagram of what is below ground. It picks up quarry ditches cut into the limestone bedrock on either side of our burial mound and even detects walls and other features within the mound itself. Last year, we also used radar sounding to see if we could locate burial chambers within the mound. One day we may be able to "excavate" a site by remote sensing alone, without ever setting spade to earth.

Remote sensing in its more sophisticated forms isn't limited to individual sites: airborne remote sensing has already led to the detection of entire buried landscapes in some regions of the world. One such technique is radar, used to detect Maya field systems in Guatemala, another is its close cousin sonar, which led to the discovery of the armed schooners *Hamilton* and *Scourge,* sunk in Lake Ontario in the War of 1812. Radar imagery employing a long wavelength that can penetrate forest canopy has recently been used to locate and map new sites around Angkor in Cambodia, throwing light on the development of the early Khmer state. Satellite imagery from the U.S. LANDSAT and French SPOT satellites has extended this technology into space. Meanwhile, space-imaging radar (SIR) deployed from the shuttle *Columbia* in 1991 has traced former river courses in China's hyperarid Taklamakan desert.

When it comes to mapping our site, the new technology takes over again. Gone are the tape measures and drawing boards; the new technology uses a video camera mounted on a long raised arm to take overlapping pictures looking straight down at the site, feeding them directly into a computer. The resulting computer-generated plans take a fraction of the time required to make a hand-drafted map and allow us to record exactly the positions of the thousands of stones that make up our burial mound.

Other innovations involve not so much sophisticated technology as new approaches and priorities. No competent archaeologist today would ignore the wealth of evidence to be obtained by sieving the soil. Excavators who chose to sieve their material a half-century ago (and not many did) would have used a ¼-inch mesh screen, whereas today, fine meshes measuring down to 500 microns (½ of a millimeter) or less are regularly used to permit a more comprehensive recovery of faunal remains, including those of small animals, like mice, voles, and shrews. Though such animals were presumably not eaten, they live in particular habitats, so the presence of their remains can be an important indicator of environmental conditions at a site. This technique is slow, but essential in cases where a single bone can be crucial. Also standard on many sites is a flotation machine, which uses a liquid (usually water) to dissolve sediments, allowing recovery of organic remains from insect parts to plant fragments. We don't only want to know what pottery people made, what houses they lived in, and what livestock they kept, but also what plants they cultivated and ate. Almost all of our knowledge about the origins of wheat and barley cultivation has come to us by careful excavation and sieving or flotation of deposits at key Near Eastern sites such as Jericho and Abu Hureyra.

Some ancient seeds can easily be identified by eye, but to study them properly (and to classify the less obvious fragments) requires a microscope and a laboratory. Seeds now go to the lab to be studied along with pollen, which has been analyzed for more than 80 years, and newer interests such as phytoliths, the microscopic silica structures that give plants their stiffness. Like pollen, phytoliths are durable and survive after all other parts of the plant have decayed. Whereas pollen, because it is airborne, tells us what plants grew in the vicinity of a site, phytoliths show us what plants the ancient occupants actually brought to it. They can also tell us what parts of a plant were present, like grain for eating or stalks for thatching or animal bedding.

Alongside seeds, pollen, and other plant remains, we find laboratory technicians specializing in dendrochronology, dating based on patterns of growth variation in tree rings, or palaeoclimatology, the study of ancient climates and climatic change. Many of these draw on techniques developed with no archaeological application in mind. One of the most important techniques in modern palaeoclimatology, for example, is oxygen-isotope analysis. This relies on the discovery that oxygen exists in two stable forms with different numbers of neutrons and hence different atomic mass. The proportions of the two forms, oxygen-16 and oxygen-18, vary according to global temperature (warmer means higher ^{16}O, colder means higher ^{18}O). Marine organisms incorporate both forms of oxygen in their shells, recording the $^{16}O/^{18}O$ proportion. After the organism dies, its shell falls to the sea floor and is preserved in the sediments. By determining the $^{16}O/^{18}O$ proportion in shells from sediment cores extracted from the sea floor, it is possible to trace changes in global temperature.

This technique has revolutionized our understanding of world climate, and in particular of the famous Ice Ages. Fifty years ago the best interpretation of the Ice Ages was still one published by German geologists Albrecht Penck and Eduard Brückner in 1909. They believed that there had been not just one Ice Age but a series of four, which they named Günz, Mindel, Riss, and Würm after rivers in the Alps (the most recent being the Würm; the North American equivalents were Nebraskan, Kansan, Illinoian, and Wisconsin). Since then better techniques for coring in ocean floors (an innovation of oil exploration) and advances in nuclear physics made oxygen isotope analysis possible. We now know that there were not four successive Ice Ages, but actually around 20 such cold periods spanning more than two million years. We can also chart exactly how the average global temperature changed, period by period and degree by degree, during that enormous expanse of time. Ice cores in Greenland and Antarctica have given similar results, oxygen being a major component of water. They show how frighteningly rapid—an increase in the mean annual temperature of 7°C, or 12.6°F, in 50 years—was the change in the fluctuating climate at the end of the last Ice Age some 11,600 years ago.

While palaeoclimatology and pollen analysis tell us what was going on in the environment, microstratigraphy (microscopic study of the nature and composition of minute sequences of soils and surfaces) can tell us in detail what was happening in a particular rock-shelter or room, such as which areas of a building were for living or sleeping, which were open courtyards, and what fuel was being burned on the fire. To do this, a section of sediment has to be consolidated in situ by applying resin, then removed as a block to a laboratory where a thin section of it can be examined under a microscope. In northern Syria, microstratigraphy at several early city sites has detected a layer of dust, suggesting widespread fallout and burning around 2350 B.C. This was initially interpreted as a volcanic event, but a more recent, tentative suggestion is that a meteor impact might have been the cause.

So far, we haven't said much about artifacts, but they are as much the focus of attention as they ever were. A whole battery of techniques—including optical emission spectrometry (OES), X-ray fluorescence spectrometry (XRF), neutron activation analysis

(NAA), and atomic absorption spectrometry (AAS)—is now available to tell archaeologists what their artifacts are made of and, in some cases, where they come from. Each technique has its own range of applications, whether it be to metals, stone, amber, or shell. One early and still important example of this kind of study was the analysis of obsidian from sites in the Near East and Mediterranean. Obsidian was used like flint in many prehistoric societies, but it comes from only a limited number of sources. Hence analysis (by XRF, NAA, and AAS, among others) made it possible in many cases to match obsidian from archaeological sites to sources. This revealed far-flung trade patterns, connecting sites in southern Iran to sources in eastern Turkey, and demonstrated beyond question that by the end of the Upper Palaeolithic, 10,000 years ago, Aegean sailors were already crossing from mainland Greece to the obsidian-rich island of Melos.

Without doubt the greatest advance in archaeological technology over the past 50 years has been in dating. Today it is hard to imagine archaeology without the huge battery of scientific dating techniques, from reliable workhorses such as radiocarbon, to uranium-series, fission-track, potassium-argon (K-A), thermoluminescence (TL), optically-stimulated luminescence (OSL), and electron-spin resonance (ESR) dating, to various experimental methods (such as cation ratio or chlorine-36) that researchers are using in trying to crack the problem of dating rock art.

Radiocarbon overturned many chronological schemes painstakingly assembled by prehistorians over the previous 100 years.

In 1949, Willard F. Libby published the first radiocarbon dates, and announced to the world the discovery of his new method. A chemist, Libby had spent the war years researching cosmic radiation, and established that cosmic rays hitting the atmosphere created radioactive carbon (^{14}C) at a constant and predictable rate. Carbon (both "ordinary" ^{12}C and radioactive ^{14}C) is present in all living things; plants take up carbon dioxide during photosynthesis, herbivores eat plants, and carnivores eat herbivores. Carbon-14, however, is unstable and decays at a steady rate. After an organism dies, the ^{14}C in its tissues is no longer replenished and the clock begins ticking. Libby realized that the age of organic materials could be determined from the amount of residual ^{14}C they contained. The discovery revolutionized prehistoric archaeology, and in 1960 Libby was awarded a Nobel Prize for his work, the only time anyone has been so honored for an archaeological achievement.

Yet the introduction of radiocarbon dating didn't go smoothly. When it was used to date Egyptian historical material, such as samples of wood thought to be contemporary with the pyramids, the radiocarbon dates were too recent. Was the method at fault, or was the Egyptian chronology in need of radical revision? The answer came when tree rings from the bristlecone pine, which grows at high altitude in the White Mountains of California, were radiocarbon dated. The annual rings in the trees could be counted, giving an exact calendar year. Comparisons of tree-ring and ^{14}C dates from the same samples showed that, yes, radiocarbon dating yielded dates that were too recent, but also gave the means to correct or "calibrate" them. Tree-ring sequences are now used to calibrate radiocarbon dates back to 6000 B.C. and similar pairs of radiocarbon and uranium-series dates, from samples of ancient coral reef near Barbados, have now provided an even longer calibration curve going back to around 40,000 years before the present.

Radiocarbon overturned many chronological schemes painstak-

ingly assembled by prehistorians over the previous 100 years. In Europe, for example, archaeologists such as V. Gordon Childe in the 1920s to 1940s had built up a chronology that relied on the assumption that most innovations (such as metallurgy) had arisen in the Near East and only later had spread to Europe. Childe and others used comparisons with Near Eastern sites and artifacts to date European prehistory. Where there are actual imports—Mycenaean pottery from the Greek mainland found in Egyptian tombs, for example—these schemes can be made to work, but in most cases the supposed links to the Near East were only the vaguest of stylistic parallels. For as long as this climate of thought existed, it was difficult to believe that western Europeans had ever invented anything. With radiocarbon dating, all that changed. Specious links, such as that claimed for northwestern European megaliths and monumental structures in the eastern Mediterranean, were broken. It was soon shown, for example, that Stonehenge was older than the Bronze Age citadel of Mycenae, not a dim reflection of it in a barbarous, distant land. For the first time it became possible to date layers and artifacts on their own terms, to place the chronology of Australia or North America alongside that of historic Egypt or Mesopotamia; and to delve far back into prehistory, to date the end of the last Ice Age and the beginnings of agriculture in the Near East. Refinements have recently allowed radiocarbon dating to be applied to thorny questions such as the authenticity of the Turin shroud, now widely believed to be a thirteenth-century fabrication. Today, only a tiny fragment of carbonbearing material is needed, making it possible to radiocarbon date French Palaeolithic cave paintings, such as those of the Chauvet Cave in southern France, now known to be 32,000 years old. Initial estimates on stylistic grounds had suggested the Chauvet paintings were less than two-thirds that age.

However spectacular the technological successes of the past half-century, archaeology, as in the 1950s, is primarily about people and past societies. Thus it is with great excitement that archaeologists have been watching developments in one of the newest of all scientific pursuits: the study of human DNA. One of the big questions in archaeology has always been relatedness: to understand whether a group of people buried in adjacent graves in a cemetery might be members of a single family; to know whether two contemporary peoples making differently patterned pots were in fact entirely different in origin; to discover whether agriculture was brought to Europe by farmers from the Near East; and to determine whether the Americas were colonized across the Bering Strait only once or on many occasions.

For archaeology, two types of DNA analysis have been employed. First, attempts have been made to extract DNA from ancient human remains. Archaeologists sat up and took notice when Swedish scientist Svante Pääbo announced in 1985 that he had succeeded in extracting

2,400-year-old DNA from an Egyptian mummy. The expectations this early success generated died away to some extent as problems of contamination became more and more apparent. The method has been given a recent fillip, however, by the announcement that Pääbo and his colleagues have succeeded in extracting DNA from Neandertal remains and found it to be significantly different from that of modern humans. If this is shown beyond question, then one of the longest-running enigmas in human evolution—whether Neandertals were a separate species or figure in our ancestry—will have been finally resolved.

Second, DNA has been studied through sampling modern populations of "indigenous" peoples (those known not to be recent immigrants). Biological anthropologist Robert Williams has sampled blood from thousands of American Indians and found they divide into two groups, with a third group formed by Eskimo-Aleut. Williams argues from this that America was settled by three separate incoming groups. Not everyone accepts these conclusions—and it is still early days for the study of ancient populations through DNA analysis—but here we see new techniques answering

the age-old questions that lie behind so much archaeology: where are we from, and how did we come to be here?

The introduction of new techniques of many and varied kinds is perhaps archaeology's greatest success of the past 50 years. The discipline remains at heart a humanity or social science, but the new techniques allow archaeologists to ask new questions and to get new answers to old ones, squeezing ever more information out of a dwindling number of sites, as growing numbers of them are lost to development, looting, and natural processes such as erosion. But this technology doesn't come cheap. As archaeology becomes more and more sophisticated and better tooled, it also becomes more expensive, and as the quest for adequate funding becomes more intense, so does the need to convince the world at large that it is worth the cost.

CHRIS SCARRE is Deputy Director of the McDonald Institute for Archaeological Research at the University of Cambridge and editor of the Cambridge Archaeological Journal. *A specialist in French prehistory, he has written widely on archaeology and ancient history. This is the last in a series of articles documenting 50 years of archaeological achievement.*

Space Age Archaeology

Remote-sensing techniques are transforming archaeology.
Excavations may become less essential as researchers explore hidden
sites and examine buried artifacts without unearthing them

by Farouk El-Baz

The Empty Quarter of Arabia, or Ar Rub'al-Khali, is truly deserted. Covering some 777,000 square kilometers, this wasteland is infamous as a harsh environment, devoid of life. Lore has it, however, that the region hosted much kinder conditions in the recent past. Travelers are told of the lost city of Ubar, a legendary oasis along the frankincense trade route that the Koran describes as the "City of Pillars." T. E. Lawrence (perhaps better known as Lawrence of Arabia) himself hoped to find this "Atlantis of the Sands" but was unable to—and the search continues today.

The quest for Ubar recently made progress when images from a space shuttle and from Landsat satellites revealed an array of thin lines converging to a point nestled among the 200-meter-high dunes of this mysterious desert. Researchers looking at the pictures theorized that the hub of the ghostly spokes might be a cemetery or a city—and the hunt for Ubar was on again. Expeditions were mounted in 1990 and 1991, and excavations along a road are now unearthing the long-concealed structures of a walled city.

On the other side of the world, advanced technology has led scientists to the remains of a very different ancient era. This time the clue came from ground-penetrating radar—an instrument that emits radar waves into the earth and records the returned echoes. Different echoes reveal distinct layers of soil and rock or, in this case, fossilized remains of dinosaurs. Paleontologists have excavated the remains of one of these plant-eating, ground-shaking creatures—called seismosaurs—in the desert of New Mexico.

Whether deployed in space or on the earth's surface, remote-sensing instruments are becoming standard archaeological tools. Many archaeologists, trained to use a pick and shovel and to hold the artifacts they describe, are not yet comfortable with these techniques. Nevertheless, those who use remote-sensing instruments have begun to accumulate a wealth of new and unusual evidence. Perhaps as important, some have been able to gather priceless knowledge without disturbing fragile sites—a requirement that is increasingly expected in this era of conservation.

A Very Recent History

Although aerial photographs have been available since the early years of this century, remote sensing of the earth was truly born in December 1968, when Apollo astronauts telecast the first view of the planet from the vicinity of the moon. An astonished audience watched the beautiful blue sphere rise above the lunar horizon in the black void of space. Astronauts on later earth orbital missions reported seeing the Great Wall snaking across the mountainous terrain of China and the Great Pyramid gracing the Giza Plateau west of the Nile River. A new way of looking at the earth began to emerge: researchers considered how to perceive structures and landscapes from afar with advanced technologies and how to uncover hidden details.

In 1972 the National Aeronautics and Space Administration initiated the Landsat program to scan and study agricultural areas. By recording the intensity of infrared rays reflected by vegetation, NASA scientists could estimate crop yields. The healthier the crop of wheat, for example, the more vigorous the reflection. The earth could now be viewed, within the electromagnetic spectrum, as a patchwork of luminous reds, yellows, blues and greens. Gradually, researchers realized that these images were of value to other disciplines, including geology, geography and archaeology. By the late 1970s a few archaeologists were employing Landsat images to help determine the location of Maya ruins in the dense jungles of the Yucatán Peninsula and ancient structures in the plains of what was once Mesopotamia.

Remote Sensing from Space...and on Earth

Landsat Three of these digital-imaging satellites were launched in the 1970s into near-polar orbits. Multi-spectral scanners on the satellites measured the radiation in four bands of the electromagnetic spectrum reflected by various materials on the earth's surface. The scanners transmitted the data to ground stations.

Thematic Mapper This instrument was carried on Landsat 4 and Landsat 5 in the 1980s. Its sensor obtained 30-meter-resolution images in seven spectral bands: three in visible light (blue, green and red), one in near infrared, two in mid-infrared and one in thermal infrared. Thematic Mapper images could therefore detect a wider range of variations in the spectral response of surface materials.

SPOT Unlike the experimental Landsat, this series of imaging satellites was designed to be fully operational. Rather than scanning the scene with a moving mirror, as in the case of Landsat, SPOT sensors use linear-array "push broom" technology, which adds to the geometric fidelity of the images. Furthermore, the system has pointable optics to allow side viewing for stereo or three-dimensional imaging.

Radar Imaging radar instruments transmit microwaves toward the surface of the earth and record the echoes. Echoes from rocky terrain are generally strong, or "bright," in an image; those from smooth surfaces are weak, or "dark." Different combinations of wavelengths and polarization

can be used to produce color images that emphasize particular features. In addition, radar images enhance such linear features as faults and escarpments. They showed, for example, several generations of a segment of the Great Wall of China that were not identified by other imaging systems.

Corona The U.S. government has recently declassified photographs obtained by "spy satellites" between 1960 and 1972. These black-and-white views have resolution as fine as one meter. Their ability to present scenes in stereo allows for simple measurements of surface elevations—important information for archaeological investigations. Commercial satellites may soon obtain images from space having one-meter resolution. Four industrial consortia plan to launch and operate systems to provide such data.

Electromagnetic Sounding Equipment These instruments measure differences in electrical or magnetic properties between surface and subsurface soil and other features, such as rocks or buried walls. They can sense to a depth of about six meters. Researchers use these devices to map layers of soil or subsurface cavities.

Ground-Penetrating Radar This low-frequency radar is capable of "seeing" into the ground. Conventional radar uses microwaves, which can penetrate only a few centimeters into most soils. Ground-penetrating radar, however, employs frequencies closer to those used by FM radio or

television stations, allowing waves to travel, most commonly, down to 10 meters below the surface. When these pulses pierce the earth, they pass through various layers of soil, sand, clay, rock or man-made material. Each interface between these layers produces an echo. The deeper the boundary, the longer its echo takes to return to the surface—thereby indicating the depth of the buried object.

Magnetometers These instruments identify subsurface features that have a magnetization different from that of the surrounding soil. The "proton magnetometer—the form most often used by archaeologists—can measure tiny variations in the magnetic field caused by changes in magnetization, particularly those caused by the presence of a hearth.

Resistivity Instruments These tools introduce electrodes into the ground and measure the difference in electrical potential between them. As researchers move the electrodes along a site, they record differences in resistivity—clues to buried artifacts.

Seismic Instruments Archaeologists use seismometers much like those that detect and record vibrations caused by earthquakes. These archaeological instruments, however, are sensitive to artificially generated sound waves. The motion and travel time of a wave and its echoes are recorded on charts, which cumulatively present a seismic picture of the subsurface. Various seismic instruments can reach much deeper than other sensors.

In the 1980s archaeologists familiar with Landsat began to utilize pictures with even higher resolution. Thomas L. Sever, an archaeologist and remote-sensing expert at the NASA Stennis Space Center in Mississippi, and Payson D. Sheets, an anthropologist at the University of Colorado, were among those who pushed the technology to another level. By requesting the installation of infrared sensors on airplanes, they were able to

record "an odd, twisting line" in the Tilarán area of northwestern Costa Rica. The infrared photographs showed that the mark ran across hills and valleys. Sever and Sheets noted at the time that they suspected it was not a natural feature but a prehistoric road. They were correct. Later fieldwork proved the existence of footpaths that were between 1,000 and 2,000 years old, linking cemeteries, villages and quarries.

Although ancient roads can be observed in satellite images—as in the case of the Empty Quarter of Arabia—the details unveiled by the infrared aerial photographs were even more precise. Thus, Sever and Sheets had little trouble finding the structures once they set out on foot. Sever went on to identify prehistoric roads in Chaco Canyon, N.M., showing that the Chaco civilization was hardly isolated but rather part of a vast trade network in the North American Southwest. This approach to finding ancient cities has become commonplace for archaeologists.

In 1986 the National Center for Space Study in France provided the next advance in satellite remote sensing: SPOT. Its multispectral images could capture objects or areas 20 meters wide, and the panchromatic data recorded objects as small as 10 meters. (In contrast, the first three Landsat sensors were able to detect objects 80 meters in size or larger; the later two missions could resolve items as small as 30 meters in size.) The SPOT images do not offer as much detail as aerial photographs do, but they cover much larger areas, allowing regional investigations. James R. Wiseman of Boston University was one of the first researchers to employ this technology. His team studied SPOT images of the landscape in northwestern Greece and discovered the ancient coastline of Ammoudhia Bay, the home of an important bygone port. The researchers were able to map inland tidal channels as well as former inlets.

Uncanny Promise

Perhaps the greatest tool for archaeology comes from so-called imaging radar. This technology's unique ability to penetrate underneath desert sands and to unveil ancient topography has astonished experts—including its designers, Charles Elachi and his colleagues at the Jet Propulsion Laboratory in Pasadena, Calif. Imaging radar was first used on board the maiden flight of the space shuttle in November 1981. The Shuttle Imaging Radar experiment (SIR-A) provided numerous images of the eastern Sahara. Three years later SIR-B also obtained images of the Arabian Peninsula, as did the radar's most recent incarnation—the Spaceborne Imagining Radar (SIR-C) in April and October 1994. Sir-C beamed the images in digital form to receiving stations on the ground for direct analysis by computer. By including both the horizontal and vertical polarizations, SIR-C brought out more details of the imaged regions.

The SIR-A images of the Western Desert of Egypt, near the border with Sudan, had particular significance for my own research. This terrain is covered by a thick layer of sand, topographically distinguished only by low hills. But the radar unveiled the long-empty beds of three great rivers, which ranged from eight to 20 kilometers in width. The intervening hills appeared to have been islands created by fluvial erosion. Field excavation later showed that the radar waves had penetrated five meters into the sand to reveal the banks of these ancient waterways. Archaeologists then unearthed hand axes, proving that humans lived there some 200,000 years ago.

The discovery provided the data that teams of archaeologists, geologists and biologists needed to verify their hypothesis about the evolution of this part of the Sahara, just west of the Nile. The Western Desert is today the driest place on earth. Nevertheless, researchers suspected that between 5,000 and 11,000 years ago, the local climate was wetter; before that, a dry climate prevailed. These alternating cycles were thought to date back 320,000 years. Imaging radar clinched the case by revealing vast river courses from the wet periods.

The ability to determine the presence of invisible rivers, in turn, allowed archaeologists to develop a more complete picture of early Egyptian civilization. Fred Wendorf of Southern Methodist University, who has conducted many investigations in the Western Desert, concludes that about 11,000 years ago, rainfall increased from near zero to 100 to 200 millimeters a year. This shift permitted the growth of grasses and thorn trees—much like those thriving in such environments as California's Death Valley. Wendorf believes that although the climate was unstable and fraught with droughts, the indigenous people developed a complex economy based on herding.

The rainy era ended 5,000 years ago—the date that marks the initiation of Egyptian civilization. It is my opinion that the two events are inextricably related. Climate change gradually brought extreme aridity to the eastern Sahara, perhaps prompting a mass migration to the only dependable source of water, the Nile. The banks of the Nile, however, were already teeming with a sedentary

population. It may have been the dynamic convergence of these two peoples that planted the seeds of ancient Egypt.

The ancient "river" people lived in harmony with the ebb and flow of the Nile. They measured the strength of annual floods and ingeniously lifted water from the river to channel it to their fields. Their thoughts were directed toward the earth, which they tilled with great expertise. Those who came from the west had "desert wisdom." They learned how to live with erratic rainfall and where to seek greener pastures. To escape the scorching heat of the sun, they moved at night and were adept in astronomy. These nomadic people kept their sights turned upward, contemplating man's place in the universe—a philosophical orientation that permeates the recorded history of Egypt.

The arrival of desert people on the banks of the Nile increased the regional population, requiring better social organization to produce enough food. The cultural interaction of the two groups created a vigorous new society; it was this cross-fertilization that ignited the spark of civilization in ancient Egypt.

Back Down to Earth

The least explored application of remote sensing for archaeology takes place on the ground: the use of hand-held sensors. Typically, when archaeologists study a site, they divide it into a grid to guide digging, which often proceeds at each point of intersection. The approach leaves much to chance. Hand-held sensors, however, can direct archaeologists to the exact location of an artifact, limiting the area that has to be disturbed and saving time.

Anna C. Roosevelt of the Field Museum in Chicago has used such tools to great advantage, experimenting with various combinations. Roosevelt has been at the forefront of this technological advance—and she has made important discoveries about the settlements and lifestyles of prehistoric peoples in the Brazilian Amazon.

One of the cultures Roosevelt studied was a mound-building chiefdom that subsisted on fishing and the cultivation and

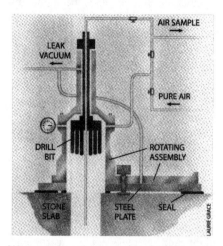

[A] remote investigation was undertaken on the second of two sealed pits containing disassembled royal barges of Pharaoh Khufu. To avoid environmental damage, remote sensing was used on the second barge. A specially designed air lock prevented introduction of foreign matter into the pit. A steel plate was sealed to the stone; a rotating assembly could turn 90 degrees to align holes in the plate and stone for drilling or to cover the hole in the fixed plate, sealing the work surface so that drills or probing heads could be safely changed.

collection of plants on the island of Marajó, at the mouth of the Amazon River. She used a series of portable tools to discern the location and nature of the mounds. A proton magnetometer scan of several three-hectare-wide mounds that ranged in height from seven to 10 meters delineated the large, fired-clay hearths of many houses. Ground-penetrating radar revealed disturbed soil layers. Electromagnetic equipment indicated conductivity changes below the surface, marking locations of strata. In addition, instruments measuring electrical conductivity resistance mapped horizontal and vertical stratigraphic shifts caused by buried earth platforms, garbage fill and the hearths. Devices that measured the refraction of seismic waves detected several building stages and located the original ground on which the mounds were built.

Taken together with excavations, the insights gleaned from these technologies allowed Roosevelt to form a picture of life along the banks of the Amazon between 500 A.D. and the arrival of Europeans in the mid-1500s. Marajoaran peoples lived in separate and warring chiefdoms, harvested fruits and food crops, and built their extensive mounds

to raise their settlements out of the swamps. For centuries, they would build one house on top of an older one. Roosevelt has argued that the Marajoarans' sophisticated culture was indigenous, thus challenging the long-standing theory that the lush life of the forest prevented Amazonian Indians from evolving complex societies.

Work near Santar´em in northern Brazil led Roosevelt to another discovery that is overturning thinking about Amazon habitation. It has been an entrenched anthropological conclusion that Indians from Mexico or Peru introduced pottery making into the Amazon. But Roosevelt's team uncovered evidence of a thriving pottery-using, fishing population in place 7,000 years ago. Ground-penetrating radar revealed numerous domestic features, and resistivity and seismic surveys detected the initial layers of occupation, which produced the early radiocarbon and thermoluminescence dates of the pottery. Because the Amazon pottery later found at several other sites predates other Western Hemisphere pottery by thousands of years, the research has changed the picture of early American cultural development.

The Craft of Conservation

Archaeological sites are easily destroyed once they have been excavated, because they become exposed to the elements, to visitors and, often, to looters. It is becoming disturbingly clear that cultural patrimony is under siege, as magnificent monuments—from Angkor in Cambodia to Machu Picchu in Peru—crumble. Modern archaeologists must increasingly consider how to preserve sites they have unearthed or how to examine sites without touching them.

My first experience using remote sensing in this way came in 1987 during work on the Great Pyramid at Giza. Built by Pharaoh Khufu—or, as the Greeks called him, Cheops—some 4,600 years ago, the pyramid had two sealed chambers near its base. Excavation of one began in 1954, and archaeologists soon discovered inside it a disassembled barge, 43.4 meters long and 5.9 meters wide. It took 18 years to excavate and as-

semble this royal bark, which was ultimately housed in a special "Boat Museum" constructed on the site. Opened to visitors in 1982, the boat became a popular attraction.

It also diminished. By some estimates, the barge has shrunk about a half a meter since it was placed in the museum. Conservators believe this deterioration is caused by the environmental conditions inside the building, which differed from those of the sealed chamber. It was thought that a second, unopened chamber also contained a boat, so I was asked to develop a plan to study the sealed environment—and to determine how best to preserve the boat that was already on exhibit.

In 1987 the Egyptian Antiquities Organization, the National Geographic Society and the Center for Remote Sensing at Boston University agreed to apply remote-sensing techniques to study the second chamber. Because the first chamber had been hermetically sealed, it seemed logical that an air sample from the second one could produce data on the composition of the earth's atmosphere 4.6 millennia ago. I called on Bob Moores, a Black and Decker engineer who had worked on the lunar-surface drill used by the Apollo astronauts, to drill a hole without affecting the pristine environment. Moores designed an airlock that allowed cutting through the rock without mixing the air inside with the air outside. We used ground-penetrating radar to determine the shape of the chamber and to select a proper drilling site.

After two and a half days of drilling, we penetrated the 159-centimeter-thick rock cap. We then inserted a probe into the chamber and sampled air from three levels. Next, we lowered a camera into the enclosure, discovering hieroglyphs on the chamber walls and the anticipated second royal bark. The analysis of the air samples—as well as a view of moisture marks on the walls and of a desert beetle crawling about—testified to the fact that the modern environment was somehow reaching the chamber. But it was not necessary to excavate and further endanger the bark, and so we sealed the hole and left the royal history in the same state as we found it.

A team of archaeologists in England has recently been able to conduct a similar nondestructive study. Using remote-sensing instruments, the scientists are mapping a buried Roman city under the village of Wroxeter, locating streets, shops and what may be a church—all without disturbing the village and pastures that overlie the city. Computer models offer a compelling illustration of what this densely populated city must have looked like.

In the next century, remote sensing will continue to offer researchers a virtual archaeological reality, one that is needed to preserve the fragile environment of the earth and of historical sites. In exploring the mysteries that may lie beneath our feet, we may learn as much from what we do not touch as we do from what we hold in our hands.

The Author

FAROUK EL-BAZ is director of the Center for Remote Sensing at Boston University. He received his undergraduate degree from Ain Shams University in Cairo and his Ph.D. in geology from the University of Missouri. He has taught at Assiut University in Egypt and at the University of Heidelberg in Germany and has held positions at Bell-Comm, at the Smithsonian's National Air and Space Museum (where he established and directed the Center for Earth and Planetary Studies) and at Itek Optical Systems. His research focuses on the interpretation of satellite images, the application of space photography to desert studies and the use of remote sensing in archaeology and geology.

Further Reading

GROUND-PENETRATING RADAR SIMULATION IN ENGINEERING AND ARCHAEOLOGY. D. Goodman in *Geophysics*, Vol. 59, No. 2, pages 224–232; February 1994.

REMOTE SENSING AND THE ARCHAEOLOGY OF THE SILK ROAD. E. Pendleton Banks in *Current Anthropology*, Vol. 36, No. 3, page 520; June 1995.

HIGH-RESOLUTION SATELLITE IMAGERY IN ARCHAEOLOGICAL APPLICATION; WITH A PHOTOGRAPH OF THE STONEHENGE REGION. Martin J. F. Fowler in *Antiquity*, Vol. 70, No. 269, pages 667–670; September 1996.

THE USE OF SATELLITE IMAGERY AND DIGITAL IMAGE PROCESSING IN LANDSCAPE ARCHAEOLOGY: A CASE STUDY FROM THE ISLAND OF MALLORCA, SPAIN. A. M. Montufo in *Geoarchaeology*, Vol. 12, No. 1, pages 71–92; January 1997.

A Wasp's-Nest Clock

With a highly unusual dating technique, two Australian researchers have identified what may be the world's oldest portrait of a human.

By Rachel F. Preiser

The rock outcroppings of the Kimberley region of northwestern Australia are painted, pecked, and engraved with vestiges of aboriginal art. Unfortunately, except for the odd charcoal sketch, most aboriginal rock art is nearly impossible to date—it is often colored with ocher, a mineral pigment that lacks the organic carbon compounds required by radioactive-dating techniques. Without an absolute scale, archeologists have had to rely on informed guesswork to date most aboriginal art. But that may soon change. Some Australian researchers have found a way to use fossilized wasps' nests to determine the age of ancient art.

Grahame Walsh, a rock-art specialist at the Takarakka Rock Art Research Center at Carnarvon Gorge, was studying the Kimberley paintings when he noticed that a nearby wasp's nest he had assumed to be of recent origin was in fact fossilized. Wasps' nests—made of a loosely packed fabric of sand, silt, and pollen grains—are not generally durable. But Walsh found that silica carried by water apparently seeped through the sandstone overlying the rock shelters and filled in the pores in the nest, reinforcing it to withstand the ravages of time.

Walsh realized that the sand grains worked into the nest would make it possible to date the nest. He contacted Richard Roberts, a geologist at La Trobe University in Melbourne who specializes in reading these grainy timepieces using a method known as optical luminescence dating. Radiation from radioactive trace elements in the sand bombards the grains. The radiation causes atoms in the grains to spit out electrons that become trapped in imperfections in the grains' crystalline structure. Here the displaced electrons remain until ultraviolet radiation in sunlight frees them from their crystal prisons. As the electrons return to more stable positions, each emits a photon of light. By exposing sand grains to light and measuring the intensity of the light emitted by the grains, geologists can estimate how long ago they were last exposed to sunlight.

Two years ago Roberts joined Walsh on an expedition to Kimberley in search of petrified wasps' nests built on top of rock art. While clambering around the rocky outcroppings, the researchers came across two fossilized nests overlying a mulberry-colored painting of a human figure whose elongated body, narrow head, and semicircular headdress suggested it belonged to a style believed by most archeologists to date back some 5,000 years. The researchers pried the fossilized nests free and extracted sand grains from their cores.

Using luminescence dating, Roberts discovered that the nests were more than 17,000 years old. That makes the underlying aboriginal rock painting the oldest depiction of a human figure in the world. Roberts believes the figure may actually be much older than the nest, since the Ice Age had reached its height at that time and the Kimberley region would thus have been arid and inhospitable to humans.

A fossilized wasp's nest lies just to the left of the painted figures. (Photo © Richard Roberts)

"Presumably the paintings were made during a previous, wetter period," says Roberts, "perhaps 25,000 to 30,000 years ago or even earlier, before the peak of the last glacial maximum." If he's right, the mulberry-colored figure may rival the oldest known paintings of animals—from the Chauvet cave in France—thought to be about 30,000 years old.

Although too sparse to date, the pollen found in the petrified nests can be used to identify the plants the wasps visited while building their homes many thousands of years ago. The nests Walsh and Roberts found contain mostly eucalyptus pollen and smatterings of pollen from an array of flowering plants and grasses. For Roberts, that makes the nests a still more important record, enabling a detailed reconstruction of the environment in which the ancient artists lived. "My feeling is that the greatest global application of the approach will be to examine past vegetation histories and infer past climate from preserved nests," says Roberts. "That wasn't the main aim of our project—the presence of pollen was pure luck but the combination of being able to date the rock art and reconstruct past environments makes wasp nests extremely versatile time capsules.".

From *Discover*, November 1997, p. 42. © 1997 by Rachel F. Preiser. Reprinted with permission of *the author*.

Profile of an Anthropologist

No Bone Unturned

Patrick Huyghe

The research of some physical anthropologists and archaeologists involves the discovery and analysis of old bones (as well as artifacts and other remains). Most often these bones represent only part of a skeleton or maybe the mixture of parts of several skeletons. Often these remains are smashed, burned, or partially destroyed. Over the years, physical anthropologists have developed a remarkable repertoire of skills and techniques for teasing the greatest possible amount of information out of sparse material remains.

Although originally developed for basic research, the methods of physical anthropology can be directly applied to contemporary human problems.... In this profile, we look briefly at the career of Clyde C. Snow, a physical anthropologist who has put these skills to work in a number of different settings....

As you read this selection, ask yourself the following questions:

- Given what you know of physical anthropology, what sort of work would a physical anthropologist do for the Federal Aviation Administration?
- What is anthropometry? *How might anthropometric surveys of pilots and passengers help in the design of aircraft equipment?*
- What is forensic anthropology? *How can a biological anthropologist be an expert witness in legal proceedings?*

Clyde Snow is never in a hurry. He knows he's late. He's always late. For Snow, being late is part of the job. In fact, he doesn't usually begin to work until death has stripped some poor individual to the bone, and no one—neither the local homicide detectives nor the pathologists—can figure out who once gave identity to the skeletonized remains. No one, that is, except a shrewd, laconic, 60-year-old forensic anthropologist.

Snow strolls into the Cook County Medical Examiner's Office in Chicago on this brisk October morning wearing a pair of Lucchese cowboy boots and a three-piece pin-striped suit. Waiting for him in autopsy room 160 are a bunch of naked skeletons found in Illinois, Wisconsin, and Minnesota since his last visit. Snow, a native Texan who now lives in rural Oklahoma, makes the trip up to Chicago some six times a year. The first case on his agenda is a pale brown skull found in the garbage of an abandoned building once occupied by a Chicago cosmetics company.

Snow turns the skull over slowly in his hands, a cigarette dangling from his fingers. One often does. Snow does not seem overly concerned about mortality, though its tragedy surrounds him daily.

"There's some trauma here," he says, examining a rough edge at the lower back of the skull. He points out the area to Jim Elliott, a homicide detective with the Chicago police. "This looks like a chopping blow by a heavy bladed instrument. Almost like a decapitation." In a place where the whining of bone saws drifts through hallways and the sweet-sour smell of death hangs in the air, the word surprises no one.

Snow begins thinking aloud. "I think what we're looking at here is a female, or maybe a small male, about thirty to forty years old. Probably Asian." He turns the skull upside down, pointing out the degree of wear on the teeth. "This was somebody who lived on a really rough diet. We don't normally find this kind of dental wear in a modern Western population."

"How long has it been around?" Elliott asks.

Snow raises the skull up to his nose. "It doesn't have any decompositional odors," he says. He pokes a finger in the skull's nooks and crannies. "There's no soft tissue left. It's good and dry. And it doesn't show signs of having been buried. I would say that this has been lying around in an attic or a box for years. It feels like a souvenir skull," says Snow.

Souvenir skulls, usually those of Japanese soldiers, were popular with U.S. troops serving in the Pacific during World War II; there was also a trade in skulls during the Vietnam War years. On closer inspection, though, Snow begins to wonder about the skull's Asian origins—the broad nasal aperture and the jutting forth of the upper-tooth-bearing part of the face suggest Melanesian features. Sifting through the objects found in the abandoned building with the skull, he finds several loose-leaf albums of 35-millimeter transparencies documenting life among the highland tribes of New Guinea. The slides, shot by an anthropologist, include graphic scenes of ritual warfare. The skull, Snow concludes, is more likely to be a trophy from one of these tribal battles than the result of a local Chicago homicide.

"So you'd treat it like found property?" Elliott asks finally. "Like somebody's garage-sale property?"

"Exactly," says Snow.

Clyde Snow is perhaps the world's most sought-after forensic anthropologist. People have been calling upon him to identify skeletons for more than a quarter of a century. Every year he's involved in some 75 cases of identification, most of them without fanfare. "He's an old scudder who doesn't have to blow his own whistle," says Walter Birkby, a forensic anthropologist at the University of Arizona. "He know's he's good."

Yet over the years Snow's work has turned him into something of an unlikely celebrity. He has been called upon to identify the remains of the Nazi war criminal Josef Mengele, reconstruct the face of the Egyptian boy-king Tutankhamen, confirm the authenticity of the body autopsied as that of President John F. Kennedy, and examine the skeletal remains of General Custer's men at the battlefield of the Little Bighorn. He has also been involved in the grim task of identifying the bodies in some of the United States' worst airline accidents.

Such is his legend that cases are sometimes attributed to him in which he played no part. He did not, as the *New York Times* reported, identify the remains of the crew of the *Challenger* disaster. But the man is often the equal of his myth. For the past four years, setting his personal safety aside, Snow has spent much of his time in Argentina, searching for the graves and identities of some of the thousands who "disappeared" between 1976 and 1983, during Argentina's military regime.

Snow did not set out to rescue the dead from oblivion. For almost two decades, until 1979, he was a physical anthropologist at the Civil Aeromedical Institute, part of the Federal Aviation Administration in Oklahoma City. Snow's job was to help engineers improve aircraft design and safety features by providing them with data on the human frame.

One study, he recalls, was initiated in response to complaints from a flight attendants' organization. An analysis of accident patterns had revealed that inadequate restraints on flight attendants'

jump seats were leading to deaths and injuries and that aircraft doors weighing several hundred pounds were impeding evacuation efforts. Snow points out that ensuring the survival of passengers in emergencies is largely the flight attendants' responsibility. "If they are injured or killed in a crash, you're going to find a lot of dead passengers."

Reasoning that equipment might be improved if engineers had more data on the size and strength of those who use it, Snow undertook a study that required meticulous measurement. When his report was issued in 1975, Senator William Proxmire was outraged that $57,800 of the taxpayers' money had been spent to caliper 423 airline stewardesses from head to toe. Yet the study, which received one of the senator's dubious Golden Fleece Awards, was firmly supported by both the FAA and the Association of Flight Attendants. "I can't imagine," says Snow with obvious delight, "how much coffee Proxmire got spilled on him in the next few months."

It was during his tenure at the FAA that he developed an interest in forensic work. Over the years the Oklahoma police frequently consulted the physical anthropologist for help in identifying crime victims. "The FAA figured it was a kind of community service to let me work on these cases," he says.

The experience also helped to prepare him for the grim task of identifying the victims of air disasters. In December 1972, when a United Airlines plane crashed outside Chicago, killing 43 of the 61 people aboard (including the wife of Watergate conspirator Howard Hunt, who was found with $10,000 in her purse), Snow was brought in to help examine the bodies. That same year, with Snow's help, forensic anthropology was recognized as a specialty by the American Academy of Forensic Sciences. "It got a lot of anthropologists interested in forensics," he says, "and it made a lot of pathologists out there aware that there were anthropologists who could help them."

Each nameless skeleton poses a unique mystery for Snow. But some, like the second case awaiting him back in the autopsy room at the Cook County morgue, are more challenging than oth-

ers. This one is a real chiller. In a large cardboard box lies a jumble of bones along with a tattered leg from a pair of blue jeans, a sock shrunk tightly around the bones of a foot, a pair of Nike running shoes without shoelaces, and, inside the hood of a blue windbreaker, a mass of stringy, blood-caked hair. The remains were discovered frozen in ice about 20 miles outside Milwaukee. A rusted bicycle was found lying close by. Paul Hibbard, chief deputy medical examiner for Waukesha County, who brought the skeleton to Chicago, says no one has been reported missing.

Snow lifts the bones out of the box and begins reconstructing the skeleton on an autopsy table. "There are two hundred six bones and thirty-two teeth in the human body," he says, "and each has a story to tell." Because bone is dynamic, living tissue, many of life's significant events—injuries, illness, childbearing—leave their mark on the body's internal framework. Put together the stories told by these bones, he says, and what you have is a person's "osteobiography."

Snow begins by determining the sex of the skeleton, which is not always obvious. He tells the story of a skeleton that was brought to his FAA office in the late 1970s. It had been found along with some women's clothes and a purse in a local back lot, and the police had assumed that it was female. But when Snow examined the bones, he realized that "at six foot three, she would have probably have been the tallest female in Oklahoma."

Then Snow recalled that six months earlier the custodian in his building had suddenly not shown up for work. The man's supervisor later mentioned to Snow, "You know, one of these days when they find Ronnie, he's going to be dressed as a woman." Ronnie, it turned out, was a weekend transvestite. A copy of his dental records later confirmed that the skeleton in women's clothing was indeed Snow's janitor.

The Wisconsin bike rider is also male. Snow picks out two large bones that look something like twisted oysters—the innominates, or hipbones, which along with the sacrum, or lower backbone, form the pelvis. This pelvis is narrow and steep-walled like a male's, not broad and shallow like a female's. And the sciatic notch (the V-shaped space where the sciatic nerve passes through the hipbone) is narrow, as is normal in a male. Snow can also determine a skeleton's sex by checking the size of the mastoid processes (the bony knobs at the base of the skull) and the prominence of the brow ridge, or by measuring the head of an available limb bone, which is typically broader in males.

From an examination of the skull he concludes that the bike rider is "predominantly Caucasoid." A score of bony traits help the forensic anthropologist assign a skeleton to one of the three major racial groups: Negroid, Caucasoid, or Mongoloid. Snow notes that the ridge of the boy's nose is high and salient, as it is in whites. In Negroids and Mongoloids (which include American Indians as well as most Asians) the nose tends to be broad in relation to its height. However, the boy's nasal margins are somewhat smoothed down, usually a Mongoloid feature. "Possibly a bit of American Indian admixture," says Snow. "Do you have Indians in your area?" Hibbard nods.

Age is next. Snow takes the skull and turns it upside down, pointing out the basilar joint, the junction between the two major bones that form the underside of the skull. In a child the joint would still be open to allow room for growth, but here the joint has fused—something that usually happens in the late teen years. On the other hand, he says, pointing to the zigzagging lines on the dome of the skull, the cranial sutures are open. The cranial sutures, which join the bones of the braincase, begin to fuse and disappear in the mid-twenties.

Next Snow picks up a femur and looks for signs of growth at the point where the shaft meets the knobbed end. The thin plates of cartilage—areas of incomplete calcification—that are visible at this point suggest that the boy hadn't yet attained his full height. Snow double-checks with an examination of the pubic symphysis, the joint where the two hipbones meet. The ridges in this area, which fill in and smooth over in adulthood, are still clearly marked. He concludes that the skeleton is that of a boy between 15 and 20 years old.

"One of the things you learn is to be pretty conservative," says Snow. "It's very impressive when you tell the police, 'This person is eighteen years old,' and he turns out to be eighteen. The problem is, if the person is fifteen you've blown it—you probably won't find him. Looking for a missing person is like trying to catch fish. Better get a big net and do your own sorting."

Snow then picks up a leg bone, measures it with a set of calipers, and enters the data into a portable computer. Using the known correlation between the height and length of the long limb bones, he quickly estimates the boy's height. "He's five foot six and a half to five foot eleven," says Snow. "Medium build, not excessively muscular, judging from the muscle attachments that we see." He points to the grainy ridges that appear where muscle attaches itself to the bone. The most prominent attachments show up on the teenager's right arm bone, indicating right-handedness.

Then Snow examines the ribs one by one for signs of injury. He finds no stab wounds, cuts, or bullet holes, here or elsewhere on the skeleton. He picks up the hyoid bone from the boy's throat and looks for the tell-tale fracture signs that would suggest the boy was strangled. But, to Snow's frustration, he can find no obvious cause of death. In hopes of identifying the missing teenager, he suggests sending the skull, hair, and boy's description to Betty Pat Gatliff, a medical illustrator and sculptor in Oklahoma who does facial reconstructions.

Six weeks later photographs of the boy's likeness appear in the *Milwaukee Sentinel.* "If you persist long enough," says Snow, "eighty-five to ninety percent of the cases eventually get positively identified, but it can take anywhere from a few weeks to a few years."

Snow and Gatliff have collaborated many times, but never with more glitz than in 1983, when Snow was commissioned by Patrick Barry, a Miami orthopedic surgeon and amateur Egyptologist, to reconstruct the face of the Egyptian boy-king Tutankhamen. Normally a facial reconstruction begins with a skull, but since Tutankhamen's 3,000-year-old remains were in Egypt, Snow had to

make do with the skull measurements from a 1925 postmortem and X-rays taken in 1975. A plaster model of the skull was made, and on the basis on Snow's report—"his skull is Caucasoid with some Negroid admixtures"—Gatliff put a face on it. What did Tutankhamen look like? Very much like the gold mask on his sarcophagus, says Snow, confirming that it was, indeed, his portrait.

Many cite Snow's use of facial reconstructions as one of his most important contributions to the field. Snow, typically self-effacing, says that Gatliff "does all the work." The identification of skeletal remains, he stresses, is often a collaboration between pathologists, odontologists, radiologists, and medical artists using a variety of forensic techniques.

One of Snow's last tasks at the FAA was to help identify the dead from the worst airline accident in U.S. history. On May 25, 1979, a DC-10 crashed shortly after takeoff from Chicago's O'Hare Airport, killing 273 people. The task facing Snow and more than a dozen forensic specialists was horrific. "No one ever sat down and counted," says Snow, "but we estimated ten thousand to twelve thousand pieces or parts of bodies." Nearly 80 percent of the victims were identified on the basis of dental evidence and fingerprints. Snow and forensic radiologist John Fitzpatrick later managed to identify two dozen others by comparing postmortem X-rays with X-rays taken during the victim's lifetime.

Next to dental records, such X-ray comparisons are the most common way of obtaining positive identifications. In 1978, when a congressional committee reviewed the evidence on John F. Kennedy's assassination, Snow used X-rays to show that the body autopsied at Bethesda Naval Hospital was indeed that of the late president and had not—as some conspiracy theorists believed—been switched.

The issue was resolved on the evidence of Kennedy's "sinus print," the scalloplike pattern on the upper margins of the sinuses that is visible in X-rays of the forehead. So characteristic is a person's sinus print that courts throughout the world accept the matching of antemortem and postmortem X-rays of the sinuses as positive identification.

Yet another technique in the forensic specialist's repertoire is photo superposition. Snow used it in 1977 to help identify the mummy of a famous Oklahoma outlaw named Elmer J. McCurdy, who was killed by a posse after holding up a train in 1911. For years the mummy had been exhibited as a "dummy" in a California funhouse—until it was found to have a real human skeleton inside it. Ownership of the mummy was eventually traced back to a funeral parlor in Oklahoma, where McCurdy had been embalmed and exhibited as "the bandit who wouldn't give up."

Using two video cameras and an image processor, Snow superposed the mummy's profile on a photograph of McCurdy that was taken shortly after his death. When displayed on a single monitor, the two coincided to a remarkable degree. Convinced by the evidence, Thomas Noguchi, then Los Angeles County corner, signed McCurdy's death certificate ("Last known occupation: Train robber") and allowed the outlaw's bones to be returned to Oklahoma for a decent burial.

It was this technique that also allowed forensic scientists to identify the remains of the Nazi "Angel of Death," Josef Mengele, in the summer of 1985. A team of investigators, including Snow and West German forensic anthropologist Richard Helmer, flew to Brazil after an Austrian couple claimed that Mengele lay buried in a grave on a São Paulo hillside. Tests revealed that the stature, age, and hair color of the unearthed skeleton were consistent with information in Mengele's SS files; yet without X-rays or dental records, the scientists still lacked conclusive evidence. When an image of the reconstructed skull was superposed on 1930s photographs of Mengele, however, the match was eerily compelling. All doubts were removed a few months later when Mengele's dental X-rays were tracked down.

In 1979 Snow retired from the FAA to the rolling hills of Norman, Oklahoma, where he and his wife, Jerry, live in a sprawling, early-1960s ranch house. Unlike his 50 or so fellow forensic anthropologists, most of whom are tied to

academic positions, Snow is free to pursue his consultancy work full-time. Judging from the number of miles that he logs in the average month, Snow is clearly not ready to retire for good.

His recent projects include a reexamination of the skeletal remains found at the site of the Battle of the Little Bighorn, where more than a century ago Custer and his 210 men were killed by Sioux and Cheyenne warriors. Although most of the enlisted men's remains were moved to a mass grave in 1881, an excavation of the battlefield in the past few years uncovered an additional 375 bones and 36 teeth. Snow, teaming up again with Fitzpatrick, determined that these remains belonged to 34 individuals.

The historical accounts of Custer's desperate last stand are vividly confirmed by their findings. Snow identified one skeleton as that of a soldier between the ages of 19 and 23 who weighed around 150 pounds and stood about five foot eight. He'd sustained gunshot wounds to his chest and left forearm. Heavy blows to his head had fractured his skull and sheared off his teeth. Gashed thigh bones indicated that his body was later dismembered with an ax or hatchet.

Given the condition and number of the bodies, Snow seriously questions the accuracy of the identifications made by the original nineteenth-century burial crews. He doubts, for example, that the skeleton buried at West Point is General Custer's.

For the last four years Snow has devoted much of his time to helping two countries come to terms with the horrors of a much more recent past. As part of a group sponsored by the American Association for the Advancement of Science, he has been helping the Argentinian National Commission on Disappeared Persons to determine the fate of some of those who vanished during their country's harsh military rule: between 1976 and 1983 at least 10,000 people were systematically swept off the streets by roving death squads to be tortured, killed, and buried in unmarked graves. In December 1986, at the invitation of the Aquino government's Human Rights Commission, Snow also spent several weeks training Philippine scientists to

investigate the disappearances that occurred under the Marcos regime.

But it is in Argentina where Snow has done the bulk of his human-rights work. He has spent more than 27 months in and around Buenos Aires, first training a small group of local medical and anthropology students in the techniques of forensic investigation, and later helping them carefully exhume and examine scores of the *desaparecidos*, or disappeared ones.

Only 25 victims have so far been positively identified. But the evidence has helped convict seven junta members and other high-ranking military and police officers. The idea is not necessarily to identify all 10,000 of the missing, says Snow. "If you have a colonel who ran a detention center where maybe five hundred people were killed, you don't have to nail them with five hundred deaths. Just one or two should be sufficient to get him convicted." Forensic evidence from Snow's team may be used to prosecute several other military officers, including General Suarez Mason. Mason is the former commander of the I Army Corps in Buenos Aires and is believed to be responsible for thousands of disappearances. He was recently extradited from San Francisco back to Argentina, where he is expected to stand trial this winter [1988].

The investigations have been hampered by a frustrating lack of antemortem information. In 1984, when commission lawyers took depositions from relatives and friends of the disappeared, they often failed to obtain such basic information as the victim's height, weight, or hair color. Nor did they ask for the missing person's X-rays (which in Argentina are given to the patient) or the address of the victim's dentist. The problem was compounded by the inexperience of those who carried out the first mass exhumations prior to Snow's arrival. Many of the skeletons were inadvertently destroyed by bulldozers as they were brought up.

Every unearthed skeleton that shows signs of gunfire, however, helps to erode the claim once made by many in the Argentinian military that most of the *desaparecidos* are alive and well and living in Mexico City, Madrid, or Paris. Snow recalls the case of a 17-year-old boy named Gabriel Dunayavich, who disappeared in the summer of 1976. He was walking home from a movie with his girlfriend when a Ford Falcon with no license plates snatched him off the street. The police later found his body and that of another boy and girl dumped by the roadside on the outskirts of Buenos Aires. The police went through the motions of an investigation, taking photographs and doing an autopsy, then buried the three teenagers in an unmarked grave.

A decade later Snow, with the help of the boy's family, traced the autopsy reports, the police photographs, and the grave of the three youngsters. Each of them had four or five closely spaced bullet wounds in the upper chest—the signature, says Snow, of an automatic weapon. Two also had wounds on their arms from bullets that had entered behind the elbow and exited from the forearm.

"That means they were conscious when they were shot," says Snow. "When a gun was pointed at them, they naturally raised their arm." It's details like these that help to authenticate the last moments of the victims and bring a dimension of reality to the judges and jury.

Each time Snow returns from Argentina he says that this will be the last time. A few months later he is back in Buenos Aires. "There's always more work to do," he says. It is, he admits quietly, "terrible work."

"These were such brutal, cold-blooded crimes," he says. "The people who committed them not only murdered; they had a system to eliminate all trace that their victims even existed."

Snow will not let them obliterate their crimes so conveniently. "There are human-rights violations going on all around the world," he says. "But to me murder is murder, regardless of the motive. I hope that we are sending a message to governments who murder in the name of politics that they can be held to account."

From *Discover* magazine, December 1988, pp. 51–56. © 1988 by Patrick Huyghe. Reprinted with permission of the author.

'Let the Bones Talk' is the Watchword for Scientist-Sleuths

When the FBI moved in across the street 60 years ago, Smithsonian anthropologists began a tradition of helping to solve crimes

By Elizabeth Royte

It is late on a Thursday afternoon before Douglas Owsley can turn his attention to the cardboard box on his office floor. He shoves it toward a table and casually lifts the lid. He reaches into wrinkled white sheets and a blanket and pulls out a waxy brown skull.

Bone by bone, Owsley transfers the skeleton to his examination table. "Heavy brow, large mastoid processes, well-defined nuchal [nape of the neck] area," he murmurs, turning the skull this way and that. "Narrow nasal width, pronounced nasal spine. Definitely white, definitely male." But it doesn't take a physical anthropologist to deduce this much information. A medical examiner had supplied the man's identity. What the local pathologist wants Owsley to determine is whether this man, who had disappeared from a nursing home, had suffered any kind of trauma. The bones had been found in a wooded area near the home. It appeared that the gentleman had simply wandered off. Or had he?

Douglas Owsley works as a forensic anthropologist at the Smithsonian's National Museum of Natural History. Strong, compact and encircled by a tooled Western belt, he's the kind of person who doesn't hesitate to get down onto his bare office floor, if that's where

the next box of bones lies. His scholarly work involves prehistoric and pioneer bones in the Great Plains and more recent bones in the East. But he also does forensic work. Police departments and medical examiners across the country routinely enlist Owsley's services. They come upon bones and want to know: Who is it? What happened? A forensic pathologist—in the mode of television's Quincy—asks similar questions, but Owsley's work picks up where Quincy's leaves off.

Most of his cases originate in rural areas, because bodies that come to rest in cities are usually found before soft tissues rot away. Dogs discover a fair number of bodies. So do hunters, in the woods after the leaves have dropped, and drivers, in any season, who stop to relieve themselves in wooded sites along roadways.

Owsley works in a cluttered suite of offices on the third floor of the museum. Scientific journals line his shelves, photographs of his buddies exhuming graves hang on the walls. Outside his door, the corridors are institutionally lighted and lined with drawer after wooden drawer, stacked 14 feet high. Here the skeletons of 30,000 people are carefully arranged and catalogued. The bones—of people

ranging in age from prenatal to 90, who died between 10,000 years ago and one—hail from as far as Ecuador and Iraq, and as near as Bethesda, Maryland.

A forensic investigation usually begins with the opening of a package. Sometimes Owsley can resolve a case without even sitting down.

Police officer: is this bone human?

Owsley: No, it's pig.

Officer: Thank you, goodbye.

More often, the inquiry will take weeks or months to play out. Owsley recently finished the case of a Baltimore police officer who denied any involvement in the slaying of his girlfriend. But investigators vacuumed up tiny bone chips—about the size of pencil points—from the back floor of his pickup. Owsley examined the chips under a stereozoom microscope and determined they belonged to somebody whose skull became fragmented perimortem—at or around the time of death. He found traces of soot, lead and blood on the fragments, features consistent, as they say, with those of a bullet fired at close range. "But it's the tiny traces of blood on the bone chips that helped nail him," Owsley says. "It shows up as red rust stains under the microscope." The officer was eventually sentenced to life plus 20 years.

Photograph by Robert C. Burke

Meanwhile, Nursing Home Man lies on the table, his hand bones in one pile, his foot bones in another. Owsley sorts through the ribs, arranging 12 on the right and 11 on the left. "Hmmm," he says, not overly concerned. Then he picks up a short bone—"rabbit," he says—and sets it aside. It's not unusual to find animal bones with human: the dog that finds bones and buries them under the back porch is not discriminating.

Owsley starts to calculate the man's height, based on the length of his leg and arm bones. He looks at the points where muscles were attached to bone, to get an idea of his build. A creative forensic anthropologist may look at, for example, the ridges where muscles attach on finger bones and wonder if this unidentified skeleton once played the flute, but he'd never include such speculation in a final report. "The science on that is a little flaky," says Douglas Ubelaker, who, as the other forensic anthropologist at the museum, works about 40 law-enforcement cases a year. (He also teaches at

George Washington University.) "It could lead investigators to look for missing flute players and rule out all others."

Ubelaker and Owsley are both infuriatingly cautious. "Let the bones talk to you" is their motto. Scientists to the core, they make conclusions based solely on the evidence at hand. "You can't go on your gut feelings," says Ubelaker, sober, mustachioed and, on a summer day when the air conditioning is not working, dressed in sandals, a blue polo shirt and pleated slacks. "A prosecutor comes in, he's convinced it's this guy, and he says, 'Doc, what do you think?' There's a subtle pressure to support his opinion. But you must divorce yourself from that. I'm not an advocate for the FBI or the defense but a spokesman for the victim." I ask if he's ever been wrong. "I don't recall ever being very wrong in a forensic case, considering the evidence available at the time." Though he sounds smug, he is not. He is stating a fact. "You shouldn't be wrong on a report. I won't say it's the skeleton of a person 37 years

old, but I will say with 90 percent certainty he's between 30 and 38."

Sixty years ago, the use of anthropology to solve crimes was virtually unheard of. The law-enforcement community didn't recognize that skeletons contained clues that were inaccessible through conventional forensic examinations, and anthropologists, for their part, were reluctant to get involved in police work. Applied science—using anthropology to achieve an immediately tangible result—was somehow less pure than basic research, went the thinking.

Today, forensic anthropology is an accepted science. The American Board of Forensic Anthropology certifies new diplomates each year (Ubelaker is the current president). At the Smithsonian, forensic anthropology began in the 1930s when the Federal Bureau of Investigation moved in across the street on Constitution Avenue. Ales Hrdlicka, director of the Division of Physical Anthropology from 1903 until 1943, formalized the relationship, and in 1942

Hrdlicka's student and successor, T. Dale Stewart, began to consult regularly for the FBI. In the 1950s Stewart helped in the identification of Korean War dead. But it was the bow-tied, cigar smoking Larry Angel (SMITHSONIAN, February 1977), who worked so many cases in the 1970s that the press started calling him "Sherlock Bones."

(Other Smithsonian scientists also are taking on forensic missions. Roxie Laybourne, an ornithologist [March 1982], has taught several graduate students about identifying feathers found at plane crashes and murder scenes. And there are practitioners of forensic geology and entomology. Geologists can often tell from dirt particles in a victim's clothing where a murder actually happened. Entomologists can tell by what insects are present on a body how long the person has been dead.)

Even now it's not all smooth sailing within the scientific community. "Some anthropologists still think it's technical, not research oriented," says Owsley, heatedly, "but it *is* research oriented! The information we derive immeasurably improves our work on older skeletons. We look at Civil War digs, at whites versus blacks, old versus young, urban versus rural, rich versus poor, and we see changes in health trends. We can follow health trends through time. We see the results not only of bone cancer, but breast cancer, which metastisizes and perforates bone. We can now track the evolution of warfare among Plains Indians for 6,000 years by bone pathology."

Owsley and Ubelaker enjoy their law-enforcement cases but they both favor historical work—Owsley studying the bones of Colonial villagers and Native Americans, Ubelaker working in Ecuador and in museum collections in Europe, tracing the history of diseases. In studying ancient bones, physical anthropologists are less interested in individuals—how a man fractured his pelvis and why he was buried with his dog—than in documenting what happened to communities over time and space: what they ate, how and where they lived, what diseases afflicted them, how their life expectancy changed as they abandoned the nomadic life for agriculture.

Says Owsley, "We apply what we learn from archaeological excavations to criminal cases, and vice versa. The information flows both ways." Owsley's work with the victims of a prehistoric war who had been dismembered immediately after death proved to be invaluable experience when he worked on the case involving Jeffrey Dahmer's first victim. He analyzed hundreds of bone and tooth fragments that Dahmer had crushed with a heavy implement and scattered over a two-acre site, examined each for cut marks and determined the age and sex of the victim. The Smithsonian's Ralph Chapman clinched the identification by digitizing bitewing x-rays taken by a dentist so they could be scaled to match images from the remains. A second molar root was identical to a 90 percent probability.

Douglas Owsley grew up in a small Wyoming town, the son of a fish and game warden. He entered the University of Wyoming as a zoology major, planning on a career in medicine, or perhaps dentistry. That changed when he volunteered one summer to help George Gill, a charismatic anthropology professor, work a thousand-year-old burial site in Mexico. They mucked around mangrove swamps all day and ate huge shrimp cocktails at night. "I said to myself, 'This is the life,'" recalls Owsley, grinning. "I got completely caught up in it." He switched his major, earned his doctorate in physical anthropology under Gill at the University of Tennessee, then began teaching at Louisiana State University in 1980. The crime rate around Baton Rouge and the preponderance of bayous for dumping bodies meant plenty of hands-on forensic cases. In 1987 the Smithsonian sent out a call for a new physical anthropologist and Owsley applied. Today, Gill and Owsley continue their work together, most recently in the analysis of late prehistoric and historic period skeletons from Easter Island.

Douglas Ubelaker also slipped into anthropology after accepting, as a lark, a summer job on a dig. He was a premed student at the University of Kansas when an anthropology professor noted his muscles and invited him on a dig in the Dakotas. The keen-eyed professor was

William Bass of the University of Tennessee, who has trained the majority of the forensic anthropologists in the country. To Ubelaker, the prospect of studying centuries-old remains held a "distinct element of romance." He, too, was instantly hooked, and by the end of the summer the Ubelakers knew there would not be another doctor in the family.

Drafted in 1968, just after graduating from college, Ubelaker, was assigned to a military hospital lab in Washington, D.C. He spent his spare time working in the Smithsonian's collections, incidentally forging the alliances that would secure him a job at the museum after he earned his doctorate in Kansas.

Both Ubelaker and Owsley appreciate the mystery in their law-enforcement cases, but they try not to get too involved: the bones come and go, and often they don't find out what becomes of a case once their role—pinpointing the age of a bone's owner or suggesting a probable murder weapon—is finished. Knowing a victim's vocation and personal habits could prejudice their investigations. Working on decomposing bodies at the Branch Davidian compound in Waco, Texas, Ubelaker didn't want to know which cult members were still unaccounted for. Along with FBI agents, Texas Rangers and staff from the medical examiner's office, he sorted through hundreds of bones, which they first had to excavate from under the rubble and unexploded ordnance. He and Owsley were part of the team that then listed probable ages and sexes and matched what they could with skeletal x-rays. Keeping their minds open to any and all possibilities was essential.

Such work affects a forensic anthropologist's personal life. Investigations and testifying at trials mean time away from home. Even at home the work intrudes. At Ubelaker's Christmas tree farm in Virginia, he pokes scraps of plastic and other compounds into fires, just to see how they'll emerge. Burned drywall, it turns out, can resemble bone. So can garden hose.

"You do develop a special interest in tire irons," he adds. "I can't go into an auto supply store without evaluating the differences between them."

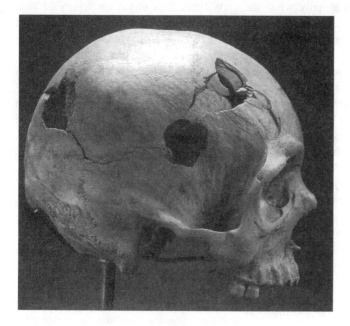

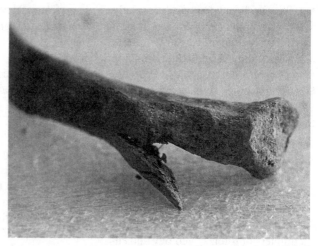

Photograph by Robert C. Burke

The knife was twisted, or the young woman victim moved as she was stabbed, splitting this section of a rib.

Photograph by Robert C. Burke

This skull was struck 19 times with the head and claw of a hammer; most of the damage is in back.

PROMOTING ACCURACY IN MYSTERIES

Sometimes, fiction overtakes fact in the museum's anthropology department. Best-selling crime novelist Patricia Cornwell consulted with Ubelaker as she worked on *All That Remains,* about a serial killer in Virginia. Cornwell spent a day with Ubelaker, looking at slides of damaged bones and trying to figure out what cut marks on a hand phalanx, a finger bone, would look like. "I asked him what a serrated knife would do," Cornwell says. "Doug told me that with a slice it's impossible to tell, because the points of the blade would cover their own tracks. Only if the bone was hacked could you tell." In her book, the heroine—Kay Scarpetta, a medical examiner—is able to determine that a bone has been hacked, a wound incurred when the victim tried to defend herself. And Ubelaker was the inspiration for the character Dr. Alex Vessey, the Smithsonian's expert bone man.

Nursing Home Man, after several hours on the table, smells warm and mammally. His bones feel greasy, which isn't unpleasant, but they're also flecked with bits of dried tissue and a waxy, light brown substance—adipocere, a byproduct of fat decomposition in moist condi-

tions. Owsley isn't wearing gloves, so I make up my mind to be brave, as well. In grad school, Owsley was assigned to work on an extremely fat woman who was found dead and in an advanced state of decomposition in the Smoky Mountains. Her body, says Owsley, was actually foaming with adipocere, and the odor was intense. "I worked for ten minutes, threw up for ten minutes, worked for ten minutes, threw up for ten." And then he never threw up again.

Owsley now looks for any "inclusions" in the cardboard box—bullets, rings, documents, a shoe. Save for the rabbit bone, the box contains only human parts. He notes taphonomic evidence, that is, any changes that affected the body after death. Such evidence may include vegetation that grew on a body as it lay under a porch, silt that settled in bone cracks when the skeleton was later dragged toward a river, a snail shell that lodged between vertebrae as the spine drifted downstream. "One of the great things about the Smithsonian," says Owsley, "is that I can pick up the phone and call a botanist to analyze the algae, a geologist for the silt and an invertebrate zoologist for the snail. Forensic anthropology combines a lot of disciplines."

Owsley holds a femur in the air. "See that lipping [bony extensions] on the end? Arthritis," he says. I pick up a fingernail from among pelvic bones and move it up to the hand pile. It's long and yellowed and thick, and it gives me more of the creeps than anything else arrayed on the table, even the equine-looking teeth.

As Owsley examines the ribs, I open a yellow envelope that came with the box. It's full of hair. "Hey," I say. "This hair is kind of dark." Owsley stops and looks over.

"No gray?"

"No, and there's plenty of it—for an old guy."

"Well," he says, "he wasn't really an old guy." The plot thickens; Owsley knows more than he is letting on. He continues, "Actually, this guy was 45." I nod. "His wife put him in the nursing home because of his diminishing mental capabilities. They suspect she was poisoning him, perhaps even while he was in the nursing home."

Now I know that we aren't looking at an elderly man with Alzheimer's who'd wandered away, gotten lost in the woods and died of a heart attack, exposure or starvation. The bones, come to think of it, do look pretty strong, despite the arthritis. Owsley tells me that toxicologists will be working up his bone marrow, looking for evidence of poisoning. Still, he's got to examine each bone for signs of trauma. Had the dead man been in a fistfight? The nose does not appear broken. The hyoid, a fragile bone in the throat, is intact, but strangulation can't be ruled out. Had he battled an attacker? The ulna—one of the forearm bones, a common spot for a parry fracture— shows no sign of trauma. Nor do the ribs, all 23 of them. Without a major bullet hole to offer immediate gratification, I can imagine this inventory becoming tedious. But Owsley doesn't let up. "You have to go all out on each case," he says. "Each person is equally important. Someone cared about him."

Sometimes, the person who cares doesn't get satisfaction for a long, long time. In January of 1978, in a small Midwestern town, the trailer home of a family named Morris caught fire. Mrs. Morris reported that there had been an explosion and that her husband had rescued her 6-year-old son from the flames, and a neighbor had rescued her 9-year-old. Her husband, Donald Morris, she said, threw her out of the trailer, then attempted to rescue her 5-year-old. But the two never made it out. The fire chief, brand-new on the job, ruled out arson. The medical examiner declared the deaths accidental and did not perform autopsies.

Morris' brother, however, told the chief of detectives that the entire case smelled fishy to him. Dan D'Annunzio, the newest detective on the staff, was as-

signed to the case. D'Annunzio brought in one arson investigator who said the fire had been set. A second expert concurred. D'Annunzio asked to have the bodies exhumed, but the medical examiner refused.

For the next 15 years D'Annunzio worked on the case whenever time allowed. In 1993 he thought he had enough to reopen the case. The county attorney told him that if he could come up with one more piece of evidence, he would do it. D'Annunzio then found the older son in a prison. The son told him that he had woken that winter night and seen his mother hit his stepfather over the head with an ashtray and then stab him repeatedly in the back as he lay on the floor.

From a high shelf in the hall, Owsley retrieves Donald Morris, neatly arranged among crisp white sheets in a large cardboard box. Owsley sits cross-legged on the floor and takes out the bones. Morris' skull is badly burned, covered with dry patches of black and white that resemble lichen. Owsley holds up a femur. "This case really talks to you. Look at how strong he was—you can see where the hamstrings were attached. Powerful man; you can just imagine him throwing his wife out the window." "Now look at this vertebra." He holds up another one. "See the cut mark?" I do: there's an angular end on the transverse process (an extension to the side) of this lumbar vertebra. I can see the sharp cuts of a knife or machete. Owsley shows me several ribs with the same markings, clear evidence of multiple stab wounds.

"This skeleton says *so* much," Owsley says, again. He's excited now, remembering the case, holding up bones left and right. "Look at the pelvis—it was cracked and then healed. Look at the nose, it's been broken. When I met Morris' brother in the courtroom, he said 'It's just like Donald is here—you know so much about him.'[#ThinSpace]" Partly on the basis of Owsley's work, a jury convicted Mrs. Morris of two counts of murder and one of arson.

Precisely because Morris' skeleton was so expressive, Owsley asked the family if the Smithsonian could have it for its collections, to use for teaching. They agreed.

That case was closed. Nursing Home Man was proving more intractable. Owsley finished examining the remains. He found no evidence of trauma, and the toxicologists found not a trace of poison in his bone marrow. The man's wife may have committed the perfect crime, but it's still too soon to tell. Owsley has started on another dozen cases—an unidentified skeleton from Northern Virginia, a young girl with cut marks on her cervical vertebrae—but he hasn't closed the book on Nursing Home Man quite yet. He's got a more powerful microscope down the hall, and he plans to look at each of the 205 bones once again.

ELIZABETH ROYTE *lives in New York City. She writes about the natural world for* Outside, *the* New York Times Magazine, Harpers *and other periodicals.*

What Did They Eat?

Eleanora Reber (Harvard)

Most archaeologists know that visible food residues can appear on potsherds, offering a possibility of dietary reconstruction. Visible residues are not, however, the only means of identifying the contents of pots. When an unglazed pottery vessel is used for cooking, lipids and water-soluble compounds from the contents absorb into the vessel walls. These absorbed residues, which are protected by the unyielding clay matrix from chemical degradation, can be extracted and identified.

MAKINGS OF PREHISTORIC STEW

As a meal is cooked in an unglazed vessel, the prehistoric cook may have added a variety of foods into a stew. From the cook's point of view, she was boiling food until properly cooked, serving, then rinsing the vessel for its next use. On the molecular level, as the foods were added to the stew, heat and the circulation of water caused fats, vitamins, starches, proteins and other substances to circulate through the water, and to be absorbed by the walls of the pot. Bacteria may have begun to work on the foods even before they were added to the pot; if the vessel was not washed for several hours following cooking, even more spoilage could occur. Water-soluble chemicals—such as most vitamins—absorbed into the pot are easily washed out by groundwater following archaeological deposition of the pot. Less water-soluble chemicals, however, once safely absorbed into the walls of the pot become a fixture until polluted by modern solvents or chemicals, or removed for study.

EXTRACTION TO RECONSTRUCTION

The procedure for residue identification involves extraction of preserved residue from the walls of a vessel. Because these residues are held in the walls of the vessel by weak chemical bonds, their recovery involves powdering 1–3 grams of the sherd, and then extracting the powder with solvent. This destructive procedure is painful for both the archaeologist and analyst, and is not undertaken lightly.

The precious residue-impregnated solvent is then evaporated to produce a tiny amount of unimpressive grease, which is injected into a chemical instrument called a gas chromatograph/mass spectrometer. This instrument separates the residue into its component compounds, and identifies each compound through its molecular fragments.

With the habits of our prehistoric cook in mind, however, it is clear that identifying diet from a residue is not a simple task. Many pottery vessels were used for more than one type of food. If a vessel was used for cooking, we need to consider the effect of heat on the foods. Furthermore, even when absorbed into a pot, some degradation of the chemicals can slowly occur. Polyunsaturated fats tend to degrade first, then monounsaturated fats, leaving the saturated fats behind. Bacterial action complicates matters further. So, the analyst looks for marker compounds—compounds that are unique to a particular food or group of foods, such as cholesterol in meat, theobromine in cocoa, or leaf waxes in turnips or cabbage. Ratios of lipids can also tell the analyst something about the basic classes of foods. If a high ratio of unsaturates to saturates survives, it suggests the presence of vegetables or grain.

IDENTIFYING MAIZE

Although analysis of absorbed residues is not infallible, and cannot identify everything cooked in a pot, the technique is already useful. Stable isotopic data give a snapshot of the residue. The presence of meat or vegetable can be determined with a fairly high degree of certainty. In an ambiguous pot it is also possible to tell whether or not food in a pot has been cooked, thereby answering questions about vessel function. If marker compounds are present, the corresponding food can be identified. Many, or perhaps even most foods may have marker compounds, but to discover this, each food must be carefully investigated. This is a worthy goal, and one that attracts students to the field, but progress is, of necessity, slow.

One archaeological application of residue is my own research, in which I am developing a technique using stable isotope and lipid analysis to identify maize residues. When established I will apply the technique to Mississippian pottery from a variety of temporal and geographical locations. The appearance of maize in residues should correspond to the change in cooking vessel thickness and temper, which has generally been attributed to the appearance of maize in the region. Thus, residue analysis can answer a variety of archaeological and anthropological questions by any researcher with questions about diet and pottery.

SAVE YOUR RESIDUES!

Once an absorbed residue is safely preserved inside the matrix of the clay, few things can remove or damage it. One of these culprits, unfortunately, is post-excavation washing or treatment of a sherd. Acid-washing and varnishing both damage absorbed residues irretrievably. Labeling a sherd with a nail polish and white-out will also contaminate residues, though they may be salvageable. Touching a sherd during excavation or storing it in a plastic bag can result in modern residues which may make the analysis of older remains difficult. A sherd submitted for residue study should not be washed, it should be touched as little as possible and stored and sent to the lab in tin foil or acid-free paper.

Eleanora Reber is presently in the doctoral program at Harvard U, Department of Anthropology. Following an undergraduate career at Beloit College as a chemistry/anthropology major, she spent time digging for contract firms. She is presently working on a preliminary study involving the identification of maize residues in pottery from around the world. One hundred sherds are needed, and analysis will be free of charge. If you have a sherd which you believe has been used to cook maize, please send samples and inquires, by March 1, to: Eleanora Reber, Dept of Anthropology, Harvard, 11 Divinity Ave, Cambridge, MA 02138; 617/495-4388, reber@fas.harvard.edu.

The Archaeologists Who Wouldn't Dig

Uncovering one of the most storied sites in antiquity—without touching a shovel

JOHN FLEISCHMAN

IN ALL OF GREEK LITERATURE, there are few places more famous than Pylos. "Sandy Pylos" is Homer's epithet in the *Iliad* for the kingdom of Nestor, the garrulous old warrior-king who gives the other Greek captains so much unwanted advice before the walls of Troy. In the *Odyssey,* Telemachus begins his search for his lost father, Odysseus, at Nestor's palace. Perched at the southwestern tip of modern-day Greece, Pylos was also the site of a scandalous event during the Peloponnesian War: the surrender, in 425 B.C., of some 120 armed Spartan officers of the hoplite infantry to the Athenians. "Nothing that happened in the war," the historian Thucydides noted, "surprised the Hellenes as much as this."

In our century nothing has matched what happened at Pylos on April 4, 1939, probably the luckiest first day on a dig an archaeologist ever had. On that morning Carl W. Blegen, the preeminent American archaeologist of the time, opened a trench through an olive grove. There, above Pylos, he struck what he later described as "the office of internal revenue" in Nestor's late Bronze Age palace. A cataclysmic fire had destroyed the palace 3,200 years earlier, but storage jars of olive oil had exploded near clay tab-

lets on which the palace financial records were kept, firing them into a crude ceramic. All told, Blegen laid bare more than 1,000 tablets covered in an early Greek script called Linear B, the earliest writing then known on the European mainland.

A terrible disappointment to some classicists (who had hoped the tablets would be filled with poetry), the decipherment of Linear B was a revelation to historians. The *wanax,* as the king of Pylos was called, had made his scribes keep lists of everything: bath attendants, bronze-shod chariot wheels, perfumed oil and postings of shepherds and coastguards. The Bronze Age Greeks, or Mycenaeans, such lists show, had created the first highly centralized civilization in Europe—a precursor to citystates, empires and nations from Athens to the Soviet Union.

For Jack L. Davis, Carl W. Blegen professor of Greek archaeology at the University of Cincinnati in Ohio, that was reason enough to revisit Pylos fifty years after his predecessor's first excavations. Davis assembled a consortium of archaeologists, historians, physical scientists and students into the Pylos Regional Archaeological Project, or PRAP, including John Bennet of the University

of Wisconsin-Madison, Susan E. Alcock of the University of Michigan in Ann Arbor, Cynthia W. Sheldmerdine of the University of Texas at Austin, Yannos G. Lolos of the University of Ioannina in Greece and Eberhard Zangger, founder of Geoarchaeology International in Zurich, Switzerland.

In archaeological parlance, PRAP is "survey." By plotting the locations of ceramics, stone tools and other artifacts that weathered out of the soil across wide areas, PRAP determines large-scale patterns of human activity. The shovel is the one tool that Davis and his fellow principal investigators do not use. PRAP does not dig.

ARCHAEOLOGISTS WHO DON'T excavate? Surely that is heresy. Yet surveys are a well-established archaeological practice. American anthropologists working in the Southwest and in Meso-America refined the technique in the 1960s and 1970s. Later, British archaeologists picked up the New World habit, wedded it to French modernist theories on the history of "ordinary" life and brought it to bear on Old World problems. Still, nothing as ambitious as the PRAP survey has ever been tried on mainland Greece. "It's one thing when you find a hundred or even a thousand artifacts in a square kilometer," Davis says of North American surveys, "but in the Aegean we're finding hundreds of thousands of artifacts in a square kilometer."

The results of that work are already available on the World-Wide Web at <http:\\classics.lsa.umich.edu\PRAP\html>. The really subversive stuff, however, is in Davis's mild-mannered book titled *Sandy Pylos,* which will be published by University of Texas Press next year. *Sandy Pylos* quietly undermines many conventional assumptions about archaeology and history. Without lifting a shovel, Davis's teams have uncovered nothing less than "the history, not just of one archaeological site, but of an entire landscape," as Davis writes in the book's foreword, "and not just in a single period, but at all times in the past."

THE LOCATION OF PYLOS WAS an ancient mystery even to the ancients. As the Greek geographer Strabo noted, quoting an old riddle: "There is a Pylos in front of Pylos and there is yet another Pylos." Even Greeks of the Classical Age knew only that Nestor's Pylos lay near the town they called Koryfasion (not to be confused with modern Koryfasio, which is somewhere else entirely).

When I decided to retrace Blegen's footsteps and talk with Davis, I had to take an all-day bus ride from smog-bound Athens across the rocky Peloponnesus to Pylos in western Messenia. Eight hours later, dehydrated and reeking of tobacco smoke, I staggered off the bus in Pylos and fell straight into the confusion over place names in modern Greece. In 1827, after the Greeks won their independence, the Ottoman town of Navarino was renamed Pylos. But Ottoman Navarino had never been ancient Pylos. The Pylos I was looking for turned out to be a short but terrifying taxi ride away: fourteen kilometers north of town, along the Bay of Navarino and then several hundred yards abruptly uphill, to the beak of a sharp ridge called Ano Englianos.

Blegen's dig is now covered by a huge, open-sided sheet-metal hangar,

erected by the Greek government to protect the low, rubble footprint of the late Bronze Age palace. The day after my arrival, I wandered through the ankle-high maze of the palace remains in search of the great central *megaron,* or throne room, where the wanax presided. From scraps of fallen plaster, Blegen had reconstructed some of the palace's brilliant decorations. There were frescoes of deer, doves, bare-chested warriors, a singer and his lyre: a splendid setting for a warrior-king—even one surrounded by accountants. Down the hall, the Linear B archives never bothered to name the king, but they did name the place.

This was Pylos, the Pylos before there were any others. Standing outside the ruin, looking across the plain below to the Bay of Navarino and the Ionian Sea beyond, I could understand why the later Greeks could not find Pylos: they were convinced that Homer's "sandy Pylos" had to be near the sea. Why Pylos was here in the hills was a question PRAP would later answer for me.

A journalist visiting a working archaeological site usually can count on a grand tour of the "dig," a tortured plot of ground covered with grid markers, tools and heaps of dirt waiting to be screened. There, in the holy trenches, he will be shown graduate students with serious sunburn working the earth with dental picks and dustpans.

Davis did not have a single trench to show me. Survey work is done by walking, he explained as we sat in the cool of the evening at PRAP headquarters in the village of Hora. Every morning between fifteen and twenty PRAP students fan out in teams across the rugged hills and coastline around the old palace. At fifteen-meter intervals they pace off precise quadrants, collecting surface artifacts and environmental data. (Areas covered with dense litter are resurveyed more intensively.) The teams press on regardless of topography, heat and the infamous Greek *macchia,* chaparral-like underbrush that grows luxuriantly even where shepherds and their goats have given up.

At day's end the PRAP walkers carry their surface finds back to a temporary museum in a Hora schoolhouse. There the finds' locations are logged in a mar-

velous computer information base and the sherds are stored in recycled five-gallon oilcans.

BROKEN POTTERY IS A VIRTUally catastrophe-proof record of human settlement. Invaders may loot precious metals and survivors may scavenge building materials, but no one ever carries off the broken pottery—no one, that is, except archaeologists. Aegean pottery types, from the truly ancient to the nearly modern, have been so thoroughly characterized that PRAP pottery experts can usually sort the fragments as easily as if they were sorting socks.

At many archaeological sites, soil stratigraphy is everything: it gives context to artifacts, showing when and how they were deposited and what the environmental conditions were at the time. But farmers have churned up Western Messenia for 6,000 years; in some places the ground has eroded so deeply that they plow up the soft bedrock marl directly for soil. Over time the surface of the soil has become a historical hodgepodge: bits of late Bronze Age oil jars are mixed indiscriminately with eighteenth-century Ottoman plates and third-century Roman roof tiles. Nevertheless, as sherds weather to the surface, they create a rough statistical model of what's below. Collected and plotted, the age-sorted sherds pile up electronically around certain sites, indicating peaks of activity and population. Survey is about finding such patterns.

READERS WHO DIP INTO SANDY Pylos for the "truth" behind Homeric epics or Greek nationalism will be swept away instead by a torrent of time rushing across Messenia. The book synthesizes new data, old documents and novel analyses, and it draws perspectives from at least a dozen disciplines. The evidence comes from everything from core drilling to medieval financial records newly uncovered from state archives in Istanbul and Italy.

The story begins with the clash of the African and Eurasian tectonic plates that pushed up the Taygetus Mountains as well as other chains running from Greece to the Balkans. Two million years of stream erosion went on to create two rugged coastal valleys, and a series of ice ages left the slopes covered with pine forests. Then, in about 15,000 B.C., people first began to leave traces of their habitation.

Evidence of farming dates from about 4000 B.C., first in the form of light tools along stream bottoms and then, after 3000 B.C., in the form of plows. In the next 1,000 years both the human population and the number of grazing livestock exploded. Those explosions set off the first of what pollen and soil samples show were four waves of dramatic environmental change, which gradually wiped out the native vegetation and stripped away most of the topsoil. The second wave coincided with the rise of Mycenaean culture in about 1400 B.C. and the third, in about 500 B.C., with the new intensive agricultural practices of the Classical world. PRAP's physical scientists charted those changes, concluding, for instance, that in the fourth century B.C. olive trees were cultivated on a quarter of the surface area of the Pylos region. The fourth, last and ongoing wave of destruction dates from modern times, with the rise of the bulldozer and the chemical sprayer.

Each wave of environmental change marks a major change in human activity, or—in the common parlance—history. Take those olive groves. Here the environmental and archaeological survey data come together in intriguing ways. Until PRAP, the early Classical period was the black hole of the Messenian past. In the eighth century B.C. Sparta swallowed up its western neighbor in a series of shadowy wars, and the Spartan grip was not broken until 371 B.C., when the Spartans were defeated by the Theban general Epaminondas at the Battle of Leuctra. The Spartans had little interest in recording their own history, much less the history of the subjugated people of Messenia. Only through the curiosity of other Greeks, particularly such nosy Athenians as Thucydides, can contemporary scholars glimpse the fate of Spartan vassals, who were reduced to the status of *perioikoi* (literally "dwellers around"), with no political rights, or to helots, who were state-owned slaves.

What were the Spartans up to for all those centuries before Messenia regained its independence?

Elsewhere in Greece at that time numerous scattered farmsteads were the agricultural rule. But in Messenia PRAP found no sherds from Spartan-era farmsteads. After reviewing PRAP's exhaustive survey records, the archaeologists Ann B. Harrison, of the J. Paul Getty Museum in Los Angeles, and Nigel Spencer, of the Institute of Archaeology of the University of Oxford in England, concluded that such farmsteads never existed on the PRAP site. Instead the population was crowded into large villages and small towns—so that their Spartan overlords could control or overawe them, presumably—and the olive groves were tended by helots. With the defeat of Sparta, PRAP's sherd patterns also show, the population spread out through the countryside.

IF THE PRAP SURVEY MARKS the changes in the landscape, it also reveals the continuities. Long before the Spartans came to Pylos, an indigenous Mycenaean palace culture arose from a scattering of small fiefdoms, then slowly formed a centralized kingdom. That evolution can be seen in sherd patterns and in the location of Bronze Age *tholos* tombs. By the late Bronze Age anyone who was anyone in Mycenaean Pylos was buried near the palace on Ano Englianos. Other secondary settlements faded out completely in the late palace period, their populations drawn away perhaps by the brighter lights of splendid Pylos.

Scouring the countryside for every sign of previous settlement, PRAP was able to locate 150 separate sites, many of which may number among the 240 places named in the Pylos Linear B tablets. By matching the restored geography to the activities recorded on the tablets, and by referring to the work of previous scholars, John Bennet (one of PRAP's resident Linear B specialists) could draw an amazingly detailed picture of the kingdom of Pylos, which covered close to 800 square miles. The kingdom had a "Hither" province of seven districts, it seems, and a "Further" province of nine,

divided by Mount Aigaleon, rising to the northeast of the palace.

Seeing that line on the map, I suddenly knew why Strabo and the Greeks of the Classical Age couldn't find Pylos. The palace was sited in the shadow of the mountain, not to keep an eye on the distant sea but to keep an eye on Hither and Further. The wanax of Pylos ruled both sides of the mountain. His palace guarded the pass between them.

But the wanax had nautical interests too. The closest thing to an amazing "find" for PRAP was the discovery of the Bronze Age harbor of Pylos. It was a manmade, 360-by-250-yard straight-sided basin created by diverting part of the Selas River across an alluvial plain. The basin is "the first and thus far only artificial port discovered in prehistoric Europe," according to Eberhard Zangger, the geoarchaeologist who headed PRAP's earth sciences team.

Although no port structures (let alone ships) have yet been found, the PRAP geologists inferred the construction of a port from core samples that bore marine remains dated to the twelfth century B.C. In the layering of fine clays and then coarse gravels, Zangger could read the sudden transformation of a calm, shallow pond into a deep basin fed by the redirected Selas surging toward its new outlet. Excavations elsewhere in Greece had revealed the Mycenaean knack for diverting streams to control floods and supply water. Here they had turned that talent to building a harbor in the shadow of the wanax's palace.

The port perished soon after the palace. Without a central authority at Pylos, the walls of agricultural terracing that surrounded the palace could not be maintained. As the walls collapsed, they spilled hillsides of rich soil into the sea, and the harbor silted shut.

THE GÖTTERDÄMMERUNG OF the Palcce haunted earlier archaeologists. Blegen read into the destruction of "Nestor's Pylos" the advent of the "Dorian" invasion, which was the traditional explanation in Classical times, as well as in Blegen's, for the overthrow of the Mycenaeans. All their great strongholds perished in the late twelfth century B.C., plunging Greece into a dark age (the Geometric period) that lasted for 500 years in Pylos. Blegen flatly declared that the great fire at Pylos ended human occupation on Ano Englianos.

"That's not what happened," Davis told me. "That's not true at any site. People just don't walk away unless a volcano goes off suddenly and they have absolutely no warning. Very often they gradually abandon their sites rather than all at once. They return to sites. They carry off stuff of value. And they build on top of the sites, often 1,000 years later."

That's what PRAP shows happened at Pylos. Life went on in the old kingdom without the wanax. PRAP walkers collected many sherds of Geometric pottery in a wide swath around the palace. Those sherds were then linked to Geometric material that Blegen recovered inside the palace ruins—sherds he had dismissed as trivial later intrusions. The pottery may have become cruder, such examples show, the agriculture rougher and the population smaller, but the locals remained, speaking Greek and worshiping the same gods.

Davis doesn't believe in a Dorian invasion or occupation. "As far as I'm concerned, there's no evidence for any displacement or entrance of foreigners at this time," he said. "The evidence points to continuity. Mycenaean pottery is related to the pottery of historical Greece. It's hard to believe it wasn't the same population."

IT'S HARD TO BELIEVE THAT ANY landcape could have as much history as Pylos. Except for a brief Messenian "independence" after the Spartan expulsion, the region has been a pawn of greater powers. Ruled from Rome and then Constantinople, Messenia was ravaged by the Heruli, the Visigoths and the Vandals, two major earthquakes and various plagues. The Middle Ages brought the Venetians for the first time, followed by a conquering Frankish knight, Geoffroi de Villehardouin of Champagne, driven by a storm to the coast south of Pylos during the Fourth Crusade in 1205. Frankish "Morea" was swept, in turn, by Catalan mercenaries, imperial troops reasserting Byzantine authority, the Black Death, the Venetians again, the Ottoman Turks (for the first time), the Venetians yet again and the Ottoman Turks (for the second time) before its liberation in 1827.

PRAP draws the historical line at Greek independence, but you might as well throw in the Second World War, the Greek civil war and membership in the European Community, which, by allowing foreigners to buy land along the coast, is unleashing rampant development on ancient sites.

The damage worries Davis, but it does not surprise him. People have lived around Pylos since the Neolithic. At least since the second millennium B.C., he figures, some of the inhabitants have come from the same, Greek-speaking stock. That is not to say the Pylians are "pure" Greek in a narrow ethnic or nationalistic sense. The population has always been well mixed, thanks to warlords, mercenaries, refugees, slaves, holy men, merchants, tourists and archaeologists. Dealing with such a mix of ancient and modern, of legends and ledgers, is the whole point of survey archaeology. In Greece "the problem confronting surveyors is not in finding artifacts," Davis writes, "but in investigating, in a systematic manner, an entire landscape full of them."

JOHN FLEISCHMAN is a freelance writer living in Cincinnati, Ohio, who specializes in archaeology. His first article for THE SCIENCES *was "The Riddle of Troy" (March/April 1994).*

UNIT 4
Historical Archaeology

Unit Selections

29. **Alcohol in the Western World**, Bert L. Vallee
30. **Reading the Bones of La Florida**, Clark Spencer Larsen
31. **Living Through the Donner Party**, Jared Diamond
32. **Case of the Colorado Cannibal**, Andrew Curry
33. **Life in the Provinces of the Aztec Empire**, Michael E. Smith
34. **Legacy of the Crusades**, Sandra Scham
35. **Israel's Mysterious Stone**, Haim Watzman

Key Points to Consider

• What is historical archaeology? Give some examples.

• Discuss the effects of the Cold War era and give their historic significance.

• Discuss the historical roots of alcohol used in ancient civilizations.

• What does historic archaeology tell us about the effects of disease brought about by European contact with the New World? Give some examples.

• How is the Donner Pass story an example of cultural historical reconstruction, even though it is not strictly archaeology?

• Who was the "Colorado Cannibal"? What is "opportunistic" cannibalism?

• Recent historical data on the Aztec provinces give a different view of the distribution of wealth and services in that empire. What are these revised views?

• How do archaeologists view the Christian Crusades of the Middle Ages? What do they view as its current historical consequence?

 **Links: www.dushkin.com/online/**
These sites are annotated in the World Wide Web pages.

GIS and Remote Sensing for Archaeology: Burgundy, France
http://www.informatics.org/france/france.html

Petra Great Temple/Technology
http://www.brown.edu/Departments/Anthropology/Petra/excavations/technology.html

Radiocarbon Dating for Archaeology
http://www.rlaha.ox.ac.uk/orau/index.html

Zeno's Forensic Page
http://forensic.to/forensic.html

How many times have you misplaced your car keys? Locked yourself out of the house? Lost your wallet? Your address book? Eyeglasses? Sometimes these artifacts are recovered and brought back into the historical present. Sometimes they are lost forever, becoming part of the garbage of an extinct culture. Have you ever noticed that lost things, when found, are always in the last place you look? Is this a law of science? Be skeptical.

Here is an opportunity to practice historical archaeology. You may wish to try this puzzler in order to practice thinking like an archaeologist. (Do not forget to apply the basics discussed in unit 1.) The incident recounted here is true. Only the names, dates, and places were changed to protect the privacy of the famous personages involved in this highly charged mystery.

Problem: Dr. Wheeler, a British archaeologist at a large university left his office on December 17, 2003, around 10 P.M. on a cold Friday evening. This was his last night to be at the university because he would not be back again until after the holidays. Right before he left his office, he placed a thin, reddish, three-ring notebook in an unlocked cupboard in his office.

Dr. Wheeler then proceeded to go directly to his designated campus parking space, got into his Mini Cooper S, and drove directly to his flat in Marshalltown Goldens. When he arrived at home he went straightaway to his study. He remained at his flat with his family and never left his flat during the entire holiday.

Dr. Wheeler and family had a jolly good holiday and Dr. Wheeler thought nothing more of his notebook until the university resumed its session on Wednesday, January 5, 2004 at the beginning of the New Year.

Upon returning to his office, Dr. Wheeler could not find his notebook in the cupboard, and he became very agitated. He chased his assistant, Miss Mortimer, around the office, wielding a wicked looking Acheulean hand-ax. Poor Miss Mortimer claimed she had no knowledge of the whereabouts of the notebook. But Dr. Wheeler had always suspected that Miss Mortimer pinched pens and pencils from his desk, so, naturally… But Miss Mortimer protested so earnestly that Dr. Wheeler eventually settled in, had a cup of tea, and decided that perhaps he had absentmindedly taken the notebook home after all.

However, a thorough search of his flat indicated that the notebook was clearly not there. It was lost! Dr. Wheeler was almost lost himself when his wife, Sophia, caught him excavating her rose garden in the vain hope that Tut, the family dog, had buried the lost article there. It was a professor's nightmare, since the notebook contained the only copy of all his class records for the entire term. What could he do? He knew he was in danger of being fired from his chair for incompetence.

So, Dr. Wheeler approached the problem in the manner of a proper, eccentric archaeologist. He had another cup of tea and generated several hypotheses about where his notebook might have gone. He tested several hypotheses, but to no avail! His notebook still remained missing. However, being the good archaeologist he is, he kept on generating hypotheses. But his notebook was still not found. Then he began to wonder if maybe the postprocessualists weren't right after all!

Dr. Wheeler was at his wit's ends, when sometimes as it happens, pure luck intervened as it often does in archaeology. You just get lucky sometimes. Everyone does. His faithful assistant Miss Mortimer received a phone call on January 9, 2004, from a woman who had found the missing notebook on the evening of December 31, 2003. The helpful lady found his notebook in a gutter! To be precise, she found it in a family neighborhood located on the corner of Olduvai Drive and East Turkana Avenue in Hadar Heights, about 1 mile away from the university. Please note that this area is in the opposite direction from Dr. Wheeler's flat in Marshalltown Goldens. The notebook was wet and muddy, and furthermore, it was wedged down into a gutter grill in the street.

Greatly relieved, the next day, January 10, 2004, Dr. Wheeler has Miss Mortimer run over to the kind woman's flat. So it was in this mysterious way that he recouped his class records. Dr. Wheeler was so delighted that when Miss Mortimer returned with the notebook, he invited her to sit and join him for a spot of tea (which was not his habit, being misogynist). Yet, Dr. Wheeler was not satisfied with merely recovering his notebook. He was curious to know what had happened to it and why! He continued to generate more sophisticated hypotheses to solve the mystery.

Challenge to the Student:

Try to place yourself in Dr. Wheeler's position. Attempt to generate your own hypotheses as to the whereabouts of the lost three-ring notebook from the night of Friday, December 17, 2003, to the time of its return to Dr. Wheeler on January 10, 2004.

How do you go about doing this? First, review everything you "believe" to be true. Be very careful and skeptical about what is true and what is not. Then convert this into your original database. From that point again set up even more hypotheses and/or make alternative hypotheses until you arrive at the simplest possible explanation. The simplest possible explanation is most likely to be the correct answer. Support your answer with your database.

Pretend that you are doing historical archaeology. Ask your living informant(s) for information first. What could you ask Dr. Wheeler? You could ask, "Did you go back to the lavatory before you left the building on December 17, 2003? Are you sure of where your motorcar was parked or could you be mistaken? What was the weather like? Was it raining? Is it possible that you in fact stopped and talked to someone on your way to your motorcar? Are you sure you were at home on December 31, 2003 and you did not go out to celebrate the New Year?" Be very precise with your questioning. Also, let your imagination run wild with possibilities. Brainstorm. Sometimes this is when you are most likely to get the answer. Creativity is the essence of all science.

Hints:

Dr. Wheeler's university office was never broken into. Poor Miss Mortimer and the kind lady who found the notebook had nothing to do with the disappearance of the notebook. Dr. Wheeler's dog Tut did not bury his notebook. So what did happen? There is in fact a correct answer that will explain the mystery. Try to find that answer! If you do this you will have to think like an archaeologist. It is a lot of fun, and it will reward you well!

Alcohol in the Western World

*The role of alcohol in Western civilization has changed dramatically during this millennium.
Our current medical interpretation of alcohol as primarily an agent of
disease comes after a more complex historical relationship.*

By Bert L. Vallee

A substance, like a person, may have distinct and even contradictory aspects to its personality. Today ethyl alcohol, the drinkable species of alcohol, is a multifaceted entity; it may be social lubricant, sophisticated dining companion, cardiovascular health benefactor or agent of destruction. Throughout most of Western civilization's history, however, alcohol had a far different role. For most of the past 10 millennia, alcoholic beverages may have been the most popular and common daily drinks, indispensable sources of fluids and calories. In a world of contaminated and dangerous water supplies, alcohol truly earned the title granted it in the Middle Ages: *aqua vitae*, the "water of life."

Potent evidence exists to open a window into a societal relationship with alcohol that is simply unimaginable today. Consider this statement, issued in 1777 by Prussia's Frederick the Great, whose economic strategy was threatened by importation of coffee: "It is disgusting to notice the increase in the quantity of coffee used by my subjects, and the amount of money that goes out of the country as a consequence. Everybody is using coffee; this must be prevented. His Majesty was brought up on beer; and so were both his ancestors and officers. Many battles have been fought and won by soldiers nourished on beer, and the King does not believe that coffee-drinking soldiers can be relied upon to endure hardships in case of another war."

Surely a modern leader who urged alcohol consumption over coffee, especially by the military, would have his or her mental competence questioned. But only an eyeblink ago in historical time, a powerful head of government could describe beer in terms that make it sound like mother's milk. And indeed, that nurturing role may be the one alcohol played from the infancy of the West to the advent of safe water supplies for the masses only within the past century.

Natural processes have no doubt produced foodstuffs containing alcohol for millions of years. Yeast, in metabolizing sugar to obtain energy, creates ethyl alcohol as a by-product of its efforts. Occasionally animals accidentally consume alcohol that came into being as fruit "spoiled" in the natural process of fermentation; inebriated birds and mammals have been reported. Humans have a gene for the enzyme alcohol dehydrogenase; the presence of this gene at least forces the conjecture that over evolutionary time animals have encountered alcohol enough to have evolved a way to metabolize it. Ingestion of alcohol, however, was unintentional or haphazard for humans until some 10,000 years ago.

About that time, some Late Stone Age gourmand probably tasted the contents of a jar of honey that had been left unattended longer than usual. Natural fermentation had been given the opportunity to occur, and the taster, finding the effects of mild alcohol ingestion provocative, probably replicated the natural experiment. Comrades and students of this first oenologist then codified the method for creating such mead or wines from honey or dates or sap. The technique was fairly simple: leave the sweet substance alone to ferment.

Beer, which relies on large amounts of starchy grain, would wait until the origin and development of agriculture. The fertile river deltas of Egypt and Mesopotamia produced huge crops of wheat and barley; the diets of peasants, laborers and soldiers of these ancient civilizations were cereal-based. It might be viewed as a historical inevitability that fermented grain would be discovered. As in the instance of wine, natural experiments probably produced alcoholic substances that aroused the interest of those who sampled the results. Before the third millennium B.C., Egyptians and Babylonians were drinking beers made from barley and wheat.

Wine, too, would get a boost from agriculture. Most fruit juice, even wild grape juice, is naturally too low in sugar to produce wine, but the selection for sweeter grapes leading to the domestication of particular grape stock eventually led to viniculture. The practice of growing grape strains suitable for wine production has been credited to people living in what is now Armenia, at about 6000 B.C., although such dating is educated guesswork at best.

The creation of agriculture led to food surpluses, which in turn led to ever larger groups of people living in close quarters, in villages or cities. These municipalities faced a problem that still vexes, namely, how to provide inhabitants with enough clean, pure water to sustain their constant need for physiological hydration. The solution, until the 19th century, was nonexistent. The water supply of any group of people rapidly became polluted with their waste products and thereby dangerous, even fatal, to drink. How many of our progenitors died attempting to quench their thirst with water can never be known. Based on current worldwide crises of dysentery and infectious disease wrought by unclean water supplies, a safe bet is that a remarkably large portion of our ancestry succumbed to tainted water.

In addition, the lack of liquids safe for human consumption played a part in preventing long-range ocean voyages until relatively recently. Christopher Columbus made his voyage with wine on board, and the Pilgrims landed at Plymouth Rock only because their beer stores had run out. An early order of business was luring brewmasters to the colonies.

Alcohol versus Water

Negative evidence arguing against a widespread use of water for drinking can be found in perusal of the Bible and ancient Greek texts. Both the Old and New Testaments are virtually devoid of references to water as a common human beverage. Likewise, Greek writings make scant reference to water drinking, with the notable exception of positive statements regarding the quality of water from mountain springs. Hippocrates specifically cited water from springs and deep wells as safe, as was rainwater collected in cisterns. The ancients, through what must have been tragic experience, clearly understood that most of their water supply was unfit for human consumption.

In this context of contaminated water supply, ethyl alcohol may indeed have been mother's milk to a nascent Western civilization. Beer and wine were free of pathogens. And the antiseptic power of alcohol, as well as the natural acidity of wine and beer, killed many pathogens when the alcoholic drinks were diluted with the sullied water supply. Dating from the taming and conscious application of the fermentation process, people of all ages in the West have therefore consumed beer and wine, not water, as their major daily thirst quenchers.

Babylonian clay tablets more than 6,000 years old give beer recipes, complete with illustrations. The Greek *akratidzomai*, which came to mean "to breakfast," literally translates as "to drink undiluted wine." Breakfast apparently could include wine as a bread dip, and "bread and beer" connoted basic necessity much as does today's expression "bread and butter."

BRYAN CHRISTIE;
SOURCE: *Food: The Gift of Osiris, Vol. 2*, Academic Press, 1977

EGYPTIAN PAINTINGS show alcohol as integral to the lives of the nobility. This depiction of wines being blended is from Amanemhat's tomb, circa 1400 B.C.

The experience in the East differed greatly. For at least the past 2,000 years, the practice of boiling water, usually for tea, has created a potable supply of nonalcoholic beverages. In addition, genetics played an important role in making Asia avoid alcohol: approximately half of all Asian people lack an enzyme necessary for complete alcohol metabolism, making the experience of drinking quite unpleasant. Thus, beer and wine took their place as staples only in Western societies and remained there until the end of the last century.

The traditional production of beer and wine by fermentation of cereals and grapes or other fruits produced beverages with low alcohol content compared with those familiar to present-day consumers. The beverages also contained large amounts of acetic acid and other organic acids created during fermentation. Most wines of ancient times probably would turn a modern oenophile's nose; those old-style wines in new bottles would more closely resemble today's vinegar, with some hints of cider, than a prizewinning merlot.

As the alcohol content of daily staple drinks was low, consumers focused on issues of taste, thirst quenching, hunger satisfaction and storage rather than on intoxication. Nevertheless, the "side effects" of this constant, low-level intake must have been almost universal. Indeed, throughout Western history the normal state of mind may have been one of inebriation.

The caloric value of nonperishable alcoholic beverages may also have played a significant role in meeting the daily energy requirements of societies that might have faced food shortages. In addition, they provided essential micronutrients, such as vitamins and minerals.

Alcohol also served to distract from the fatigue and numbing boredom of daily life in most cultures, while al-

BRYAN CHRISTIE; SOURCE: *Food: The Gift of Osiris, Vol. 2*, Academic Press, 1977

INEBRIATED REVELERS have accompanied the presence of alcoholic beverages for millennia. This painting from Khety's tomb, circa 2100 B.C., shows guests being carried away from a banquet after too much wine. Although drinking to excess was, and is, an unsafe practice, drinking any quantity of water 4,100 years ago was probably a much riskier undertaking.

leviating pain for which remedies were nonexistent. Today people have a plethora of handy choices against common aches and pain. But until this century, the only analgesic generally available in the West was alcohol. From the Book of Proverbs comes this prescription: "Give strong drink unto him that is ready to perish, and wine unto them that be of heavy hearts. Let him drink, and forget his poverty, and remember his misery no more." A Sumerian cuneiform tablet of a pharmacopoeia dated to about 2100 B.C. is generally cited as the oldest preserved record of medicinal alcohol, although Egyptian papyri may have preceded the tablet. Hippocrates' therapeutic system featured wines as remedies for almost all acute or chronic ailments known in his time, and the Alexandrian School of Medicine supported the medical use of alcohol.

Religion and Moderation

The beverages of ancient societies may have been far lower in alcohol than their current versions, but people of the time were aware of the potentially deleterious behavioral effects of drinking. The call for temperance began quite early in Hebrew Greek and Roman cultures and was reiterated throughout history. The Old Testament frequently disapproves of drunkenness, and the prophet Ezra and his successors integrated wine into everyday Hebrew ritual, perhaps partly to moderate undisciplined drinking custom, thus creating a religiously inspired and controlled form of prohibition.

In the New Testament, Jesus obviously sanctioned alcohol consumption, resorting to miracle in the transformation of water to wine, an act that may acknowledge the goodness of alcohol versus the polluted nature of water. His followers concentrated on extending measures to balance the use and abuse of wine but never supported total prohibition. Saint Paul and other fathers of early Christianity carried on such moderating attitudes. Rather than castigating wine for its effects on sobriety, they considered it a gift from God, both for its medicinal qualities and the tranquilizing characteristics that offered relief from pain and the anxiety of daily life.

Traditionally, beer has been the drink of the common folk, whereas wine was reserved for the more affluent. Grape wine, however, became available to the average Roman after a century of vineyard expansion that ended in about 30 B.C., a boom driven by greater profits for wine grapes compared with grain. Ultimately, the increased supply drove prices down, and the common Roman could partake in wine that was virtually free. Roman viniculture declined with the empire and was inherited by the Catholic Church and its monasteries, the only institutions with sufficient resources to maintain production.

For nearly 1,300 years the Church operated the biggest and best vineyards, to considerable profit. Throughout the Middle Ages, grain remained the basic food of peasants and beer their normal beverage, along with mead and homemade wines or ciders. The few critics of alcohol consumption were stymied by the continuing simple fact of the lack of safe alternatives. Hence, despite transitions in political systems, religions and ways of life, the West's use of and opinion toward beer and wine remained remarkably unchanged. But a technological development would alter the relationship between alcohol and humanity.

DISTILLATION created alcoholic drinks of unprecedented potency. This distillation apparatus appeared in Hieronymus Brunschwig's *Liber de arte distillandi*, the first book published on the subject, in A.D. 1500. The book featured these claims for distilled alcohol: "It causes a good colour in a person. It heals baldness… kills lice and fleas…. It gives also courage in a person, and causes him to have a good memory."

After perhaps 9,000 years of experience drinking relatively low alcohol mead, beer and wine, the West was faced with alcohol in a highly concentrated form, thanks to distillation. Developed in about A.D. 700 by Arab alchemists (for whom *al kohl* signified any material's basic essence), distillation brought about the first significant change in the mode and magnitude of human alcohol consumption since the beginning of Western civilization. Although yeasts produce alcohol, they can tolerate concentrations of only about 16 percent. Fermented beverages therefore had a natural maximum proof. Distillation circumvents nature's limit by taking advantage of alcohol's 78 degree Celsius (172 degree Fahrenheit) boiling point, compared with 100 degrees C for water. Boiling a water-alcohol mixture puts more of the mix's volatile alcohol than its water in the vapor. Condensing that vapor yields liquid with a much higher alcohol level than that of the starting liquid.

The Arab method—the custom of abstinence had not yet been adopted by Islam—spread to Europe, and distillation of wine to produce spirits commenced on the Continent in about A.D. 1100. The venue was the medical school at Salerno, Italy, an important center for the transfer of medical and chemical theory and methods from Asia Minor to the West. Joining the traditional alcoholic drinks of beer and wine, which had low alcohol concentration and positive nutritional benefit, were beverages with sufficient alcohol levels to cause the widespread problems still with us today. The era of distilled spirits had begun.

Knowledge of distillation gradually spread from Italy to northern Europe; the Alsatian physician Hieronymus Brunschwig described the process in 1500 in *Liber de arte distillandi*, the first printed book on distillation. By the time Brunschwig was a best-selling author, distilled alcohol had earned its split personality as nourishing food, beneficent medicine and harmful drug. The widespread drinking of spirits followed closely on the heels of the 14th century's bouts with plague, notably the Black Death of 1347–1351. Though completely ineffective as a cure for plague, alcohol did make the victim who drank it at least feel more robust. No other known agent could accomplish even that much. The medieval physician's optimism related to spirits may be attributed to this ability to alleviate pain and enhance mood, effects that must have seemed quite remarkable during a medical crisis that saw perhaps two thirds of Europe's population culled in a single generation.

Economic recovery following the subsidence of the plague throughout Europe generated new standards of luxury and increased urbanization. This age witnessed unprecedented ostentation, gluttony, self-indulgence and inebriation. Europe, apparently relieved to have survived the pestilence of the 14th century, went on what might be described as a continentwide bender. Despite the obvious negative effects of drunkenness, and despite attempts by authorities to curtail drinking, the practice continued until the beginning of the 17th century, when nonalcoholic beverages made with boiled water became popular. Coffee, tea and cocoa thus began to break alcohol's monopoly on safety.

In the 18th century a growing religious antagonism toward alcohol, fueled largely by Quakers and Methodists and mostly in Great Britain, still lacked real effect or popular support. After all, the Thames River of the time was as dangerous a source of drinking water as the polluted streams of ancient cultures. Dysentery, cholera and typhoid, all using filthy water as a vehicle, were major killers and would remain so in the West as recently as the end of the 19th century, rivaling plague in mass destruction.

Only the realization that microorganisms caused disease and the institution of filtered and treated water supplies finally made water a safe beverage in the West. Religious anti-alcohol sentiment and potable water

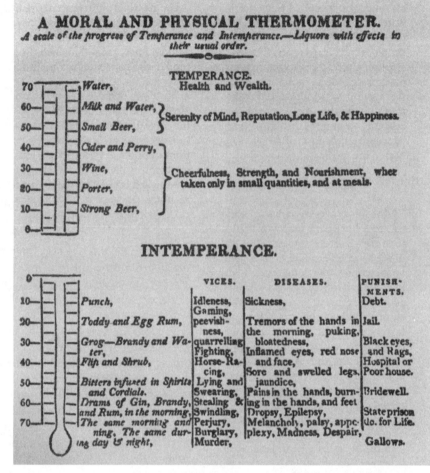

THERMOMETER ANALOGY was an attempt by physician and political figure Benjamin Rush to illustrate the effects of alcohol. Even after realizing that alcohol abuse was a disease, Rush did allow for the benefits of moderate drinking, seen in the "Temparance" section of the chart.

would combine with one other factor to make it finally possible for a significant percentage of the public to turn away from alcohol. That other factor was the recognition of alcohol dependence as an illness.

Diseases of Alcohol

Throughout the 19th century the application of scientific principles to the practice of medicine allowed clinical symptoms to be categorized into diseases that might then be understood on a rational basis. Alcohol abuse was among the earliest medical problems to receive the attention of this approach. Two graduates of the Edinburgh College of Medicine, Thomas Trotter of Britain and Benjamin Rush of the colonies and then the U.S., made the first important contributions to the clinical recognition of alcoholism as a chronic, life-threatening disease. The influence of moralistic anti-alcohol Methodism may have driven their clinical research, but their findings were nonetheless sound.

In an 1813 essay on drunkenness, Trotter described alcohol abuse as a disease and recognized that habitual and prolonged consumption of hard liquor causes liver disease, accompanied by jaundice, wasting and mental dysfunction, evident even when the patient is sober. Rush published similar ideas in America and to greater effect, as he was a prominent member of society and a signer of the Declaration of Independence. His personal fame, behind his correct diagnosis of a societal ill, helped to create viewpoints that eventually culminated in the American Prohibition (1919–1933).

Nineteenth-century studies detailed the clinical picture and pathological basis of alcohol abuse, leading to today's appreciation of it as one of the most important health problems facing America and the rest of the world. Alcohol contributes to 100,000 deaths in this country annually, making it the third leading cause of preventable mortality in the U.S. (after smoking and conditions related to poor diet and a sedentary way of life). Although the exact number of problem drinkers is difficult to estimate accurately, America is probably home to between 14 and 20 million people whose lives are disrupted by their relationship with alcohol.

LIBRARY OF CONGRESS

WOMEN'S AUXILIARY of the Keeley League supported Keeley's "Gold Cure," which claimed to cure alcoholism at the end of the last century. Dr. Leslie Keeley announced that gold salts effectively ended an alcoholic's cravings for drink. His talent was in fact marketing, not biochemistry. The Women's Auxiliary may have been responsible for whatever success Keeley had, as they provided a social support network for alcoholics struggling with their addiction. Keeley died in 1990, and his cure soon met its demise.

The overall alcohol problem is far broader. Perhaps 40 percent of Americans have been intimately exposed to the effects of alcohol abuse through a family member. And every year some 12,000 children of drinking mothers are robbed of their potential, born with the physical signs and intellectual deficits associated with full-blown fetal alcohol syndrome; thousands more suffer lesser effects. Pharmaceutical treatments for alcoholism remain impractical and inadequate, with total abstinence still the only truly effective approach.

Society and science are at the threshold of new pharmaceutical and behavioral strategies against alcoholism, however. As with any other disease, whether of the individual or the society, a correct diagnosis is crucial to treatment. Alcoholism, in historical terms, has only just been understood and accepted as a disease; we are still coping with the historically recent arrival of concentrated alcohol. The diagnosis having been made and acknowledged, continuing research efforts can be counted on to produce new and more effective treatments based on the growing knowledge of the physiology of alcohol abuse and of addictive substances in general.

Humanity at any moment of history is inevitably caught in that time, as trapped as an insect in amber. The mores, traditions and attitudes of an era inform the individuals then living, often blinding them to the consideration of alternatives. Alcohol today is a substance primarily of relaxation, celebration and, tragically, mass destruction. To consider it as having been a primary agent for the development of an entire culture may be jolting, even offensive to some. Any good physician, however takes a history before attempting a cure.

Further Reading

DRINKING IN AMERICA: A HISTORY. Mark E. Lender and James K. Martin. Free Press (Macmillan), 1987.

TOWARD A MOLECULAR BASIS OF ALCOHOL USE AND ABUSE. Edited by B. Jansson, H. Jörnvall, U. Rydberg, L. Terenius and B. L. Vallee. Birkhäuser Verlag, Switzerland, 1994.

THE ALCOHOL DEHYDROGENASE SYSTEM. H. Jörnvall, O. Danielsson, B. Hjelmquist, B. Persson and J. Shafqat in *Advances in Experimental Medicine and Biology*, Vol. 372, pages 281–294; 1995.

KUDZU ROOT: AN ANCIENT CHINESE SOURCE OF MODERN ANTIDIPSOTROPIC AGENTS. W. M. Keung and B. L. Vallee in *Phytochemistry*, Vol. 47, No. 4, pages 499–506; February 1998.

PATIENTS WITH ALCOHOL PROBLEMS, P. G. O'Connor and R. S. Schottenfeld in *New England Journal of Medicine*, Vol. 338, No. 9, pages 592–602; February 16, 1998.

The Author

BERT L. VALLEE received his M.D. from New York University in 1943 and held positions at the Massachusetts Institute of Technology before joining the faculty of Harvard Medical School in 1945. He is currently that institution's Edgar M. Bronfman Distinguished Senior Professor. Vallee's primary research has been in zinc enzymology, a field he is credited with establishing. His work on alcohol dehydrogenase, a zinc enzyme, led to his interest in the history of alcohol. The author of more than 600 scientific publications, Vallee is a Fellow of the National Acadmey of Sciences and holds numerous honorary degrees and professorships.

From *Scientific American*, June 1998, pp. 80-85. © 1998 by Dr. Bert L. Vallee, Department of Pathology, Harvard Medical School, Boston, MA 02115. Reprinted by permission of the author.

Reading the Bones of
La Florida

New approaches are offering insight into the lives of Native Americans after the Europeans arrived. Their health declined not only because of disease but because of their altered diet and living circumstances

Clark Spencer Larsen

The lives of Native Americans changed in dramatic ways after Christopher Columbus landed in the Caribbean islands in 1492. Written records paint a vivid picture of conquest and epidemics sowing death and disease among the indigenous peoples of the Americas, quickly decimating them. Until recently, in fact, almost all that was known about the biological consequences of contact with the Europeans was based on these old documents, which emphasize epidemics and population collapse. Although these texts offer an important perspective, they are not the only source of information.

Bioarchaeology, an emerging field that focuses on the study of archaeological remains, is supplementing our view of the health and daily life of Native Americans, particularly those who lived in the Spanish missions of the Southeast, in an area once known as *La Florida.* Sustained encounters between Indians and Europeans in *La Florida* began in 1565, when Pedro Menéndez de Avilés established the town of St. Augustine on the Atlantic coast in northern Florida. From there Roman Catholic priests set up a chain of missions among the Timucua and Apalachee Indians of northern Florida and the Guale Indians of the Georgia coast. At some of those places—including Santa Catalina de Guale on St. Catherines Island, San Martin de Timucua and San Luis de Apalachee—archaeologists have uncovered the ruins of large churches that served the converts. As the nucleus of each community, the church carried out important religious functions for the living; for the dead, it provided a burial ground.

Skeletons found beneath the floor of these churches have provided scholars with a surprisingly complete record of the diet and work habits of the mission Indians. Bioarchaeology is beginning to fill in the details of the historical record, offering specifics about how food sources changed and raising unexpected questions about the merits of a purely agricultural way of life—at least for the Indians who inhabited *La Florida.*

Food, obviously, is fundamental to human well-being, as it provides nutrients for growth, development and other physiological processes. Before our research, the diets of *La Florida* Indians were reconstructed from two sources: accounts by priests and other Europeans, and food remains at archaeological sites. The written records are often contradictory. Some depict little farming at the time. Others, including those examined by Grant D. Jones of Davidson College, say that indigenous peoples relied heavily on agriculture, particularly on corn.

The archaeological record is inconclusive as well. Plant remains do not always survive well, and in coastal regions they are particularly vulnerable to the destructive effects of moisture and acidic soils. Nevertheless, analysis of such evidence by C. Margaret Scarry of the University of North Carolina at Chapel Hill and Donna Ruhl of the University of Florida has revealed that native peoples ate numerous plant species, both wild and domesticated, before and after the arrival of the Europeans. But their use of corn is unclear. Excavations have revealed some kernels and cobs from late prehistoric and contact-era sites; however, the relative importance of this grain in the Indians' diet is not known.

RECONSTRUCTING DIET

To resolve some of these questions, we turned to the many bones found at these sites. Because the tissues of all living things contain stable isotopes of such elements as carbon and nitrogen, we can mea-

ROBERTO OSTI (map); SPANISH MISSIONS were established throughout what is now Florida and coastal Georgia. Serving three primary tribes—the Guale, the Apalachee and the Timucua—these missions became centers of social and religious life.

sure the amounts of these elements in bones and then use this information to reconstruct ancient diets. Differences in the ratios of two carbon isotopes, carbon 12 and carbon 13, contain a record of which plants an individual ate. Most plants are divided into two types: carbon 3 plants break down a three-carbon molecule during photosynthesis; carbon 4 plants synthesize a four-carbon molecule. The distinctive chemical signature of the C_3 and C_4 plants that a person consumes shows up in his or her bones. Virtually all plants eaten in the *La Florida* region were of the C_3 variety—including fruits, wheat, acorns and hickory nuts. The only major C_4 plant eaten by native peoples was corn.

Nitrogen isotopes provide a different set of clues. Fish bones and oyster shells in archaeological sites indicate that the Guale and other native peoples of the region ate seafood regularly—before and after the Europeans arrived. Because marine plants, such as algae, and terrestrial plants use the two stable isotopes of nitrogen—nitrogen 14 and nitrogen 15—differently, the ratios of these isotopes are different in the bones of a person who ate mostly marine foods as opposed to one who ate mostly terrestrial foods.

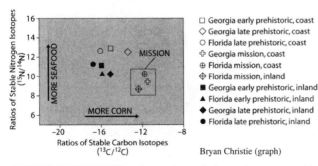

Bryan Christie (graph)

RATIOS OF ELEMENTS, such as carbon and nitrogen isotopes, provide important information about diet. Recorded in bones, these varying ratios reveal what kinds of plants or how much seafood an individual ate.

Examining the differences between carbon and nitrogen ratios in bones before and after the Europeans arrived pointed to enormous changes in the Native Americans' diets. Margaret J. Schoeninger of the University of Wisconsin-Madison, Nikolaas J. van der Merwe of Harvard University, Dale L. Hutchinson of East Carolina University, Lynette Norr of the University of Florida and I found that the variations were geographically and chronologically patterned. As would be expected, coastal people ate more seafood than inland people did, regardless of the era. The Guale Indians on St. Catherines and Amelia islands ate corn before and after the missionaries arrived. But during the mission period, they ate more than their ancestors had. Similarly, the Apalachee, who had eaten some corn before contact, seemed to eat it more after the Europeans arrived; and the Timucua, who had eaten little or no corn before contact, also adopted it after the establishment of the missions.

THE CONSEQUENCES OF CORN

The bone chemistry findings thus show that the Indians' diets changed after the Europeans came—but not for the better. Their relatively heterogeneous diet, rich in seafood and a variety of plants and animals was replaced by a more homogeneous and less nutritious diet focused on the cultivation of a single crop: corn.

Corn-dominated diets are very poor ones. Corn contains a great deal of sugar, which promotes cavities and poor oral health in general. It also contains phytate, a chemical that binds with iron, inhibiting absorption of the mineral by the body. As a result, people whose diets are heavy in corn are predisposed to anemia and the many other consequences of low iron [see "Iron Deficiency," by Nevin S. Scrimshaw; SCIENTIFIC AMERICAN, October 1991]. To make matters worse for corn-dependent populations, growth and development are hampered because corn is a poor source of calcium and of niacin, or vitamin B_3 which is necessary for metabolism. Corn is also an inadequate source of protein because, depending on the strain, it is deficient in or entirely lacking three of the eight essential amino acids: lysine, isoleucine and tryptophan.

For these reasons, some mission Indians have more, and larger, cavities than their ancestors did. Tooth decay was probably exacerbated by the consistency of their food: soft foods, such as gruel made from corn, facilitate the build-up of cavity-causing bacteria and plaque on teeth. By looking at tooth wear with a scanning electron microscope, Mark F. Teaford and his colleagues at Johns Hopkins University have shown that the foods eaten by mission Indians were softer than those their ancestors ate. We can tell this by the reduction in the number of tooth-surface features, such as pits and scratches, caused by eating hard, non-agricultural food.

In places where diet varied, this general pattern shows some interesting departures. In collaboration with Bonnie G. McEwan of the Florida Bureau of Archaeological Research, we analyzed teeth from the San Luis mission site. Later work on the teeth by Tiffiny A. Tung of the University of North Carolina at Chapel Hill indicated that people in this mission had fewer cavities than did their counterparts at other sites. This departure

Signs of Stress in a Skeleton

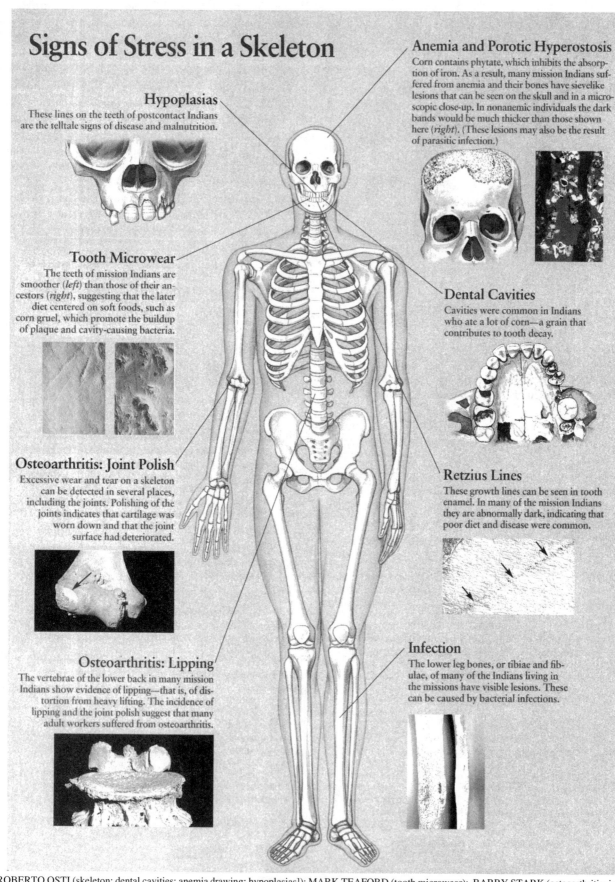

Hypoplasias
These lines on the teeth of postcontact Indians are the telltale signs of disease and malnutrition.

Tooth Microwear
The teeth of mission Indians are smoother (*left*) than those of their ancestors (*right*), suggesting that the later diet centered on soft foods, such as corn gruel, which promote the buildup of plaque and cavity-causing bacteria.

Osteoarthritis: Joint Polish
Excessive wear and tear on a skeleton can be detected in several places, including the joints. Polishing of the joints indicates that cartilage was worn down and that the joint surface had deteriorated.

Osteoarthritis: Lipping
The vertebrae of the lower back in many mission Indians show evidence of lipping—that is, of distortion from heavy lifting. The incidence of lipping and the joint polish suggest that many adult workers suffered from osteoarthritis.

Anemia and Porotic Hyperostosis
Corn contains phytate, which inhibits the absorption of iron. As a result, many mission Indians suffered from anemia and their bones have sievelike lesions that can be seen on the skull and in a microscopic close-up. In nonanemic individuals the dark bands would be much thicker than those shown here (*right*). (These lesions may also be the result of parasitic infection.)

Dental Cavities
Cavities were common in Indians who ate a lot of corn—a grain that contributes to tooth decay.

Retzius Lines
These growth lines can be seen in tooth enamel. In many of the mission Indians they are abnormally dark, indicating that poor diet and disease were common.

Infection
The lower leg bones, or tibiae and fibulae, of many of the Indians living in the missions have visible lesions. These can be caused by bacterial infections.

ROBERTO OSTI (skeleton; dental cavities; anemia drawing; hypoplasias]); MARK TEAFORD (tooth microwear); BARRY STARK (osteoarthritis; joint polish and osteoarthritis; lipping); MARK C. GRIFFIN (infection); MICHAEL SCHULTZ (anemia photograph); SCOTT W. SIMPSON (Retzius lines) from the usual pattern may have been explained by the research of Elizabeth J. Reitz of the University of Georgia, who examined animal remains at the same site. She determined that people living in San Luis had access to beef—a rare addition to the mission Indians' standard diet—and that protein may have inhibited the formation of cavities.

The tooth record has provided us with other important insights as well. Hutchison and I have found that many Indians had hypoplasias—visible lines on teeth caused by disease or malnutrition. The large size of the hypoplasias in some Indians suggests that they experienced severe or sustained illness or poor nutrition, or both. We also found evidence of disturbances in tooth development. With Scott W. Simpson of Case Western Reserve University, we studied microscopic features of teeth, looking at what are called Retzius lines—growth lines that can be seen in enamel. Although both precontact and mission Indians have abnormal Retzius lines, these malformations are more prevalent in the mission Indians.

Considered together with other evidence, the increase in abnormal Retzius lines suggests that poor diet was not the only problem facing the mission Indians. David Hurst Thomas of the American Museum of Natural History in New York City has excavated a shallow, plank-lined well in Santa Catalina de Guale that may have served as a reservoir for parasites. Although their ancestors relied on freshwater streams and springs, the mission Indians drank well water, and anyone living in the region today knows the dangers of drinking water from shallow wells: it is easily contaminated and can cause parasite infection and other problems.

The probability of rampant infection is strengthened by the fact that most of the defective tooth enamel we studied appears to have been formed during the first two years of life. This is a period when dehydration from infantile diarrhea is a primary health threat. Acute dehydration can inhibit the function of all forms of cells, including ameloblasts—the cells responsible for enamel formation. As in many underdeveloped nations today, bacteria and viruses in contaminated food and water cause infantile diarrhea. Certainly the mission would have created the kind of living circumstances that promote infantile diarrhea and the pattern of growth stress we have seen in teeth.

Other diseases, such as smallpox and measles, may have easily spread as well because the Indians were clustered together in crowded communities around the missions. Although many acute infectious diseases kill people long before their bones are affected, some infections—such as those caused by the bacterium *Staphylococcus aureus*—can travel from a soft-tissue wound to nearby bone, leaving observable lesions. Numerous lower-leg bones, or tibias, of contact-era Indians have lesions that suggest just this kind of infection.

Infection can also cause anemia because some types of parasite, such as hookworm, bleed their human hosts. Observations of mission bones indicate that such infection was common. The surfaces of many of these bones have sievelike lesions—called porotic hyperostosis—that can be caused by iron deficiency, scurvy or infection. Few precontact Indians seemed to have these lesions, probably because their diet of fish and maize together provided enough iron to stave off anemia. But the abun-

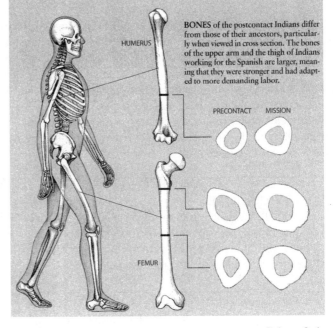

BONES of the postcontact Indians differ from those of their ancestors, particularly when viewed in cross section. The bones of the upper arm and the thigh of Indians working for the Spanish are larger, meaning that they were stronger and had adapted to more demanding labor.

Roberto Osti

dance of porotic hyperostosis in the mission Indians was most likely the result of the anemia brought on not simply by an increasingly corn-rich diet but also by intestinal infection.

Food and living conditions were not the only aspects of culture that were drastically altered for the Indians who lived in the missions. The Spanish practiced *repartimiento* draft labor in *La Florida*, which meant that able-bodied Indian men were required to work on farms, in public works and government building projects, and for the military. Indians were also required to carry heavy loads over long distances, because draft animals were not available in the region until after 1680 or thereabouts. In our studies of skeletons, we noticed that contact-era Indians had a higher rate of osteoarthritis than their predecessors did—a phenomenon we believed had been caused by the increased workload, because wear and tear on the joints can lead to osteoarthritis. But the condition is related to other factors as well. So we decided to investigate further, looking to the skeletons for more answers.

WORKING BONES

The skeleton of a living person is highly responsive to physical activity. Throughout life a person's bones change shape and structure in response to mechanical forces acting on them. Basically, bone tissue is placed where the skeleton needs it. When a person walks, for example, or stands, forces deriving from the pull of muscles or from body weight trigger cellular activity in the bone that results in skeletal remodeling. Without the proper amount or distribution of bone in key places, the force of bending or twisting could break the thigh bone, or femur.

Drawing from methods developed by civil and mechanical engineers for measuring the strength of building materials, Christopher B. Ruff of the Johns Hopkins University School of

Medicine and I have analyzed the strength of femur and humerus (upper-arm) bones from both precontact and mission sites in *La Florida*. This approach entails measuring cross-sectional geometric properties of the bones called second moments of area. Second moments of area reflect how the bone is distributed in cross section and indicate the strength or ability of the bone to resist breaking during bending or twisting. The analysis entails tracing the profile of the outer (subperiosteal) and inner (endosteal) perimeters of the bones in cross section and then calculating the biomechanical properties of the bone [*see illustration on previous page*].

AGRICULTURE among the mission Indians increased enormously after the Spanish arrived. The shift was not beneficial for the the natives of *La Florida*. Agriculture ultimately forced them to simplify their diet to such a degree that their health suffered.

We discovered that the mission Indians had stronger bones than their predecessors did: the later bones had greater second moments of area than the earlier bones. This is not to say that the bones of the mission Indians were better than those of their ancestors. Rather the bones had just adapted to new mechanical demands. Given the well-known circumstance of exploitation and the heavy workloads of the Indians laboring under the Europeans, we believe that the increases in bone strength and osteoarthritis were caused by fundamental alterations in their way of life that involved increased physical activity.

The insights afforded us by bioarchaeology confirm much of what is found in historical texts—including the forced labor of the Indians and the diseases that plagued them—but they also give us a much more comprehensive and precise picture of the past. European contact introduced hardships for the Indians on many fronts. Pestilence, poor nutrition, iron deficiency, growth disruption, infection and hard labor all took their toll. Yet despite the unfavorable state of affairs, native peoples accommodated new demands and new challenges, a story that is repeated time and again in the history of our species.

THE AUTHOR

CLARK SPENCER LARSEN directs the La Florida Bioarchaeology Project, which involves the collaboration of many scientists from the U.S. abroad. He began his studies of ancient human skeletons in his freshman year at Kansas State University, where he received his B.A. in 1974. His doctorate in biological anthropology was awarded by the University of Michigan in 1980. Larsen is Ames Hawley Professor of Anthropology at the University of North Carolina at Chapel Hill and is a research associate with the American Museum of Natural History in New York City. Larsen is currently president of the American Association of Physical Anthropologists.

FURTHER INFORMATION

THE ARCHAEOLOGY OF MISSION SANTA CATALINA DE GUALE, VOL. I: SEARCH AND DISCOVERY. David Hurst Thomas. *Anthropological papers of the American Museum of Natural History*, Vol. 63, Part 2, pages 47–161; June 12, 1987.

THE ARCHAEOLOGY OF MISSION SANTA CATALINA DE GUALE, VOL. 2: BIOCULTURAL INTERPRETATIONS OF A POPULATION IN TRANSITION. Edited by Clark Spencer Larsen. *Anthropological Papers of the American Museum of Natural History*, No. 68; 1990.

IN THE WAKE OF CONFLICT: BIOLOGICAL RESPONSES TO CONQUEST. Edited by Clark Spencer Larsen and George R. Milner. Wiley-Liss, 1994.

THE APALACHEE INDIANS AND MISSION SAN LUIS. John H. Hahn and Bonnie G. McEwan. University Press of Florida, 1988.

REGIONAL VARIATION IN THE PATTERN OF MAIZE ADOPTION AND USE IN FLORIDA AND GEORGIA. Dale L. Hutchinson, Clark Spencer Larsen, Margaret J. Schoeninger and Lynette Norr in *American Antiquity*, Vol. 63, No. 3, pages 397–416; July 1998.

SKELETONS IN OUR CLOSET: REVEALING OUR PAST THROUGH BIOARCHAEOLOGY. Clark Spencer Larsen. Princeton University Press, 2000.

Living Through the Donner Party

The nineteenth-century survivors of the infamous Donner Party told cautionary tales of starvation and cannibalism, greed and self-sacrifice. But not until now are we learning why the survivors survived.

Jared Diamond

Jared Diamond is a contributing editor of DISCOVER, *a professor of physiology at* UCLA *School of Medicine, a recipient of a MacArthur genius award, and the author of* The Third Chimpanzee.

"Mrs. Fosdick and Mrs. Foster, after eating, returned to the body of [Mr.] Fosdick. There, in spite of the widow's entreaties, Mrs. Foster took out the liver and heart from the body and removed the arms and legs.... [Mrs. Fosdick] was forced to see her husband's heart broiled over the fire." "He eat her body and found her flesh the best he had ever tasted! He further stated that he obtained from her body at least four pounds of fat." "Eat baby raw, stewed some of Jake and roasted his head, not good meat, taste like sheep with the rot."

—GEORGE STEWART,
*Ordeal by Hunger: The Story
of the Donner Party*

Nearly a century and a half after it happened, the story of the Donner Party remains one of the most riveting tragedies in U.S. history. Partly that's because of its lurid elements: almost half the party died, and many of their bodies were defiled in an orgy of cannibalism. Partly, too, it's be-

cause of the human drama of noble self-sacrifice and base murder juxtaposed. The Donner Party began as just another nameless pioneer trek to California, but it came to symbolize the Great American Dream gone awry.

By now the tale of that disastrous journey has been told so often that seemingly nothing else remains to be said—or so I thought, until my friend Donald Grayson at the University of Washington sent me an analysis that he had published in the *Journal of Anthropological Research*. By comparing the fates of all Donner Party members, Grayson identified striking differences between those who came through the ordeal alive and those who were not so lucky. In doing so he has made the lessons of the Donner Party universal. Under more mundane life-threatening situations, who among us too will be "lucky"?

Grayson's insights did not depend on new discoveries about the ill-fated pioneers nor on new analytical techniques, but on that most elusive ingredient of great science: a new idea about an old problem. Given the same information, any of you could extract the same conclusions. In fact, on page 163 you'll find the roster of the Donner Party members

along with a few personal details about each of them and their fate. If you like, you can try to figure out for yourself some general rules about who is most likely to die when the going gets tough.

The Lewis and Clark Expedition of 1804 to 1806 was the first to cross the continent, but they didn't take along ox-drawn wagons, which were a requirement for pioneer settlement. Clearing a wagon route through the West's unmapped deserts and mountains proved far more difficult than finding a footpath. Not until 1841 was the first attempt made to haul wagons and settlers overland to California, and only in 1844 did the effort succeed. Until the Gold Rush of 1848 unleashed a flood of emigrants, wagon traffic to California remained a trickle.

As of 1846, when the Donner Party set out, the usual wagon route headed west from St. Louis to Fort Bridger in Wyoming, then northwest into Idaho before turning southwest through Nevada and on to California. However, at that time a popular guidebook author named Lansford Hastings was touting a shortcut that purported to cut many miles from the long trek. Hastings's route continued west from Fort Bridger through the Wasatch mountain range, then south of

Utah's Great Salt Lake across the Salt Lake Desert, and finally rejoined the usual California Trail in Nevada.

In the summer of 1846 a number of wagon parties set out for California from Fort Bridger. One, which left shortly before the Donner Party, was guided by Hastings himself. Using his shortcut, the party would eventually make it to California, albeit with great difficulty.

The pioneers who would become the members of the Donner Party were in fact all headed for Fort Bridger to join the Hastings expedition, but they arrived too late. With Hastings thus unavailable to serve as a guide, some of these California-bound emigrants opted for the usual route instead. Others, however, decided to try the Hastings Cutoff anyway. In all, 87 people in 23 wagons chose the cutoff. They consisted of 10 unrelated families and 16 lone individuals, most of them well-to-do midwestern farmers and townspeople who had met by chance and joined forces for protection. None had had any real experience of the western mountains or Indians. They became known as the Donner Party because they elected an elderly Illinois farmer named George Donner as their captain. They left Fort Bridger on July 31, one of the last parties of that summer to begin the long haul to California.

Within a fortnight the Donner Party suffered their first crushing setback, when they reached Utah's steep, brush-covered Wasatch Mountains. The terrain was so wild that, in order to cross, the men had first to build a wagon road. It took 16 backbreaking days to cover just 36 miles, and afterward the people and draft animals were worn out. A second blow followed almost immediately thereafter, west of the Great Salt Lake, when the party ran into an 80-mile stretch of desert. To save themselves from death by thirst, some of the pioneers were forced to unhitch their wagons, rush ahead with their precious animals to the next spring, and return to retrieve the wagons. The rush became a disorganized panic, and many of the animals died, wandered off, or were killed by Indians. Four wagons and large quantities of supplies had to be abandoned.

Not until September 30—two full months after leaving Fort Bridger—did the Donner Party emerge from their fatal shortcut to rejoin the California Trail.

By November 1 they had struggled up to Truckee Lake—later renamed Donner Lake—at an elevation of 6,000 feet on the eastern flank of the Sierra Nevada, west of the present-day California-Nevada border. Snow had already begun to fall during the last days of October, and now a fierce snowstorm defeated the exhausted party as they attempted to cross a 7,200-foot pass just west of the lake. With that storm, a trap snapped shut around them: they had set out just a little too late and proceeded just a little too slowly. They now faced a long winter at the lake, with very little food.

Death had come to the Donner Party even before it reached the lake. There were five casualties: on August 29 Luke Halloran died of "consumption" (presumably tuberculosis); on October 5 James Reed knifed John Snyder in self-defense, during a fight that broke out when two teams of oxen became entangled; three days later Lewis Keseberg abandoned an old man named Hardkoop who had been riding in Keseberg's wagon, and most of the party refused to stop and search for him; sometime after October 13 two German emigrants, Joseph Reinhardt and Augustus Spitzer, murdered a rich German named Wolfinger while ostensibly helping him to cache his property; and on October 20 William Pike was shot as he and his brother-in-law were cleaning a pistol.

They cut off and roasted flesh from the corpses, restrained only by the rule that no one partook of his or her relative's body.

In addition, four party members had decided earlier to walk out ahead to Sutter's Fort (now Sacramento) to bring back supplies and help. One of those four, Charles Stanton, rejoined the party on October 19, bringing food and two Indians sent by Sutter. Thus, of the 87 original members of the Donner Party, 79—plus the two Indians—were pinned down in the winter camp at Donner Lake.

The trapped pioneers lay freezing inside crude tents and cabins. They quickly exhausted their little remaining food, then killed and ate their pack animals. Then they ate their dogs. Finally they boiled hides and blankets to make a glue-like soup. Gross selfishness became rampant, as families with food refused to share it with destitute families or demanded exorbitant payment. On December 16 the first death came to the winter camp when 24-year-old Baylis Williams succumbed to starvation. On that same day 15 of the strongest people—5 women and 10 men, including Charles Stanton and the two Indians—set out across the pass on homemade snowshoes, virtually without food and in appallingly cold and stormy weather, in the hope of reaching outside help. Four of the men left behind their families; three of the women left behind their children.

On the sixth morning an exhausted Stanton let the others go on ahead of him; he remained behind to die. On the ninth day the remaining 14 for the first time openly broached the subject of cannibalism which had already been on their minds. They debated drawing lots as to who should be eaten, or letting two people shoot it out until one was killed and could be eaten. Both proposals were rejected in favor of waiting for someone to die naturally.

Such opportunities soon arose. On Christmas Eve, as a 23-year-old man named Antoine, a bachelor, slept in a heavy stupor, he stretched out his arm such that his hand fell into the fire. A companion pulled it out at once. When it fell in a second time, however, no one intervened—they simply let it burn. Antoine died, then Franklin Graves, then Patrick Dolan, then Lemuel Murphy. The others cut off and roasted flesh from the corpses, restrained only by the rule that no one would partake of his or her own relative's body. When the corpses were consumed, the survivors began eating old shoes.

On January 5, 23-year-old Jay Fosdick died, only to be cut up and boiled by Mrs. Foster over the protests of Mrs. Fosdick. Soon after, the frenzied Mr. Foster chased down, shot, and killed the two Indians to eat them. That left 7 of the original 15 snowshoers to stagger into the first white settlement in California, after a midwinter trek of 33 days through the snow.

On January 31 the first rescue team set out from the settlement for Donner Lake. It would take three more teams and two and a half months before the ordeal was all over. During that time many more people died, either in the winter camp or while fighting their way out with the rescue teams. There was never enough food, and by the end of February, cannibalism had established itself at the lake.

When William Eddy and William Foster, who had gotten out with the snowshoers, reached the lake with the third rescue team on March 13, they found that Keseberg had eaten their sons. The Foster child's grandmother accused the starving Keseberg of having taken the child to bed with him one night, strangling him, and hanging the corpse on the wall before eating it. Keseberg, in his defense, claimed the children had died naturally. When the rescuers left the lake the next day to return to California, they left Keseberg behind with just four others: the elderly Lavina Murphy, the badly injured George Donner, his 4-year-old nephew Samuel and his healthy wife Tamsen, who could have traveled but insisted on staying with her dying husband.

The fourth and last rescue team reached the lake on April 17 to find Keseberg alone, surrounded by indescribable filth and mutilated corpses. George Donner's body lay with his skull split open to permit the extraction of his brains. Three frozen ox legs lay in plain view almost uneaten beside a kettle of cut-up human flesh. Near Keseberg sat two kettles of blood and a large pan full of fresh human liver and lungs. He alleged that his four companions had died natural deaths, but he was frank about having eaten them. As to why he had not eaten ox leg instead, he explained that it was too dry: human liver and lungs

tasted better, and human brains made a good soup. As for Tamsen Donner, Keseberg noted that she tasted the best, being well endowed with fat. In a bundle held by Keseberg the rescuers found silk, jewelry, pistols, and money that had belonged to George Donner.

After returning to Sutter's Fort, one of the rescuers accused Keseberg of having murdered his companions, prompting Keseberg to sue for defamation of character. In the absence of legal proof of murder the court verdict was equivocal, and the issue of Keseberg's guilt remains disputed to this day. However, Tamsen Donner's death is especially suspicious since she had been in strong physical condition when last seen by the third rescue team.

Experience has taught us that the youngest and oldest people are the most vulnerable even under normal conditions, and their vulnerability increases under stress.

Thus, out of 87 Donner Party members, 40 died: 5 before reaching Donner Lake, 22 in their winter camp at the lake, and 13 (plus the two Indians) during or just after efforts to leave the lake. Why those particular 40? From the facts given in the roster, can you draw conclusions, as Grayson did, as to who was in fact the most likely to die?

As a simple first test, compare the fates of Donner Party males and females irrespective of age. Most of the males (30 out of 53) died; most of the females (24 out of 34) survived. The 57 percent death rate among males was nearly double the 29 percent death rate among females.

Next, consider the effect of age irrespective of sex. The worst toll was among the young and the old. Without exception, everyone over the age of 50 died, as did most of the children below the age of 5. Surprisingly, children and teenagers between the ages of 5 and 19 fared better than did adults in their prime

(age 20 to 39): half the latter, but less than one-fifth of the former, died.

By looking at the effects of age and sex simultaneously, the advantage the women had over the men becomes even more striking. Most of the female deaths were among the youngest and oldest, who were already doomed by their age. Among those party members aged 5 to 39—the ones whose ages left them some reasonable chance of survival—half the men but only 5 percent of the women died.

The dates of death provide deeper insight. Of the 35 unfortunates who died after reaching the lake, 14 men but not a single woman had died by the end of January. Only in February did women begin to buckle under. From February onward the death toll was essentially equal by sex—11 men, 10 women. The differences in dates of death simply underscore the lesson of the death rates themselves: the Donner Party women were far hardier than the men.

Thus, sex and age considered together account for much of the luck of the survivors. Most of those who died (39 of the 40 victims) had the misfortune to be of the wrong sex, or the wrong age, or both.

Experience has taught us that the youngest and oldest people are the most vulnerable even under normal conditions, and their vulnerability increases under stress. In many natural disasters, those under 10 or over 50 suffered the highest mortality. For instance, children under 10 accounted for over half the 240,000 deaths in the 1970 Bangladesh cyclone, though they constituted only one-third of the exposed population.

Much of the vulnerability of the old and young under stress is simply a matter of insufficient physical strength: these people are less able to walk out through deep snow (in the case of the Donner Party) or to cling to trees above the height of flood waters (in the case of the Bangladesh cyclone). Babies have special problems. Per pound of body weight a baby has twice an adult's surface area, which means double the area across which body heat can escape. To maintain body temperature, babies have to in-

Manifest of a Tragic Journey

DONNER FAMILY			
Jacob Donner	M	65	died in Nov. in winter camp
George Donner	M	62	died in Apr. in winter camp
Elizabeth Donner	F	45	died in Mar. in winter camp
Tamsen Donner	F	45	died in Apr. in winter camp
Elitha Donner	F	14	
Solomon Hook	M	14	
William Hook	M	12	died Feb. 28 with first rescue team
Leanna Donner	F	12	
George Donner	M	9	
Mary Donner	F	7	
Frances Donner	F	6	
Isaac Donner	M	5	died Mar. 7 with second rescue team
Georgia Donner	F	4	
Samuel Donner	M	4	died in Apr. in winter camp
Lewis Donner	M	3	died Mar. 7 or 8 in winter camp
Eliza Donner	F	3	

MURPHY-FOSTER-PIKE FAMILY			
Lavina Murphy	F	50	died around Mar. 19 in winter camp
William Foster	M	28	
William Pike	M	25	died Oct. 20 by gunshot
Sara Foster	F	23	
Harriet Pike	F	21	
John Landrum Murphy	M	15	died Jan. 31 in winter camp
Mary Murphy	F	13	
Lemuel Murphy	M	12	died Dec. 27 with snowshoers
William Murphy	M	11	
Simon Murphy	M	10	
George Foster	M	4	died in early Mar. in winter camp
Naomi Pike	F	3	
Catherine Pike	F	1	died Feb. 20 in winter camp

GRAVES-FOSDICK FAMILY			
Franklin Graves	M	57	died Dec 24. with snowshoers
Elizabeth Graves	F	47	died Mar. 8 with second rescue team
Jay Fosdick	M	23	died Jan. 5 with snowshoers
Sarah Fosdick	F	22	
William Graves	M	18	
Eleanor Graves	F	15	
Lavina Graves	F	13	
Nancy Graves	F	9	
Jonathan Graves	M	7	
Franklin Graves Jr.	M	5	died Mar. 8 with second rescue team
Elizabeth Graves	F	1	died soon after rescue by second team

BREEN FAMILY			
Patrick Breen	M	40	
Mary Breen	F	40	
John Breen	M	14	
Edward Breen	M	13	
Patrick Breen Jr.	M	11	
Simon Breen	M	9	
Peter Breen	M	7	
James Bren	M	4	

Isabella	F	1	

REED FAMILY			
James Reed	M	46	
Margaret Reed	F	32	
Virginia Reed	F	12	
Patty Reed	F	8	
James Reed Jr.	M	5	
Thomas Reed	M	3	

EDDY FAMILY			
William Eddy	M	28	
Eleanor Eddy	F	25	died Feb. 7 in winter camp
James Eddy	M	3	died in early Mar. in winter camp
Margaret Eddy	F	1	died Feb. 4 in winter camp

KESEBERG FAMILY			
Lewis Keseberg	M	32	
Phillipine Keseberg	F	32	
Ada Keseberg	F	3	died Feb. 24 with first rescue team
Lewis Keseberg Jr.	M	1	died Jan. 24 in winter camp

MCCUTCHEN FAMILY			
William McCutchen	M	30	
Amanda McCutchen	F	24	
Harriet McCutchen	F	1	died Feb. 2 in winter camp

WILLIAMS FAMILY			
Eliza Williams	F	25	
Baylis Williams	M	24	died Dec. 16 in winter camp

WOLFINGER FAMILY			
Mr. Wolfinter	M	?	killed around Oct. 13 by Reinhardt and Spitzer
Mrs. Wolfinger	F	?	

UNRELATED INDIVIDUALS			
Mr. Hardkoop	M	60	died around Oct. 8, abandoned by Lewis Keseberg
Patrick Dolan	M	40	died Dec. 25 with snowshoers
Charles Stanton	M	35	died around Dec. 21 with snowshoers
Charles Burger	M	30	died Dec. 29 in winter camp
Joseph Reinhardt	M	30	died in Nov. or early Dec. in winter camp
Augustus Spitzer	M	30	died Feb.7 in winter camp
John Denton	M	28	died Feb. 24 with first rescue team
Milton Elliot	M	28	died Feb. 9 in winter camp
Luke Halloran	M	25	died Aug. 29 of consumption
William Herron	M	25	
Samuel Shoemaker	M	25	died in Nov. or early Dec. in winter camp
James Smith	M	25	died in Nov. or early Dec. in winter camp
James Smith	M	25	died in Nov. or early Dec. in winter camp
John Snyder	M	25	killed Oct. 5 by James Reed
Jean Baptiste Trubode	M	23	
Antoine	M	23	died Dec. 24 with snowshoers
Noah James	M	20	

crease their metabolic rate when air temperature drops only a few degrees below body temperature, whereas adults don't have to do so until a drop of 20 to 35 degrees. At cold temperatures the factor by which babies must increase their metabolism to stay warm is several times that for adults. These considerations place even well-fed babies at risk under cold conditions. And the Donner Party babies were at a crippling further disadvantage because they had so little food to fuel their metabolism. They literally froze to death.

But what gave the women such an edge over the men? Were the pioneers practicing the noble motto "women and children first" when it came to dividing food? Unfortunately, "women and children last" is a more accurate description of how most men behave under stress. As the *Titanic* sank, male crew members took many places in lifeboats while leaving women and children of steerage class below decks to drown. Much grosser male behavior emerged when the steamship *Atlantic* sank in 1879: the death toll included 294 of the 295 women and children on board, but only 187 of the 636 men. In the Biafran famine of the late 1960s, when relief agencies tried to distribute food to youngsters under 10 and to pregnant and nursing women, Biafran men gave a brutally frank response: "Stop all this rubbish, it is we men who shall have the food, let the children die, we will make new children after the war." Similarly, accounts by Donner Party members yield no evidence of hungry men deferring to women, and babies fared especially poorly.

Instead, we must seek some cause other than male self-sacrifice to account for the survival of Donner Party women. One contributing factor is that the men were busy killing each other. Four of the five deaths before the pioneers reached the lake, plus the deaths of the two Indians, involved male victims of male violence, a pattern that fits widespread human experience.

However, invoking male violence still leaves 26 of 30 Donner Party male deaths unexplained. It also fails to explain why men began starving and freezing to death nearly two months before women did. Evidently the women had a

big physiological advantage. This could be an extreme expression of the fact that, at every age and for all leading causes of death—from cancer and car accidents to heart disease and suicide—the death rate is far higher for men than for women. While the reasons for this ubiquitous male vulnerability remain debated, there are several compelling reasons why men are more likely than women to die under the extreme conditions the Donner Party faced.

The Donner Party records make it vividly clear that family members stuck together and helped one another at the expense of the others.

First, men are bigger than women. Typical body weights for the world as a whole are about 140 pounds for men and only 120 pounds for women. Hence, even while lying down and doing nothing, men need more food to support their basal metabolism. They also need more energy than women do for equivalent physical activity. Even for sedentary people, the typical metabolic rate for an average-size woman is 25 percent lower than an average-size man's. Under conditions of cold temperatures and heavy physical activity, such as were faced by the Donner Party men when doing the backbreaking work of cutting the wagon road or hunting for food, men's metabolic rates can be double those of women.

To top it all off, women have more fat reserves than men: fat makes up 22 percent of the body weight of an average nonobese, well-nourished woman, but only 16 percent of a similar man. More of the man's weight is instead made up of muscle, which gets burned up much more quickly than does fat. Thus, when there simply was no more food left, the Donner Party men burned up their body reserves much faster than did the women. Furthermore, much of women's fat is distributed under the skin and acts as heat insulation, so that they can withstand cold temperatures better than men can. Women don't

have to raise their metabolic rate to stay warm as soon as men do.

These physiological factors easily surpass male murderousness in accounting for all those extra male deaths in the Donner Party. Indeed, a microcosm of the whole disaster was the escape attempt by 15 people on snowshoes, lasting 33 days in midwinter. Of the ten men who set out, two were murdered by another man, six starved or froze to death, and only two survived. Not a single one of the five women with them died.

Even with all these explanations, there is still one puzzling finding to consider: the unexpectedly high death toll of people in their prime, age 20 to 39. That toll proves to be almost entirely of the men: 67 percent of the men in that age range (14 out of 21) died, a much higher proportion than among the teenage boys (only 20 percent). Closer scrutiny shows why most of those men were so unlucky.

Most of the Donner Party consisted of large families, but there were also 16 individuals traveling without any relatives. All those 16 happened to be men, and all but two were between 20 and 39. Those 16 unfortunates bore the brunt of the prime-age mortality. Thirteen of them died, and most of them died long before any of the women. Of the survivors, one—William Herron—reached California in October, so in reality only 2 survived the winter at the lake.

Of the 7 men in their prime who survived, 4 were family men. Only 3 of the 14 dead were. The prime-age women fared similarly: the 8 survivors belonged to families with an average size of 12 people, while Eleanor Eddy, the only woman to die in this age group, had no adult support. Her husband had escaped with the snowshoers, leaving her alone with their two small children.

The Donner Party records make it vividly clear that family members stuck together and helped one another at the expense of the others. A notorious example was the Breen family of nine, every one of whom (even two small children) survived through the luck of retaining their wagons and some pack animals much longer than the others, and through their considerable selfishness toward others. Compare this with the old bachelor Hardkoop, who was ordered out of the Keseberg family wagon and abandoned to die, or the fate of the young bachelor Antoine, whom none of the hungry snowshoers bothered to awaken when his hand fell into the fire.

Family ties can be a matter of life and death even under normal conditions. Married people, it turns out, have lower death rates than single, widowed, or divorced people. And marriage's life-promoting benefits have been found to be shared by all sorts of social ties, such as friendships and membership in social groups. Regardless of age or sex or initial health status, socially isolated individuals have well over twice the death rate of socially connected people.

For reasons about which we can only speculate, the lethal effects of social isolation are more marked for men than for women. It's clear, though, why social contacts are important for both sexes. They provide concrete help in case of need. They're our source of advice and shared information. They provide a sense of belonging and self-worth, and the courage to face tomorrow. They make stress more bearable.

All those benefits of social contact applied as well to the Donner Party members, who differed only in that their risk of death was much greater and their likely circumstances of death more grotesque than yours and mine. In that sense too, the harrowing story of the Donner Party grips us because it was ordinary life writ large.

From *Discover* magazine, March 1992, pp. 100-107. © 1992 by Jared Diamond. Reproduced with permission of the author.

Case of the Colorado Cannibal

Alferd Packer may have eaten his snowbound fellow prospectors, but did he murder them?

◆

by ANDREW CURRY

THERE'S AT LEAST ONE THING all the experts agree on: Alferd Packer was a hungry guy. Ever since the well-fed guide walked out of the San Juan Mountains in 1874, more than two months after his prospecting party had gotten lost in a snowstorm, the case of the Colorado Cannibal has horrified—and captivated. Though Packer was convicted of murdering his five companions in 1873, he claimed till his dying day that another member of the party, Shannon Bell, went crazy and killed the others with an ax. Packer then shot the ax wielder in self-defense and ate all five—not a crime in desperate circumstances.

In the decades since Packer's death in 1907, the Colorado Cannibal has become a fixture in the lore of the Wild West, inspiring books, songs, memorials, and even a musical. In recent months, his appetite has moved from the realm of bad puns and cannibal kitsch to archaeological debate, with new evidence that some say proves the hapless prospector may have been a man-eater, but he wasn't a murderer.

Packer's problems started when his party tried to cross the San Juan Mountains in southwestern Colorado in the dead of winter. When Packer stumbled, alone, into the Los Pinos Indian Agency after 57 days in the snowbound mountains, all he wanted was a good, stiff drink. His lack of interest in breakfast wasn't the only clue that something might be amiss. Though he'd been nearly broke when he left, he paid for his whiskey with a wad of cash. When questioned, Packer claimed he had been abandoned by his companions and had no idea what had happened to them. A search party was soon organized, and a suddenly nervous Packer started spinning a new story. Two of the men had died of hunger and were eaten by the other four. A third man was accidentally killed, and beefy redhead Shannon Wilson Bell shot the youngest member of the party, George "California" Noon. With no one left but Bell and Packer, presumably eying each other hungrily over a flickering campfire, Packer shot Bell in self-defense, covering up the remains, and taking a large piece of Bell with him.

Not surprisingly, the Packer-led search party found nothing. But once the snow melted, it was only a matter of time. Hopelessly iso-lated in the dead of winter, the riverbank crime scene was something of a backwoods thoroughfare in the summer months. In search of mountain vistas to draw, an artist for *Harper's Magazine* came across what was left of the bodies in late August 1873, more than three months after Packer had made his way out of the pass. "They were lying in a gloomy, secluded spot, densely shaded by tall trees, at the foot of a steep hill near the bank of the Gunnison River," begins the *Harper's* account, complete with lurid illustrations of the badly decomposed bodies. "Marks of violence on each body indicated that a most terrible crime had been committed there. The bodies lay within a few feet of each other, in their blankets and clothes. There had been no attempt to conceal the remains."

Packer was arrested, but escaped, living on the lam for nine years until he was spotted in a Wyoming saloon by itinerant merchant "Frenchy" Carbazone in 1883 and sent back to Colorado for trial. In his second confession, he told the tale he would (mostly) stick with until his death. Lost in the mountains, stumbling along snowy ridgelines, and boiling rosebuds and pine gum after their food ran out, the prospecting party made camp on the banks of the Gunnison River. Packer grabbed his gun and went off alone to see if he could find a way out. He returned to a horrific scene: Bell, he told the court, surrounded by four hacked-up corpses, was munching on a piece of leg meat. Spying Packer, the crazed Bell came at him with a hatchet. According to Packer, "I shot him sideways through the belly, the hatchet fell forwards. I grabbed it and hit him in the top of the head."

The frontier jury didn't buy his self-defense story, and sentenced Packer to hang. As legend has it, an angry judge thundered, "There was seven Democrats in all of Hinsdale County, and you ate five of them. I sentence you to be hung by the neck until you are dead, dead, dead, as a warning against further reducing the Democratic population of this county!"

Though a technicality let Packer slip the noose, he spent 18 years in jail. Paroled in 1901, Packer died six years later of "trouble and worry," according to his death certificate. He maintained his innocence until the end.

Time turned the hungry prospector into an unlikely Western folk hero. The Colorado Cannibal was a source of pioneer pride and quickly became one of the best-known and documented American cannibalism cases. Soon Packer's name started popping up all over the state. Students at the University of Colorado at Boulder have been eating at the Alferd Packer Grill since the 1960s—the El Canibal burrito is a favorite—and in 1982 a bust of the prospector was installed in the Colorado State Capitol.

Packer's legend has also fed pop culture references. While still University of Colorado film students, the creators of the animated comedy series *South Park* filmed a decidedly low-budget *Alferd Packer: The Musical!,* and folk singer Phil Ochs penned "The Ballad of Alferd Packer" in 1964. The chorus: *They called him a murderer, a cannibal, a thief / It just doesn't pay to eat anything but government-inspected beef.* And of course there's been a thriving trade in tacky Packer-abilia, from Packer preserves to bumper stickers and T-shirts.

But it wasn't until 1989, when George Washington University law professor James Starrs decided to dig up the victims' bones in the interest of science, that Packer's case transcended colorful frontier lore and became the center of a scholarly debate. Starrs is known for digging up notorious bodies, including Lizzie Borden's parents and the outlaw Jesse James. His most recent high-profile crime case, last December, called into question the identity of the Boston Strangler. Starrs says that though "there wasn't that much meat in the case for teaching purposes," Packer's self-defense claim piqued his legal curiosity. After learning that the bodies had been buried together in a grave just outside of Lake City, Colorado, Starrs organized a team to exhume the remains.

Legend has it that Judge Melville B. Gerry took Packer to task for eating Democrats. During the New Deal, Colorado Republicans formed "Alferd Packer Clubs." Members swore to "eliminat" at least five Democrats.

Analysis of the bones revealed ample evidence of violence. "There was plenty of blunt-force trauma, and plenty of sharp-force trauma," says Michigan State University forensic anthropologist Todd Fenton, who worked on Starrs' team. "We were able to conclusively answer one question—almost every piece of meat on the bodies was removed." Other grisly finds: most of the cut marks were on the victims' backs, possibly implying that the killer was reluctant to look his friends-cum-food in the face, and dozens of hack marks on the arms and head of the party's youngest member, indicating a heroic, if futile, struggle. Starrs concluded Packer was the killer, arguing that an old war wound would have made Bell a bad ax-murderer, unable to overpower the younger Noon. More than a decade later, Starrs has yet to publish his findings, though Fenton plans to publish the data this year, with the appetite for information about cannibalism at an all-time high. Fenton and others hope a well-documented cannibalism case might better inform the current debate over man-eaters in the American Southwest. "Cannibalism is very hot right now, but all the stuff in the anthropological debates so far has dealt with inferences. Until now, we haven't had an accepted case of known cannibalism," says Fenton who remains cautious. "They'll eat you up, those cannibalism guys."

Once his investigation was complete, Starrs re-buried the bones. The man who owned the land then dropped a massive steel plate atop the burial site, sealing it off from relic hunters and future investigators alike.

But the Starrs inquiry only whetted the appetites of Packer aficionados. After years of research, a team of historians and scientists announced recently that Packer was telling the truth. Using an electron microscope to analyze soil samples taken from the graves of the victims, Museum of Western Colorado curator and historian David Bailey says lead fragments found near Bell's bones match samples from a Colt revolver excavated nearby five decades ago and said to have belonged to Packer. The badly damaged gun, a rusted-out .38 caliber Colt pistol, was found on Cannibal Mesa near the Lake City massacre site in 1950. Popular with prospectors of the time, the pistol still had three bullets in its five chambers. "The lead in the gun was unique, and the lead found under the body was the same type," Bailey says. "We now know [Bell] was shot. It gives a lot of credence to Packer's story."

Bailey's case rests on what he claims is a bullet hole in Bell's hipbone, though Starrs, whose team took the photographs Bailey is working from, insists the hole was made by animals gnawing on the bones. "It wasn't a bullet hole at all—it was a carnivore gnaw mark. It had none of the classic marks of a bullet hole," Starrs scoffs. "The most likely scenario is that Packer killed all five with an ax. Packer was quite a con artist, and apparently he's still at it."

But one man's carnivore is another's gun, and Bailey has mustered documentary evidence to show that the hole in Shannon Bell's hip was put there by a desperate Packer. Trial testimony from a member of the local coroner's party that first investigated the crime scene noted "a piece of hip bone, with a bullet through it, [that] lay near one of the bodies; also a pocketbook with a bullet hole through it was found."

"It was a weird place for a hole to be—it's possible the bullet hole went through afterwards," Bailey says. "[Starrs] proved they were traumatized and murdered, but he didn't prove who did it. The historical record is mostly conjecture, and now we've taken it beyond that with science."

With the bones most likely crushed under thick steel, there may be no way to bury the debate for good. But Packer will surely continue to eat away at the imagination. "It's the cannibalism aspect—it's our darkest human fear, so people tend to joke about it," says Bailey. "The dark nature of humanity really fascinates people."

ANDREW CURRY *is an associate editor at* U.S. News and World Report.

Life in the Provinces of the Aztec Empire

The lives of the Aztec common people were far richer and more complex
than the official histories would have us believe

By Michael E. Smith

In 1519, when Hernán Cortés led his army into Tenochtitlan in the Valley of Mexico, that Aztec city was the capital of a far-flung tributary empire. The emperor Motecuhzoma sat atop a complex social and political hierarchy, and the Aztec populace owed allegiance and tribute to nobles at several levels. Below the emperor were the kings of subject city-states. The Aztec dominion employed a policy of indirect rule, and imperial authorities supported local dynasties so long as they delivered their quarterly tribute payments on time. Officials recorded these payments in documents such as the Codex Mendoza [see "The Codex Mendoza," by Patricia Rieff Anawalt and Frances F. Berdan; SCIENTIFIC AMERICAN, June 1992]. Local nobles, who lived in both urban and rural areas, were subjects of their city-state king. At the bottom of the hierarchy were the commoners, whose tribute payments supported all these nobles.

Aztec commoners must have had a heavy tribute obligation. How were they able to meet their payments? First of all, there were millions of commoners, so the tribute burden was spread over a large population. During the 1970s, surveys of patterns of settlement turned up the startling discovery that the Aztec period witnessed one of the major population explosions of antiquity. The number of people in the Valley of Mexico, the heartland of the Aztec Empire, increased from 175,000 in the early Aztec period (A.D. 1150–1350) to nearly one million in the late Aztec period (A.D. 1350–1519). Similar patterns of growth occurred in other parts of Aztec territory as well.

The Aztec population explosion placed a heavy stress on the environment of central Mexico. New villages and towns sprung up everywhere, and all available land was cultivated, often at considerable labor expense. Wherever possible, farmers built dams and canals to irrigate cropland; they also built terraced

stone walls on hillsides to make new fields; and they drained the swamps outside Tenochtitlan to create raised fields (*chinampas*), one of the most highly productive agricultural systems of the ancient world. These intensive farming practices transformed the central Mexican countryside into a managed landscape of cultivation.

What were the effects of tribute extraction, population growth and agricultural intensification on the Aztec common people? Did these processes leave people impoverished and powerless, or did they allow commoners to prosper and thrive? Few of the available written accounts have information on conditions beyond the imperial capital, and thus it is up to archaeologists to study these questions.

Until very recently, no major archaeological excavations had been carried out at Aztec sites. Most Aztec cities and towns either were destroyed during the Spanish Conquest or were occupied and then buried under later settlements. The few surviving sites were small, unassuming peasant villages. Most archaeologists working in Mesoamerica bypassed Aztec sites on their way to the spectacular jungle ruins of classic-period Maya civilization. Aztec sites were deemed either too difficult to excavate or too small to bother with. This neglect came to an abrupt end in 1978, when the Mexican government mounted an extensive excavation of the Great Temple of Tenochtitlan. Situated in the middle of Mexico City today, the magnificence of this structure, and the richness of the offerings associated with it, awakened a new interest in Aztec society. Unfortunately, these excavations did not provide much new information about the commoners or life in the provinces.

To address these issues, my wife, Cynthia Heath-Smith, and I embarked on archaeological projects at rural and urban sites in

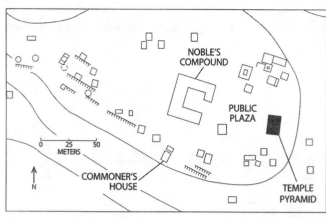

MARKET PLAZA in the 15th-century Aztec town of Cuexcomate teemed with vendors, buyers and artisans. Here commoners could trade craft goods made in their homes—mainly textiles—or salt and painted pottery imported from the Valley of Mexico and other areas, obsidian blades from regions hundreds of kilometers away and needles and other bronze objects from western Mexico. Local produce and goods such as woven mats, baskets, corn-grinding tools and tortilla griddles were also displayed and traded. A map of the center of the modern dig site at Cuexcomate indicates the location of the temple pyramid, a noble family's compound and commoners' dwellings, as well as other buildings and the more distant terraced fields and rural dwellings.

the modern Mexican state of Morelos. Located just south of the Valley of Mexico, this was the first area outside the valley to be conquered when the Aztecs began their military expansion in the 1430s.

We first excavated two rural sites—Capilco and Cuexcomate—southwest of the modern city of Cuernavaca. Later we turned to the Aztec city of Yautepec in north-central Morelos. By excavating the houses of both rich and poor, we have found that provincial society was far more complex than previously thought. Aztec peasants were not simple farmers whose lives were dominated by the need to pay tribute to their elite overlords. Commoners living in both rural and urban areas of the provinces made heavy use of a thriving marketing system. They exchanged craft goods produced in their homes for a variety of foreign goods, and most of this economic activity was accomplished outside imperial control and ignored by early writers on the Aztecs.

PEASANT LIFE

Archaeologists have found that excavations of houses and associated remains often provide the best data on ancient social and economic patterns. Capilco and Cuexcomate were good examples because traces of house walls were visible above the ground, and we did not have to waste time trying to find buried structures. Capilco was a village with 21 houses, and Cuexcomate a town with more than 150 structures, including temples, storehouses and ritual dumps. Houses at these sites were small (with a mean area of 15 square meters) and built of adobe brick walls supported on stone foundations. We excavated test pits in

29 houses selected at random. We then chose 10 of these for more complete clearing of architecture and associated deposits. These excavations allowed us to refine the Aztec chronology by splitting the late Aztec period into two subperiods—late Aztec A (A.D. 1350–1440) and late Aztec B (A.D. 1440–1519)—to yield a more detailed analysis.

Capilco was founded by a few peasant families in the early Aztec period. The population explosion began in the late Aztec A period, when Cuexcomate was founded and both settlements grew rapidly. The residents of these communities could not support themselves using rainfall agriculture alone, so they had to intensify their agricultural practices. Farmers built terraces on slopes and in ravines to create additional, more productive plots in which they grew maize, beans and cotton. Houses at these sites were not packed very closely together, and open areas were probably devoted to farming.

Cotton was an important crop in this part of the Aztec Empire, and household production of cotton textiles soon became the major craft. Every excavated house yielded large quantities of ceramic artifacts used in the hand spinning of cotton. Bead-like spindle whorls provided weights for the twirling wooden spindle, and small bowls with tripod supports were designed to control the spindle. Documentary sources state that all Aztec women, from the lowest slave to the highest noblewoman, spun and wove cloth. Cotton textiles had two economic functions beyond use as clothing. First, they were the most common item of tribute demanded by both city-states and the Aztec Empire. Second, they served as a form of money in the marketplaces, where they could be used to obtain a range of goods and services.

In addition to textiles, some residents of these sites manufactured paper out of the bark of the wild fig tree, as attested to by "bark beaters" made of basalt. The Aztecs used paper to make books of picture-writing and to burn in ritual offerings.

The many ceramic vessels used and discarded at each house were probably purchased in the marketplaces. Although local potters produced a full range of vessels, people often bought many decorated foreign pots. About 10 percent of all ceramic vessels excavated from these sites had been imported from the Valley of Mexico and other areas. These vessels did not have any functional superiority to the wares made locally, and people must have simply enjoyed using a variety of decorated serving bowls.

In addition to ceramic vessels, people had other foreign goods in their homes. We recovered thousands of broken obsidian blades, whose closest geologic source was 100 kilometers away. Obsidian blades, which had extremely sharp cutting edges, served in many household and craft activities. Needles and other items of bronze were imported from western Mexico. People obtained salt from the Valley of Mexico, where specialists extracted it by boiling and evaporating the saline lake water. Salt was transported in distinctive ceramic basins, and in every excavated house we found many shards of these vessels. The market system connected the inhabitants of these rural sites to the rest of the Aztec Empire and beyond.

These excavations also revealed something of the noneconomic life of Aztec peasants. For example, every house con-

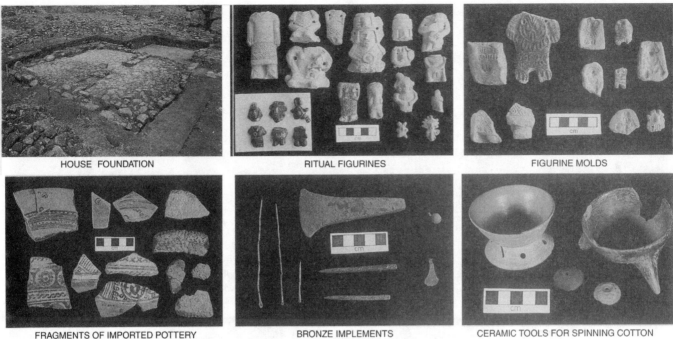

| HOUSE FOUNDATION | RITUAL FIGURINES | FIGURINE MOLDS |
| FRAGMENTS OF IMPORTED POTTERY | BRONZE IMPLEMENTS | CERAMIC TOOLS FOR SPINNING COTTON |

Photography by Michael E. Smith

The photographs above show artifacts unearthed in the modern Mexican state of Morelos from trash middens adjacent to Aztec dwellings of the 12th through 16th centuries.

tained a variety of incense burners and small ceramic figurines in the forms of humans and deities. These artifacts played a role in domestic rituals, which focused on purification and curing. Such ceremonies complemented the more spectacular public celebrations that took place at the towering temple pyramids in the larger cities and towns. Early Spanish priests described in detail the Aztec public religion, and excavation of the Great Temple has shown where these activities occurred. Before the recent excavations of houses, however, scholars had no idea of the nature of domestic rituals.

Not surprisingly, the larger town of Cuexcomate was a more complex community than Capilco. The town was laid out around a public plaza with a small temple pyramid on its east side. Across the plaza from the temple was a distinctive residential compound that, at 540 square meters, was significantly larger than the other houses. Its rooms were elevated above ground level by stone platforms. The compound employed finer construction materials and methods than most houses, including ample use of lime plaster. These features, combined with a floor plan that corresponds to the layout of Aztec palaces, led us to conclude that the compound was the residence of a noble household.

The artifacts left by the nobles who lived in this compound differed in quantity but not in kind from the artifacts found in the dwellings of commoners. For example, this structure yielded significantly greater numbers of imported and decorated ceramics than did the commoners' houses, as one might expect. Nevertheless, nobles did not have exclusive use of any category of artifact. We uncovered the most costly imported goods, such as polychrome bowls from the religious center of Cholula, bronze objects and jade jewelry, at both common and

noble residences, showing that both groups had ready access to the extensive Aztec marketing system of central Mexico.

> TYPICAL PEASANT HOUSE was small (roughly 15 to 25 square meters) and probably had two doors and no windows. Many activities, such as the ubiquitous weaving, took place in patios between the dwellings. Houses were furnished with mats and baskets; a simple shrine with two or three figurines and an incense burner adorned one wall. The absence of hearths is puzzling; quite possibly cooking was done, as it is in traditional villages today, in a lean-to against the back of the house.

The conquest of this region by the Aztec Empire around A.D. 1440 ushered in the late Aztec B period. Soon after, the noble's compound at Cuexcomate was abandoned, and a new, smaller elite compound was built on the north side of the plaza. Populations continued to grow; Cuexcomate expanded from 200 to 800 persons, and Capilco grew from 35 to 135 persons in the late Aztec B period. Agricultural workers constructed extensive terracing to keep up with population growth, but farming reached a point of diminishing returns as all available land was terraced.

Artifacts and architecture provide clues to ancient standards of living, and evidence at these sites points to a significant decline between periods A and B. For example, nobles as well as commoners had fewer imported goods and fewer decorated ceramic vessels in

161

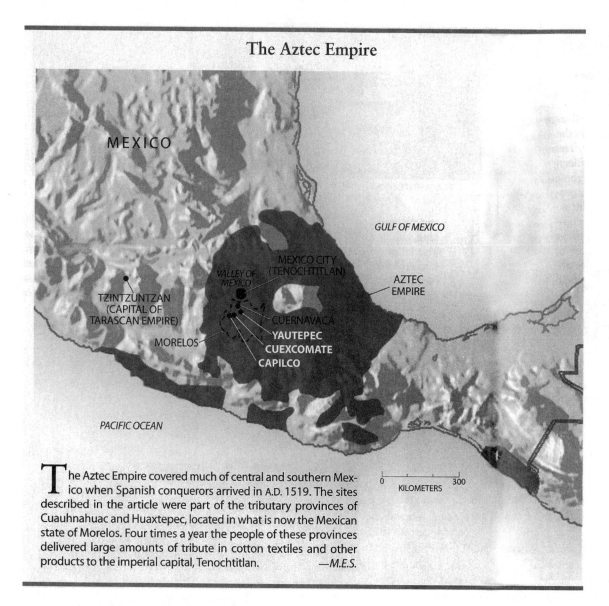

The Aztec Empire

The Aztec Empire covered much of central and southern Mexico when Spanish conquerors arrived in A.D. 1519. The sites described in the article were part of the tributary provinces of Cuauhnahuac and Huaxtepec, located in what is now the Mexican state of Morelos. Four times a year the people of these provinces delivered large amounts of tribute in cotton textiles and other products to the imperial capital, Tenochtitlan. —M.E.S.

the later period. Wealth indices, which we calculated from the quantities of valuable artifacts found at each house, showed a consistent decline. Some commoners tried to compensate for their economic difficulties by increasing their production of textiles. At each site, the houses with the most cotton spinning artifacts were the ones with the lowest wealth indices. In other words, the poorest households put the greatest efforts into craft production, probably to compensate for low crop yields or a lack of land. This pattern has occurred in many parts of the world when overpopulation and land scarcity have led to declining standards of living.

URBAN LIFE

To round out our study of provincial life, we turned to Yautepec, the capital of a powerful city-state in Aztec times. Former Aztec cities in central Mexico are still occupied today, with the ancient ruins buried under layers of historical and more modern settlement. The early Spaniards built Christian churches on top

of the remains of Aztec pyramids and placed their own towns over the Aztec cities. In this respect, Yautepec is unusual. There the Spanish settlement covered only part of the city. In 1989 Hortensia de Vega led a team of archaeologists from Mexico's National Anthropology Institute in the excavation of a large mound at the edge of modern Yautepec. This mound turned out to be the ruin of the royal palace of Yautepec. It is the only Aztec palace to be extensively excavated. We were invited to join the work at Yautepec to study houses from other parts of the ancient city.

At that time, very little was known about Aztec cities except for Tenochtitlan. Although archaeologists had collected surface artifacts from cities in the Valley of Mexico, no one had excavated any urban Aztec houses. The first field season, in 1992, we devoted to a surface survey that established the size and extent of the Aztec settlement. Even within the modern town it was not difficult to trace the extent of ancient Yautepec, which covered just over two square kilometers. In 1993 we returned to excavate houses. We began by digging test pits in open fields and vacant lots and succeeded in locating and uncovering seven houses and their yard areas.

The Yautepec excavations encountered quite dense concentrations of artifacts, and in six months of fieldwork, we recovered 1.2 million potsherds and nearly 50,000 obsidian artifacts, mainly blades and other tools. The classification and study of these materials are still in progress, but preliminary results reveal some fascinating similarities and differences with respect to the earlier findings at Cuexcomate and Capilco.

INTENSIVE AGRICULTURAL PRACTICES evolved to meet the demands of the expanding Aztec population in the 15th century. Farmers built terraced fields—called checkdam terraces—in otherwise unusable ravines to trap the soil eroding in seasonal streams that arose during the heavy rains. The farmers piled up stones, one row at a time, and the terrace formed itself from the erosion as soil washed down the hillside. Each row of stones was set just behind the previous row, without the use of mortar. Thus, the terrace walls sloped rather steeply, and the heavy rains often caused breaches. In the terraces they created in this way, the farmers grew primarily maize, beans and cotton.

Of the seven houses excavated at Yautepec, five were small dwellings of commoners, which had an average size of 26 square meters. Like their rural counterparts, the houses were built of adobe bricks placed on foundation walls of stone cobbles. We also excavated an elite residence that was much larger (430 square meters) than the common houses and made greater use of lime plaster and dressed stone masonry. Another house was a poorly preserved structure of intermediate size (80 square meters) whose class affiliation is not clear.

Yautepec commoners, like their country cousins at Capilco and Cuexcomate, had ready access to foreign goods. The same kinds of imported ceramics, obsidian, salt, jade and bronze were found in residences at Yautepec. We cannot make quantitative comparisons, however, until all artifact studies have been completed. A number of technical analyses currently under way will determine the places of origin of the raw materials used for various artifacts at Yautepec. At this point, we do know that most of the obsidian came from a source near Pachuca, a city north of the Valley of Mexico. We are applying x-ray fluorescence techniques to determine the geologic sources of the remaining obsidian artifacts. Compositional studies of ceramics, including thin-section petrography and neutron-activation analysis, will help distinguish wares manufactured in the Yautepec Valley from those imported from other parts of central Mexico.

One set of analyses recently completed illuminates the origins of the bronze artifacts. Dorothy Hosler of the Massachusetts Institute of Technology analyzed the chemical composition, design and metallurgical properties of metal artifacts

from all three of the sites. These objects include sewing needles, awls, bells and tweezers, all composed of copper-tin or copper-arsenic bronze alloys. Morelos was not a metal-producing zone in ancient times, and these artifacts closely resemble the bronze artifacts made in the Tarascan Empire of western Mexico.

Hosler has completed the first application of lead isotope analysis to ancient Mesoamerican metallurgy by sampling ore sources in several areas and artifacts from a variety of sites, including Yautepec. A number of the Yautepec bronze objects match ore samples from the Tarascan territory. Although written sources report that the Aztecs and Tarascans were constantly at war, the excavations nonetheless provide clear evidence that Tarascan bronze and obsidian were traded across the border and that they made their way into the homes of provincial commoners through the Aztec marketing system.

Yautepec, unlike the rural sites, had numerous craft industries in addition to domestic textile production. Several households made obsidian blades, and a few excavations uncovered evidence of the production of lip plugs, ear plugs and other obsidian jewelry. We also recovered molds used to make ceramic spindle whorls and figurines. Although these molds are not abundant, they were found in many different excavations at Yautepec. Bark beaters for the manufacture of paper were also present. At this point, it appears that many of the common households at Yautepec produced various craft items in addition to cotton textiles.

PROVINCIAL AZTECS

What do these excavations tell us about the people who lived in the provinces of the Aztec Empire? The overall impression is that provincial commoners were relatively prosperous, enterprising people. In spite of an economic decline after conquest and incorporation into the Aztec Empire, commoners in both urban and rural settings still enjoyed access to a wide range of imported goods. These goods were obtained through the markets. Both documentary and archaeological data indicate that the Aztec market system operated largely outside state control. The markets connected people in even the smallest peasant villages with the larger informal Aztec economy of central Mexico. Family members engaged in a variety of craft activities to produce goods to sell in the markets. At sites in Morelos, the most important of these products were cotton textiles manufactured by women in their homes.

Written sources tell us that Aztec commoners were subject to nobles, who owned most of the land and monopolized power within the city-states. Archaeological excavations suggest that at least in several provincial settlements, this burden was not excessive. There is no evidence to suggest that nobles controlled craft production or exchange. The people in the provinces managed to achieve a degree of economic success through channels unconnected to the state and unreported in the official histories of the Aztecs. Illuminating the lives of these previously invisible people is one of the rewards of being an archaeologist today.

THE AUTHOR

MICHAEL E. SMITH *is a professor in the department of anthropology at the State University of New York at Albany. Born in the Philippine Islands, he received his undergraduate degree from Brandeis University and, in 1983, his doctorate in anthropology from the University of Illinois. Before joining the faculty at S.U.N.Y., Smith taught at Loyola University in Chicago. His research focuses on the archaeology and ethnohistory of postclassic central Mexico. The excavations described in this article were funded principally by the National Science Foundation and the National Endowment for the Humanities.*

FURTHER READING

ARCHAEOLOGICAL RESEARCH AT AZTEC-PERIOD RURAL SITES IN MORELOS, MEXICO, VOL. 1: EXCAVATIONS AND ARCHITECTURE. M. E. Smith. University of Pittsburgh Memoirs in Latin American Archaeology, No. 4, 1992.

ECONOMIES AND POLITIES IN THE AZTEC REALM. Edited by Mary G. Hodge and Michael E. Smith. Institute for Mesoamerican Studies, State University of New York at Albany, 1994.

THE AZTECS. Michael E. Smith. Blackwell Publishers, 1996.

COPPER SOURCES, METAL PRODUCTION, AND METALS TRADE IN LATE POSTCLASSIC MESOAMERICA. Dorothy Hosler and Andrew Macfarlane in *Science,* Vol. 273, pages 1819–1824; September 27, 1996.

Legacy *of the* Crusades

The ruins of castles on hillsides throughout the Middle East are mute
reminders of a bloody chapter in medieval history.

by Sandra Scham

A STORY IS TOLD IN KERAK, a small city in Jordan dominated by a well-preserved crusader castle, about the fortress'
most notorious denizen, Reynauld of Chatillon. According to
this tale, the Hajj route to Mecca during Reynauld's time, the
late twelfth century A.D., passed beneath his castle walls. Attracted by the richness of one caravan, Reynauld swooped down
on the unfortunate pilgrims, capturing all and relieving them of
their worldly goods. At the end of his foray, he found, to his immense glee, that one of his hostages was the sister of the legendary Islamic leader Saladin. Reynauld's fellow crusaders
were appalled by his brazen violation of a rather tenuous truce.
Baldwin IV, king of Jerusalem, sent a message forthwith, demanding that Reynauld release his distinguished prisoner. Reynauld's answer reflects his customary bravado: "You are king
of Jerusalem," he wrote, "but I am king in Kerak."

Kerak, though, never had a king, a fact well known to both
Reynauld and the local guides who repeat this story. Nevertheless, although it was within the boundaries of the crusader
kingdom of Jerusalem, Kerak was also far enough away from
the center of power to enable its ruler to do pretty much as he
pleased—that is, summarily executing prisoners, whether they
were men, women, or children, in the most brutal manner imag-
inable. Reynauld eventually got his just desserts, and has the dubious distinction of being the only important crusader to have
been personally executed by Saladin.

The castle of Kerak is built on a spur to take advantage of the
natural defense accorded by this topography. The town of Kerak
has grown all around the spur and it is usually a lively tourist
destination. I visited the site, familiar to me from previous sojourns in Jordan, on a beautiful day this past summer, when one
would normally expect to see tour buses and guides hustling
large groups through the castle gates. The streets were empty.
Abdul Hamied, one of Kerak's more knowledgeable local
guides, explained, "Tourism in Jordan is down by 70 percent-I

worked only seven days this year." Jordan is feeling the effects
of the prolonged Israeli-Palestinian struggle, despite the fact
that it has been relatively free from conflict itself.

T he castle of Kerak in Jordan was once
home to notorious crusader knight
Reynauld of Chatillon, who preyed on
pilgrims traveling to Mecca. A popular
tourist destination in modern times, the
castle has recently seen a drop in visitors
because of the ongoing Israeli-
Palestinian conflict.

Reflecting on battles both past and present, and the physical
legacy of these conflicts ever-present in the landscape, I asked
Hamied what he learned about crusader history growing up in
Kerak in the shadow of this looming medieval structure. "We
were taught that they came from Pharaoh's Island [off the coast
of the Sinai Peninsula] and built this line of castles here [from
Aqaba to Turkey] to control the trading business," he replied.
"When these crusaders came, they came as invaders—killing
thousands. And they were not coming for religion or 'holy war.'
It was an economic war that used religion."

Aziz Azayzeh, another guide at Kerak, agrees with this assessment. "As a Jordanian, I learned in school that the crusaders
came and took our lands just because of greed and gave us
nothing in return." Both men, however, true to their professions,
say similar things about the crusader sites. Azayzeh continues,
"Later, when I studied more about them, I think they did give us
something—they were good architects. You know Saladin was

smart. He asked the best architects and artists from the crusaders to stay and work." Hamied is more philosophical: "The crusaders—they came as invaders, the Romans came as invaders, in Hellenistic times also. The big powers everywhere—they look to their own interests, but they left something behind for us at these places."

Listening to these remarks, as I stood at the summit of Kerak, I recalled a conversation I had with a colleague before leaving the United States. Salman Elbedour, an American psychology professor who is also an Israeli Bedouin, told me that there is a "Crusader Complex" in the Middle East. Consequently, it was no surprise to him that President Bush's rather bizarre juxtaposition of ideas, promising to rid the world of the perpetrators of violence in the name of religion, while at the same time labeling the American incursion in Afghanistan a "crusade," was perceived as a major affront by the Arab world. Elbedour and other Muslims, whose ancestors lived in the very heart of crusader territory, see the crusaders as the ultimate vicious usurpers. Archaeologist Adel Yahyeh, who lives in Ramallah on the West Bank, adds, "When we were children in Palestine, our nightmares were about monsters coming after us, wearing crosses on their chests. We even started to see Israeli soldiers that way—strange as it seems."

*"Y*ou go to Lebanon, Syria, Jordan today...you can see that many of the crusaders stayed and married, and that today we are a mixture of people."*

Crusader sites, like the crusader tradition, inspire a variety of emotions and thoughts. The castles are what most people think of when they envision the crusader period (1097-1291), and many Arabs, says Yahyeh, take a measure of pride in them, since it was the Arabs who liberated the castles from their Christian enemy. But there are other effects of the period to be considered, as well. "You go to Lebanon, Syria, Jordan today...you can see that many of the crusaders stayed and married, and that today we are a mixture of people," says Azayzeh. This casual statement actually reflects the focus of a great deal of new archaeological activity relating to crusader sites in the region. Although it was long believed that European culture did not penetrate rural areas in the Levant, excavations of villages and farmsteads with crusader architecture, sugar refining equipment (a fairly new industry in the medieval period), and a general increase in pig bones at rural sites now indicate otherwise.

OF COURSE, Muslims are not the only ones to have suffered at the hands of the crusaders. Eastern Orthodox Christians and Jews have their own perspectives on this period. As Jörg Bremer, a German historian and journalist who is now living in Jerusalem, says, "Today, we talk of special [collective] memories of the Crusades." Jews see the Crusades, he continues, "as having started in Germany with killing of Jews." Then, there is "the tradition of the Eastern Church relating to the sack of Byz-

antium" (by crusaders in 1204—when it was an entirely Christian city). Finally, he speaks of the revival of crusader consciousness among Muslims who see "the state of Israel today as neo-crusader."

Bremer is a latter-day member of the Order of the Knights of St. John (the Hospitallers), as were his ancestors, and explains, "The Hospitallers were in the Holy Land long before the Crusades and were not called 'knights' until the real crusaders came." Hospitaller tradition, he says, avers that "we were the only European group that was allowed to stay [after the crusaders were defeated]." Bremer laments the fact that the Hospitallers, originally a peaceful group, were forced by the coming of the Templars to bear arms. The Templars were founded in 1119 for the purpose of defending Christian pilgrims in the Holy Land, while the Hospitallers, so-called because their principal mission was to care for the sick, did not become a military order until 1130, some 60 years after having been founded in Jerusalem.

The historical and cultural legacy of the Crusades is accompanied by a concrete, or rather stone, legacy, dotting hillsides throughout the Middle East. Less obvious than the isolated castles like Kerak are the crusader remains in the cities, many of which were built upon in subsequent eras. Jerusalem and Akko (Acre), the two most important cities of medieval times, are replete with varied examples of crusader architecture. In Jerusalem, the centerpiece of the crusader kingdom, many sites were modified by the crusaders, but they built from the ground up as well. Not surprisingly, most of these activities centered on churches; the complete rebuilding of the Church of the Holy Sepulchre was a major project. The church was consecrated in 1149, a half-century after the crusaders first seized Jerusalem, and stands today largely in its crusader form.

Akko's harbor served as the primary port of entry for pilgrims to the Holy Land. Today, local residents take a plunge into the Mediterranean from the city's crusader fortifications.

Despite this fact, many members of Eastern Orthodox denominations think of the Church of the Holy Sepulchre as Byzantine. "It was first built in the fourth century, and there are still Byzantine structures," explains Ardin Sisserian, an Eastern Orthodox gatekeeper and guide at the Church. The reason for his de-emphasis on crusader architecture here may have something to do with tensions between the Catholics, "whose ancestors came with the sword and the Cross," says Sisserian, and the other four faiths that have access to the Church—all Eastern Christian.

Bremer encountered similar tensions when he and other modern Hospitallers asked to pray at Jerusalem's twelfth-century Church of St. John the Baptist, patron saint of their order. Although the Greek Orthodox Church now owns the structure, it was once so important to the Hospitallers that they maintained guards there after the expulsion of other crusaders and the re-taking of Jerusalem by Saladin in 1244. The Hospitallers were denied permission to pray there until 2001, when, Bremer says, they went to Greek Orthodox officials to open what he calls a "diplomatic channel," with the formal admission that "this part of our history is horrible" and that they wanted to go "on the record as recognizing special ties with the Eastern Church." As a result, Bremer says, they "could pray in the church for the first time in 800 years."

These days, most visitors to the Church of the Holy Sepulchre appear to be Israelis rather than Christian pilgrims—who, like many others, are leery of coming to what they perceive to be a war zone. Among the groups speaking Hebrew and touring the church on one Shabbat (Jewish Sabbath) afternoon were several people wearing yarmulkes, as well as seemingly secular Jews. A nonreligious member of a group of mixed religious and secular students, Hagai Dror, explained, "Christians today seem closer to Jews than Muslims do. We see these sites as European, and many of us who have a European background are interested in them." His friend, Gal Ariely, added, "The main reason we are here is because we live here. This is my city, and it's my duty to know about it." This last statement reflects the sense of ownership that many young Israelis feel about Jerusalem. Yossi is an ultra-orthodox Jewish resident of the Mt. Zion's Diaspora Yeshiva, which is housed in a building that was at one time a fourteenth-century crusader monastery. Yossi, who had a strictly religious education in Jerusalem, says that he knows nothing about crusaders except that "I live in a crusader house."

THE CITY OF AKKO was the last major crusader foothold in Palestine—finally falling to the Muslim forces in 1291, after 100 years of renewed crusader rule. Akko's crusader remains can now be seen below the city's current street level in the northern part of today's walled Old Town. It's a fascinating labyrinth of underground structures unearthed by excavations that began in the late 1950s and continue today. There are barracks for the knights, a hall of the crusader palace, an underground sewage system with a number of public toilets, and portions of crusader streets and walls—all visible beneath the bustling Ottoman city above.

Akko's Ottoman structures, largely built on top of the crusader ruins, represent the Arab character of the city, past and present. The people who live in most of the houses in the Old City, however, were moved there from the Galilee after 1948 (the year of the establishment of the state of Israel), when Akko's older indigenous Arab population fled the city. Ron Be'eri, an archaeologist from the University of Haifa who works at Akko, says that the people who live there today "feel little connection with the city's history" and generally view the historical character of their own houses as an annoyance. Considered abandoned property owned by the State of Israel, these places are occupied mostly by Arab renters who are not permitted, even if they have the funds, to buy them. They are also not permitted, because these are historic structures, to alter them in any way. Consequently, most of the Old City's residences are in great disrepair.

Nevertheless, Erica Gal of the Akko Development Corporation insists that Akko's locals take an interest in the heritage of their city. "Schools visit the subterranean [crusader] site all the time and, from the fifth grade, local students take a course called 'Akko, My Town' in which they learn all of the local history." She does suggest that visits by local people to Akko underground may be limited by the fact that they must buy tickets to gain access to it. Be'eri believes that "very few" of the Old City's residents have ever visited the crusader site, but this may reflect their hostility toward "heritage sites" in general, given their experience with them, rather than any residual resentment of crusaders.

Although the schools of Akko may take an interest in crusader sites as part of the local history, education in most of Israel, as distinct from Jordan, glosses over the crusader occupation. "We learn nothing about this period in school," says Salman Elbedour, who received an Israeli education. According to Israeli archaeologist Adrian Boas, the crusader period, which is his area of specialization, is not a favored subject for Israeli historians and archaeologists, although he points out that a recent crusader exhibit at the Israel Museum in Jerusalem drew large crowds. As to the historical antagonism, "If you asked the average Jew here about this," he says, "they wouldn't have a clue what you were talking about." Attitudes toward crusader sites in Israel are a reflection of cultural ties to, or antipathies toward, the Crusades as well as individually held beliefs. Boas, originally from Australia, says that his interest in the Crusades and crusader sites comes "from basically having grown up in an Anglo-Saxon country. As a child, I was always interested in the medieval period." Elbedour says that he has no interest in visiting crusader sites. Bremer, who has visited the sites, says that many of the castles look "so militant—like tank posts on top of a hill."

While Boas admires the "tactical advantages" of Kerak and other spur castles, he says that he is most impressed with Belvoir, a Hospitaller castle overlooking the Jordan River and the Damascus to Jerusalem Road. In this case, the strategical importance of Belvoir's location in the past is repeated in the present as today, it overlooks the boundaries between Israel and the West Bank, and Israel and Jordan. One of the earliest examples of the "concentric castle" or castrum, a building with one fortification wall entirely enclosing another, Belvoir remains one of the most remarkable buildings of this type.

On the coast south of Akko is probably one of the few crusader sites in the Middle East that is regularly visited by people who live there. Elbedour admits to having been to only one crusader site, Caesarea, but only "because it's on the [Mediterranean] Sea." Although the town witnessed few historical events in the past, some crusader buildings at Caesarea have an interesting modern history. One of them, the citadel, became a mosque after the defeat of the crusaders. With the founding of the state of Israel and subsequent displacement of the local population of Muslims, the mosque became a restaurant and bar, a state of affairs that was bound to offend those Muslims remaining in the region. The restaurant, called "The Castle," is now closed.

Caesarea's crusader—and Roman-era ruins were restored to attract foreign tourists. Its location on a stretch of sandy Mediterranean beach makes it popular with Israeli visitors.

Caesarea, according to Pennsylvania State University archaeologist Ann Killebrew, was among those sites that the Israel Antiquities Authority decided early on to develop. Crusader remains and Roman ruins, although they do not precisely reflect the ethnic or religious character of the country today, were restored specifically to attract foreign tourists, she says. In the 1990s, Caesarea was further embellished as a result of the government's efforts to provide employment to workers from the nearby town of Or Akiva. As a result, says Killebrew, the site has been "completely uncovered, and has become unattractive to tourists."

Some writers who have recently looked at the legacy of the Crusades, such as Karen Armstrong (*Holy War*) and, to a lesser extent, Bernard Lewis (*What Went Wrong?*) believe they are the source of the troubles afflicting the Middle East today. Whether or not the Crusades were responsible for bringing West and East together or, conversely, the origin of the struggles now taking place in the region, it seems certain that a crusader legacy, lasting almost 1,000 years, is not a media fantasy. In few places in the world is ancient history given such immediacy as in the Middle East. The founding of the state of Israel in 1948 was partially predicated on the biblical history of the region during the Iron Age—a period some 3,000 years in the past. A trauma that is only 900 years old is relatively recent in a place where history is marked by millennia rather than centuries.

SANDRA SCHAM, *a contributing editor for* ARCHAEOLOGY, *is an archaeologist who has been living and working in Israel since 1996. A former curator of the Pontifical Biblical Institute Museum in Jerusalem, she is currently affiliated with the department of anthropology at the University of Maryland at College Park.*

Israel's Mysterious Stone

Researchers battle over the authenticity of an ancient inscription

BY HAIM WATZMAN

JERUSALEM

When Edward L. Greenstein, professor of biblical studies at Tel Aviv University, opened his newspaper one Tuesday in January, he was surprised to find front-page news from his field. Three scientists from the Geological Survey of Israel, a government research institute, had reported a major discovery: a black sandstone tablet engraved with ancient Hebrew letters.

According to the scientists, the stone and its inscription date to the ninth century BC and are apparently a remnant of the Holy Temple that, according to the Bible, King Solomon constructed in Jerusalem. That would make it the first material evidence ever found of the existence of the Temple. The discovery, Mr. Greenstein realized, would challenge the theories of "minimalist" scholars, who contend that Solomon's reign and other parts of biblical history might never have happened.

Far from just an academic dispute, the issue has profound religious and political implications. The hill in Jerusalem where Solomon is said to have built his temple has become a flashpoint in the Israeli-Palestinian conflict. Jews regard the site, which they call the Temple Mount, as sacred, and some fundamentalists want to rebuild the Holy Temple there. But the spot, now the site of the Dome of the Rock and the Al Aqsa mosque, is the third holiest in the Islamic world. The Muslim religious authorities who control it deny that a Jewish temple ever stood there.

Mr. Greenstein took a closer look at the photograph in the paper. "I had some time, and ancient Semitic texts is one of my areas of expertise, so I copied out the letters on a pad. And certain things struck me wrong," he said.

Fact or faked? An apparently ancient stone tablet, slightly larger than a sheet of office paper, describes repairs made to Solomon's Temple.

Mr. Greenstein was among several scholars here who took their concerns to the press. Around the world, other textual scholars have also detected problems with the inscription, ones that lead many to call the tablet a forgery. In fact, *Biblical Archaeology Review* has offered a $10,000 reward for someone who can duplicate the chemical signature of the "ancient" tablet. But the geologists who studied the stone stand by their conclusions, leading to a showdown between humanities researchers and scientists about who can best judge the authenticity of ancient material.

ANONYMOUS SOURCE

Rumors of the discovery first started circulating more than a year ago, yet details of the inscription emerged only in January, when the geological-survey scientists published their finding in their institute's journal, *Current Research*. The tablet had been delivered to the institute

for analysis by agents of an anonymous antiquities collector.

The scientists analyzed the chemical composition of the tablet's surface, looking in particular at the patina that had formed on top of the sandstone. Such coatings often develop on ancient materials as their surface reacts with the air or with the ground in which they are buried. Among other tests, they sent samples of the patina to a laboratory in Miami for radiocarbon dating. This technique can measure the age of organic material, such as the carbon in the patina, and it indicated that the patina is more than 2,000 years old. The geologists concluded that "artificial production ... in recent years is not impossible, but seems to us not very probable.... [W]e propose that stages ... of the formation of the tablet predate 2,250 years BP [before present]." In other words, according to the scientists, the inscription is most likely genuine.

But the government survey geologists were not the only ones to be contacted by agents of the mysterious collector. According to press reports, scholars specializing in the vocabulary and syntax of ancient texts, and others whose expertise is paleography (the study of the physical forms of ancient writing) were shown the tablet at clandestine meetings in hotel rooms in Israel. Even then some suspected a forgery. It was not until the geologists' report was published, though, that the textual scholars could examine the inscription, with the help of the photograph in the institute's journal.

The text of the inscription commemorates repairs to the Temple. While the name of the king who had the inscription carved does not appear—it would most likely have been on a corner of the tablet that had broken off—from the context it is clear that the biblical king in question is Jehoash, whose reign of Judah is generally dated by historians to 836-798 BC. It closely parallels the account of these repairs given in the biblical Book of II Kings, Chapter 12, described also in II Chronicles, Chapter 24.

TOO GOOD TO BE TRUE

It was that closeness to the biblical text that aroused the suspicion of Nadav Neeman, a historian of the biblical period at Tel Aviv University. The find seemed too good to be true. In 1998, he had published an article in a Dutch biblical-studies journal, *Vetus Testamentum,* about the sources that the author of the Book of Kings had used in composing his work. Relying on differences of vocabulary and syntax in sections of Kings, Mr. Neeman theorized that the author of those sections had based his work on various texts available at the time. In particular, Mr. Neeman surmised that King Jehoash had placed a plaque in the area of the Temple to commemorate his renovation project and that the author of Kings had borrowed from that inscription. Royal inscriptions marking the important works of kings are a well-known genre of the ancient Middle East, though at that point none from the kingdom of Judah had ever been found.

Mr. Greenstein also found the inscription's similarity to the biblical text suspicious. But several other textual anomalies jumped out at him as he transcribed the text from the newspaper photograph onto a legal pad. By the time he had gone through the text, six major problems and a number of minor ones emerged, he says.

For example, one is the use of the phrase *bedeq habayit.* In modern Hebrew, this phrase has come to mean "renovations" or "home repairs." But the literal meaning is "breach in the house"—that is, cracks in the Temple walls. The Book of Kings thus uses the verb "to strengthen" in association with

this phrase, meaning "to repair the breach in the house." But the verb used in the Jehoash inscription is "to do"—to do the breach in the house. That only makes sense, says Mr. Greenstein, if the person who wrote the text is using the phrase in the modern way, meaning "to do the renovations." Mr. Greenstein sees such evidence as a sign of a forger who knew enough chemistry to fool the geologists but not enough biblical Hebrew to fool the textual scholars.

Another problem he found was in the use of the word *edut.* The Jehoash inscription uses this word in the sense of "testimony," its meaning in modern Hebrew. But in parts of the Bible thought to date from the First Temple period, says, Mr. Greenstein, "*edut* means 'covenant,' while 'testimony' is signified by a related but distinct word, *ed.*"

The inscription has also been criticized by paleographers, who argue that the form of the ancient Hebrew letters is not appropriate to the time and place of King Jehoash. Frank Moore Cross, an emeritus professor of Hebrew at Harvard Divinity School, is publishing his paleographic analysis of the stone in a forthcoming issue of *Israel Exploration Journal.* In an e-mail message to *The Chronicle,* he says that "the script of the Plaque is not ninth-century Hebrew script (which we know well) but a mixture of ninth-century Phoenician, Moabite, and Old Aramaic scripts, [and] that the spelling does not follow in two cases the spelling rules used in pre-Exilic Hebrew texts...."

"Any one of these howlers would demonstrate the spurious character of the inscription on the sandstone plaque," he writes.

Both Mr. Greenstein and Mr. Cross have told the Israeli press that the chemical and geological results cannot, by themselves, validate the find. If the text does not match what humanities scholars know about the ancient Hebrew language and alphabet, the results obtained by the "hard sciences" must be mistaken, they say. Both suggest that the Israeli geological-survey scientists did not perform sufficiently rigorous tests. The geological survey's analysis has been criticized in detail by the chairman of Tel Aviv University's department of archae-

ology and ancient Near Eastern cultures, Yuval Goren, in an article posted on a site called the Bible and Interpretation (http://www.bibleinterp.com/articles/alternative_interpretation.htm).

Mr. Goren points out that royal inscriptions are generally engraved on basalt. He says that the choice of sandstone in this instance is no coincidence. It is much easier to apply a fake patina to sandstone, Mr. Goren argues in his paper. He offers a step-by-step process by which, he says, the patina could have been applied, weathered, and aged.

The authors of the Israeli geological-survey paper, Shimon Hani, Amnon Rosenfeld, and Michael Dvorachek, are government employees and are not permitted to speak to journalists directly. But a scientist close to them says that the geologists stand by their results and that Mr. Goren's critique is "garbage."

$10,000 PRIZE

The scientist supports the geologists' claim that some of the chemical characteristics of the patina would be nearly impossible to fake. Even the doubters accept the geologists' dating of the patina to the ancient period, though they say that patina from some other object could have been applied to the inscription.

Beyond that, the geologists also reported that the patina contains minute globules of pure gold, measuring from one to a few microns in size. Formation of such globules of gold, the geologists write in their paper, requires temperatures of more than 1,800 degrees Fahrenheit, and their distribution in the patina indicates a natural rather than an artificial process. The geologists suggest that the globules may have formed, and adhered to the inscription, when the Temple, which contained gold objects and decorations, was burned by the Babylonians, according to the Bible.

The scholars in the humanities simply don't know enough chemistry to judge the scientists' results, the scientist close to the Israeli geologists suggests. But Mr. Cross says that he has an undergraduate degree in chemistry, did postgraduate work in the field, and knows it quite well.

Hershel Shanks, editor of the magazine *Biblical Archaeology Review,* published in Washington, says that he finds the textual evidence of a forgery compelling. He also points out, though, that he knows of no other cases in which an ancient patina of this type has been successfully faked. In the current issue of the magazine he is announcing a $10,000 prize for anyone who can convincingly fake a patina of the type found on the Jehoash inscription.

Microscopic globs of gold embedded in the tablet's surface could have come from the burning of gold objects when the Temple was destroyed. But skeptics say that the gold bits reflect the process used to fake the stone's patina.

Everyone involved agrees that the find is especially problematic because it was not excavated in a methodical archaeological dig where scientists could record its context and surroundings. Such context is important for dating and authenticating ancient objects. Still, antiquities are valuable, and as a result there is a thriving black market in them,

and that market has always been a source of both important finds (such as the Dead Sea Scrolls) and forgeries. It is little surprise that the tablet's provenance remains obscure: According to Israeli law, all antiquities are public property. Private excavations and the sale of antiquities are felonies. The law is so strict that even the marketing of forgeries and replicas can land you in jail.

TESTING THE STONE

When rumors of the existence of the Jehoash inscription began circulating, the Israel Antiquities Authority, the statutory body charged with protection of archaeological objects, began an investigation that eventually led to an antiquities collector, Oded Golan, who acknowledged having the inscription in his possession, although he denied being its owner. Mr. Golan is now under investigation, and the sandstone plaque has been turned over to the antiquities authority, which has established two committees to study the object. One will be responsible for chemical and geological analysis, and the other will examine the textual and paleographical issues the inscription raises. The stone may be sent overseas for further chemical tests. While the committees have no deadline

for submitting their report, Osnat Goaz, the spokesman for the authority, says that the process will probably take a number of weeks.

That will provide time for tempers to cool and egos to calm, says Gabriel Barkay, an archaeologist from Bar-Ilan University. Mr. Barkay says that the textual and paleographic arguments made against the tablet's authenticity so far are weak. None of them is unambiguous, and, he adds, a forger could have opened any modern Hebrew dictionary to find out the biblical sense of *bedeq habayit.* He views the chemical analysis as compelling.

Yet the field of archaeology has known many forgeries, he acknowledges, and it will take time and study to reveal the truth about the Jehoash inscription.

For now, Mr. Barkay remains undecided. Despite his skepticism about the textual and paleographic arguments made to date, he does think that such research is more important than the work of chemists and geologists.

"An inscription is made by man, not by nature," he points out, "and so the natural sciences have to take second place to the humanities."

UNIT 5

Contemporary Archaeology

Unit Selections

Key Points to Consider

- Discuss NAGPRA and give some examples of different views on this subject.

- Why do both ethnographers and archaeologists go into the field to gather the same data? How do these approaches differ? What is their impact on the native people?

- What is the latest word on the controversial skull known as "Kennewick Man"? Does "Kennewick Man" belong to archaeologists or "the American Indians"? How old is the skull?

- Who are the *Mochica* people of ancient Peru? How is this an example of salvage archaeology? How did the excavation of this site reveal the art, rituals, and religion of these ancient peoples? Give examples.

- What is the archaeology evidence for the existence of the *Biblical James?* According to the Christian Bible, James was supposed to be the brother or cousin of Jesus Christ. Does the evidence confirm the existence of these religious persons? If not, why? Give examples.

- How do archaeologists handle being involved in the highly charged warfare in the Middle East? How do they handle their own political involvement? Please discuss.

- What happened if archaeologists themselves lie about their findings to suit their own purposes? Give an example of this based on the findings of the Nazi-death camps.

- Discuss the findings of archaeologists studying central Nevada. How are these artifacts reminders of the recent Cold War? Will humankind learn its lesson or will there still be a Nuclear Holocaust? Discuss.

 **Links: www.dushkin.com/online/**
These sites are annotated in the World Wide Web pages.

Ancient World Web
http://www.julen.net/ancient/

Archaeology and Anthropology: The Australian National University
http://online.anu.edu.au/AandA/

WWW: Classical Archaeology
http://www.archaeology.org/wwwarky/classical.html

The origins of contemporary archaeology may be traced back to the nineteenth century. Several currents of thought and beliefs coalesced in that unique century. Some say it started with a French man named Boucher de Perthes who found odd-shaped stones on his property, stones that could comfortably be held by a human hand. Undoubtedly, thousands of other people made such finds throughout history. But to Monsieur de Perthes, these stones suggested a novel meaning. He wondered if these odd rocks might not be tools, made by humans long lost in the mists before history.

Other exciting changes were occurring in the epistemology of the nineteenth century that would soon lend credibility to this hypothesis. In 1859 there was the publication of On the Origin of Species by Charles Darwin. In this book (which, by the way, never mentioned humans or any implied relationship they might have to apes) Darwin suggested a general process that became known as natural selection. The theory suggested that species could change gradually through time in response to the environment. This was an idea counterintuitive to scientific thought. Even biologists believed that species were immutable. But it changed forever the nature of the way human beings regarded their place in nature. If species could change, then the implication was so could humans. And that idea knocked humankind down from its loft and into the archaeological record.

There was the concurrent emergence of the idea of uniformitarianism, which implied that Earth was old, very old, perhaps hundreds of thousands of years old. (It is, in fact, about 5 billion years old.) But with this idea, the revolutionary possibility that human beings could have existed before history became more plausible. Such a serious challenge to the established wisdom that Earth was only about 6,000 years old additionally contributed to this new age of speculation on the meaning of being human.

The newly emerging science of paleontology and the discovery and recognition of extinct fossil species seriously challenged the traditional elevated status of human beings. Nineteenth-century philosophers were forced to reexamine the nature of humanity. Among the intellectuals of the Western world, the essential anthropocentrism of the Christian view gradually shifted to a more secular view of humankind as part and parcel of nature. Therefore humans became subject to the rules of nature and natural events, without reference to a theology.

So it was then, within this new nineteenth-century enlightenment, that Boucher de Perthes suggested his hypothesis regarding the antiquity of his stone tools. The time had come, and others answered that they too had found these same odd-shaped stones and had thought similar thoughts. The study of archaeology had begun.

As a science evolves, it naturally diversifies. There is now worry that archaeologists will specialize themselves right out of the mainstream of anthropology. But the shared cultural concept and holistic approach tend to maintain this traditional relationship. That is not to deny that mainstream archaeology is now being pulled in many different directions.

The saving grace in contemporary archaeology may be found in the current trend of moving toward a more public archaeology. There is an awareness that archaeologists should tell more stories. Or talk about their own digs and portray a larger picture that says something more than the sum of tedious detail. And above all, stop talking inbred lingo to each other. Now is the time to start a give-and-take dialogue with the public.

Article selections deal with the interest in the preservation, conservation, reconstruction, and transformation of archaeological sites into the present for the educational and aesthetic value of the sites themselves. This is the direction of contemporary archaeology. More attention must be directed toward the financing of archaeological endeavors as well as the incorporation of alternate sources of labor in these new political times.

Ethical questions must be faced. An archaeological site should be viewed as nonrenewable resource. What of the needs of developers? It is their livelihood to do this work even if it means destroying archaeological sites. What of the rights of landowners versus persons with a perceived historical ownership of the same land? Archaeological excavation itself is the systematic destruction of sites and their ecological context. Anything overlooked, mislaid, not measured, or in some way not observed is a lost piece of the past. If the information is never shared with an audience, it is a complete loss.

Burying American Archaeology

On November 16, 1990, Congress passed the Native American Graves Protection and Repatriation Act (NAGPRA). One controversial provision of the act requires the return, on request, of skeletal remains and burial goods to Native Americans who can prove cultural affiliation with the materials.

by Clement W. Meighan

In 1991 the West Virginia Department of Transportation and a committee of Indians and non-Indians claiming to represent Native American viewpoints signed an agreement whereby everything unearthed in advance of road construction near the 2,000-year-old Adena mound was to be given up for reburial within a year. "Everything" included not only cremated bones but artifacts such as chipping waste, food refuse, pollen samples, and soil samples. The $1.8 million rescue excavation was federally funded in the interest of science. Yet nothing of tangible archaeological evidence was to be preserved. In addition, Indian activists were paid by the state to monitor the excavation and to censor "objectionable" photographs or data appearing in the final report. The activists also insisted that, following an alleged ancient custom, human remains be covered with red flannel until reburial and that no remains, including artifacts, be touched by menstruating women.

Millions of dollars have now been spent to inventory collections and to interpret and administer the legislation.

American Indians, Australian aborigines, and ultraorthodox Jews in Israel have all attacked archaeology in recent years and continue to seek restrictions on archaeological study. In North America, the argument has been put forward that the archaeological study of ancient Native American people is a violation of the religious freedom of living Indians. Some Indian spokesmen have claimed their right, on religious grounds, to control archaeological study and specimens regardless of the age of the remains, the area from which they come, or the degree of claimed Indian ancestry.

In my view, archaeologists have a responsibility to the people they study. They are defining the culture of an extinct group and in presenting their research they are writing a chapter of human history that cannot be written except from archaeological investigation. If the archaeology is not done, the ancient people remain without a history.

A number of confusions have led to the present conflict over archaeological study of Native American remains. One is the assumption of direct genetic and cultural continuity between living persons and those long deceased. Who knows whether the Indians of 2,000 years ago believed that a corpse must be covered with red flannel and not touched by menstruating women? As if to emphasize their contempt for real ancestral relationships, the activists who demanded reburial of the remains from the Adena mound included Indians from tribes as far away as northwestern Washington, as well as non-Indians. Meanwhile, the views of a local West Virginia tribe that favored preservation of the remains were ignored.

A year before the government passed the Native American Graves Protection and Repatriation Act. According to preliminary interpretations of this law, some sort of relationship must be shown between claimants and the materials claimed. However, no line has been drawn at remains over a certain age, despite the obvious impossibility of establishing a familial relationship spanning 20 or more generations of unrecorded history. Millions of dollars have now been spent to inventory collections, including those containing items thousands of years old, and to add a corps of bureaucrats to interpret and administer the legislation. An enormous amount of scientists' time is also being diverted from research that might otherwise be done on those bones and artifacts soon to be lost to repatriation.

One wonders why museum directors are so eager to relinquish the holdings for which they are responsible. Museums house a great variety of collections and their directors are rarely trained in any of the natural sciences or have any special interest in physical anthropology. Being, for the most part, public institutions, they are dependent on good public relations, which can be undermined by activists. Like politicians, museum directors seem all too willing to satisfy activists by dissatisfying scientists. Meanwhile, in university departments of anthropology, physical anthropologists are normally outnumbered by cultural anthropologists. The latter have little interest in osteological collections; more important to them is maintaining good relations with the living tribes with

whom they work. As a group, cultural anthropologists include a considerable number of politicized academics. Many of them welcome an opportunity to demonstrate their solidarity with an allegedly oppressed minority, especially when it means insisting that the latter's native religion be respected. Since their own research will not be adversely affected, they have nothing to lose. Political correctness has rarely been so all-around satisfying.

Scholars and scientists often thought of themselves as helping the American Indian to preserve his heritage.

It is questionable whether Indian activists and politicized professors and curators could succeed in influencing politicians and administrators if the latter found their claims to be utterly implausible. Even the most cynical and opportunistic lawmakers would not want to be observed supporting self-evidently absurd demands. Yet the multiple laws inhibiting archaeological research, physical anthropology, and museum studies have all been instigated and justified in the name of Indian religious beliefs. This is remarkable for a number of reasons. First, no other religious group in the United States has been given the same protection. Second, most Indians no longer hold these beliefs. Third, Indian knowledge of the traditions of their ancestors is derived in large part from the collections and scholarship that the activists among them are now seeking to destroy.

That measures hostile to science have gained so much ground in this nation's legislative bodies, universities, and museums—and on so flimsy a basis—suggests that there has been a sea change in the opinions and sentiments that have hitherto guided the public in support of scientific endeavor. The New Age disposition to invoke or invent beliefs

no one really holds, and to maintain that they are of a value at least equal to, if not supremely greater than, those that account for the triumph of Western civilization, is given concrete expression in the repatriation movement. Conversely, the success of this movement will further reinforce these newly fashionable doubts about the value of Western science in particular and rational thought in general.

Reasonable doubts have been raised about whether the large quantity of bones tucked away in museum drawers and cabinets are really of scientific value. In fact, these are frequently studied by physical anthropologists and their students. The techniques of statistical research require as large a sample as possible so that generalizations can be well-formulated. In addition, bones that have already been examined may be needed again when new analytic techniques are developed. Only recently has it been possible to extract antibodies and genetic material from ancient bones, making it possible to trace the evolution of specific human diseases. Future laboratory advances in dating bones and in determining the source of artifact materials will also require these objects to be available for study. Finally, the bones belonging to particular tribes are precisely those that are most valuable to historical studies of those tribes.

But even if it were true that the bones, once examined, need never be studied again, the demand that they be reburied conflicts with the scholarly requirement to preserve data. If research data are destroyed, there can be no basis on which to challenge honest but possibly erroneous conclusions. Reburying bones and artifacts is the equivalent of the historian burning documents after he has studied them. Thus, repatriation is not merely an inconvenience but makes it impossible for scientists to carry out a genuinely scientific study of American Indian prehistory. Furthermore, it negates scientific work that has already been done, since the evidence on which that work was based is now to be buried.

Repatriation also raises other issues. It is a violation of a museum's public trust to give away materials that it has held legally and at public expense. A similar violation is involved when a museum has received these materials from a private donor or at a private donor's expense. In particular, such action ignores many Indians who donated or sold materials on the understanding that these items would go into a permanent repository for the benefit of future generations of Indians.

An entire field of academic study may be put out of business. It has become impossible for a field archaeologist to conduct a large-scale excavation in the United States with-out violating some law or statute. The result is that archaeology students are now steered away from digs where they might actually find some American Indian remains. American archaeology is an expiring subject of study—one in which new students no longer choose to specialize. Instead, they specialize in the archaeology of other countries, where they will be allowed to conduct their research and have some assurance that their collections will be preserved.

Scientific disciplines are not immune to change, but the scientific ideal is that these changes are the consequence of new discoveries and theories driven by developments internal to science, and not imposed from without. It may therefore be questioned whether the repatriation movement is not a massive invasion of the freedom of scholarly and scientific disciplines to define their own goals and chart their own course.

What the activists know about the Indians' past depends almost entirely on the records of European explorers, missionaries, and settlers, and on the studies of past and present historians, ethnographers, anthropologists, and archaeologists. These scholars and scientists often thought of themselves as helping the American Indian to preserve his heritage. A great many Indians, past and present, shared or share that conviction. It would be interesting to know whether a majority of living persons of Indian descent actually favor reburial or the continued preservation, display, and study of Indian remains and artifacts.

From Archaeological Ethics, edited by Karen D. Vitelli, 1996, pp. 209-213. Published by AltaMira Press, A Division of Sage Publications, Inc. Originally from Archaeology magazine, November/December 1994. © 1994 by Joan Meighan. Reprinted with permission of the Archaeological Institute of America.

Ownership and Control of Ethnographic Materials

SJOERD R JAARSMA

U of Nijmegen/Papua Heritage Foundation

What has changed most about ethnographic research in the present age of globalization is not the way academic anthropologists deal with the communities they study, but how members of those communities deal with their anthropologists. A few years ago, I met with a group of anthropologists, ethnomusicologists, archivists and librarians to consider the problems relating to the disposition of ethnographic field materials. We concluded that basic questions like "Who owns the information?" and "Should everything be accessible?" should be reconsidered not only by academic anthropologists, but also by the communities being studied.

Ever since fieldwork became the preferred approach to gathering ethnographic information, the quality and quantity of research data being gathered has increased radically. Present-day students have both the training and equipment to make the most of their temporary stay in the field. Yet, the way we relate to the people we study has changed little since the first anthropologists left for the field in colonial days. Most fieldwork still follows the same general pattern. Anthropologists go into the field and gather their material, usually explaining that it will be used to write a book. Having gathered the material needed, they leave, establishing their careers on the

merits of the research done. While these days a copy of the thesis written is sent back to local informants, research data will remain under the anthropologists' care and control. Access to raw field materials rarely is granted to others, including members of the study community, during an anthropologist's lifetime.

Indigenous Access and Control

Until recently, people in the field rarely were able to follow up on any of the issues dealt with in the published research results, let alone seek access to the data gathered by the researcher. Equally, they were unable to point out the lack of balance in "services rendered" that surrounds this pattern of research. Even today, with more rules and regulations in place, local grip on field research remains limited. Unless the local community sponsors the research being done, it has few means for managing the flow of research information.

Two issues that academic anthropologists can no longer ignore stand out. First, the flow of information going in and out of any fieldwork location is, as a rule, hugely unbalanced. Second, very little thought has been given so far to control over and access to the data gathered while in the field.

A world growing ever smaller makes it easier for anthropologists to visit the field and keep in contact. Likewise, informants may keep in touch with the anthropologists via phone, email, visits, or communication through family or friends. The Internet allows people to access materials even from the field. The ease with which information can be shared makes the control over data gathered by individual anthropologists an ever more relevant issue.

Value of Information

Ethnographic information, like all information, has a market value, even if anthropologists are not used to thinking in such terms. Although ethnobiologists appreciate the need to establish an equitable tradeoff based on the value placed on indigenous knowledge concerning plants and medicines, the opposite is well-known too. First World musicians still harvest indigenous songs written down by ethnomusicologists to include in their compositions. Sampled compositions sell millions of CDs without revenues flowing to the original indigenous artists or mention being made of their contributions.

Ethnography affects the nature of indigenous knowledge itself. Anthropologists' published materials place indigenous knowledge, previously protected by individual ownership, in the public domain. For example, written records of land ownership differ from "traditional" oral discourse on such matters. Access to the written records by anthropologists shifts the power balance inherent in the use of knowledge. Here, too, the disposition of control over and access to indigenous knowledge is of paramount importance.

Effects on Anthropology

Recently indigenous peoples have become aware that they have a right to exercise control over their own cultural resources. Conferences like the 1993 First International Conference on the Cultural and Intellectual Property Rights of Indigenous Peoples sponsored by the UN provide a forum on these rights. Similarly, the 1991 Native American Graves Protection Act has established indigenous control over ethnographic artifacts in museums and the disposition of burial sites. Such rights will only expand further.

What does this mean for anthropological fieldwork? With anthropologists studying ever more critically aware and emancipated communities, they will be held accountable for their responsibilities concerning the data gathered. Laws will circumscribe rights to the data gathered. Though not written with anthropologists in mind, these laws apply to the anthropologists' research. Similarly, a foreseeable increase in sponsoring of research by indigenous communities themselves will affect the way anthropologists deal with data.

Needed Action

The field data presently in the possession of anthropologists and stored by them in archives and libraries should be made more readily accessible. Implicitly, this means sorting out and protecting ownership rights to knowledge recorded in the field notes, sifting out potentially harmful and damaging information and safeguarding future research interests. This is best done by the original researcher, as archivists and librarians, or even fellow anthropologists, rarely share the knowledge necessary to do this properly.

It is better to plan all this at the start of fieldwork than put it in place afterward. Therefore not only the setup of field-work, but also training for fieldwork, should be reviewed in such a way that safeguarding the informant's interests in the data becomes second nature to anthropologists.

Anthropologists are entrusted to use and work with other people's knowledge, but "ownership" remains limited to what they add as interpretation. They have to acknowledge that the communities being studied have equal if not greater legitimate rights to the ethnographic materials gathered. These rights are only mitigated by an obligation to prevent damage deriving from any access provided to the material. If the academic community does not make itself and the data anthropologists gather accessible and accountable, it may eventually be forced to do so.

Sjoerd R Jaarsma specializes in the history of anthropology and comparative ethnography of New Guinea. He discusses the implications of indigenous rights to ethnographic knowledge and field materials. Also see Jaarsma's edited volume Handle with Care: Ownership and Control of Ethnographic Materials *(2002).*

Last Word on Kennewick Man?

A court ruling on the controversial remains pleases archaeologist James Chatters.

On August 30, Judge John Jelderks of the U.S. District Court of Oregon ruled against the government's 1996 decision that declared the 9,400-year-old skeleton known as Kennewick Man to be Native American, a classification which would require the remains to be turned over to a coalition of tribes for reburial. James Chatters, archaeologist and author of *Ancient Encounters: Kennewick Man and the First Americans* (New York: Simon and Schuster, 2001), identified the remains when they were found on the banks of Washington's Columbia River in 1996. He talked with ARCHAEOLOGY about the recent ruling and the larger issues raised by Kennewick Man.

What was your reaction to Jelderks' ruling?

I experienced a tremendous feeling of relief, followed by a sense of validation that taking a stand for science, and advocacy for Kennewick Man, had been the right things to do. The decision validated all that the plaintiffs [eight scientists who wished to study the remains], attorneys, and I have gone through for the past six years.

What do you think of the media coverage surrounding this issue?

It's been mixed. Some media outlets have shown a clear understanding of the issues and intent of the lawsuit and are consistently accurate in their reporting. Others, particularly tabloids, political talk shows, and many prominent eastern newspapers, fixated on the "Science-versus-Indians" angle and clung to the erroneous idea that Kennewick Man was Caucasian and that we wanted to study him for that reason. Several big papers, including the *New York Times* and *Washington Post,* really attacked us on the red herring of race.

Why do you think race became such a flash point with Kennewick Man?

You really should ask the people for whom that was an issue. To me, the significant point of the discovery is that Kennewick Man and his contemporaries differ greatly from all present-day peoples. It reopens the question of how and by whom the Americas were peopled. Race is an issue of the present that should not be extended into the distant past.

You were investigated by the FBI for possible involvement in the disappearance of some of the Kennewick Man bones, which were later found in the local sheriff's office. Can you tell us something about that experience?

I only learned of the investigation indirectly and was never questioned. Even so, it was very intimidating. At any one time I'm working on collections of bones for half a dozen or more projects, any or all of which agents could have seized in their quest for the missing femur fragments.

What's your position on the Native American Grave Protection and Repatriation Act (NAGPRA)?

We need a law like NAGPRA. We can't silently condone desecration of Indian graves and keep the bones of people's known kin on museum shelves and expect the general populace to see living Native Americans as fellow human beings. But NAGPRA is being misapplied as a license for tribes to take control of any and all early skeletons, and, as we are seeing increasingly, any and all archaeological materials.

When do you think repatriation and reburial are appropriate?

When any fair person would agree that the culture practiced by the dead was directly antecedent to that of a modern tribe, that tribe is most likely to know how the deceased would like to be treated in death. But that connection only rarely goes back beyond a few hundred to a thousand years. For the preceding 6,000 years, when no cultural link exists, the dead could be ancestors of anyone of Indian ancestry, including most Hispanics and a significant proportion of African Americans and Whites.

Where do you see Kennewick Man in another six years?

I'd like to see him securely preserved, like the Cro-Magnon and Neanderthal fossils of Europe, as a national treasure at the Smithsonian, where future generations could learn from him through ever-improving technologies. But if this case is appealed, or if the federal government or tribes attempt to bypass Jelderks' decision by changing regulations or the law, he might remain in limbo, or dissolve underground.

Tales from a Peruvian Crypt

The looting of a prehistoric pyramid stimulates an operation in salvage archeology, with unexpected scientific dividends

Walter Alva and Christopher B. Donnan

Walter Alva, a native of Peru, has participated in numerous excavations on that country's north coast and is the director of the Museo Brüning at Lambayeque. Coauthor Christopher B. Donnan is a professor of anthropology and director of the Fowler Museum of Cultural History at the University of California, Los Angeles. They are the coauthors of Royal Tombs of Sipán *(Los Angeles: Fowler Museum of Cultural History, University of California, 1993).*

In the fertile river valleys that relieve Peru's arid coastal plain, mud-brick pyramids stand as the most visible evidence of the prehistoric Moche civilization, which flourished between the first and eighth centuries A.D. Rising out of agricultural fields in the Moche River valley, the massive Pyramid of the Sun was the largest structure ever built in South America. With a ramp that led up to small buildings on its flat summit, it stood about 135 feet high and sprawled over 12.5 acres at its base. It once contained more than 130 million sun-dried bricks. Some of it has eroded away naturally while part was demolished in the seventeenth century by Spanish entrepreneurs in search of rich burials or other treasures.

About ninety-five miles north of the Pyramid of the Sun, in the Lambayeque River valley, the Moche cemeteries and three pyramids near the village of Sipán have long been the target of looters. Over the years they have dug many deep holes with picks and shovels in hopes of locating intact tombs containing ceramic vessels, shell and stone beads, and rarer ornaments of silver and gold. By November 1986, they had nearly exhausted the cemeteries, and one group of treasure seekers decided to focus on the smallest pyramid. Working at night to avoid police detection, they dug a series of holes, but found little of value. Then, on the night of February 16, 1987, at a depth of about twenty-three feet, they suddenly broke into one of the richest funerary chambers ever looted, the tomb of an ancient Moche ruler.

The looters removed several sacks of gold, silver, and gilded copper artifacts. They also took some ceramic vessels, but they broke and scattered many others in their haste. Almost immediately the looters quarreled over the division of the spoils, and one of them tipped off the police. The authorities were able to seize some of the plundered artifacts, but only a pitiful amount was salvaged from the find. The rest disappeared into the hands of Peruvian collectors or was illegally exported for sale in Europe, Japan, and the United States.

Building on civilizations that preceded them in coastal Peru, the Moche developed their own elaborate society, based on the cultivation of such crops as corn and beans, the harvesting of fish and shellfish, and the exploitation of other wild and domestic resources. They had a dense, socially stratified population, with large numbers of workers devoted to the construction and maintenance of irrigation canals, pyramids, palaces, and temples. Their lords apparently received food and commodities from their subjects and distributed them to lesser nobles and to the potters, weavers, metalworkers, and other artisans who created luxury objects for the elite. In sculptures, decorated ceramics, and murals, archeologists have glimpsed many complex scenes of Moche life, including hunting, combat, and ceremonial practices.

The luxury items from Sipán that were confiscated by the police, including hollow gold beads of various shapes and sizes, hinted at the magnificence of the plundered burial, which must have belonged to one of the Moche elite. More fortune-hunters descended on the site in search of overlooked valuables. They hacked at the tomb walls and sifted through the excavated dirt. By the time the police secured the area, little was left except a boot-shaped hole. Nevertheless, with armed guards stationed around the clock, we hastily organized an archeological survey to learn everything possible of scientific value (author Walter

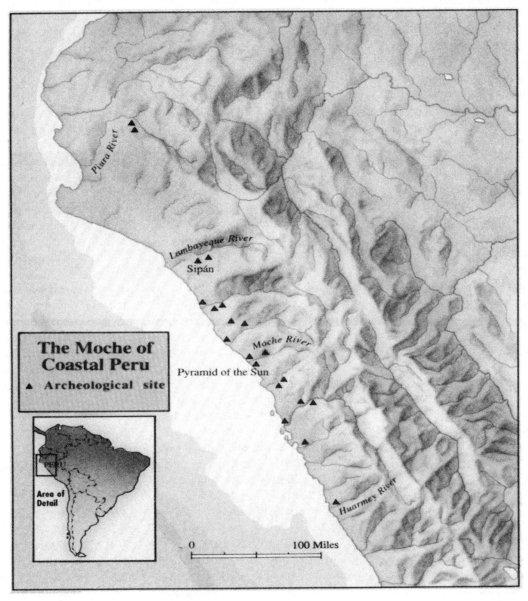

The Moche of Coastal Peru
▲ Archeological site

Area of Detail

0   100 Miles

Joe LeMonnier

Alva directed the project; coauthor Christopher B. Donnan was one of the many participants).

We began by making a contour map of the three pyramids and what remained of their ramps and adjacent plazas. The small pyramid, where the tomb had been found, was riddled with looters' tunnels, but in some places, the piles of dirt they had excavated helped preserve the original contours. The tunnels also enabled us to examine the internal construction. The pyramid and the rest of the complex evidently had been built and rebuilt over a long period of time, undergoing many changes as the various parts were en-

larged. The small pyramid seems to have gone through six phases, beginning in the first century A.D. and ending about 300.

Although the burial chamber had been gouged out of shape, we were able to determine that it had originally been roofed with large wood beams, which had decomposed. To our great surprise, we were able to uncover some of the tomb's contents that had been missed by the original looters and the subsequent gleaners. Clearing along one side of the chamber, we found the remains of a large, gilded copper crown decorated with metal disks; four ceramic jars mod-

eled in the shape of human figures; and a copper mask with inlaid turquoise eyes. In excavating these, we also discovered a heavy copper scepter forty inches long, pointed at one end and bearing a three-dimensional architectural model on the other. The model depicted a platform with a balustrade, surrounding an open-front building with one back wall and a peaked roof supported by posts. Seventeen double-faced human heads decorated the roof ridge, while depicted in relief on the wall was a supernatural creature, half feline and half reptile, copulating with a woman on a crescent moon.

Knowing that the pyramid would be further plundered once we left, we decided to open up a new section to methodical excavation, choosing a ten-by-ten meter (1,076-square-foot) area near the summit. Here we came upon a place where the mud brick had been carved out and refilled in ancient times. Digging down, we found eight decomposed woodbeams, similar to those that had roofed the looted burial chamber. Buried beneath these, in the debris of what had been a small rectangular chamber, we found 1,137 ceramic bowls, jars, and bottles. They portrayed a variety of human figures: warriors holding war clubs and shields, nude prisoners with leash-like ropes around their necks, musicians with drums, and seated figures wearing beaded pectorals (biblike coverings). Some were arranged in symbolic tableaux, for example, musicians and prisoners ringing and facing noble personages.

As we removed the ceramics, we found several pieces of copper and, finally, a man's skeleton lying jack-knifed on its back, with chin, knees, and arms pulled in toward the torso. Since the Moche customarily buried their dead in a fully extended position, we interpreted this individual to be a sacrificial victim, whose body had been shoved into the small chamber as part of the ritual offering.

Even as these offerings were being excavated, we discovered a second, larger rectangular area that appeared to have been carved into the pyramid and refilled. As we carefully excavated this, we found, about thirteen feet below the original surface of the pyramid, the skeleton of a man wrapped in a cotton shroud. He lay stretched out on his back and wore a gilded copper helmet. Over the right forearm, which rested on his chest, was a round copper shield. A little below we found the remains of seventeen parallel beams that, we dared hope, lay over a major, undisturbed burial chamber.

The discoveries that subsequently emerged surpassed our dreams. Buried in the chamber were the remains of a wood coffin that contained the richest grave offerings ever to be excavated scientifically in the Western Hemisphere.

The body of a man between thirty-five and forty-five years of age had been laid to rest with a feathered headdress, banners of cloth with gilded copper decorations, beaded pectorals, nose ornaments and necklaces of gold and silver, ear ornaments of gold and turquoise, face coverings of gold, a gold backflap and a silver backflap that would have been hung from the belt, and countless other precious objects. In his right hand the deceased had held a gold and silver scepter topped with a large rattle, and in his left hand, a smaller scepter of cast silver. In relief on the rattle, which was shaped like an inverted pyramid, were scenes of an elaborately dressed warrior subjugating a vanquished opponent. The sculpted head of the smaller scepter echoed this theme.

Working six days a week, it took us four months to document and safely empty the delicate contents of the tomb. As our original budget became exhausted, we received some partial funding from a brewery and a truckload of noodles donated by a pasta manufacturer. At one point we were paying the fieldworkers with a combination of cash and noodles. We eventually secured new support from the Research Committee of the National Geographic Society and were able to proceed with further excavation.

All the while we had been working and moving equipment around the coffin burial, we had been walking only inches above hundreds of ceramic vessels, two sacrificed llamas, a dog, and the burials of two men, three women, and a child of nine or ten. Although we do not know this for sure, the men and the child might have been buried as sacrifices to accompany the principal figures. The remains of the females, however, were partly decomposed at the time they were placed in the tomb, as evident from the way the bones were somewhat jumbled. They had probably died years earlier and their remains maintained elsewhere until this final interment.

As we excavated the tomb and cataloged its contents, we couldn't help wondering who was the important personage buried there. The key to the answer was a major photographic archive of Moche sculpture and drawings at the University

of California at Los Angeles. As the tomb was being excavated, photographs of the objects were sent to UCLA for comparative study.

Many of the objects in the coffin suggested the man buried there was a warrior. The archive of Moche art contains hundreds of depictions from which we can reconstruct a sequence of Moche militarism and ceremonial activity. We can see processions of warriors carrying war clubs, spears, and spear throwers, perhaps on their way to battle. We can see warriors in combat, apparently away from settled areas. The essence of Moche combat appears to have been the expression of individual valor, in which warriors engaged in one-on-one combat, seeking to vanquish, rather than kill, an opponent. The victor is often shown hitting his opponent on the head or upper body with the war club, while the defeated individual is depicted bleeding from his nose or losing his headdress or other parts of his attire. Sometimes the victor grasps his adversary by the hair and removes his nose ornament or slaps his face.

As far as we can tell, the Moche warriors fought with one another, not against some foreign enemy. Once an opponent was defeated, he was stripped of some or all of his clothing and a rope was placed around his neck. The victor made a bundle of the prisoner's clothing and weapons and tied it to his own war club as a trophy. After a public parading of the spoils, the prisoners were arraigned before a high-status individual and finally brought back to the Moche settlements or ceremonial precincts. There the priests and their attendants sacrificed them, cutting their throats and drinking the blood from tall goblets. The bodies were then dismembered and the heads, hands, and feet tied individually with ropes to create trophies.

Many representations of the sacrifice ceremony exist in Moche art. Although they vary, not always depicting all personages in the ceremony, apparently three principal priests and one priestess were involved, each associated with specific garments and ritual paraphernalia. The most important was the "warrior priest," generally depicted with a cres-cent-shaped nose ornament, large circular ear ornaments, a warrior backflap, a scepter, and a conical helmet with a crescent-shaped ornament at its peak. A comparison of these and other details with the contents of the tomb convinced us that the individual buried there was just such a warrior priest.

When the sacrifice ceremony was first identified in Moche art, in 1974, no one could be sure it was a real practice, as opposed to a mythical event. Now we had archeological evidence that this was an actual part of Moche life. Here was one of the individuals who presided over the sacrifices. Further, because the limited numbers of objects salvaged from the looted tomb were similar to some of those we had excavated, we could conclude that the looted tomb also must have belonged to a warrior priest.

As if this were not enough, during the excavation of the warrior priest's tomb, we located another suspected tomb elsewhere on the pyramid. We held off excavation until work on the earlier find was nearly complete. The knowledge we gained made it easier to anticipate the sequence of excavation. Again we found the residue of a plank coffin containing the rich burial of a man between thirty-five and forty-five years old. Among his grave goods was a spectacular headdress ornament of gilded copper, in the form of the head and body of an owl from which arched long banks with suspended bangles, representing the feathered wings. Nearby we found the remains of four other individuals: a male between fourteen and seventeen years of age, two females in their late teens or early twenties, and an eight- to ten-year-old child. Buried with the child were a dog and a snake.

The contents of this tomb were only a little less lavish than those of the warrior priest. They suggest that the principal individual was another of the priests depicted in the sacrifice ceremony—one we call the "bird priest." The major clue was the large owl headdress. He was also buried with a copper cup near his right hand, similar in proportion to the cups portrayed in pictures of the sacrifice ceremony.

Having identified these individuals as participants in the sacrifice ceremony, we began to wonder if such ceremonies took place in Sipán itself. The answer was soon revealed when, about eleven yards from the bird priest's tomb, we found several small rooms that contained hundreds of ceramic vessels, human and llama bones, and miniature ornaments and implements, mixed with ash and organic residues. Among the human remains were hands and feet, quite possibly the trophies taken from dismembered sacrificial victims. Altogether these looked to be the residue of sacrifice ceremonies, which the Moche apparently carried out at Sipán, as no doubt they did at their other centers.

The looted tomb, the two excavated tombs, and the sacrificial offerings all seem to date to about A.D. 290. While excavating the offerings, we found a fourth, somewhat earlier tomb containing the remains of a man between forty-five and fifty-five years old, also richly endowed with grave goods, including a necklace of gold beads in the form of spiders on their webs, anthropomorphic figures of a crab and a feline, scepters, an octopus pectoral with gilded copper tentacles, and numerous other ornaments and objects. Nearby we found the body of a young, sixteen- to eighteen-year-old woman next to a sacrificed llama. This tomb may also have belonged to a warrior priest, but not all the identifying elements are there. Possibly, this is simply because it dates to an earlier period than the depictions we have of the sacrifice ceremony, which are all after A.D. 300.

Moche civilization collapsed suddenly, sprobably as a result of one or more of the natural cataclysms that periodically devastate coastal Peru—earthquake, flooding, or drought. The Moche had no writing system, so they left no records we can hope to decipher. They disappeared before Europeans reached the New World and could leave us eyewitness accounts. Yet with the scientific excavation of these royal tombs, we have gained an intimate portrait of some of their most powerful lords. Work at Sipán continues, now at a promising location near the tomb of the bird priest. As we dig more deeply, we look forward to our next encounter.

Reprinted with permission from *Natural History*, May 1994, pp. 26-30, 33-34. © 1994 by the American Museum of Natural History.

Guardians
of the
Dead

Peru's citizens' brigades patrol a coastal landscape in
an effort to curb a growing national industry—looting.

by ROGER ATWOOD

ALEAN MAN IN HIS 50S with skin-burnished from a life-time working in sugar cane fields, Gregorio Becerra remembers the days when his father used to bring home ancient ceramic pots to their home in the village of Úcupe. Birds, faces, fruits, animals—the whole pantheon of Moche pottery themes stood on their living room shelf, where his father would place the perfectly preserved vessels he and his buddies dug up. "Everyone had a few pots in his house. They were nice decorations," says Becerra.

But sometime around 1990, all that changed. "It became a business," he recalls. "Outsiders came. They came from the city, and you'd see them out in the hills digging up everything they could find. They'd take it all away and sell it."

And so the modern looting industry came to little Úcupe and a hundred villages like it up and down the coast of northern Peru. People who used to excavate pots as a back-lot hobby or family activity at Holy Week, as much a part of local social life as fishing or football, watched first with bafflement and then anger as professional grave robbers descended on their lands to search for pieces to supply the international market for Peruvian antiquities.

Poor, neglected, hurt by the fall of sugar prices, these villages suddenly found themselves living literally on top of a commodity hotter than sugar ever was: Moche ceramics from the first millennium A.D. that, for a time, had collectors in their thrall, fetching prices in New York that for the best pieces could surpass $30,000.

Now Becerra is the leader of his village's *grupo de protección arqueológica,* or *la grupa,* a citizens' patrol armed with binoculars, a dirt bike, one revolver, and one shotgun but whose most important weapon is the eyes and ears of people living in the village's adobe houses. The brigade's mission is to stop people from occupying the land and plundering what lies beneath it. The patrol chases away bands of looters, or surrounds them, seizes their tools—shovels, poles, buckets—and ties up their wrists with rope until the police come.

> The Brüning Museum warehouse is filled with Moche and Chimú ceramics excavated by archaeologists, seized by patrols, or donated by guilt-stricken collectors.

Walter Alva, director of the new Museum of the Royal Tombs of the Lord of Sipán in the town of Lambayeque, 30 miles north of Úcupe, organized eight such patrols in the early 1990s in response to the phenomenal growth of commercial looting in the Moche heartland. In doing so, he took a cue from rural Peru's long tradition of ragtag peasant militias known as *rondas campesinas,* which have fought scourges ranging from cattle rustlers to Shining Path Maoist guerrillas. This time the enemy was looters prospecting for ancient art, and it was ironically Alva's own 1987 excavation of the tombs at Sipán that helped inspire the plundering.

On February 6 of that year, looters digging at Sipán's burial mound, or *huaca,* struck a tomb where a Moche lord had been buried around A.D. 300. They carried out about a dozen rice sacks full of gold and silver artifacts, somewhere between 200 and 300 objects in all, and smashed or discarded hundreds more either inadvertently or because they didn't think they were good enough to sell. Police stopped the pillage and notified Alva, who, under constant harassment from townspeople who wanted to ransack the site, began excavating where the looters had left off. He found a dozen more tombs, two as rich in artifacts as the looted one. Alva's excavations brought new insights into the social complexity of the Moche, who ruled the north coast from about A.D. 100 to 700.

Meanwhile the looted artifacts had already hit the market, whetting the appetite of collectors as never before. Once an exotic niche product, Peruvian artifacts became almost overnight one of the hottest items in the international antiquities trade. "It was a gold rush," recalls Alva. "It's been a constant struggle against looters ever since." More has been destroyed in Peru in the past 40 years than in the previous 400, he claims.

I HAD COME TO ÚCUPE because I wanted to see if what Alva and his followers were doing was actually effective in stopping the rampant looting.

Archaeologist Carlos Wester, who helped Alva and Alva's late wife, Susana Meneses, develop the patrols and is now acting director of the Brüning National Archaeological Museum in Lambayeque, led me to the top of an unmolested 1,800-year-old Moche *huaca* less than a mile from Úcupe. As such mounds go it was pretty small, maybe three stories high, overlooking the *algarrobo*·trees, grazing goats, and the village in the distance.

"The patrols have really worked," said Wester. "If you come here to loot, they'll chase you out before the police even get here. People have become aware of the value of preserving the *huacas*. Inside this one, there are probably some good things. Someday we'll excavate it, but until we do it's well protected."

In Úcupe, Wester introduced me to Becerra and another patrol leader, Gilberto Romero. I returned by bus a few days later to see the patrol in action. The road to Úcupe passed through a moonscape of barren hills before reaching the lazy Zaña River where the women of Úcupe were washing clothes while children splashed among water lilies and goats nibbled weeds by the banks. The village itself is a collection of single-story brick and adobe houses along the main road; dirt streets lead away through farms and sand dunes to the Pacific coast a few miles away.

Romero met me at the bus stop. A man with a gravelly voice and a sleepy smile, his manner was so mild that I was surprised to learn he doubled as a security guard for the local sugar cooperative and, as such, was licensed to carry a gun. He is the only member of the patrol who regularly carries a weapon, although he told me that he had never shot directly at looters. "This isn't war," he said.

Becerra, Romero, and I hired a motorcycle fitted with a passenger seat wide enough for the three of us. With a young driver named Julio, we bumped along a rutted dirt road past fields of spicy red pepper plans and sugar cane. Now and then Romero would point out a bare hill and explain that it was not a hill. It was another *huaca,* weathered by many centuries of wind and sun. "We have virgin *huacas,* never been touched and known only to us," said Romero, shouting above the sound of the engine.

A Chavín-era wall, dating from about 200 B.C., was excavated in the 1980s. It was later reburied to protect its priceless murals from the elements. Patrols now guard it from pillagers, who would cut it up and sell the pieces to dealers in Lima.

The Úcupe *grupa* was created in July 1994, Romero told me. "There are about 20 of us active in the *grupa*, but directly or indirectly I would say 90 percent of the people in the town collaborate with us. There are always a few who still want to dig up pots to sell, but we keep an eye on them. If we see somebody looting, we call the [Brüning] museum, and it calls teh police. If the police can't get here fast enough, we hold them ourselves. A month ago we detained three looters and their tools. We let down our guard for an hour and before we knew it hey were digging. It's like that here. You go to lunch and you come back, and there they are, digging. It's always people from outside, mosly from Cayaltí."

The market town of Cayaltí, with a population of about 10,000, lies 12 miles northeast of Úcupe. It is built around a rambling, wooden plantation mansion with peeling yellow paint. In the late 1960s, a left-wing government confiscated the house and the surrounding sugar plantations and turned them over to a workers' cooperative. Thirty years later the cooperative went bankrupt, and residents say the town has been struggling ever since. "No jobs here. Nothing to do," said a young man in the town square.

Cayaltí is known throughout the region as a looting center, a town where plundered antiquities are bought and sold with impunity. It's a busy town of woodworking shops and stands selling pirated videos, where fruit sellers and prostitutes in clingy black pants stand in the street and little cafes sell sandwiches and warm Cokes. One day as Wester and I drove into town, he pointed to two men walking beside a horse-drawn cart. "The older one, he's been arrested several times for looting," he said. "We know who he is."

Social hierarchy in Cayaltí is no longer based on sugar but on loot, with grimy tomb-diggers at the bottom, small-time dealers above them, and at the top, antiquities traders who sell to Peruvian and occasionally European collectors who come to town to buy. Two carpentry shops serve as fronts for the antiquities business. A taxi stand at the edge of town is known as a distribution center.

I wandered alone through Cayaltí, posing as a buyer and asking around for *antiguedades*. It didn't take long before a dealer led me to an alley behind his house, where he offered me point-bottomed Inka pots, a broken Moche portrait vessel, and an exquisite little ceramic jar no bigger than a perfume bottle in the shape of a spondylus seashell. All freshly dug up, he told me. (I bought an Inka pot and the broken portrait vessel for the equivalent of $3 each and took them to Alva at the National Museum in Lima, where he confirmed they were authentic. I donated them to the museum.) The dealer wanted to know if I was a museum director. Like loot sellers everywhere, he boasted that he sold his best pieces to museums. The son of the late owner of Lima's Gold Museum, he told me, occasionally came to town in a big black car to see what he had to offer.

The hills outside Cayaltí are pockmarked with holes left by looters and strewn with human bones, empty water bottles, and worthless bits of ancient textile. *"Aquí todo el pueblo huaquea"* (everybody loots here), the dealer told me, including the former president of Cayaltí's sugar cooperative, who was arrested in 1996 along with four other men for looting.

The people of Úcupe speak with disgust about places like Cayaltí. "No respect for their ancestors," an Úcupe woman told me as we waited for a bus. Archaeologists and the brigade have made the people of Úcupe more aware of their cultural heritage. "When I was a boy, people knew nothing about the importance of these objects we found," said Becerra. "We didn't know what the pre-Columbian cultures were. Moche, Chimú, Chavín, we'd never heard those names. Now everyone knows them. They teach them to the children in school."

Úcupe and Cayaltí are also divided by a bitter land feud. Farmers in tranquil Úcupe fear that Cayaltí people will descend on their lands and then petition a judge for legal title. Whole towns are born this way in Peru. Squatters take over idle private land by the light of the moon, and months or years later they ask that their settlement be incorporated as a town.

"People come from Cayaltí saying they want to work on the farms," said Romero. "Some of them have family members here. But to us, everyone who comes from Cayaltí is a looter." Becerra added, "We have extinguished looting in this area, because after the looters come the cattle rustlers, the thieves, and the land invaders. All the bad elements."

Some 350 people are now actively involved in the brigades. Alva calculates they have seized about 3,200 objects from looters. He also knows their efforts have pushed the problem elsewhere. Partly because of police and *grupa* pressure, and partly because the tastes of international collectors have changed, the professionals are moving south.

IT'S TOUGH WORKING in the north these days. You can get arrested," says 23-year-old Robin. In Italy he would be a *tombarolo*, in Guatemala an *estelero*; in Peru he's a *huaquero*, a professional grave robber who has been digging up tombs almost every night since his early teens. He loves his job and lives in a small brick house with his wife and two daughters in a town north of Lima. He earns a little money on the side driving a taxi.

Robin and his buddies now work mostly in the Cañete area south of Lima, where there are no citizens' patrols, less police interference, and abundant ancient textiles of the kind that bring big bucks on the international art market—$10,000 for good ones, a quarter of a million for the very best. I met Robin and his colleagues through a collector friend. It took some persuading but he finally agreed to take me along on a nighttime raid. I told him I wouldn't buy anything or join in the digging. I just wanted to watch and take notes. They agreed.

We met late in the afternoon and took a bus south. There were four of us: Robin, two other looters named Remi and Harry, and me, a 39-year-old American reporter who drew a lot of stares as we crowded onto the bus with armfuls of shovels and tools. We got out at an empty stretch of highway some 80 miles south of Lima and walked for nearly an hour across cotton fields illuminated by moonlight. A few dogs barked but we encountered no one as we walked. Eventually we came to a tree. Sitting on its gnarled roots, we chewed coca leaves. About 100 feet away rose the Inkaera *huaca* they were about to assault.

The looters drank cane liquor and talked about strange and beautiful things they had found over the years—perfectly preserved pots, color-spangled weavings, piles of human bones and skulls. Robin told of a weaving that bore the image of a huge condor with outstretched wings.

They also talked about the fickle spirits of the dead. The *huaca* was a living force, with jealousies and resentments, moments of generosity, and fits of spite. "If you act greedy, the *huaca* won't give you anything," said Robin. "You take too much, and it will close up and never give you anything again."

"But it warns you," added Remi. "When the coca leaf tastes sweet, the *huaca* is about to give you something."

The looters particularly liked this *huaca;* it was relatively untouched, and they knew, having dug into it before, that the tombs within were not too deep. But, unusual for the south coast, there was some police presence here. Police had chased them away before, and Robin only barely escaped arrest one night at a burial site in the area. They told me the ground rules: no flash pictures (the flash might attract police), make as little noise as possible, and if you must talk, whisper.

I followed them to the *huaca* and sat on the chalky surface as they began their work. Shaped like a kidney, it stood about 40 feet high and stretched a quarter of a mile end to end. First they plunged metal poles into its smooth, bald surface to locate tombs. When they hit nothing but sand, they moved on. If the pole suddenly met no resistance, that meant they had hit an empty pot, probably within a tomb. And if the pole made a certain muffled crack, that meant they had hit human remains. The excruciating crack of metal hitting bone made me recoil.

After an hour of sinking their poles and making mental notes of where they had hit bodies, they began to dig—fast. In 15 minutes, they excavated a hole six feet deep; in half an hour, they had broken into tombs ten feet down. These seemed to belong to Inka commoners, simple graves with gourds containing peanuts or bird bones, woven bags, and coils of string. There were knitting instruments, broken ceramics, a child's tiny bone flute with a string attached. I looked at all this in the moonlight, fascinated, disgusted and saddened. They couldn't sell this stuff, and they were throwing it into heaps of debris.

"We know what people are buying and what they don't want," said Robin. "We leave a lot of stuff because we can't sell it. It's hard to sell ceramics these days. Too much of it is on the market. These days buyers want textiles and more textiles." They often get specific requests relayed from collectors through middlemen—customized looting.

Within a few hours they had ripped into half a dozen tombs and the remains of adults and children who had lain together for 500 years were scattered all over the *huaca*. The looters grasped human skulls by the hair and chucked them out like basketballs. They shoveled out bones, some with bits of desiccated human tissue still attached.

At about 4 A.M. they found what they wanted—an Inka weaving. At the bottom of a hole nine feet deep, using a flashlight, they could see the fabric wrapped around a bundle that surely contained human remains. In the light they could see the deep red and ocher of the fabric. "Look at those colors! We've got a good one," said Robin. "I'm going to dig around the sides, carefully so as not to damage the weaving. If you rip it out, you'll destroy it." Another half-hour of digging and he pulled the weaving free and clambered out of the pit. He held it up to the flashlight and shook it, releasing a cloud of dust. It was indeed a lovely piece, a design of red, yellow, blue, and beige diamonds. It was a shirt, almost perfectly intact, with a hole for the head and two for the arms. It probably belonged to a boy or a young man. The bones of the body it had wrapped lay at the bottom of the pit; a femur, a spine, a skull gazing up at the stars.

"This is the best thing we've found in two weeks," said Robin. They were all the more lucky because the pole had not pierced the fabric. They gathered their tools and put the weaving in a knapsack. As we walked back across the fields, they anxiously discussed how much money the textile might bring them. A thousand dollars, maybe $1,500.

As the sun came up we flagged down a bus making the all-night trip from Cuzco to Lima. Back in the small house where Remi lived, the men spread out the weaving on the dirt floor. They were tired but excited as they made calls with Robin's cell phone to find a buyer. By 9 A.M., they had one, a smuggler they knew only as Lucho, and asked him to come see it. "Believe me,

it's a good piece, *una belleza,*" said Robin. "We're not going to bring you all the way down here for something that's not worth it."

That was when I had to leave. I could not be present at the deal because Lucho might not like it. Would he be armed? I asked. No, he does not carry a weapon, but he is an important buyer and might feel uncomfortable having someone he doesn't know present, Robin explained.

The looters told me later that they asked for $1,500, but Lucho bargained them down to $1,000. The weaving would be on a plane out of Peru within days.

I had asked the looters how they felt about digging up bodies. "When you first start doing this, it makes you nervous," Remi said. "Digging up bones, you think you're going to incur a curse. But after a while it becomes easy. You don't even think about it."

"But," I inquired, "doesn't it bother you personally? I mean, how would you like it if someone dug up your grave and stole everything your family had put in it?" They looked at each other nervously, and then at me as if suddenly they wished I weren't there. Then Remi said, "Around here there is no other kind of work."

ROGER ATWOOD *is a journalist writing on the antiquities trade with a fellowship from the Alicia Patterson Foundation. He can be reached at atwoodsy@aol.com*

In a Box

The case of the ossuary and the rules of archeology

JOHN J. MILLER

THE final scene in *Raiders of the Lost Ark* shows workers boxing the Ark of the Covenant and wheeling it into the middle of an impossibly huge warehouse—an object of incomprehensible significance is lost forever. It's a bit of ironic humor at the end of a rollicking movie.

What's not funny, however, is that the same fate might have awaited the most interesting Biblical object to surface in some time, a first-century ossuary with a tantalizing inscription: "James, son of Joseph, brother of Jesus." If these words are authentic, they represent the earliest historical reference to Jesus outside of the Bible. And yet the most important professional organizations for scholars in the field of Biblical history have policies that ban them from studying the object or even acknowledging its existence.

That's because the ossuary—a limestone box that might have housed the bones of James—emerged from the antiquities market rather than an archeological excavation. Somebody had looted it and sold it. Robbing ancient sites is illegal everywhere, but it is not always against the law to traffic in old objects with a shadowy past. About 15 years ago, an Israeli collector of antiquities bought the James ossuary for a modest price. He didn't know of its importance until recently, when he let French epigraphist André Lemaire take a close look. Lemaire's conclusions vouching for its authenticity were released on October 21, and they have gripped the imagination of Christians (and others) around the globe.

The Archaeological Institute of America and the American Schools of Oriental Research would prefer that they hadn't. The AIA and ASOR publish the most influential scholarly journals in their field and host the most important conferences. They also have rules against taking note of objects that lack a legitimate provenance—these items can't be written about in their publications or discussed at their meetings, at least not until an unaffiliated journal has explored it first, breaking the embargo. It conveys a bizarre sense of moral purity, not unlike refusing to open a *Playboy* centerfold but peeking after it's been displayed. More critical, though, is that this attitude threatens to deprive us of real knowledge about the past.

Everybody who cares about the study of history agrees that the looting of archeological sites is a menace. There is nothing new about it. Ancient objects are looted because people and museums want to own them, and a robust trade in antiquities has arisen to meet these desires. But "the field of archeology is substantially injured by people who loot," says Patty Gerstenblith, a law professor at DePaul University and a former trustee of the AIA. "Collectors and dealers provide the incentive to engage in this practice." Colin Renfrew, a prominent archeologist at Cambridge, is even more blunt: "Collectors are the real looters."

In 1985, the Getty Museum bought a 2,500-year-old Greek statue without a provenance for an estimated $10 million. Does injecting so much cash into the antiquities trade actually promote looting? Surely it does. Yet there's no easy way to suppress it—and the hope that it might be eliminated is not realistic. The notion that a scholarly boycott can have any impact is sheer fantasy.

Items of unusual interest inevitably appear in the marketplace. In 1947, a Bedouin boy went searching for a lost goat in the hills near Qumran. He didn't find his goat, but he did come across a cave full of ancient manuscripts. In Bethlehem, he and a friend hocked a few of them for about $14. Other caves were eventually found to contain more than 800 manuscripts—and today the Dead Sea Scrolls are recognized as the most important cache of Hebrew and Aramaic documents ever uncovered. The Israeli government now owns most of them, and they are available for scholars to study—but only because a kid looking to make a buck (or a shekel) looted them and a few buyers knew they were valuable.

Archeologists would much rather find objects in the ground. For them, the context of a site is often more important than its content. "A piece of charcoal might be of greater importance than a hoard of gold coins," Avner Raban of the University of Haifa has written. Scholars want to know all sorts of things: How were the objects arranged, where did human hands last touch them, what's that charcoal doing there? Archeologists look for answers when they conduct scientific excavations. Just as a new car loses value the moment it leaves the lot, ancient objects lose archeological value when they're moved. Looters simply grab and run, which also diminishes the worth of a site as a whole: It is no longer a pristine conduit for information about the past. Imagine if the ossuary box had been discovered during a proper dig. There might have been bones inside. "Maybe somebody could have done a facial reconstruction of James, or even a DNA analysis," notes Larry Herr of the Canadian University College in Alberta. (Armenian Christians claim that James's bones rest in their Jerusalem cathedral.)

It may be unfortunate that professionals did not excavate the ossuary, but it is fortunate that the thing exists at all.

An archeologist didn't uncover the ossuary, so opportunities to learn more about it are gone. It will also have permanent doubters. According to one theory, the box itself is old but the inscription phony. "The only way to guarantee something's genuine is to dig it up," says Ellen Herscher, a Washington, D.C.-based archeologist affiliated with the AIA. Adds Gerstenblith, the DePaul professor, "The box [by itself] really doesn't tell us much we didn't already know because most people accept the historicity of Jesus."

It may be unfortunate that professionals did not excavate the ossuary, but it is fortunate that the thing exists at all. The precise relationship between Jesus and James is an old debate. Protestants tend to think they shared the same parents; Roman Catholic theologians, sticking to their belief in Mary's perpetual virginity,

have suggested that Jesus and James were cousins. The words on the box would seem to cast doubt on this latter interpretation, though it remains possible that Jesus and James were children of the same father but not the same mother (which is what the Eastern Orthodox Church teaches). At any rate, it gives scholars and the rest of us plenty to mull over.

But for an unconventional channel, the public might have remained in the dark about the box. André Lemaire published his research in *Biblical Archaeology Review,* a maverick magazine that ignores the dictates of the AIA and ASOR and presents scholarly information to interested lay readers. Its editor, Hershel Shanks, abhors looting—as well as the attitudes of the professional organizations. "Many academics like to vilify the antiquities market," says Shanks. "They need to realize that there are bad collectors and good collectors. The bad collectors are the ones who buy things and stash them in their basements. The good ones open their collections to researchers and eventually donate what they own to public institutions."

Demonizing collectors as a class simply increases the incentives for the good ones to turn bad and the bad ones to stay that way. It's no accident that the owner of the ossuary has chosen to remain anonymous. He's trying to be a good collector by letting the world know what he owns, but he also doesn't want to be attacked as a grave robber by academic archeologists.

Scorn for the antiquities trade may actually complicate the problems archeolo-

gists want to address. If the marketplace were legitimized, more collectors would conduct their business in the public eye. That would hurt forgers because buyers would place a greater emphasis on authenticated items.

The real answer is not simply to tolerate the market but to embrace it by permitting the direct sale of artifacts to the public. This is apostasy among many professional archeologists, but the benefits would be enormous. If they were allowed to sell some of what they dug up, they would have more money for the protection of existing sites and the exploration of new ones. Most looters are peasants trying to earn a little extra money; they might be just as glad to be hired as diggers at excavation sites.

This would solve another problem. Museums around the world are running short on space to store all the items that archeologists unearth. The University of Arizona museum, for instance, has 20,000 pieces of pottery kept out of sight in two old buildings that lack proper environmental controls. "About a third of our collection has been damaged, and there are collections elsewhere that have been completely destroyed by this same process," said museum official Miriam Nickerson in the *Arizona Daily Star.* The situation is even more desperate in developing countries. It would make sense for them to discriminate between which objects must be held and which might be sold.

It's been said that archeologists handle priceless objects for poor pay. If they could attach a few price tags, though, we'd all wind up the richer for it.

From the *National Review*, November 25, 2002, pp. 26-28. © 2002 by National Review, Inc., 215 Lexington Avenue, New York, NY 10016. Reprinted by permission.

Land Can Be Divided. Histories Cannot.

By Amy Dockser Marcus

Even as Israelis and Palestinians move closer to reaching a final agreement on their territorial conflict, a new battlefield is emerging. This time the dispute is not over events of the past 50 years, but of the past 4,000.

Land can be divided—that, of course, will be the main topic of President Clinton's peace summit with Israeli Prime Minister Ehud Barak and Palestinian leader Yasser Arafat this week. But in an area that has seen so many different conquerors, it's much harder to parcel out history, especially the kind of history that touches not just on both groups' sense of national identity, but the core of their religious faiths. This history is suddenly up for reinterpretation now, given how scientific advances have transformed the discipline of archaeology. And the fight to control the past is just as volatile and dangerous as the fight to control the land, as I discovered on a visit to the Temple Mount in Jerusalem, where tensions are running high over an archaeological dispute.

The Muslim Waqf, or religious trust, has been digging outside of Solomon's Stables, an underground vault where a new mosque is being built. The Palestinians employed by the trust to excavate the area have disposed of thousands of tons of dirt—and, along with it, the Israelis claim, artifacts that date from the time King Solomon's Temple stood there.

Eilat Mazar, an Israeli archaeologist who is spearheading a lobbying effort among Israeli parliament members to halt the digging, says more is at stake here than the loss of important cultural artifacts: The Palestinians, she contends, are purposely trying to erase any presence of Jewish history from the mount. "They aren't interested in finds connected to any time earlier than the Islamic period and especially not any finds that relate to Judaism," Mazar says.

More than 100 miles away, at the Israeli city of Kaztrin on the Golan Heights, it is the Israelis who are accused of being insensitive to another people's past. Archaeologists have been reconstructing an ancient synagogue, and, in doing so, removing a later, Mamluk-era mosque. The mosque will be recorded in any reports that the archaeologists publish about the Kaztrin finds, but this part of Katzrin's past isn't readily available to foreign tourists or to Israelis who visit the site, which focuses on representing early Jewish village life. "Unless the tour guide at the site says 'There was also a Mamluk Muslim village here,' the public won't see it," says Ann Killebrew, an archaeologist at the University of Haifa who helped excavate the site. "The people in charge of sites choose what they think is important and ignore the rest. In that way, history is removed."

Archaeology, like politics, is complicated. Many sites, like Solomon's Stables and Katzrin, are about more than one past. Ancient cities were often built on top of the ruins of another. Joel Singer, the lead negotiator of the Israeli-Palestinian peace process in the mid-1990s, explained to me that Israel tried to keep control over sites of importance in Jewish history, but it wasn't easy. "Ancient sites often have several layers," Singer says. "One can be Jewish, another Muslim, a third from the Crusader period. How do you decide how to divide this?"

After the Israelis signed peace treaties in the early '90s with the Palestinians and Jordanians, many archaeologists had high hopes that a more complete history of the region could be told: Instead of working within their own countries, they would be able to cross borders and compare finds. And while some of this kind of exchange has happened—resulting in new areas of inquiry and radical rewritings of biblical history—all too often the various countries have substituted a cultural war for the territorial one, feeling increasingly threatened by the spectacle of each other's historical pageants.

Rarely are the excavations free of political overtones. In recent years, the Palestinians have been trying to establish their links to the tribes that originally lived in the part of Canaan that the Bible calls the Promised Land. The Palestinian Ministry of Culture sponsored a Canaanite festival two years ago, and a popular Palestinian newspaper ran a lengthy series detailing Palestinian links with the Canaanites. At Bir Zeit University in Ramallah, visitors can see Palestinian pottery collected by archaeology students.

The researchers say that Canaanite potters working thousands of years ago used the same ceramic styles and clay sources as modern Palestinian potters, demonstrating the cultural continuity between the two groups.

Many Israelis see this differently—not simply as a Palestinian attempt to document ancient links with the land, but as a challenge to Israeli identity at a time when the country is taking security risks by giving back territory. And in recent months, the Israelis have started to fight back, sponsoring seminars to counter the idea that many biblical tales lack archaeological proof.

The more excavation that goes on, though, the more biblical stories are being held up to scrutiny. In Egypt, some archaeologists are digging at a cemetery belonging to the workers who constructed the pyramids—and coming up with an alternative narrative to the story of Exodus. There's no historical record of the event, beyond the biblical tale of the Jews' flight from slavery in Egypt to freedom, which has long been of intense interest to tourists. The story has never been viewed with much enthusiasm among Egyptians, though. "Exodus is not an Egyptian story," explains Kent Weeks, an American archaeologist affiliated with American University in Cairo.

Now a more complicated picture is emerging from the discovery, just a few miles from the Sphinx, of tombs filled with small statues, engravings and elaborate hieroglyphics. The picture is not the familiar story of enslaved laborers cringing under a pharaoh's whip, but of local Egyptian workers who enjoyed high status. Some of the inscriptions reveal that workers served as witnesses in business contracts, a role slaves were barred from fulfilling. Forensic examinations of the skeletal remains indicated that they were well cared for.

Zahi Hawass, the official keeper of the pyramids, tried to explain to me how much biblical narratives and ancient traditions have erroneously shaped outsiders' perceptions of Egypt. He recalled Menachem Begin's visit as Israeli prime minister to Egypt more than 15 years ago, and still bristled at how, upon seeing the pyramids, Begin turned to his hosts and said excitedly, "We built those, you know." Hawass told me "no one wants to

acknowledge that the Egyptians built the pyramids," adding that the discovery of the cemetery will allow the Egyptians to show that the pyramids were built by artisans helped by peasants who were drafted into service.

Every site is a potential source of tension.

Similar emotions fire the Israelis and Palestinians in their eight-year fight over the control of other biblical archaeological sites. Hamdan Taha, who heads the department of antiquities in the Palestinian National Authority, sits in his Ramallah office surrounded by pottery shards, antique oil lamps and other finds and pulls out a map of the West Bank. He points to Sabastiyah, site of the capital of the northern kingdom of Israel during biblical times and also a central site in the Roman era. Now a Palestinian village, Sabastiyah is in a section of the West Bank controlled by the Palestinians. But the ancient ruins, which tell of the comings and goings of many peoples over the course of history, remain under Israeli control. "We want to develop the site as a national park but we can't," says Taha, who envisions this as one of many important sites for Palestinian tourism. "It isn't logical to separate modern Sabastiyah from its history. We understand that we have to divide Palestine with the Israelis. We don't want to divide Palestine's history."

Taha insists that the Palestinians want to tell the stories of all the people who once lived on the land, including the Israelites. "We think it is time to do archaeology free from the pressure of ideology," he says, but then finds himself conceding that, as a Muslim, he thinks that Islamic Arab culture is the most important in Palestine.

In that light, every site is a potential source of tension. One morning I drove out to Mount Ebal, the place the Bible says Israel first became a nation, and is now a contested zone in the West Bank. It is formally under Palestinian political administration but still within Israeli security control.

The Israeli archaeologist excavating the site, Adam Zertal, has persuaded a European Christian group to contribute

money for the reconstruction of what he believes is an altar. He wants to open the area for Israeli tourism. Jewish settlers in the area are raising money to expand and improve the road leading there, hoping that even if land is returned to the Palestinians, the site will remain Israeli. "This is our past," says Shuki Levin, who was serving as the security head for the Jewish settlements in the region. "And our past should remain in our hands."

No one wants to see the history of their people's presence in the ancient Middle East written out of the narrative that is emerging from the latest archaeological discoveries. Until now, the Israelis have controlled the interpretation of most biblical sites in the contested areas of Jerusalem and the West Bank, but that is about to change. As more land comes under Palestinian control, so do more antiquities. The Palestinians have made it clear that they want all artifacts found in the West Bank returned to them. That includes ancient Hebrew and Aramaic manuscripts and other finds that directly relate to the Israeli historical narrative.

Back at the Temple Mount, it becomes evident that those who believe the most difficult aspect of the Arab-Israeli conflict will be over once the land is divided are in for a rude awakening. Not far from where the Waqf is digging at Solomon's Stables is a small museum opened in 1922 and run by the Islamic Council. It was set up to house artifacts related to holy places in Jerusalem, and the museum has an impressive collection of hundreds of Korans, colorful tiles and beautifully carved cedar wood used in mosques. But there is no sign that any other religion considers Jerusalem a holy city. "In Jerusalem, the Romans were here, the Persians were here, the Jews were here," says Khidr Ibrahim Salamah, who runs the museum. "But just because you were here doesn't mean you should be in the museum."

Walking among the remnants of centuries of religious fervor, Salamah recounts how he tried to bring an exhibition of 19th-century photographs of Jerusalem by the British-born photographer Mendel John Diness to the museum. The Islamic Council refused to give its permission. It turns out that some of the photographs were of the old Jewish quarter in Jerusalem, something the Islamic council did not want presented. "It seems we cannot live together, even in a museum," Salamah says.

And the truth is that the latest archaeological finds have too often been used as a weapon. The discovery of the cemetery of the pyramid builders in Egypt does not just give us a side of history that was missing; it also allows the Egyptians to challenge the Israeli interpretation of the biblical tale and, by extension, the modern Israeli claims to the land they fled to. The Palestinian embrace of a putative Canaanite past is another way of continuing the fight with the Israelis long after the ink on a peace treaty has dried.

But it doesn't have to be this way. Archaeology can also create a new narrative, a different past, and, by doing this, create the possibility of a different future.

The best place to see this is not inside Israel, but at Mount Nebo in Jordan, on the outskirts of the Promised Land—the spot where the Bible says Moses got his first and last glimpse of Canaan. A survey of the surrounding area has turned up more than 600 sites of archaeological interest going as far back as 18,000 years to the Paleolithic prehistoric period. The archaeologists who are excavating the site have asked Jordan's king for permission to turn Nebo and the surrounding area into an archaeological park.

From the summit's edge, it is possible to see the hills of Amman, once the capital of the ancient Ammonites. Further in the distance is Jericho, where the Canaanites had lived. The outline of Bethlehem also appears, with Herodion, the fortress of the great builder King Herod, next to it. And there, shimmering elusively on the horizon, is Jerusalem, the city that King David made his capital after moving from Hebron.

The archaeologists working at these various sites told me that the ancient Middle East was in some ways very similar to the modern one. The Israelites, Canaanites, Ammonites and Edomites fought each other, competed over land and accused each other of perfidy. But the archaeology being done in the valley below this mountain also has demonstrated that there was extensive trade and common artistic, cultural and religious traditions among the peoples of these cities. Archaeology does not have to be a new battlefield; it can also offer some common ground. You can see the outlines of it from the top of Nebo, but you have to know where to look.

Amy Dockser Marcus is a senior writer at Money magazine and author of the recently published book, "The View From Nebo: How Archaeology Is Rewriting the Bible and Reshaping the Middle East" (Little Brown).

Germany's Nazi Past

The Past as Propaganda

*How Hitler's archaeologists distorted European
prehistory to justify racist and territorial goals.*

Bettina Arnold

The manipulation of the past for political purposes has been a common theme in history Consider Darius I (521—486 B.C.), one of the most powerful rulers of the Achaemenid, or Persian, empire. The details of his accession to power, which resulted in the elimination of the senior branch of his family, are obscured by the fact that we have only his side of the story, carved on the cliff face of Behistun in Iran. The list of his victories, and by association his right to rule, are the only remaining version of the truth. Lesson number one: If you are going to twist the past for political ends, eliminate rival interpretations.

The use of the past for propaganda is also well documented in more recent contexts. The first-century Roman historian Tacitus produced an essay titled "On the Origin and Geography of Germany." It is less a history or ethnography of the German tribes than a moral tract or political treatise. The essay was intended to contrast the debauched and degenerate Roman Empire with the virtuous German people, who embodied the uncorrupted morals of old Rome. Objective reporting was not the goal of Tacitus's *Germania;* the manipulation of the facts was considered justified if it had the desired effect of contrasting past Roman glory with present Roman decline. Ironically, this particular piece of historical

propaganda was eventually appropriated by a regime notorious for its use and abuse of the past for political, imperialist, and racist purposes: the Third Reich.

The National Socialist regime in Germany fully appreciated the propaganda value of the past, particularly of prehistoric archaeology, and exploited it with characteristic efficiency. The fact that German prehistoric archaeology had been largely ignored before Hitler's rise to power in 1933 made the appropriation of the past for propaganda that much easier. The concept of the *Kulturkreis,* pioneered by the linguist turned-prehistorian Gustav Kossinna in the 1920s and defined as the identification of ethnic regions on the basis of excavated material culture, lent theoretical support to Nazi expansionist aims in central and eastern Europe. Wherever an artifact of a type designated as "Germanic" was found, the land was declared to be ancient Germanic territory. Applied to prehistoric archaeology, this perspective resulted in the neglect or distortion of data that did not directly apply to Germanic peoples. During the 1930s scholars whose specialty was provincial Roman archaeology were labeled *Römlinge* by the extremists and considered anti-German. The Römisch Germanische Kommission in Mainz, founded in 1907, was the object of numerous def-

amatory attacks, first by Kossinna and later by Alfred Rosenberg and his organization. Rosenberg, a Nazi ideologue, directed the Amt Rosenberg, which conducted ethnic, cultural, and racial research.

Altered prehistory also played an important role in rehabilitating German self-respect after the humiliating defeat of 1918. The dedication of the 1921 edition of Kossinna's seminal work *German Prehistory: A Preeminently National Discipline* reads: "To the German people, as a building block in the reconstruction of the externally as well as internally disintegrated fatherland."

According to Nazi doctrine, the Germanic culture of northern Europe was responsible for virtually all major intellectual and technological achievements of Western civilization. Maps that appeared in archaeological publications between 1933 and 1945 invariably showed the Germanic homeland as the center of diffusionary waves, bringing civilization to less developed cultures to the south, west, and east. Hitler presented his own views on this subject in a dinner-table monologue in which he referred to the Greeks as Germans who had survived a northern natural catastrophe and evolved a highly developed culture in southern contexts. Such wishful thinking was supported by otherwise reputable archaeologists. The *Research Report of the Reichsbund for German Prehistory,* July to December 1941, for example, reported the nine-week expedition of the archaeologist Hans Reinerth and a few colleagues to Greece, where they claimed to have discovered major new evidence of Indogermanic migration to Greece during Neolithic times.

This perspective was ethnocentric, racist, and genocidal. Slavic peoples occupying what had once been, on the basis of the distribution of archaeological remains, Germanic territory, were to be relocated or exterminated to supply true Germans with *Lebensraum* (living space). When the new Polish state was created in 1919, Kossinna published an article, "The German Ostmark, Home Territory of the Germans," which used archaeological evidence to support Germany's claim to the area. Viewed as only temporarily occupied by racially inferior "squatters," Poland and Czechoslovakia could be reclaimed for "racially pure" Germans.

Prehistoric archaeologists in Germany who felt they had been ignored, poorly funded, and treated as second-class citizens by colleagues specializing in the more honored disciplines of classical and Near Eastern archaeology now seemed to have everything to gain by an association with the rising Nazi party. Between 1933, the year of Hitler's accession to power, and 1935, eight new chairs were created in German prehistory and funding became available for prehistoric excavations across Germany and eastern Europe on an unprecedented scale. Numerous institutes came into being during this time, such as the Institute for Prehistory in Bonn in 1938. Museums for protohistory were established, and prehistoric collections were brought out of storage and exhibited, in many cases for the first time. Institutes for rune research were created to study the *futhark,* or runic alphabet in use in northern Europe from about the third to the thirteenth centuries A.D. Meanwhile, the Römisch Germanisches Zentral Museum in Mainz became the Zentral Museum für Deutsche Vor- und Frühgeschichte in 1939. (Today it has its pre-war title once again.)

Open-air museums like the reconstructed Neolithic and Bronze Age lake settlements at Unteruhldingen on Lake Constanz were intended to popularize prehistory. An archaeological film series, produced and directed by the prehistorian Lothar Zotz, included titles like *Threatened by the Steam Plow, Germany's Bronze Age, The Flames of Prehistory and On the Trail of the Eastern Germans.* The popular journals such as *Die Kunde (The Message),* and *Germanen-Erbe (Germanic Heritage)* proliferated. The latter publication was produced by the Ahnenerbe ("Ancestor History") organization, run as a personal project of Reichsführer-SS and chief of police Heinrich Himmler and funded by interested Germans to research, excavate, and restore real and imagined Germanic cultural relics. Himmler's interests in mysticism and the occult extended to archaeology; SS archaeologists were sent out in the wake of invading German forces to track down important archaeological finds and antiquities to be transported back to the Reich. It was this activity that inspired Steven Spielberg's *Raiders of the Lost Ark.*

The popular journals contained abundant visual material. One advertisement shows the reconstruction of a Neolithic drum from a pile of meaningless sherds. The text exhorts readers to "keep your eyes open, for every *Volksgenosse* [fellow German] can contribute to this important national project! Do not assume that a ceramic vessel is useless because it falls apart during excavation. Carefully preserve even the smallest fragment!" An underlined sentence emphasizes the principal message: "Every single find is important because it represents a document of our ancestors!"

Amateur organizations were actively recruited by appeals to patriotism. The membership flyer for the official National Confederation for German Prehistory (*Reichsbund für Deutsche Vorgeschichte*), under the direction of Hans Reinerth of the Amt Rosenberg, proclaimed: "Responsibility with respect to our indigenous prehistory must again fill every German with pride!" The organization stated its goals as "the interpretation and dissemination of unfalsified knowledge regarding the history and cul-

tural achievements of our northern Germanic ancestors on German and foreign soil."

For Himmler objective science was not the aim of German prehistoric archaeology. Hermann Rauschning, an early party member who became disillusioned with the Nazis and left Germany before the war, quotes Himmler as saying: "The one and only thing that matters to us, and the thing these people are paid for by the State, is to have ideas of history that strengthen our people in their necessary national pride. In all this troublesome business we are only interested in one thing—to project into the dim and distant past the picture of our nation as we envisage it for the future. Every bit of Tacitus in his *Germania* is tendentious stuff. Our teaching of German origins has depended for centuries on a falsification. We are entitled to impose one of our own at any time."

Meanwhile archaeological evidence that did not conform to Nazi dogma was ignored or suppressed. A good example is the controversy surrounding the Externsteine, a natural sandstone formation near Horn in northern Germany In the twelfth century Benedictine monks from the monastery in nearby Paderborn carved a system of chambers into the rock faces of the Externsteine. In the mid-1930s a contingent of SS Ahnenerbe researchers excavated at the site in an attempt to prove its significance as the center of the Germanic universe, a kind of Teutonic mecca. The excavators, led by Julius Andree, an archaeologist with questionable credentials and supported by Hermann Wirth, one of the founders of the SS Ahnenerbe, were looking for the remains of an early Germanic temple at the Externsteine, where they claimed a cult of solar worshipers had once flourished. The site was described in numerous publications as a monument to German unity and the glorious Germanic past, despite the fact that no convincing evidence of a temple or Germanic occupation of the site was ever found.

So preposterous were the claims made by Andree, Wirth, and their associates that numerous mainstream archaeologists openly questioned the findings of the investigators who became popularly known as *German omanen* or "Germanomaniacs." Eventually Himmler and the Ahnenerbe organization disowned the project, but not before several hundred books and pamphlets on the alleged cult site had been published.

By 1933 the Nazis had gone a step further, initiating a movement whose goal was to replace all existing religious denominations with a new pseudopagan state religion based loosely on Germanic mythology, solar worship, nature cults, and a Scandinavian people's assembly or *thing,* from which the new movement derived its name. Central to the movement were open-air theaters or *Thingstätten,* where festivals, military ceremonies, and morality plays, known as *Thingspiele,* were to be staged. To qualify as a Thingstätte, evidence of significant Germanic occupation of the site had to be documented. There was considerable competition among municipalities throughout Germany for this honor. Twelve Thingstätten had been dedicated by September 1935, including one on the summit of the Heiligenberg in Heidelberg.

The Heiligenberg was visited sporadically during the Neolithic, possibly for ritual purposes; there is no evidence of permanent occupation. It was densely settled during the Late Bronze Age (1200–750 B.C.), and a double wall-and-ditch system was built there in the Late Iron Age (200 B.C. to the Roman occupation), when it was a hillfort settlement. Two provincial Roman watchtowers, as well as several Roman dedicatory inscriptions, statue bases, and votive stones, have been found at the site.

When excavations in the 1930s failed to produce evidence of Germanic occupation the Heiligenberg was granted Thingstätte status on the basis of fabricated evidence in the published excavation reports. Ironically, most of the summit's prehistoric deposits were destroyed in the course of building the open-air arena. The Heiligenberg Thingstätte actually held only one Thingspiel before the Thing movement was terminated. Sensing the potential for resistance from German Christians, the Ministry of Propaganda abandoned the whole concept in 1935. Today the amphitheater is used for rock concerts.

Beyond its convenience for propaganda and as justification for expansion into countries like Czechoslovakia and Poland, the archaeological activities of the Amt Rosenberg and Himmler's Ahnenerbe were just so much window dressing for the upper echelons of the party. There was no real respect for the past or its remains. While party prehistorians like Reinerth and Andree distorted the facts, the SS destroyed archaeological sites like Biskupin in Poland. Until Germany's fortunes on the eastern front suffered a reversal in 1944, the SS Ahenerbe conducted excavations at Biskupin, one of the best-preserved Early Iron Age (600–400 B.C.) sites in all of central Europe. As the troops retreated, they were ordered to demolish as much of the site's preserved wooden fortifications and structures as possible.

Not even Hitler was totally enthusiastic about Himmler's activities. He is quoted by Albert Speer, his chief architect, as complaining: "Why do we call the whole world's attention to the fact that we have no past? It's bad enough that the Romans were erecting great buildings when our forefathers were still living in mud huts; now Himmler is starting to dig up these villages of mud huts and enthusing over every potsherd and stone axe he finds. All we prove by that is that we were still throwing stone hatchets and crouching around open fires when Greece and Rome had already reached the highest stage of culture. We should really do our best to keep quiet about this past. Instead Himmler makes a great fuss about it all. The present-day Romans must be having a laugh at these revelations."

"Official" involvement in archaeology consisted of visits by Himmler and various SS officers to SS-funded and staffed excavations, like the one on the Erdenburg in the Rhineland, or press shots of Hitler and Goebbels viewing a reconstructed "Germanic" Late Bronze Age burial in its tree-trunk coffin, part of the 1934 "Deutsches Volk—Deutsche Arbeit" exhibition in Berlin. Party appropriation of prehistoric data was evident in the use of Indo-European and Germanic design symbols in Nazi uniforms and regalia. The double lightning bolt, symbol of Himmler's SS organization, was adapted from a Germanic rune. The swastika is an Indo-European sun symbol which appears in ceramic designs as early as the Neolithic in western Europe and continues well into early medieval times.

German archaeologists during this period fall into three general categories: those who were either true believers or self-serving opportunists; those (the vast majority) who accepted without criticism the appropriation and distortion of prehistoric archaeology; and those who openly opposed these practices.

Victims of the regime were persecuted on the basis of race or political views, and occasionally both. Gerhard Bersu, who had trained a generation of post–World War I archaeologists in the field techniques of settlement archaeology, was prematurely retired from the directorship of the Römisch Germanische Kommission in 1935. His refusal to condone or conduct research tailored to Nazi ideological requirements, in addition to his rejection of the racist Kossinna school, ended his career as a prehistorian until after World War II. The official reason given for the witchhunt, led by Hans Reinerth under the auspices of the Amt Rosenberg, was Bersu's Jewish heritage. By 1950 Bersu was back in Germany, again directing the Römisch Germanische Kommission.

It should be noted that some sound work was accomplished during this period despite political interference. The vocabulary of field reports carefully conformed to the dictates of funding sources, but the methodology was usually unaffected. Given time this would have changed as politically motivated terms and concepts altered the intellectual vocabulary of the discipline. In 1935, for example, the entire prehistoric and early historic chronologies were officially renamed: the Bronze and pre-Roman Iron Ages became the "Early Germanic period," the Roman Iron Age the "Climax Germanic period," the Migration period the "Late Germanic period," and everything from the Carolingians to the thirteenth century the "German Middle Ages."

It is easy to condemn the men and women who were part of the events that transformed the German archaeological community between 1933 and 1945. It is much more difficult to understand the choices they made or avoided in the social and political contexts of the time. Many researchers who began as advocates of Reinerth's policies in the Amt Rosenberg and Himmler's Ahnenerbe organization later became disenchanted. Others, who saw the system as a way to develop and support prehistory as a discipline, were willing to accept the costs of the Faustian bargain it offered. The benefits were real, and continue to be felt to this day in the institutions and programs founded between 1933 and 1945.

The paralysis felt by many scholars from 1933 to 1945 continued to affect research in the decades after the war. Most scholars who were graduate students during the 12-year period had to grapple with a double burden: a humiliating defeat and the disorienting experience of being methodologically "deprogrammed." Initially there was neither time nor desire to examine the reasons for the Nazi prostitution of archaeology. Unfortunately prehistoric archaeology is the only German social-science discipline that has still to publish a self-critical study of its role in the events of the 1930s and 1940s.

The reluctance of German archaeologists to come to terms with the past is a complex issue. German prehistoric archaeology is still a young discipline, and first came into its own as a result of Nazi patronage. There is therefore a certain feeling that any critical analysis of the motives and actions of the generation and the regime that engendered the discipline would be ungrateful at best and at worst a betrayal of trust. The vast majority of senior German archaeologists, graduate students immediately after the war, went straight from the front lines to the universities, and their dissertation advisers were men whose careers had been determined by their connections within the Nazi party.

The reluctance of German archaeologists to come to terms with the past is a complex issue.

The German system of higher education is built upon close bonds of dependence and an almost medieval fealty between a graduate student and his or her dissertation advisor. These bonds are maintained even after the graduate student has embarked on an academic career. Whistle-blowers are rare, since such action would amount to professional suicide. But in the past decade or so, most of the generation actively involved in archaeological research and teaching between 1933 and 1945 have died. Their knowledge of the personal intrigues and alliances that allowed the Nazi party machine to function has died with them. Nonetheless, there are indications that the current generation of graduate students is beginning to penetrate the wall of silence that has surrounded this subject since 1945. The remaining official documents and publications may allow at least a partial reconstruction of the role of archaeology in the rise and fall of the Nazi regime.

The future of prehistoric archaeology in the recently unified Germany will depend on an open confrontation with the past. Archaeologists in the former East Germany must struggle with the legacy of both Nazi and Communist manipulation of their discipline. Meanwhile, the legacy of the Faustian bargain struck by German archaeologists with the Nazi regime should serve as a cautionary tale beyond the borders of a unified Germany: Archaeological research funded wholly or in part by the state is vulnerable to state manipulation. The potential for political exploitation of the past seems to be greatest in countries experiencing internal instability. Germany in the years following World War I was a country searching for its own twentieth-century identity. Prehistoric archaeology was one means to that end.

Proving Ground
of the Nuclear Age

*The mangled artifacts and lunar landscape of the Nevada Test Site are a
vivid testament to the advent of atomic weaponry.*

By William Gray Johnson and Colleen M. Beck

The desert flats of central Nevada offer an eerie landscape of twisted I-beams, bent towers and deformed bridges, frame buildings ripped apart, and stretches of land scarred by craters—one so vast it rivals depressions on the moon. Welcome to the Nevada Test Site, 1,350 square miles of landscape indelibly marked by hundreds of atomic bomb experiments. Here, for some 40 years during the Cold War between the West and the former Soviet Union and its allies, scientists experimented with various forms of nuclear weaponry. Today, with moratoriums on both underground and above ground testing, the Test Site is a silent wasteland, its devastation a legacy of that time.

We work for the Desert Research Institute (DRI), a branch of the University of Nevada system set up in 1959 to investigate arid land problems such as water availability and air quality. Since then our focus has broadened to include past environments and archaeology. Working for the United States Department of Energy (DOE), which owns the Test Site, and for state and private agencies in Nevada, we also regularly study Native American cultures as well as early settlements of miners and ranchers. The Native American ruins span some 10,000

years and include scatters of stone artifacts and pottery, occasionally associated with rock-shelters, caves, and rock outcrops decorated with petroglyphs and pictographs. Most of the mining and ranching occurred between 1905 and 1940, and claim markers and shafts can be seen in the hilly regions nearby, where springs, stone and wood cabins, out-houses, corrals, and fencing still remain.

We began recording these sites in 1978 in an effort to help the DOE comply with the National Historic Preservation Act of 1966, which directs federal agencies to inventory archaeological and historical property under their jurisdiction and to determine the effects of their activities—in the DOE's case the testing of nuclear weapons—on these properties. It soon became clear that what remained of the testing program itself was the most important component of the archaeological record. Like most artifacts left unused on the landscape, the Test Site structures and associated debris have begun to disappear. Weathering, recycling of items, and the need to reuse areas for other activities are slowly stripping the landscape of its Cold War artifacts. In 1982 Nevada's State Historic Preservation Office acknowledged the

years of testing as an important period in the state's history and recommended that specific artifacts be preserved as testaments to the nuclear bomb experiments spawned by the Cold War.

In 1988 we proposed to the DOE that we survey the area. The proposal was well received, and in 1991 we were asked to evaluate two structures, a 1,527-foot tower used in a study of radiation released from an unshielded reactor, and an underground parking garage tested for possible lateral and vertical displacement in a nuclear blast. We felt both were eligible for the National Register of Historic Places, the official list of the nation's cultural resources deemed worthy of preservation. Soon after we were asked to inventory all Test Site structures to determine their eligibility for the National Register. This program continues today. Surprisingly, many of the artifacts and even some of the structures we have researched are not recorded in any official documents. Instrumentation stands and temporary storage bunkers, for example, were important for the instruments they held or stored, but were not considered worth documenting.

To enter the Test Site, one takes U.S. Highway 95 north from Las Vegas to Mercury, a complex of scientific labora-

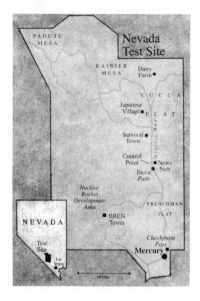

tories and warehouses, a building that houses radiation monitoring equipment and staff, dormitory-style housing, a cafeteria, a post office, a fire station, a hospital, a bowling alley, and a chapel. This is where scientists and support staff lived and worked during the nuclear testing period, which began January 27, 1951, with an air-drop event code-named Able. Above ground testing ended in 1963 with the Limited Test Ban Treaty, which prohibited atmospheric, underwater, and outer-space nuclear testing. The current moratorium, which includes underground testing, took effect October 2, 1992. It has been extended twice, most recently to October 1995. Scientists still work here, but their efforts are focused on tracking residual radiation in the environment and cleaning it up. Mercury is still closed to the casual tourist, and a gate is manned by guards 24 hours a day. The DOE began conducting public tours in the early 1980s in recognition of the need to communicate the nature and extent of the testing program and in acknowledgment of the taxpayers' contributions to the program. Monthly tours continue to be available to individuals and groups.

Those who visit the site follow the Mercury Highway north. A sign indicates that cameras are not allowed in the forward areas. Another warns workers to be cautious of posted radiation areas. Driving through Checkpoint Pass, a guard station no longer used, one enters Frenchman Flat, a dry lake bed surrounded by rolling hills leading to distant mountains. Blown-out buildings and twisted metal litter the landscape. Fourteen aboveground nuclear devices were detonated here; Grable, Priscilla, and Met were the code names of three. The largest, Priscilla, left most of the wreckage. Bunkers, motels, and homes, grouped at different distances from ground zero, were subjected to a blast equivalent to 37,000 tons of TNT. A steel-reinforced, concrete-sided bank vault at the center of the blast survived pressures of 600 per square inch. We have recommended that the entire area be considered a historic district.

Continuing north, the highway cuts through Yucca Pass and a collection of gray windowless buildings that once served as the Test Site's electronic Control Point. Nearby, a faded sign on a boulder-covered hill identifies the site of News Nob, "where on April 22, 1952, the American press and radio first covered, and the nation first viewed by the medium of television, the firing of a nuclear device known as 'Operation Big Shot.'" At the foot of the hill are 11 rows of weather-beaten benches where reporters and dignitaries observed multiple explosions, some as close as 14 miles away.

Yucca Flat, whose cratered surface resembles the surface of the moon, witnessed more aboveground and underground tests than Frenchman Flat. One huge crater, known as Sedan, measures 320 feet deep and 1,280 feet across, and is a regular stop on the DOE tours. It was created in the Plowshare Program, a project designed to find peaceful uses for nuclear bombs, such as large-scale excavation. (A redigging of the Panama Canal was under consideration at the time.) Sedan Crater was listed on the National Register last year, the first Test Site area to be so designated.

Yucca Flat bears the remains of two-story houses located 6,600 and 8,000 feet southeast from ground zero of a test code-named Apple II. They were part of "Survival Town," a 1995 Civil Defense exercise designed to study the durability of typical civilian buildings subjected to nuclear weapons. Test targets also included industrial buildings and shelters, electrical power systems, communications equipment, a radio broadcasting station, trailer homes, fire equipment, cars, and food supplies placed at varying distances from ground zero. The force of the blast was the equivalent of 29,000 tons of TNT. Only the two-story houses and the frames of a few ranch-style homes survived.

Yucca Flat was also the site of radiation experiments. Bare Reactor Experiment, Nevada, or BREN, was part of Operation Ichiban, a program intended to determine radiation exposures experienced by the survivors of the Hiroshima and Nagasaki bombings. In these tests an unshielded reactor was placed in an elevator that rode up and down a 1,527-foot tower. The reactor released radiation on a mock Japanese village whose frame houses contained dosimeters for measuring exposure. Raising or lowering the reactor enabled scientists to change the angle and range of the radiation. Ichiban data allowed scientists to determine relationships between radiation doses and health problems associated with radiation sickness. Though the tower was moved to another part of the Test Site in 1965, our research at the Japanese village and the relocated tower has determined that both are National Register candidates. Also eligible is an experimental dairy farm designed to study the effects of radioactive fallout on the fodder-cow-milk food chain. A number of small dairy farms were located downwind from the Test Site, and there was concern at the time that children drinking milk from these dairies might be affected by the fallout.

Farther north, Rainier Mesa rises 7,000 feet above sea level. Underground nuclear testing began here in 1957. Code-named Rainier, the first blast shook the mesa and surrounding areas with the force of 1,700 tons of TNT. Rainier Mesa and its neighbor, Pahute Mesa, were the sites of numerous underground tests. Some nuclear devices were placed on long shafts, others in tunnels. We know of underground bunkers, similar to bomb shelters, and we have heard about structures shaped like submarines with periscoping elevators. What condition are they in today? We hope to find out. Elsewhere there are remarkable structures associated with nuclear rocket development. We believe they too are significant.

Is this archaeology? We think it is. Our instincts lead us to believe that these artifacts of the Cold War are historically important and need to be studied. Can anyone honestly call them nonarchaeological? Scholars traditionally time-trek through millennia. Casually discussing similarities between the migrations of hunters and gatherers of 50,000 years ago and the peopling of the New World at the end of the last Ice Age some 10,000 years ago, they have grown accustomed to thinking in large blocks of time. It is the short blocks of time, especially our own, that we have difficulty understanding.

WILLIAM GRAY JOHNSON, assistant research professor with the Desert Research Institute, is in his third year of investigating the Nevada Test Site's historic structures. COLLEEN M. BECK, associate research professor at the Institute, has published on prehistoric and historic cultures in the Andes and the western United States. *The authors would like to thank the U.S. Department of Energy for funding the research that made this article possible.*

Index

Index

N

NASA (National Aeronautics and Space Administration), 115
Nassaney, Michael, 28
National Center for Space Study, 117
National Confederation for German Prehistory, 194
National Historic Preservation Act of 1966, 197
National Register of Historic Places, 197
Native American Graves Protection and Repatriation Act (NAGPRA), 174–176, 178, 179
Native American ruins, artifacts in, 197
Native Americans, living conditions of, after the arrival of Europeans, 146–150
natural selection, 86, 87
Nazis, of Germany, 193–196
Neeman, Nadav, 170
Nefertari, tomb of, 33
neutron activation analysis (NAA), 112–113
Nevada Test Site, atomic weaponry in, 197–199
Neves, Walter, 65
New Kingdom, pharaohs of, in the Valley of the Kings, 33
New World, question on who were first people in the, 61–65, 66–69
New York, Fresh Kills landfill in, 91–98
Nimrud, 9, 10
Nineveh, 9, 10
nitrogen isotopes, 146–157
Norr, Lynette, 147
North American Inuit women, as toolmakers, 84
Nursing Home Man, 128, 130, 131

O

O'Connell, James, 88
Olduvai Gorge, Tanzania, 12
"Operation Big Shot," 198
Operation Ichiban, 198
optical emission spectrometry, 112–113
optical luminescence dating, 120
Osiris, 31, 38
ossuary, and the rules of archaeology, 188–189
Ötzi, 50–54
Owen, Linda, 79, 81, 82
Owsley, Douglas, 127–131
Oxford Illustrated Prehistory of Europe, The (Cunliffe), 46
oxygen-isotope analysis, 111

P

Pääbo, Svante, 114
Packer, Alfred, as the Colorado cannibal, 157–158
palaeoclimatology, 112
Palestinian civilians, under Israeli occupation curfew, 29, 30
Pálsson, Gísil, 5
papyri, 9
Pavlov, Upper Paleolithic life of, 78, 80, 81
Pax Chaco (Lekson), 48

peasant life, of the Capilcos and the Cuexcomates, 160–162
Penck, Albrecht, 111
Persian Empire, 193
Peruvian Pyramid, 180–183
pharaonic tombs, in the Valley of Kings, 31–41
photo superposition, 125
physical anthropology, 122
physiological factors, affecting deaths of members of the Donner Party, 155
physiological mechanism, of menopause 87
phytoliths, 71, 111
Piggott, Stuart, 12
pioneers, of the Donner Party, 151–156
Piperno, Dolores, 70, 71, 73
"pithouses," 6
Pitt-Rivers, Augustus, 10–11, 12
plant remains, research on, for history of the Iceman, 49–54
plaster sling missiles, 45
Plowshare Program, 198
plunderers, of the tomb of Ramesses the Great, 34
porotic hyperostosis, 148, 149
postmenopausal women, extended role of, 88
"pot polish," 76
poverty, warfare and, 48
Prehistoric Cannibalism at Mancos (White), 76
prehistoric cooking, 132–133
prehistoric pueblos, 45
present-day relevance, of archaeology, 25, 27–28
Price, Douglas, 46
Pylos Regional Archaeological Project (PRAP), 134–137
Pyramid of the Sun, 180
pyramids, 8–9; of Sipán, Peru, 180–183

R

race, the Kennewick Man and, 179
radar, 111
radiocarbon dating, 52, 63, 113
Rainier Mesa, 198–199
Ramallah, under Israeli occupation curfew, 29–30
Ramesses II (the Great), 31–41
religion, alcohol and 142–144
remote sensing, 111; techniques of, 115–119
repatriation movement. *See* Native American Graves Protection and Repatriation Act
Research Committee of the National Geographic Society, 182
residue identification, procedure of, 132
resistivity instruments, 116
Retzius lines, 148, 149
"revisionist," 21
Reynauld of Chatillon, 165
Roberts, Richard, 120–121
Rock Outcroppings, of Kimberly, Australia, 120–121
rondas campesinas, 184
Roosevelt, Anna C., 21–22, 23, 117–118
royal tombs, traditional designs of, 34
Ruff, Christopher B., 149–150
Rush, Benjamin, 144

S

sacrifice ceremony, representations of, in Moche art, 182–183
salvage, of Peruvian pyramids, 180–183
satellite imagery, 111
satellite remote sensing, 117
Sauer, Carl, 70–71
Schele, Linda, 47
Schliemann, Heinrich, 10, 12
Schmidl, Alexandra, 52
second moments of area, bones and, 150
seismic instruments, 116
self-sacrifice, in Donner Party, 151–156
Sever, Thomas L., 116–117
Shang civilization, 8
sharing, importance of, among !Kung bushmen of the Kalahari Desert, 99–105
Sheets, Payson D., 116
Shuttle Imaging Radar (SIR-A) experiment, 117
Siberian women, as toolmakers, 84
Simpson, Scott W., 149
"sinus imprint," 124–125
Sipán, Peru, 180–183
sites, of earliest humans, in America, 67
Six Day War of 1967, 57
skeleton, signs of stress in, 148
Smithsonian anthropologists, and the FBI, 127–131
Snow, Clyde C., 122–126
Soffer, Olga, 78–83
Solomon's Stables, 190
somatotype, 3
Spindler, Konrad, 49
SPOT satellite, 111, 116, 117
Staphylococcus aureus, 149
Starrs, James, 158
starvation, among the Donner Party, 151–156
Stewart, George, 151
Stewart, T. Dale, 129
Stone Age, 11
stone ossuary, of the Common Era, 59
stone toolmaking, among women, 84
Sumer civilization, 46
Sumerian civilizations, 8; prehistoric warfare among, 47

T

Tanakh, 55
tangibility, of archaeology, 25, 26–27
taphonomy, 102
Teaford, Mark F., 147
Testimony of the Spade, The (Bibby), 16–17
Theban Necropolis, 35, 37
thematic mapper, 116
Thomas, David Hurst, 149
Thompson, Thomas, 56
toolmakers, women as, 84–85
Toth, Nicholas, 75, 77
Trotter, Thomas, 144
Troy, city of, on northwestern Anatolian Coast, 10
tryptophan, lack of, in corn, 147
Turner, Christy G., 74, 75–76, 77

Test Your Knowledge Form

We encourage you to photocopy and use this page as a tool to assess how the articles in *Annual Editions* expand on the information in your textbook. By reflecting on the articles you will gain enhanced text information. You can also access this useful form on a product's book support Web site at *http://www.dushkin.com/online/*.

NAME:

DATE:

TITLE AND NUMBER OF ARTICLE:

BRIEFLY STATE THE MAIN IDEA OF THIS ARTICLE:

LIST THREE IMPORTANT FACTS THAT THE AUTHOR USES TO SUPPORT THE MAIN IDEA:

WHAT INFORMATION OR IDEAS DISCUSSED IN THIS ARTICLE ARE ALSO DISCUSSED IN YOUR TEXTBOOK OR OTHER READINGS THAT YOU HAVE DONE? LIST THE TEXTBOOK CHAPTERS AND PAGE NUMBERS:

LIST ANY EXAMPLES OF BIAS OR FAULTY REASONING THAT YOU FOUND IN THE ARTICLE:

LIST ANY NEW TERMS/CONCEPTS THAT WERE DISCUSSED IN THE ARTICLE, AND WRITE A SHORT DEFINITION:

We Want Your Advice

ANNUAL EDITIONS revisions depend on two major opinion sources: one is our Advisory Board, listed in the front of this volume, which works with us in scanning the thousands of articles published in the public press each year; the other is you—the person actually using the book. Please help us and the users of the next edition by completing the prepaid article rating form on this page and returning it to us. Thank you for your help!

ANNUAL EDITIONS: Archaeology 04/05

ARTICLE RATING FORM

Here is an opportunity for you to have direct input into the next revision of this volume.
We would like you to rate each of the articles listed below, using the following scale:

1. **Excellent: should definitely be retained**
2. **Above average: should probably be retained**
3. **Below average: should probably be deleted**
4. **Poor: should definitely be deleted**

Your ratings will play a vital part in the next revision.
Please mail this prepaid form to us as soon as possible.
Thanks for your help!

RATING	ARTICLE	RATING	ARTICLE
	1. Metaphors We Dig By		37. Ownership and Control of Ethnographic Materials
	2. The Awful Truth About Archaeology		38. Last Word on Kennewick Man?
	3. The Quest for the Past		39. Tales From a Peruvian Crypt
	4. Distinguished Lecture in Archaeology: Communication and the Future of American Archaeology		40. Guardians of the Dead
			41. In a Box
			42. Land Can Be Divided. Histories Cannot
	5. First Lady of Amazonia		43. The Past as Propaganda
	6. Archaeology's Perilous Pleasures		44. Proving Ground of the Nuclear Age
	7. The Travails and Tedium of Conflict-Zone Fieldwork		
	8. All the King's Sons		
	9. Prehistory of Warfare		
	10. The Iceman Reconsidered		
	11. In the Beginning Was the Word		
	12. Who Were the First Americans?		
	13. Who's On First?		
	14. The Slow Birth of Agriculture		
	15. Archaeologists Rediscover Cannibals		
	16. New Women of the Ice Age		
	17. Woman The Toolmaker		
	18. Why Women Change		
	19. Yes, Wonderful Things		
	20. Bushmen		
	21. Camera Bodies		
	22. High-Tech "Digging"		
	23. Space Age Archaeology		
	24. A Wasp's-Nest Clock		
	25. Profile of an Anthropologist: No Bone Unturned		
	26. 'Let the Bones Talk' Is the Watchword for Scientist-Sleuths		
	27. What Did They Eat?		
	28. The Archaeologists Who Wouldn't Dig		
	29. Alcohol in the Western World		
	30. Reading the Bones of La Florida		
	31. Living Through the Donner Party		
	32. Case of the Colorado Cannibal		
	33. Life in the Provinces of the Aztec Empire		
	34. Legacy of the Crusades		
	35. Israel's Mysterious Stone		
	36. Burying American Archaeology		

(Continued on next page)

BUSINESS REPLY MAIL
FIRST CLASS MAIL PERMIT NO. 551 DUBUQUE IA

POSTAGE WILL BE PAID BY ADDRESEE

McGraw-Hill/Dushkin
2460 KERPER BLVD
DUBUQUE, IA 52001-9902

ABOUT YOU

Name   Date

_____

Are you a teacher? ☐   A student? ☐
Your school's name

_____

Department

_____

Address   City   State   Zip

_____

School telephone #

_____

YOUR COMMENTS ARE IMPORTANT TO US!

Please fill in the following information:
For which course did you use this book?

_____

Did you use a text with this ANNUAL EDITION?   ☐ yes ☐   no
What was the title of the text?

_____

What are your general reactions to the *Annual Editions* concept?

_____

Have you read any pertinent articles recently that you think should be included in the next edition? Explain.

_____

Are there any articles that you feel should be replaced in the next edition? Why?

_____

Are there any World Wide Web sites that you feel should be included in the next edition? Please annotate.

_____

May we contact you for editorial input?   ☐ yes ☐   no
May we quote your comments?   ☐ yes ☐   no